RWANDA MEANS THE UNIVERSE

ALSO BY JACK KRAMER

Travels with the Celestial Dog

RWANDA MEANS THE UNIVERSE

A NATIVE'S MEMOIR OF BLOOD AND BLOODLINES

LOUISE MUSHIKIWABO

AND

JACK KRAMER

ST. MARTIN'S PRESS ≋ NEW YORK

East Providence Public Library
Weaver Memorial Library

967.571
MUS

B+ T 12/5/06 26.95L

RWANDA MEANS THE UNIVERSE. Copyright © 2006 by Louise Mushikiwabo and Jack Kramer. All rights reserved. Printed in the United States of America. No part of this book may be used or reproduced in any manner whatsoever without written permission except in the case of brief quotations embodied in critical articles or reviews. For information, address St. Martin's Press, 175 Fifth Avenue, New York, N.Y. 10010.

www.stmartins.com

Map by Jeffrey L. Ward

Book design by Kelly Too

Library of Congress Cataloging-in-Publication Data

Mushikiwabo, Louise.
    Rwanda means the universe : a native's memoir of blood and bloodlines / Louise Mushikiwabo and Jack Kramer.—1st ed.
        p. cm.
    ISBN-13: 978-0-312-20959-9
    ISBN-10: 0-312-20959-2
    1. Mushikiwabo, Louise.   2. Rwanda—History—Civil War, 1994—Personal narratives.   3. Rwanda—History—Civil War, 1994—Atrocities.   4. Genocide—Rwanda.   5. Tutsi (African people)—Crimes against—Rwanda—History—20th century.   6. Hutu (African people)—Rwanda—Politics and government—20th century.   7. Rwanda—Ethnic relations—History—20th century.   I. Kramer, Jack. II. Title.

DT450.435.M875 2006
967.57104'31—dc22   2005057441

10 9 8 7 6 5 4 3 2

3 1499 00413 3507

To my sister, Anne-Marie Kantengwa, whose courage to
pick up pieces has kept the family name alive,
To our brother, Lando Ndasingwa, whose name
has become a family name,
To all our brothers and their wives,
To our husbands, Joseph and Norman,
To our parents, Bitsindinkumi and Nyiratulira, and
their grandchildren; their love sustains us all.

—Louise

In memory of

Cadre Kidane Kiflu, K.I.A.
Lt. Jettie Rivers, USMC, K.I.A.
Malcolm Cowley

—Jack

· CONTENTS ·

RWANDA

UGANDA

DEMOCRATIC REPUBLIC
OF THE CONGO

Kagitumba

Muhabura Volcano

Karisimbi Volcano

Kagitumba River

Akagera

AKAGERA

Ruhengeri

Gabiro

Akagera River

VIRUNGA MOUNTAINS

Byumba

NATIONAL

Gisenyi

Nyabarongo River

*Lake
Muhazi*

PARK

Lake Kivu

Kabuye

Kayonza

★ Kigali

Gitarama

*Lake
Mugesera*

Kibuye

*Idjwi
Island*

*Lake
Rweru*

Kibungo

Gikongoro

Cyangugu

Butare

Kansi

TANZANIA

BURUNDI

| 0 Miles | 25 | 50 |

| 0 Kilometers | 50 |

Bujumbura

© 2005 Jeffrey L. Ward

OUR SINGLE INTENT

In 1994, in the highlands of Central Africa, the Rwandese state executed a planned operation that exterminated three-quarters of an already endangered people. It all went on in public. It struck children dumb as they watched neighbors run, watched playmates scramble and run, watched grandmothers stumble and try to run. Some onlooking kids giggled nervously. Some just giggled. Some hooted. State executioners and local volunteers swarmed over the landscape, house to house, hut to hut, hedge to hedgerow, catching and dispatching more than three times as many people as al Qaeda did when it dropped the World Trade Center.

That's not how many they killed altogether. That's how many they killed every day—ten thousand a day, more than three times the 9/11 toll.

Picture it: Summertime in the country. Summertime in Vermont. Cows. Hayricks. Hedgerows. Rwanda in April is a few degrees warmer. Some hedgerows are nearly hectic with flowers. But in a nation otherwise much the size and green mountain feel of Vermont in summer, twin towers of humanity go down over three times a day, every day, for one hundred days. Death thus hiccups close to a million times before it's over. It was a more efficient—that is, faster, cheaper—killing rate than the Nazis ever managed.

This book does not detail that crime. Within the frame of one farmer's family, it digs at its roots; it ends when the evil blooms. The narrator is one of the farmer's grown daughters. Her story is fact. If it reads at times like fiction, it could be that memory packed deeply away doesn't always come out neatly colored inside the boundaries of biography or history or newspaper features.

We take from this no license to invent. The irreducible difference between fiction and nonfiction isn't how they read. It's the difference between material fact and imaginary fact. We imagine no fact.

. . .

IN 1924, TERROR SEIZED A CLUTCH OF SCHOLARS TROWELING THE DEAD SEA BASIN. Learned students of divinity, they were searching for no less than Sodom itself, the city so deeply evil that God destroyed it. They found some shards, and on this slim evidence it hit them with holy force that they'd actually found the place, that they were gazing on original iniquity, and in insolent violation of Genesis 19, in which God warns the faithful not to look back on the evil city lest they be turned to pillars of salt. Furiously, they backfilled the dig, packed up, and motored off.

The sin God found in Sodom is the bible's ultimate expression of evil. Is genocide the modern world's ultimate evil? Do many today—even among today's scholars—avert their eyes from it with the same almost magical horror that led the faithful to avert their eyes from the evil God found in Sodom? Is this aversion to look on something repellent on our doorsteps some of the reason that "Never again!" is losing its exclamation point? Might Bergen-Belsen, Bosnia, Rwanda, the Sudan (for that matter, the World Trade Center) be our modern become postmodern Sodoms? Are they that far beyond the pale?

Yes. No one should try to explain them away. Genocidal Rwanda confounds the Rwandese. It's not a murder mystery; it's a mass murder mystery. It isn't a safe postal zone. It's neighbors killing neighbors, every day, all day, all through neighborhoods more like our own than we might like to think. It's been enough at times to make the two of us—one long used to Rwanda and terror, the other to Africa and war—want to book one-way tickets out.

Regardless, no place is so far beyond the pale that plain facts don't apply.

IN 1959, IN 1963, IN 1968, AND AGAIN IN 1973, EPIDEMICS OF MASS MURDER HAD already seized the country. Today, scholars in the new field of Holocaust studies find these earlier episodes, like the 1994 event, more characteristic of the industrial world than of the Dark Continent. Scholars have identified in them distinct features of modern genocide, by which they mean that far from a burst of tribal war, or tribal hysteria, or the work of deranged Jacobins, the killings were systematically planned by the state and engineered to exterminate a minority.

The Nazis' formula for mass murder was to ply an already bigoted public with lies and propaganda in order to create a climate that allowed them to round up hated groups and kill them in camps. Totalitarian Rwanda gave the technique its own twist. It used lies and propaganda to convince the public itself to commit most of the murders—or, more specifically, to convince the Hutu majority (long ago Rwanda's serfs) to kill the Tutsi minority (long ago Rwanda's warrior-gentry). First the state indoctrinated, then it passed small arms and orders down a formal chain of command, then neighbor went about the business of killing neighbor.

That state is now defunct, but its big power patrons remain big and powerful, and they routinely discount the crime: "Those two tribes have been at war for centuries."

Those precincts *are* scarred by centuries of war—but not between "those two tribes." And war isn't another word for genocide. This much is fact: Centuries before white men ever showed up, distinctive warrior castes ruled a patchwork of kingdoms in East Africa's Great Lakes highlands. Torment, cruelty, and blood feuds were common in these realms, the upshot of intrigue or perversion in the tightly regimented courts or of feudal war between kingdoms.

But not communal war within kingdoms. The Spartans of the ancient Peloponnese may have seen themselves forever at war with their serfs. Rwanda's warrior-gentry did not. For the most part, their enemies were rival kingdoms, against which Tutsi gent and Hutu serf fought side by side—not altogether unlike noble and serf in feudal Christendom. Toxic Hutu hatred for Tutsi people didn't boil up until Belgian colons—dizzy with Darwin and seized by fashion—recast Rwanda in terms of lesser men and supermen. As they depicted matters, the warrior minority was a distinct race, genetically superior to the Hutu peasantry. Righteously sermonizing missionaries concocted bizarre theories of Tutsi origins (Iceland, Atlantis), and when in the early thirties Hitler's Germany began issuing racial pass cards, so did Rwanda's white authorities. You were either Hutu or Tutsi—and it mattered. No surprise, much of the gentry, especially Tutsi royalists, bought into this nonsense, which tended to confirm creaky creation myths just when they should have been outgrown.

After World War II, Africa rallied for independence. In Rwanda the movement was Tutsi-led, and this dismayed Rwanda's colons no end. It was plain that their infatuation with the Tutsi "race" had gone unrequited, that in Tutsi eyes they were birds of the same feather as the missionaries Melville found sermonizing in the South Seas—of whom he said they weren't so much civilizers as "snivelizers." Worse, Hitler's disgrace in Europe made an embarrassment of their old distorted stereotypes.

So the colons dropped old stereotypes and adopted new ones. In a clumsy about-face, they switched from anti-Hutu to anti-Tutsi. Depending on the demands of the moment, *Tutsi* became a word meaning either "stingy," or "cruel," or "shifty," or you name it. For the past half century, white planters had exploited Hutu peasants. As white authority now spelled matters out to a still unschooled majority of Hutu peasants, holding souls in serfdom was an evil peculiarly inherent in "the Tutsi race." During the fifties, colonial officials sacked legions of educated Tutsi civil servants, hired legions of hastily educated Hutu replacements, and drew up plans to grant independence to an authoritarian Hutu regime. Racial pass cards remained law to the bloody end of the Belgians' watch in 1961, and would remain law after the new Hutu elite they schooled took over Rwanda.

To this elite, newly powerful, jealous of its power, uncertain, and schooled to hate anyone Tutsi, the Belgians left a bitter ethnic gospel in which to indoctrinate the Hutu public. Pogroms chased more than a third of the Tutsi minority into exile between 1959 and 1961—the period planned for Belgium gradually to cede control. A quarter century later, a totalitarian Hutu regime was in place. It was largely shaped, nurtured, and sponsored by the big powers, and especially by France, which had replaced Belgium as Rwanda's patron. Faced with opposition both Hutu and Tutsi, the state put Western cash and Western techniques—techniques now ripe with pop music and talk radio—to work inflaming the public against anyone it didn't like, and especially those with depraved Tutsi genes. Using Western cash to buy small arms—machetes, AKs, banana clips, all purchased at bulk rate—state functionaries organized local folk to commit mass murder. It would not be witch doctors in jungle huts who would teach the dark medicine of hate and mass killing. It would be educated cheerleaders at pep rallies.

Mothers with babies swaddled to their backs began hacking at mothers with babies swaddled to their backs. Schoolchildren killed schoolchildren. Cassocked priests took up the club. Throughout the killing, European, U.S., and United Nations staff on the ground reported its progress. Canadian military officers on the ground saw surveillance planes built to NATO specifications flying overhead, apparently monitoring the slaughter, and Western officials, including U.S. officials, were in nearly constant cell phone contact with the genocide's impresario, Théoneste Bagosora. At this point Rwanda's effective head of state, Bagosora was a retired colonel, well educated, fluent in French, trained in France, a family man close to his French priest, who lent him inspirational works, among them, *Mein Kampf.*

America's news business paid more attention, during this period, to a celebrity murder, a celebrity drug overdose, a celebrity figure-skating scandal. It paid more attention to a refugee crisis after the genocide than it did to the genocide itself.

HOW WE TELL THE STORY

This book is a collaboration. Distinctly different faculties frame the story through a single set of eyes. A writer from a family with a distinguished literary background collaborates here with a writer without such—and since the African is the one from a literary family, you could even say that the words are hers, the music, his. Of course, that's a conceit, but it's closer to the mark than reading our book as the ghostwritten memoir of a nonwriter.

We press no argument. We do, however, indulge argument. In fact, we indulge some furious argument. Our story is a human story, told by a human. Confusion, passion, argument are all human and part of the picture of the narrator as she wonders, burns, learns, doubts, grows, changes.

The only imaginary characters are birds. Aside from these demons who visit, all the characters are real. When anything is imagined, we say so explicitly. "I imagine . . ." or "I picture . . ." When anything is a matter of opinion, we say that explicitly. Even though a memoir is by nature a volume of feeling and opinion as well as fact, we write, "I think" or "feel" or "believe." Rumor we ignore—except when it's a matter of substance and so widespread that its currency itself must be noted. Then we quote "Radio Trottoir"—which is what Rwandese who speak French call gossip picked up on the track. As for those matters of fact, the narrator simply calls them as she recalls having seen or heard or read them, and whenever the matter of fact is also an event of record, she recalls where she saw or heard or read it. That's not to say memory has perfect vision. It's notorious for thinking it can see better than it can. A face glimpsed long ago and far away may merge with others and appear as one. But aside from such possible meldings in the deep and personal backdrop, no characters are composites. A few characters who appear once, briefly, and in personal settings have had their names changed.

Likewise, the demands of storytelling, rather than academic style, have determined whether we source literary matter or not, and storytelling has also determined our language. We aren't academics. We don't descend to the demotic; we are the demotic. There is no need to make things up. Only remember Edward R. Murrow's plea (broadcast even as *The New York Times* was burying the story), "I pray you to believe what I have seen at Buchenwald."

These features should suggest neither scholarship nor objectivity. We hold to them only because they help us in our single intent—to tell the story of a certain people in a certain place, at a certain time, through certain eyes. In so doing, we hold to Rwandese oral tradition. How we tell the story serves no other purpose.

Rwandese oral tradition is also important in other respects.

For one, Hutu and Tutsi storytellers spin the same tales. They share the same gods, spirits, and demons. In daily passing remarks, they even share the same images of one another. Simply (and crudely and falsely) put, Tutsi means tall, thin, severe; Hutu, short and happy. This makes a rich playing field for what Freud calls "the narcissism of minor differences"—which as a national affliction is no minor matter. Heedless, Rwandese have since Belgian days trafficked daily in these minor differences, picked at them daily—and so, at times, do we. Let the reader beware.

For another, there is no Hutu or Tutsi tongue. Kinyarwanda, in all its shared nuance, is uniformly the tongue of both. The most immediate example is our book's title. In Kinyarwanda, the literal meaning of the word "Rwanda" is "the universe" or "the big world" or simply "the world." The usage dates from days when Rwanda was the only world the Rwandese knew, and there was no distinction between the country and the universe. A man from one hill might ask a man from another, "How are things in your Rwanda," meaning "in your world." Or he might say of a cow, "She's as big as Rwanda," meaning as big as the universe. Rwanda was the universe, the universe was Rwanda, and the Rwandese have never forgotten that original meaning. In fact, they may still call truly big things "as big as Rwanda," meaning the universe, not the tiny country that even the most benighted now know their state to be. Why does the old meaning hang stubbornly on? It's hard to say. Perhaps the answer is simply this: Rwanda, once so alone, then so aloofly above the swamps and the dry savannah below, was ultimately hit so hard by the larger world . . . and Rwandese don't like picturing themselves as victims. Perhaps in remembering that Rwanda is the universe, Rwanda sees itself not as a victim of the world, but as a part of it, that what the universe has done to Rwanda, it is doing to itself. Rwanda is the universe. The universe is Rwanda.

In good part, Kinyarwanda—along with its oral tradition—is what distinguishes and unites the Rwandese as a nation. We urge you to become familiar with three of its words in three characteristically Bantu forms:

Bahutu   Rwanda's old peasantry; its masses; the plural of . . .
  Muhutu: in the old days, a peasant or serf; also . . .
  Hutu: the adjective.
Batutsi   Rwanda's old gentry; in Swahili, **Watusi**; the plural of . . .
  Mututsi: in the old days, a lady or a gent; also . . .
  Tutsi: the adjective.
Bazungu   white people; the plural of . . .
  Muzungu: a white person; also . . .
  Zungu: the adjective.

You may wonder why words we assign to the old days matter so much today. Indeed, herein lies our story. . . .

PART I

COUNTDOWN TO APOCALYPSE

A Crime Reconstructed in Six Days
Saturday, April 2–Thursday, April 7, 1994

· 1 ·

IN-LAWS, OUTLAWS, AND A PRATFALL FROM GRACE

I met a man once who told me about a pigeon that his cook fixed for him in Cairo. He said it looked as if the houseboy had just shot the bird with a pellet gun and it crash-landed on his plate. Its drumsticks were splayed, head twisted sideways, wings akimbo, tail in the air.

That's pretty much how Juvenal Habyarimana met his end. Shot from the sky like a pigeon.

He dies, and wherever you look, tender shoots come suddenly and enormously abloom. For something like four years, and on his orders, men and women credentialed in the cultivation of hate had been seeding poison in neat rows, and now for an even one hundred days and uncountable nights, their business blooms, boiling at last into a crime that spreads beyond your ability to comprehend.

From too far to see much or know much, I find it floating through my imagination, a bloom of algae suddenly sickly green on hills that roll like liquid swells. Up close, it stares back, an ooze with eyes called "genocide." Blooms of bobbing corpses foam up on the cold roaring feeders of the Nile. There's nowhere to hide.

But that's when he dies, and those hundred days after, and just now, that's not what's on my mind. What's on my mind just now is those last few days before he dies. I don't know why.

Juvenal Habyarimana and I were countrymen. We were *Banyarwanda*, people of the mountain nation called Rwanda. We were Africans. So let's see if I can draw you a picture of my brother African as he was during those last six days I can't get off my mind anyway. Let's look at the picture he presents before his big bang, before he goes nose-first into the mess he's made and his bird-beaked soul flutters up in thin air.

This can be tricky. You think back to his last few days, and it's hard keeping your mind off what's coming, for him and for us. But why not try? After all, right there, just then, watching him go about his business that first week of April 1994, who knows he's a man on the cusp?

Well, clearly somebody knows. Somebody's about to shoot him out of the sky. And besides the shooters, a few other personalities might well know something's up. For all we know, one of them is Juvenal Habyarimana.

He's quick. Never has this man been easily blindsided. He may well have an inkling. But put me there, or you, and we'd have no inkling at all. So let's look at the man we the ignorant might witness during the last few days before he makes that last lurid appearance on the slick pages of *Jeune Afrique,* his tasteful Afro still neatly carved, his head cleanly cleft at the neck by the force of the crash, sitting wide-eyed on its left ear just meters short of his pride, his swimming pool.

He stands trim, square, proud, his necktie smartly knotted, his head firmly on his shoulders. He steps out like Johnnie Walker on the whiskey bottle. His eyes are clear, intelligent.

His smile is healthy, white, genuine. His manners attend so considerately. He actually listens. He cares who you are. In just a few weeks, King Baudouin of the Belgians will look up in silence as he's told what Juvenal Habyarimana was up to behind closed doors. At last his royal highness will speak. "But he was such a *Christian. . . .*"

Some soldiers can make a career of standing at attention. Good soldier Habyarimana has made a career of paying attention. He's risen from the ranks by drinking in every drop of detail, and he's risen far. He springs from the poorest of the already poor people who make up the great mass of our nation.

JUVENAL H, CONFOUNDER OF CARTOONS

We call his people Bahutu. They call themselves Bahutu. Nobody else knows their name. Nobody knows our name. At least not where I'm at work that final week of his life, worlds away from Africa in a strange land of Post-it notes and drive-thru banks.

"How can things get so all, like, *nuts*?" asks a voice at work. "In Africa. On the news. Or was it the Jiffy Lube? *USA Today* in the waiting room? No. It was my podiatrist friend, Lorraine. A news junkie, world class. Now who is it you are? The Hottentots?"

As I said, nobody knows our name.

It's been a charged few months, following a charged year. No sign that this will be *the* week, Juvenal's week, our week, but all the same, come Thursday an occupational hazard gets the best of me. I'm a translator. I get paid to be picky with words, and I'm not handling the week as well as I should. Thursday noon, I'm standing at the elevator with Bea from Benefits. She's a mild woman who always smiles and nods and likes to get familiar. She asks the usual topsy-turvy questions, and I find myself explaining, in a tone I'm certain is all too picky, "I'm *Tutsi*. The minority people. The other people are *Hutu*. Which is an adjective, not a noun. The noun is *Bahutu*. *Batutsi*."

"Oh precious," she says. "Thank you so much. Now I remember. Saw it just the other night on Fox Five. The Hutsie are the other ones. The poor ones. Poor, short, and not exactly stocky, but they do have this, well, *issue with weight*. You're like the rich ones. The tall ones. Skinny. So when are we going to see some flesh on those bones, young lady?"

So there you have it, no one knows our name, but all the same, there's a cartoon doing the rounds: Hutu means the masses, squat and sturdy. Tutsi means patrician, tall, slight, and you will please ignore the tendency of patrician teeth to stick out. Thursday after work I find myself silently lecturing produce at the Safeway. "There just aren't many rich Batutsi anymore," I silently instruct a bin of indolent cabbages. They seem not to pay much attention, so I turn to some equally inattentive eggplants. "As far back as the fifties, figures show Bahutu doing about the same as Batutsi." Facts and figures document my lessons, fastidiously honed footnotes pump through my head.

"And you chattering onions there: This business about a Hutu 'issue with weight.' I'd say more Bahutu are underweight than overweight." Indeed, plenty of Bahutu are hungry these days.

For that matter, plenty of Batutsi are hungry these days. Right enough, some Batutsi are skinny for no other reason than genes. But hunger has slimmed all our people. Hunger is in our souls, in the souls of all of us, Batwa (Rwanda's pygmies), Bahutu, Batutsi.

You see it especially in our worship of amplitude, and especially in the eye our men have for cows. Time was, the gift of a cow from a Tutsi lord was one way a Hutu man won rank, a step toward becoming Tutsi, which some did. Even as I fill my cart with Sara Lee, my brothers in Africa are grooming their cows to a sleek sheen, lotioning them with butter. They can pay a woman no greater compliment than to call her a cow. They would admire Big Bea from Benefits.

LIKE MOST BAHUTU, HABYARIMANA CONFOUNDS THE HUTU CARTOON. HE'S NEITHER short nor all that heavy. Even as he ages, he's built just fine, and looking smart hasn't hurt this *bella figura* one bit. He's married well. Agathe Kanziga is not a daughter of the Batutsi. Like him, she's Hutu. But she's far better educated than most Batutsi, and in the mystery-ridden ways of our nation, she is also higher born than most.

This latter-day queen would be higher born than most of us once-patrician Batutsi even if her republic had not stripped us of all station (no, worse, of all credit) after the Belgians began handing them power in 1959. Her line of Bahutu once ruled a princely state, and lineage shows in her bearing. Married to this highborn Hutu woman, Juvenal Habyarimana has risen from the poorest of the already poor Bahutu and become His Excellency, president of the last African nation to be discovered by Europe, the last successfully to be made a colony of Europe, our Rwanda, at bay with the mountain gorilla in Africa's high interior.

SMELTER OF IRON, CARVER OF TERRACES

I grew up in Habyarimana's Rwanda. When Albert Einstein was born in the industrial-strength Rhineland of 1879, our nation had yet to be glimpsed by a single white person. For years, soot-belching freighters had been plying the sea-lanes from Brindisi and Suez to Mombasa. From booming Mombasa, the Uganda Railway regularly chugged up past booming Nairobi to our very gates in the Uganda highlands.

Where we heard you knocking, but you couldn't come in. Behind those gates, locked tight, we were a stubborn people, and not simply stubborn but illiterate, and not simply illiterate but innumerate. We couldn't count.

Another decade comes and goes. Young Colette is enumerating her beaux. Young Albert is working differential equations. We can still barely count.

White people—Zungu people, Bazungu—remain something we know the way we know that our paramount chief, our *mwami,* is divine. In Paris, photographs are starting to move. In Berlin, a man named Benz is designing an automobile. In Cleveland, a black child who will one day devise the traffic light enters school. We remain ignorant of the wheel, a people still unseen by even one Muzungu.

And yet . . . Presume if you will that we're aboriginal, some elusive stone-age remnant whose scant numbers and simple ways let us hunt and gather in deep secrecy. In the event, we're neither much of a secret nor graced with Pleistocene charm. With iron we've long since been smelting in bush forges, we've long since—centuries since—felled most of our forests. We're isolated, a small place adrift in wilds without end, but our isolated valleys are crosshatched with irrigation channels, our hills stepped in painstaking terraces. Our cows give rich milk, our bees fine honey. Our women weave fine basketry.

For nearly half your nineteenth century, the rifle-armed merchants of two different Muslim worlds have been heading for us from two different directions. From the north out of Ottoman Cairo marches the expanding merchant world of the Nile. From the east marches the expanding merchant world of Zanzibar. As John Wilkes Booth fires his derringer at Ford's Theatre, hired Arab gunmen are circling us, dragging the endless wilderness about us for slaves and ivory as they eye what they call our "infidel sultanates."

Nor are they alone in their designs. More than a quarter century before Colette begins to flirt, that most moody of Lytton Strachey's *Eminent Victorians*, General Gordon, declares he wants to trade his command at Khartoum for Mombasa, the better to reach what he reckons the Nile's true prize, our highlands. In 1884, Bismarck summons a council of Zungu cannibal chiefs. He bills it "the Conference of Berlin." The idea is to carve up Africa without carving up each other. It works—though with each cut, the Zungu chiefs eye each other intently. After securing some prime cuts for the Reich, *der Reichskanzler* has "Ruanda-Urundi" for dessert. That's nine years before a single German ever sets foot on our soil. Still, you wouldn't want to call us a triple-canopied secret. Nor would you want to call our population scant, nor our economy aboriginal. Aboriginals, anthropology tells us, need vast tracts to feed tiny bands. It took all of aboriginal Britain to feed fewer souls than live in twenty-first-century Swansea. Yes, we can barely count. We're lost in an Africa thick with hyenas and thin with people. Still, our lost sultanates have put themselves together so complexly and so obsessively that in our fastness, we have for centuries been feeding a population among the densest on earth, as dense as the Yangtze, as dense as the Ruhr. We are, in our inspired improbability, that thoroughly African.

DEAR CONSTANCE, TRUE TO HER NAME

Mama and Papa could count but they had nine children anyway; nine kids, Mama, Papa, and guests in mud-brick quarters eighteen feet by eighteen feet with no electricity, no toilet, no running water. This was 1961, the year I was born, last of the nine.

I studied. At six I minded the nuns as if stepping out of line meant breaking my mother's spine. At sixteen I studied for my diploma as if holy salvation hung in the balance, and gaped as, late in a season of long rains, our book-struck brother Lando, eleven years my senior, suddenly sprouted wings and soared off on a thunderhead of scholarship.

One minute I saw him sitting cross-legged in the shade of ripe sorghum, reading anything and everything, dog-eared comic books, *Scaramouche*, Saint-Simon, Simenon. The next minute he was up and off, gone. Just like that, he jumped a puddle and turned midleap into a Tutsi-skinny stork; and not just any stork (for we have an abundance, saddle-billed, yellow-billed, open-billed, all homebound residents), but one of those long-legged, pale-arctic storks that leave us every Easter to roost in the chimney pots of strange northern places.

Right there in midair, I lost my favorite storyteller. Right there, our Lando snatched a stipend on the wing and soared off to a distant ice palace called Montreal, there to temper his African fever for words in a blue diamond realm of books and plays and music. There I resolved to join him.

We were Tutsi, but we were also *Tsobe*. My clan, my Tutsi father's clan, storky brother Lando's clan, the clan of our fathers, was the Batsobe. Our clan inheritance was the lore and ethic of illiterate scholars, *abiru*, who committed volumes of beauty and knowledge to memory, drawing on it as if they had a library card to the human brain.

The White Fathers couldn't teach in our native Kinyarwanda, the tongue that most pleased me, most pleases me, a tongue we Batutsi seem to have learned centuries ago from our sister Bahutu. Instead I studied in French, and as I studied, Habyarimana and his cronies began cutting Batutsi out of the school system. With luck, I went to university anyway and studied English and English literature. I tried for one foreign grant after another until at last I turned twenty-four and luck favored me with a scholarship and full stipend to the University of Delaware.

Everything was set. My passage was paid, cash on the line, departure date three days hence. The U.S. Embassy, then famously proprietary with its visas, said mine was in hand; all I had to do was bring in my passport for stamping. Except that I didn't have a passport. I had applied weeks earlier to the minister of education because that's how you had to do it. You couldn't just pay a fee, fill out a form, and wait. You had to have a proper reason, certified by a government minister, who would then okay the application for a passport. Now, three days before departure, with ticket and visa in hand, a letter finally turns up in our box at the post.

"We regret to inform you that you are not permitted to pursue your studies overseas."

Nobody in the family was in the public eye. That wasn't the problem. The problem was that the state had leaped beyond keeping us out of school. Now we couldn't leave the country.

At this, big sister, solid big sister, all six feet three and thirty-two years of her, marched into the passport agency as if she had six legs with which to march. The passport agency, fittingly enough, was an adjunct of the secret police, on the ground floor of secret police headquarters. Secret police headquarters was an inconspicuous little building like a malignant little ulcer on the Rue du Marché. Inside of me, I was frightened to death. I think that inside, big sister was frightened to death. All the same, she barreled in—and there at a scuffed metal desk in a bureau full of scuffed metal desks was

Constance. Like all the other apparatchiks sitting grimly behind those desks, she was of course Hutu, but years ago and worlds ago, amid the cloisters of the Lycée Notre Dame de Citeaux just the next hill over, she and schoolmate Anne-Marie had lunched together most every day at a mess-hall table full of jokes, books, and bowls of mission porridge.

"*Constance,*" said Anne-Marie, as if there were nothing irregular about a Tutsi woman waltzing into secret police headquarters to chat.

"*Anne-Marie,*" said Constance, caught off guard, and thus as forgetful that nature (as official science then had it) abhors any friendship between Muhutu and Mututsi.

"Oh, I'm so lucky," said Anne-Marie. Office work had stopped. Men in suits behind desks were broadcasting venom with their eyes. Who was this Tutsi-tall woman? Big sister dropped her voice. "You're a lifesaver, Constance. Sister needs a passport. Now."

"Get out of here," said Constance. "Now." Then, dropping her voice: "Come back tomorrow morning. Ten." The office was dusty with years of accumulated bureaucracy. Bulging file boxes climbed to the ceiling, daring overhead fans to swat them. Vagrant memos shambled on currents of hot air. The officials here could have no idea that the education minister had blocked my passport. "Constance, sister's problem is your problem," said Anne-Marie. Constance smiled stiffly, and big sister alternately backed out and walked out, as I tripped awkwardly after her, forever adjusting my step to hers, so keen to get out of there.

Dear Constance, true to her name; she came through, and so off I flew, on a wing and a stipend to America before the minister of education ever knew this cockatoo had flown the coop. For two years I went to university, and for another four years I worked as a French translator in Washington, enjoying its fountains, its libraries, its toilets. But never once did I think about applying for citizenship. I already had a home. My home was in Africa. Aunties and uncles. Friends and cousins. In-laws and cherished outlaws. ("Outlaws?" says a lady at the hairdresser. "You mean, really, *outlaws*?" Yes, ma'am, *cherished* outlaws, but that's a story for later.) Nephews. Nieces. Seven brothers and a sister, an especially big sister. Mother, her spine unbroken. And then suddenly, the very next morning after Juvenal H plummets, my life is emptied. Drained. My home is gone. My Rwanda is gone.

THE LITTLE GRASS SHACK

Right up to the minute Juvenal Habyarimana's head rolls to a stop next to his pool, his mentor and model is the most powerful man in Africa, the tyrant of Zaire, our next-door neighbor, Mobutu Sese Seko. Mobutu doesn't look like much. He looks like an accountant and he steals like one. But a full quarter century ago, his fortune was reckoned at more than three billion dollars, and since then his net worth hasn't exactly been shrinking. By stealing all this from his nation he has inspired a new word, a word for our day, *kleptocracy,* and he's the star Habyarimana follows.

Alas, Habyarimana is a thief of more modest means. Above all, his dictatorship is not absolute. To some limited extent he must answer to the people, whose lot began crumbling when coffee prices crashed in the eighties. To keep hungry Rwanda at bay, he's got to keep Rwanda distracted with patriotics—and by jingo his propaganda machine can make bully work of patriotics. It can rally fresh-faced boys to murder.

Habyarimana has also to answer to the Bazungu who bankroll him. Embarrassed by news reports of state-sponsored hate crimes, they've been leaning on him to give a little. Which isn't easy, because there's still another group to which he must answer—the Hutu syndicate that's the muscle behind his presidency. As these connected Bahutu see matters, bargaining is a zero-sum game they can only lose, because right now Rwanda, as a franchise, is all theirs. Worse, this syndicate is more his wife's crowd than his. When he married her, she was the daughter of a powerful mountain family; now some say she's the most powerful single soul in all Rwanda, a queen upon whom her husband depends utterly for the network of fixers, informers, and enforcers that keeps him going. With coy modesty that simply underscores their wealth and their muscle, the boys who hold Habyarimana nearly captive call themselves the *Akazu*—"the little grass shack."

But who's to say a president can't put on a nice show? Habyarimana makes his subjects wear tiny pins featuring his handsome likeness. He travels. He has his own French aircraft with three French pilots who see to it that the twin-jet Dassault is kept spotless. Right next to the airfield he's built a splendid palace, with its own chapel (where his wife of distinguished lineage daily says her rosary) and a swimming pool.

Comes then Wednesday morning of Easter week, 1994. April 6. He climbs aboard his Dassault. His pilots plot a bearing due east for the Indian Ocean port of Dar es Salaam ("haven of peace," in Arabic), where a clutch of East African bosses are getting together to dutch-uncle some peace and quiet in torment-ridden Rwanda. Here he agrees without wrangling to honor a firm and final deal, the terms of which he's wrangled with bitterly for more than a year, right up to this month. The world applauds.

Or maybe I should say that applause politely clatters from those obscure corners where an informed few notice such events. For months, the world's iota-that-notices has been fearing massacres on a massive scale in Rwanda. Some have been fearing what they call "genocide."

To my ear, at this moment, the word has a clinical clink. I know what it means. That's how I make a living. But translation itself can be something of a clinical craft. I know the word as translators know it. I don't even know much about the pogroms. In 1973, when I was eleven, I was chastened by one, and I was afraid, but even then I never heard a cross word. I'd lived all my life with Bahutu; our hill, like all the hills of Rwanda, had far more Bahutu than Batutsi. Papa never told us much about how the Bahutu hated us, nor did Mama; they didn't even tell me much about the pogrom that ran them off their first farm in 1959, two years before I was born.

Now, in the early nineties, Habyarimana's tyranny of the majority has been acting out a morality play much bandied about by young students of political philosophy—the one in which a nation's citizens vote to guillotine everyone who's, say, knock-kneed or short-limbed or short-tempered, then justify this business on the grounds that it was all done democratically, in a free and fair election. We carry pass cards identifying us as the hated Batutsi—and when things get bad, we never leave home without that card. As frightening as it is to get ID'd as a hated Mututsi, it's worse to get caught pretending you're not a Mututsi. When Habyarimana's crowd needs scapegoats, the specter of pogrom whistles through Tutsi homesteads. Every day, we're subject to petty terror. "Will our little Batutsi please stand up?" says the nun to her class. "So we can see who you are? Thank you so much."

A focused few know also that a Tutsi gang attacked and grabbed a small corner of the north back in 1990. The renegades came from Uganda, to which pogroms had chased their parents, and in which Batutsi are unwanted. The iota that notices knows how the Habyarimanas and their syndicate answered the attack with gun battles that ended indecisively, and with a publicity campaign that has succeeded brilliantly. They know that by now the boys from the little grass shack have convinced the majority that we, the genetically malign 14 percent, are plotting to reduce them once again to the formal peonage of olden days.

THE HABYARIMANAS' HATE-FARMERS PLOW RICH SOIL, TURNED AND MULCHED AND LONG manured by Zungu colons. Race proud and supremely race conscious, these early Bazungu planted self-hate deep in the soul of the Bahutu, teaching them in extravagantly imagined detail how far superior were we of the minority Batutsi, we warriors and poets. Then the Axis was crushed, Fascism lost its vogue, and our colons about-faced, becoming latter-day champions of the downtrodden, priming the Bahutu with rage, teaching them in extravagantly imagined detail how we the degenerate had long ago held them in serfdom. Then they turned power over to the Bahutu.

That was 1959. The pogroms that followed came in waves. Mama and Papa had to run from one with my sister and seven brothers. The youngest was Wellars, still an infant, squalling. They lost their farm and all their cash, left behind in a bureau drawer as they bolted in panic out the front and onto the bed of a borrowed flatbed lorry. But that was before I was born, a silent picture in my head, Wellars's infant mouth open wide in a squall that's utterly silent. I never got caught in anything like that, and between the pogroms, there were days when a few Batutsi could do well in business or in the pay of Bazungu. We were drivers, doctors, bookkeepers.

This is not one of those days. For six months at least, the syndicate's propaganda apparatus has been in high dudgeon. People are awash in paranoia. In 1990, the propaganda machine's leading lights published something they called "The Ten Commandments of the Bahutu," among which are injunctions to see every Mututsi as an enemy, to see every Muhutu who marries a Mututsi as a traitor, to avoid "contamination" with Batutsi, to "show Batutsi no pity." Now they're preaching those commandments from every state pulpit and from some churchly ones as well. Pogroms have been breaking out all across the country.

Silent pogroms. Silent for me as for most of the world. In their way, they do touch me. They knot my stomach. But these killings are mostly in the bush. They don't cut me or kill mine. I'm working in Washington. What I pick up are rumbles. I get rashes.

SHADOWS OF CRUSHING COLLECTIVE MASS

Mme. Habyarimana's clique—the "zero network" that runs the little grass shack—is drawn entirely from the majority Bahutu, but it's nonetheless just that, a clique, a coterie, regularly resented by the Hutu masses. Like some yellow dog worrying a bone, the hungry Hutu peasant absently worries his sack of mealie from the Akazu larder—and every sack counts. The grass shack's ability to dole out patronage is its ticket to survival. The bargain Habyarimana is striking will mean a grim cut in the patronage that is its lifeblood.

Regardless, today in Dar es Salaam on the palm-balmy coast of the Indian Ocean, he seals the deal, committing his syndicate-state to stop dragging its feet. As he sees matters, he has no choice. His bankers don't like being embarrassed, and with coffee prices still wretched, Rwanda is broke. He'll stay president, but with nearly 40 percent of the army manned by Batutsi, thus guaranteeing the pogroms will end. Most of the iota that watches is smiling—nervously.

Not Habyarimana. By some accounts, he's been in a wired daze for the entire week. There's no telling whether it's the daze of a man bewildered or a man aware. It could be either. He boards his craft for home.

At about 8:15 P.M. on April 6, his Dassault begins its glide to the airstrip. It's in clear sight of his French pilots. Just short of the runway, two Russian SAM 16 ground-to-air missiles suck skyward. Most evidence (but not all) will point to a launch site somewhere inside a security zone razor-wired and heavily patrolled by his elite Presidential Guard. A missile strikes. The plane explodes. Most of the fuselage crashes through the president's own garden wall, tail up, nose down, just short of his swimming pool. Everyone aboard is killed.

But I'm letting events get ahead of themselves.

So far as I know, there were no pogroms the week before he crashed and burned, yet in my mind, the events of this headlong week stampede like beasts in the night. Some empty-eyed thing hidden in thorn and known only to malice spooks herds of no known species. Shadows of crushing collective mass thunder blindly, in an ultimate direction known only to providence, and in the rush, dust clogs my throat dry and I lose something, something I'm forever scrambling to find without ever knowing what it is.

Yes, you could argue that what I lose sight of is what I won't look at, and I won't deny that I have trouble accepting what happened. Yes, people at times ask, gingerly, whether those events are in fact too much to acknowledge. But I acknowledge them. I do. I know what happened—but as far as that goes, not everyone close to me died, and right now isn't the time to go into all that. That's not what gets lost in the rush of events. It's something else.

Sometimes my skin bothers me. I itch. These days I worry those six days like some yellow dog worrying her mange. I want to start on Saturday, April 2, and follow that week for clues, follow it one day at a time.

2

Day One: The Bankers Are Restless

SATURDAY, APRIL 2, 1994. Memory fails. It hears but it can't see. Then it sees but can't hear. For a split second it sees a lakefront spa called Gisenyi. For more than half a century, Gisenyi has dreamed that it's Babar the elephant's storybook Celesteville. It's a mirage of Celesteville. It fizzes off.

I'm sharing a flat with my friend Mauwa. She's Congolese. Our flat's in Maryland, in Silver Spring just outside Washington, and that's where I am just now, at home, dialing the phone, and something is assaulting my ear, high treble tones digitally generated by AT&T: 0-1-1 for an overseas line, 2-5-0 for Rwanda, 8-2-0-5-0 for the bar at Chez Lando. A few hard-knocking clicks; the line goes dead. "The circuits are busy in the country you're dialing. If you'd like to place a call . . ."

Who turned the sound up to such a harshly brilliant pitch? I try again: 0-1-1 . . . The phone rings, summoning up my touchstone, my brother, Africa.

" 'allo . . ." With one word, the pitch drops to the ultimate comfort of that low rumble. With one word, I sense his presence, long since morphed from stork to buffalo.

"Lando."

"Loulou! By Kabenga, what a treat. Went to the wedding, little sister. The one at Ruzindana's place. What a treat . . ."

"I'm sure," I lie.

"Well, you know how it is. . . ."

"Mmmh," I say. That's a word in our language, a word with many meanings—approval, interrogation, surprise, scepticism, pleasure—and I mean this *mmmh* to signal disbelief. "So. Nothing to fret about."

"Mmmh," he says. I can almost see his brows conceding. In our language, brows concede. "Well of course, there's this. And that. This in the air, that in the air. Nerves. But let me tell you about the wedding, little sister. This is what? Saturday? So it must have been Thursday last. Everybody was there. Joseph. Mama Nana. Nana . . . no, not Nana. Mama Nana put the kids with . . ."

"Never leaves them alone these days, does she?"

"Put them with Eugénie. All three. Safari, Shara, Nana."

Tricksome Lando. With downright offhand insolence, he ignores my question, using his assuring rumble to distract us from the nerves he at once acknowledges and dismisses as mere "*nervosité.*"

Static on the line. It cracks with *nervosité.* Something is going to happen. Something some of us sometimes fool ourselves into thinking we can pick out—a war, a riot, a coup. In our spleens we sense something else, sense it the way a cat senses an earthquake. My family, my brothers, my sister, my mother. They're living atop a primal, shifting fault.

Damn Lando. Stubborn Lando. Even his name. A stubborn mark of the Flemings on our once-Belgian colony. It's short for Landoald. We also carry in stock full lines of Frodualds, Ferdinands, Sylvesters, and Sixberts. Even a Festus or two.

I repeat: "So there's nothing to worry about?" I won't be put off. I need to know. They always protect me, the youngest. *Loulou.* I'm Louise.

"The 'orizon, Loulou. We have to keep our eyes on—"

I cut him off. "But of course. The horizon. We all know about that. About keeping our eyes on the horizon."

He laughs. At himself. It's a running joke, and his, not mine, Lando playing the part of some arch professor of physics droning on in singsong: "The 'orizon, class, is an imaginary line. As one approaches this line, it recedes into the distance. The more rapidly one approaches, the more rapidly it recedes." Lando has always had a weakness for the silly, and that's all this is, nothing more intended, but something makes this one a running joke that won't quit running. We fools, forever chasing the promise of the day when a Rwanda now so laced with hate is ready, willing, and able to put itself through some detox. We fools, we running dogs of Faith. Forever chasing a mechanical rabbit we call the horizon.

PHONE SIGNALS BREAK UP; RECALL BREAKS UP. SIGHT AND SOUND FAIL TO MATCH. WHAT my memory sees instead of Lando on the phone is wind-bitten peaks above that dreamy town called Gisenyi, favored retreat of Akazu barons, same time, same day. Lando is talking to me from the bar of a lodge he runs on the road east out of Kigali-ville—our scant pretender to national capital-ship. Gisenyi is even smaller, and a good five hours the other way, on a lake at the end of a road with too many heart-stopping switchbacks, through too many mountain defiles, a gravel road. My memory hears Lando's voice, deep and full of gravel. It sees Gisenyi emerging through moving mountain clouds.

Something is going on down there in Gisenyi, and I want to listen in, but what my memory still hears is Lando on the line: "And a glad thing it was, little sister. Getting away from it all."

I try to picture him. I picture Gisenyi instead. Gisenyi is where the Akazu goes to get away from it all. Lando fades; I lose him. Gisenyi emerges brilliantly from clouds—Gisenyi this same day, Saturday, April 2, 1994.

FROM THE CAPE TO CAIRO
(BY WAY OF CELESTEVILLE)

They say Kenya's White Highlands, due east of us across Lake Victoria, got their name from the second sons of British lords who made those hills their playground. Likewise, highland Gisenyi on the Rwanda shore of Lake Kivu, on our western frontier with the Congo, once provided a setting in which footloose continentals with excess marginal income could blow their wealth like soap bubbles. Crystalline Kivu sits in the mountain-bound interior of Africa, but squint and you could mistake it for Lake Como. Here in deepest Africa, Gisenyi's wealth-besotted creators had the brass to defy nature at her most emphatic, taking as models the more modern suburbs of Montreux and Monte Carlo. Art Deco villas and a few small hotels rise on landscaped bluffs. Bright umbrellas promoting Martini, Ricard, Pernod dance about cafés once smart, garlanding a brief boulevard that runs along the lake. Much of it went up during the jazz age, and who cares if Gisenyi's almost brilliant crowd played the jazz age ghostly white. The wonder is that aristos of such blinding bias played the jazz age at all. That in itself must have been transforming; you can do worse than the likes of Bix Beiderbecke.

For years, they say, Gisenyi was a treasured destination for adventurers and scoundrels—Belgian, Italian, French, German. I picture them plying the boulevard—the "corniche," they still call it—in insolent Bugattis, Bentleys, even the occasional Packard, pretending they aren't on the make, pretending they're just easing through Babar's lovely Celesteville along with the rhinos, the hippos, and the crocs (oh my). Lakeside Gisenyi's draw between the wars seems to have been such that after the second one, it drew the almost brilliant back. It became a favored stop on the boat-plane route from the Cape to Cairo, a perfect spot to put in for sundowners (whiskey light on water, gin light on tonic) between lakes Tanganyika and Victoria, now to the tune of the Dorseys, Bing Crosby, and "I'll be seeing you / In all the old familiar places. . . ."

Hardly familiar for me. It was 1977 when I first saw the place. I was sixteen, one of the new girls come to board at the Lycée Notre Dame d'Afrique at the Nyundo mission just outside of town—or I should say, above town. The corniche impressed me, but I wasn't a footloose continental with excess marginal income to blow. The nuns impressed me more.

By now, Celesteville has gone much to mold, but it's still there, and it's to this town that the United Nations' special representative for Rwanda, soon to be an official referee of doom, has traveled today, April 2.

In the same way that the Vatican calls its ambassadors "papal nuncios," the UN calls its ambassador here its "special representative." Like those second sons of British lords who needed something to do with their lives, this man too is the kinsman of a notable—a notable of Cameroon, in this case—and needs something to do with his life.

By most accounts, he's not doing it well. By some accounts, he's an incompetent, given to chummy drinking parties with the Habyarimana crowd. Picture the papal nuncio in Berlin toasting Octoberfest 1935 with Goebbels, right after the Nuremberg laws stripped German Jews of their rights. For all its dereliction then, was the Vatican any more derelict than the UN is now?

The name of the UN's nuncio is Jacques-Roger Booh-Booh. His job amounts to little more than making sure Habyarimana gets the aide-mémoire when UN brass in New York hear yet again that Habyarimana is shredding human rights too indiscreetly. The job's one requirement is looking neutral. Booh-Booh only manages neutral distance from Habyarimana when Habyarimana is trying to avoid him. Which is just what's afoot right now. For nearly two weeks, His Excellency, M. Booh-Booh has been failing and failing again to set up a rendezvous with His Excellency, the president of Rwanda. He must tell him that the UN is losing patience. For months, Habyarimana has been finding excuses to avoid making reforms he promised in writing at parleys in a town at the foot of Mount Kilimanjaro. The deal inked there is falling apart.

STRUGGLES IN THE DUST

Those parleys were refereed by the UN, and they were three-way. The three parties were the Akazu state; the renegades (armed, Tutsi-led); and the unarmed domestic opposition.

As a result of some modest headway in the talks, some leaders of the domestic opposition became ministers in two (get ready for this) "negotiated

interim governments, pending national elections agreed upon in principle." For all this diplo-spoken legal authority, the two governments had
hardly any real authority. Habyarimana was still the president, and most
key ministries were under Akazu control—as they remain right up to this
month, April 1994.

The name of the town that hosted the sessions was Arusha; it sits on the
high, dry savannah beneath Kilimanjaro. Here's what the three sides were
after there:

The domestic opposition—almost entirely Hutu—wanted to secure real
democracy and rehabilitate southern Bahutu.

The armed renegades—the Inkotanyi—wanted to secure the return of
refugees chased from Rwanda since the sixties plus political participation
for ethnic and political minorities.

The third side—the Akazu state—wanted to secure itself.

The reality was somewhat closer to this: A big rhino—the Akazu state—
was in a hot, grit-bitten fight with two little rhinos—namely, the unarmed
domestic opposition and the armed Inkotanyi renegades. The two little
ones together weren't as big as the big one. At least, that's how I paint the
picture. However you paint it, the UN was in Arusha trying to apply diplomatic theory to a rhino fight.

The big rhino held good ground. It was the State, after all. It was exercis-
ing state powers. Its propaganda apparatus had the public in a hammer-
lock, and the world's big powers were backing their fellow regime-in-power
with guns and with money. That's why I can call it the big rhino. And that's
why the renegades were one of the little rhinos. Nobody backed them except Uganda—which had its reasons. For years, Uganda had been hosting
refugees from Rwanda. Uganda reckoned, reasonably, that helping these
refugees get back to Rwanda was one way to get rid of them.

Nor was the big rhino stupid. It didn't just rage and paw the dust. It was
educated. It knew how to rage in snorts and bellows diplomats understood.
With footwork uncommon to rhinos, it made nice diplomatic points. It
bellowed, for instance, that democracy hardly requires guaranteeing a minority a portion of the armed forces—which is just what the Tutsi-led renegades in fact wanted. They wanted nearly half the military—a share far out
of proportion to the Tutsi share of the population.

But the Inkotanyi renegades could likewise dance a nice rhino minuet.
They said they needed nearly half the military because otherwise the daily
abuse and the monthly pogroms would just go on. More crucially, the renegades had something rare for rhinos—some eyesight. Their charges didn't
have nearly the thunder or genuine force the big rhino could muster, but
they connected. As the big rhino stood stupefied (like most rhinos, it was

nearly blind), the little one would charge suddenly out of the dust and connect. It was maddening.

All through the talks, the Habyarimanas' *ducs* were putting together hate
groups. The groups were aimed at Batutsi, but the Habyarimanas' crowd is
good at turning hate groups against anyone it doesn't like. The Akazu ducs
have only to label undesirables *ibyitso*. The word means "accomplices." It's
become code for every Rwandese standing up to the regime for whatever
reason. It doesn't matter if a Muhutu marked for Akazu slander hates the
Batutsi. He becomes their accomplice. All through the talks, nameless assassins were regularly dispatching Hutu opposition leaders to that realm
where the Church resides triumphant—running them down, beating them,
shooting them as they opened their gates.

No one agrees on either the center or the frontiers of this syndicate that
runs Rwanda, but everyone knows it as the Akazu, the little grass shack, an
outfit so manifest I give it that uppercase *A*. The Akazu has no official structure, no official chief, no public charter . . . and its meaning in Kinyarwanda,
"the little grass shack," is about as unofficial and modestly lowercase as you
can get. But the modesty is patently—no, ostentatiously—false, a device for
highlighting power. The Akazu is muscular. It may not proclaim itself officially and publicly, but it enjoys far more power than any publicly chartered outfit in Rwanda. It has earned its uppercase *A*.

The charmed circle at its center goes by various monikers, at times *le
réseau zéro*, "the zero network," at times, and more simply, "the network,"
at times "*le clan de madame*," meaning Mme. Habyarimana, the president's
wife, Agathe Kanziga, a quiet queen who murmurs words whose malice we
all strain to make out. Beyond its grip on legitimate business, government,
and the military, the Akazu is also an enterprise dealing variously in extor-
tion, bank fraud, embezzlement, drug trafficking, and trade in endangered
animals. A few Akazu ducs even enjoy, like the criminal seigneurs of Corsica, a true princely past; in their case, the "grass shack" business is an in-
joke whose mock modesty most especially highlights their wealth, power,
and patrician lineage.

No, they aren't Tutsi patricians. They're proudly Hutu, a name that for
years meant peasant. But nobody ever said the Great Lakes are a simple
place, or ever have been, or ever will be. The lineages of these few Akazu
Bahutu may go back further than Tutsi bloodlines, to Bantu from West
Africa who in the deep millennial past may have been the ones who brought
kingship to Rwanda. It's said that the old seigneurs of backcountry Corsica,
like the backcountry signori of Calabria and Sardinia, cultivated underworld reflexes to snap back at greater powers (Paris, Rome, Savoy) that
owned them on paper. Thus did the highborn families of these backcountry

ducs (then they weren't even called Hutu) likewise cultivate underworld reflexes to snap back at the overlordship of the central court—the Tutsi
court—at Nyanza.

So no, they aren't Tutsi, and what does it matter? Now their turf is not
just their ancestral backcountry, the high mountains of the north, but all of
Rwanda, and this is where Rwanda departs sharply from the likes of Corsica
and Calabria. The Akazu runs Rwanda openly, which is just fine with Paris,
now playing the big brother role that Belgium is gladly giving up. Meantime, the days of Rwanda's Tutsi aristos are at least three decades gone.
These days the only Rwandese Batutsi to worry about are deserters from
Uganda's army, waging guerrilla war on the Uganda frontier.

FOR THE ZUNGU MONEYMEN WHO BANKROLL HABYARIMANA, THE ULTIMATE BROKERS IN
this ménage, the assassinations and the pogroms have been exceptionally
embarrassing, at least when they find their way into *Le Monde*. Publicity
tends to make the bankers as edgy as Habyarimana's crowd gets when the
family jewels are threatened. In fact, it was heat from Habyarimana's white
backers that forced him to sit down and bargain in the first place, and now,
as a result of the deals he struck, not only Booh-Booh but an armed UN observer team is on station, so that even more Akazu indelicacies are finding
their way into *Le Soir, Die Welt, The Financial Times*.

There's something I must say here: Habyarimana surely knows why
Booh-Booh is after him. For weeks he's been avoiding the man. From
where he sits, getting rid of the entire UN team would be ideal. But he
must likewise reckon that the UN can't be put off forever, and who
knows—looking at it from where Habyarimana sits—maybe dinner and
drinks with Booh-Booh could be turned to presidential advantage. So all of
a sudden yesterday—April Fool's Day, in fact—Booh-Booh found himself
summoned to Habyarimana's Gisenyi retreat, where the presidential family will be spending Easter weekend.

Booh-Booh's first invitation is for lunch at the villa of an Akazu baron.
Habyarimana is here, but it doesn't look promising for UN business. There
are just too many guests for Booh-Booh to speak frankly to the president.

For their part, milords have business to go over with Booh-Booh. One
matter above all seems on their minds, a matter they don't have to spell out
because it's so clearly understood: Rwanda is more than some garden-
variety banana republic. Right enough, it's a totalitarian state with a totalitarian state's standard cast of malcontents: inhabitants of one region (in
Rwanda's case, the Nduga south) who don't like how most of the pork goes
to the president's cronies in another region (in Rwanda's case, the Akazu
north); minority people who don't like how the president is employing the

jobless by putting them to work killing minority people; intellectuals who aren't wild about a one-party state in which everyone is expected to wear a pin featuring the maximum man; and that gang of deserters from Uganda's army who claim they're Rwandese and think they could do a better job running the place.

But Habyarimana is no comic dictator, and Booh-Booh isn't here to play his foil. The president is shrewd, intelligent. Under him, Rwanda became a showcase for development finance, and until the coffee crash it still was. People in Rwanda have gotten rich on fees, commissions, and kickbacks. A few in France and Belgium have gotten richer. Hundreds of millions in contracts and subcontracts are at stake. French contracts, German, Belgian, Italian, Dutch—all subsidized by those governments. Lectern high, Eurocrats rhapsodize about how their generous subsidies are helping yet another of Africa's struggling states. They edit from their rhapsodies a stipulation in the paperwork: The subsidized state in Africa must contract with companies from the subsidizing state in Europe, regardless of price, regardless of quality. After the second or third expense-account sundowner at Chez Lando's bar, they calculate just how much business these subsidies for Africa will mean for *their* companies, back home in Euroland, and especially for plants having trouble keeping up with global competition, plants that might otherwise have to lay workers off—workers who vote.

Yes, you can argue that these Eurocrats are shortsighted, that the result can only be Euro-industry that's even less competitive because it's become hooked even more on subsidies. But that's the long run. Hitler couldn't see the long run when his finance minister told him he had to slow arms production. In fact, he sacked the man, the same man who had broken the back of Germany's backbreaking inflation. Likewise these Eurocrats can't see it. Especially when the short-run result is not only jobs, but a chance to award these African contracts to pet companies smart enough to have donated to the campaign funds of well-placed Euro-politicos. And the chance to dish out favors to Africrats who behave—not to speak of Africrats ready to kick back a cut of this largesse that Americans call "payola," Arabs call "baksheesh," and we call "ruswa"—though truth be told, those aren't words any of these gents would use. "Carrying charges" is closer to the mark. Or even more discreetly, "cost-plus."

This afternoon's luncheon crowd cannot, of course, put it to Booh-Booh just this way, but most likely he gets the picture: All this is now in jeopardy because sharing power means sharing patronage and the Akazu needs every bit of patronage it has. There isn't even enough credit left on the books to keep smuggling weapons out of apartheid South Africa, which dearly loves the business and would bend over backward to accommodate if only it could see some cash. So much has been achieved, Habyarimana's crowd likes to tell anyone who will listen. So much has been achieved, they surely repeat to captive guest Booh-Booh. So much is threatened, they forever complain, by the greed of what they are fond of calling *inyangarwanda,* "enemies of the nation."

Enemies of the state, they say. Greed, they repeat. A menace to society. Lest such reminders be lost on the man from Cameroon, they invite him to get together again for supper, this time at the president's Gisenyi villa.

THE UN'S NUNCIO DRAWS A LINE IN THE SAND

SATURDAY EVENING. Chez Habyarimana, the best crystal is out, Arpège is in the air, and here in deepest Africa, houseboys have undraped the reproduction Louis Quatorze, the reproduction Louis Quinze, the genuine Louis Farouk.

For all the seeming mismatch of gilded settees in a bush-bound setting, this lush evening in Gisenyi is in fact made for the Louis this, the Louis that, and above all for the Louis Farouk—this last a decorative style inspired by Egypt's last and Hollywood-smitten king, who died in corpulent exile, face-down in a plate of macaroni, on the Côte d'Azur. Thick Louis Farouk carpets rife with nylon cherubs, run off in Belgian nylon mills, recall the fraction of eighteenth-century France that was powdered and pompadoured. As do harshly gilt Louis Farouk mirrors, cabinets, and dainty divans stapled together in today's most high-tech German joineries. From Luanda to Basra to Vladivostok, this polyurethane-luxe has come to represent not the corrupt excesses of Europe, but high civilization. It furnished Tito's bunker; at this 1994 moment, it furnishes Saddam Hussein's. It's the otherwise feckless Farouk's gilded legacy to the revolutionary third world.

Tonight, amid this grandeur that he and his stand to lose, Habyarimana is in a humiliating fix. Thieves and creditors alike are at the gate. Stalling for time, he's either edged up to or outright signed agreements-in-principle that he should never have gotten anywhere near: a so-called broad-based government in which he would remain president, but at the cost of emasculation as Rwanda's all-powerful politico. (His propaganda apparatus exclaims in righteous outrage at how the minority Batutsi, so lamented in the Zungu press, once decorated their king's war drum with the testicles of their enemies.) His army would be only 60 percent his. His officer corps would be only half his. All the way down the line patronage would be slashed—and this just as his people all the way down the line are insisting it's time for their cut of the cow.

Significant concessions—but not real ones. He could never let that happen. It would be suicide, the end of what some call his crowd's *"pot aux roses."* He could agree in principle. But he's conceded no real power. He can't.

Tonight his people bombard Booh-Booh. Impossible, they tell Booh-Booh, as Queen Agathe nods in agreement. Out of the question. Unfair.

Indeed, so unfair and so outrageous that even in this authoritarian state, the press has warned the president bluntly that he'd best shift course or outraged citizens will bounce him from power. The press is owned by the barons who dine here this very evening.

April evenings in Gisenyi are cool, but the heat is relentless, and Booh-Booh has a job to do. He has a message to deliver to these people, and by jove, he will deliver it. Does he stand accused in some circles of cutting these people too much slack? He will issue them a cold ultimatum.

To be fair, some credit for the cold ultimatum must go to his Egyptian boss, UN secretary-general Boutros Boutros-Ghali. After months of threats he has not backed up, Boutros-Ghali has at last decided that enough is enough: If the stalling and the abuse don't end, the UN mission will. And Booh-Booh lets this evening's crowd know exactly what that means. There must be no ambiguity. We don't know his exact words, but we do know the unflinching thrust of his message: Listen, ladies and gents, the UN has been watching what's going on here in Rwanda, and if you don't cut it out, we're not going to watch anymore.

3

Day Two: Arcadia Adrift

SUNDAY, APRIL 3, 1994. *"Salut!"* Today is Easter, and the paschal joint is on the spit. The tender scent of roasting flesh is carried on breezes refreshed by this the season of the short rains. If momentarily there's a bit too much fat in the fire, it's cut by an abundance of oleander, Orangina, and chilled white wine. Vivaldi drifts through eucalyptus groves.

I drift with Vivaldi on a breeze, and high above the Arcadian Easter below. It's a perk that goes with being no more than an idea in the ether of this real afternoon in this real garden on this too-real day. I drift where I please. In hard material fact, I'm years and worlds away, hurtling through a black hole in an underground train in the final days of the second millennium, but I've somehow gotten the big idea that I've etherized, become an errant notion adrift above Africa on Easter Sunday 1994, and so here I drift.

It's not hard at all. Nor is it at all unpleasant imagining the earthly delights below. I know this garden. Barely three months ago, in December of '93, I was here, actually here, strolling as now these Easter guests actually stroll. Then it was Christmas. Now it's Easter already, and beyond what I see, I see more. Some of those down there I hold close. I know what's on their minds. Back at work after Christmas, I began running up long-distance calls to their houses, offices, bosses, friends; calls full of static, over cold oceans.

Now here I drift on a zephyr. I must be careful not to get gusted away as I describe what I see. I must ground my perceptions in established fact. Some Bahutu like to say we Batutsi care about nothing but fact. They say we're cold. They accuse us of hiding our feelings, of controlling every facial tick. They claim that the imperative to maintain control is drilled into us like please and thank you. They may be right. We strive not to laugh, and never to cry, and these days when we do laugh, it's often a dark laugh, to keep from crying. The picture of someone gushing her story appalls me. Nosey people give me hives. I feel as if they're trying to trap me, get me to drop my guard, induce me to make a mistake. Certainly since the events of 1994, I feel a great reluctance to say more than I intend to say, when I intend to say it, and right now I feel as if I've had a bit too much white wine. I must be careful describing what I see.

I see a uniformed maidservant trunding a tea cart about a lawn. I see children of all ages and all colors, in shorts and in pinafores, tearing paths through guests on a broad verandah and across a broad lawn. It's the lawn of the Canadian consul's residence, an idyll set in soaring stands of eucalyptus whose aroma eddies with the faintest whiff of diesel fumes. The adults nearly match the children in variety. In one corner of the lawn, marked by cigar smoke and the acrid pungency of Gauloises, men in linen cluster, black men, white men, Indians, Arabs. Over there by a punch bowl is a cluster of women, marked by Easter colors and a light cloud of cologne. On the terrace, those not quite adult take each other's measure and parade as cool as the breeze.

What is it about such young people that gives some a beauty we're tempted to call deadly no matter what their innocence? Among those almost grown, two seem to float, a girl diving sleekly into the pool and a boy playing badminton on the lawn. She's at least six feet tall. Her blue-eyed friend looks a bit younger; he's well over six feet. Their skin is of the hue Gauguin captured in the South Seas, and their features, too, look like those captured by Gauguin in his Tahitian interludes—though perhaps with a touch of El Greco's astigmatism, for much about these two is somehow stretched out.

Among the women at the punch bowl there seems to be some stiffness. We all know these affairs. You most likely find yourself in a group whose members come from several countries; only a few of you know each other. You explain how you've ended up in this small African state at war with itself, and the others nod politely, as if in agreement, as if to say, yes, you're right, that is how you ended up here. I know just one woman in this group, a matronly Muzungu named Hélène. I can almost hear her explaining, as I have often heard her explain, how she was once a staffer at the American embassy, a librarian, and how she's not American, she's Canadian, French-Canadian. The others likely nod in agreement. It's protocol at such gatherings, nodding in polite agreement to the commonplace: Yes, you are from Canada. Yes, you are a librarian. You look like a librarian. She does look like a librarian. She wears glasses on a chain about her neck.

What makes this group different is that these women grip their drinks so tightly. (Don't they know? A wineglass can shatter if you grip it too tightly.)

It's not so much the war that unnerves them. The war is confined to a corner of the north, and for the past few months, even there, a cease-fire has silenced the guns. What's unnerving are reports from the countryside, and for that matter from roads nearby, that people are getting beaten, that people are dying. A stray soul here, a half-dozen there, luckless sojourners caught by mobs. Dead, and not in battles, in massacres of ordinary folk, farmers, farmers' wives, farmers' children. The state announces it isn't happening. Relief workers dig up bodies. The state says it knows nothing about it. There's a domestic opposition, unarmed and cowed; it protests. Here and there, opposition chiefs have been showing up dead in the roads; the gendarmerie says the crimes have the earmarks of professional assassination. You wonder where the gendarmerie gets the candor for statements so impolitic, if not downright dangerous.

I can't hear what the wives are saying, but they must certainly chat about what it's like to be a minority in this minority-conscious country. It's a favored topic among this set. Someone will undoubtedly ask Hélène; she's been here longer than most. "What can an outsider know?" she generally says in reply to such questions. She's not naturally a guarded person; she has become guarded. An elegant woman joins the group. A man passes. She addresses him. "Darling Gerald . . ."

The clutch of men on the lawn ebbs and flows about a dark and heavy African who seems at one moment tall, then short, as he shifts his weight from one leg to the other. He strides from the group to greet a short, square white man with a clipped goatee ("*Joyeuses Pâques, Jacques,*" the African booms), and it becomes clear he's crippled. Up and down he pitches as he reaches for the outstretched hand of the newcomer.

"*Bonne fête, Lando,*" booms this fellow named Jacques, who stands about Lando's height when big brother's weight is on his short leg.

Our Jacques. Our Lando. Lando is at an age when middle-age spread challenges the belt, and his belt line is pitched at an angle reflecting his affliction. For years, I looked up at him from down low. Now I see him as if from above, and I try to direct him. "Go there, Lando. No, there, there by the jacaranda. You'll be safe there." He doesn't hear me.

Children rip and tear with scant inhibition, but among the older ones, the young adults, the stiffness that goes with their age seems more marked than usual. The slight blue-eyed giant returns from the punch bowl with two glass cups and an awkward effort to break the tension. Glancing over at the invisible cloud of cologne above the women, he asks who sprayed the insecticide.

"That's not funny," says his lovely friend.

Among the men, too, there are tries at humor, but here it's even darker, the humor of neighbors sandbagging for a hurricane.

"So. At last. Peace on the horizon," says Jacques, and laughs. Jacques is Jacques Roy, a lawyer from Quebec. He first met Lando years ago, in Montreal. It was in Montreal also that Jacques met that librarian over there, Hélène.

Lando then was a university student trying to scare up the wherewithal to stage productions by African playwrights. He was a storyteller then; he's a storyteller now, however preoccupied he is these days, and this day in particular. He is also now minister of labor in Rwanda's quasi-working "broad-based" cabinet, the cabinet's only Tutsi minister, representing an opposition party that the Habyarimanas were forced to accept at the peace talks beneath Kilimanjaro.

Those talks have long since produced what should be a deal. It's even been signed. But signed and enforced are worlds apart. What's going on now is the big stall. If Juvenal H ever quits stalling, opposition parties will have a bigger say. Lando is one of two candidates for speaker of the assembly when that happens. If it happens. The embassy types know full well how powerless Lando is. They know he will likely never be speaker, and he may not have long to live. When I left for Washington just after Christmas, we agreed he'd call me every weekend, when the rates are low. I've never been able to wait for the weekend. I call him when the rates are high. I'm going broke and I don't care.

Lando badgers the embassy types, trying to get them to talk. Years ago, when I was too young to understand, I asked him the secret of telling good stories. He told me it was listening, and that's what he's trying to do, but just now, that's what they want to do, listen, and they're the determined ones. They're as determined to get stories from him as I was as a kid, as I still am.

Except that with me, there's no morbid curiosity. With them, there is. This big crippled Falstaff knows something alien to them—alien to me— what it's like to get yanked from your family and thrown in prison, there to be subject to sweet Jesus knows what. He never really tells us. Only in the most cryptic way, hastening from the subject: "You've got to have courage, Loulou. Remember that."

Until 1990, our Lando was a stranger to public life. He'd been a saloon keeper, a playwright, a producer and director of stage plays, known mostly for a production of Marcel Pagnol's *Topaze* that ran for two years in the few lonely theaters of this remote African place. Then came prison, for politics in which he'd in fact had no part. When he got out, he bellied into politics with all the reckless purpose of his pained stride, and today at the Canadian consul's residence, tales of Lando's quixotic sallies at fate provide material for the gallows humor in which some men somehow find some kind of comfort.

Prime fodder for such manly palaver is Lando's knack for meeting all the wrong people. As he puts it, "low friends in high places"—the most notable and most recent of which is Mobutu Sese Seko, the top sugar of Zaire, Africa's second largest state after the Sudan.

Poor Mobutu. There must be men more wicked in Africa, but such is his notoriety that he has no peer in the African mind. Let's overlook for now that in the popular mind he's the man in a leopard-skin fez who killed his first wife with his own hands while she was pregnant. Better yet, let's assume the business about killing his wife is simply a canard. In the Lingala tongue, which travels the Congo River as Swahili follows the Indian Ocean, he's still Mobutu Sese Seko Kuku Ngbendu wa za Banga, which translates as "all-powerful ruler whose endurance and rigid resolve propel him from conquest to conquest, leaving fire in his wake." Wife-killer or not, he's one who inspires such tales, a man whose name should translate as "deadly presence in human form which strikes with sudden hunger and sucks dry the nation's patrimony."

TO THE WORLD'S PRESS, MOBUTU IS KNOWN AS THE WORLD'S PREMIER KLEPTOCRAT, SPIRitual heir to Belgium's King Leopold, who raped the Congo so thoroughly (natives who didn't collect enough rubber for him famously lost their hands) that he may become known as the premier kleptocrat of all time. To Africa, Mobutu is all that within the soul of a black mamba, a man for whom participatory democracy means that you participate by speaking your mind, he participates by arranging for a Berliet lorry to run you down.

Mobutu, it turns out, is, in addition to this, an aficionado of *la blague*. *La blague* is the bantering nonsense that goes with a couple of drinks or supper, in short, every saloon keeper's stock-in-trade. Not surprisingly, saloon keeper Lando has a name for it, and on the day of the rendezvous in question, Mobutu's protégé Habyarimana was showing off Rwanda's master of pointless banter. As Habyarimana must have seen matters, Mobutu getting Lando as a bantering partner would be something like an aficionado of the kitchen dicing carrots with a master of the blade. As Lando saw it, it was something like dicing carrots blindfolded.

It happened about six months before this Easter party. Habyarimana flew Lando and some other opposition leaders to Mobutu's private realm within a realm at Gbadolite, in the north of what was still Zaire. Quite aside from showing off, what Habyarimana seems to have had in mind was using Mobutu to pressure the opposition to get off his back. Mobutu wanted to shoot *la blague*.

"I hear you've got a way with the white ladies," said Mobutu, still trim in his declining years, to our homely Lando, already struggling with middle age. "Some taste they've got." As he spoke he cast a long look at Lando's belly. To which Lando instantly objected, "Now just a minute. Everyone knows I run a chophouse. What would it say about our cookery if my belly didn't have something to show for it?"

"So what do you think?" said Mobutu. "Could you, say, interest a nice Zungu lady in marrying the president of Zaire?"

"*Mais certainement, monsieur le président.* But tell me this: How are you going to protect me from all the jealous ladies of Zaire?"

No surprise, Mobutu liked that, and so will the men at this Easter party, as if that were the best of Lando's salt. What impressed me when I heard the story was that, through all the banter, Habyarimana kept his focus, never even chuckling the sycophant's chuckle, just forever interrupting: "You're pushing too hard, Lando. Push will come to shove."

Lando says that at last he muttered that he was obliged to speak for his party.

"Regardless, you're all pushing too hard; push will come to shove."

"Think of it this way," said Lando. "A legitimate opposition is good for you. It gives you legitimacy."

Mobutu directed a poker face at Lando, what some people call the face of a dog with eyes. For one long minute he said nothing, then, "My son, you're still too young. You still don't know Africa."

It's more chilling than comic, this story six months old, so filled with African self-hate, but gallows humor is the order of the day, and this clutch of men will surely laugh, and laugh again, until at last the equatorial sun makes ready its metronomic tick below the horizon.

Over at the punch bowl, Hélène, the librarian from Canada, must make up her mind when to call it an evening. She excuses herself, then walks over to collect her husband, the still-laughing Lando, and their children, the blue-eyed giant Patrick and his friend, his sister, six-foot Malaika.

"So beautiful," says their grandmother when she's alone on a back porch with a friend, away from prying eyes that might see her dragging on one of her tiny pipes. "So beautiful. And I'm not prejudiced."

4

DAY THREE: A BLACK MAMBA SUMMONS
OUR PRESIDENT TO ITS LAIR

SILVER SPRING, MARYLAND, MONDAY, APRIL 4, MORNING. Yesterday my phone line cum lifeline to Africa was gripped by some strange humming charge, and today I should go to work but I don't. I stay home and dial for hope. And dial. No luck. No line. Just that strange humming charge, and "If you'd like to place a call. . . ." I try Lando at work. No line. I try Lando at home. Nothing. I try Hélène. Nothing. I doodle. The word *Kigali*. Dot the *i*. Dial. The word *Gisenyi*. Dot the *i*. Dial. The dot gets bigger, and aha! Gisenyi is to the left of Kigali, just as it is on the map, west of Kigali. Dial. Connect the dots, the winding mountain road from Kigali to Gisenyi. Lac Kivu. Dial. Doodle. Mountains above Kivu. Sketch them in. Our old school there. The mission. Sketch the bell. There's no trouble in the world, just scratch paper, number two pencils, and idle time. A tiny volcano joins the map. A little gorilla dances atop. Dial. I'm becoming quite the cartographer; I add Lake Edward, the Ruwenzori hills, and their Semliki River, proud with lions (as if it were the Nile); Lake Albert.

PROFESSIONAL GEOGRAPHERS, A LITERAL LOT, HAVE TROUBLE HEARING RWANDA DE-scribed as a backwater. To them, *backwater* isn't a social term, it's a term of place. They'll tell you we lie high and green above Africa at the headwaters, the *head*waters, of the Nile, and for that matter, at the headwaters of the Congo as well.

How I wished as a child that I were a peregrine falcon or an osprey or even a hawkish little kestrel. Sometimes, in idle moments, I'm still a tardy schoolgirl, striding along some dust-bright track. The lightest zephyr billows my dress, a raft of books balances itself atop my head, and here I stop, let slip my books, and gaze up to where a hawk surveys what the geographers map.

Just as happily I'd have been a black-shouldered kite, or a griffin, or any number of soaring buzzards. The soaring fish eagle that sweeps down on our lakes sees it all with ginlike clarity, beginning in the south with two end-on-end finger lakes, Malawi and Tanganyika. From there, she sees the watershed stretch upcountry to Gisenyi's Kivu, then lakes Victoria, Edward, and Albert, where the papyrus-laced Nile alternately plunges and ambles out of wet Uganda, down in cataracts to and through the sere expanses of the Sudan.

The French call our lake lands *"la crête Congo-Nil,"* the crèche of the two great rivers. The scholarly term is *interlacustrine.* Some call it Africa's backbone: The string of lakes pool in the hollows of a three-thousand-mile spine of mountains thrown up by the Great Rift on its monumentally fractious passage from far inland East Africa to the Holy Land. Ever-shrinking bands of pungent, bush-wise pygmies, ever-shrinking herds of pygmy elephant, haunt mahogany forests. Clouds of flamingos waft in enormous skies. Halogen-eyed leopards of the night make their home among bracken and marigold, as do bushbuck, duiker, mongoose, fat rats, and high-strung forest antelopes whose bucks sport high-spiraling horns.

Few tsetse flies up here, few malarial mosquitoes; instead the owl, the tree cobra, the beetle. In backwaters and hidden marshes where peasant farmers have not yet crowded we have hippo pools and hog wallows; some remaining woodland; dappled light falling on dappled kid and dappled cat.

Here in sun you see a flattened tin:

LONGEVITY BRAND

FULL CREAM

SWEETENED CONDENSED MILK

The label is printed in Vietnamese and Mandarin; the product is packaged in Holland.

There in shadow is a clear, cold watercourse. Shadows dodge through timber. Cobwebs stretch across glens. Here the mountain gorilla holds out, besieged by hungry humans who climb with hoes and pangas. Pangas are what we East Africans call machetes.

These are the Virungas, their foothills and scarped plateaus. Their greatest peak, snow-crowned four thousand five hundred meters up, is Karisimbi. Their jewel is an actively rumbling leviathan, Mount Nyiragongo, mother of the great god Gongo, swathed in smoke and mist and steam, looking down on a nation already among the world's highest.

And the world's most densely peopled. Today's density is due in good part to lifesaving drugs imported years ago by mission dispensaries. (Where we desperate Africans sought the potions as graven images of the mission's God, magic idols to which we swarmed.) But the ancient and courtly realms of Uganda, Rwanda, and Burundi (our twin to the south) can't pin it all on mission medicine. Unlike much of Africa, unlike the wide lands surrounding us, these isolated highlands were densely peopled for centuries before modern drugs made them even more densely peopled. Cheek-by-jowl with primeval Africa is terraced hill after terraced hill.

Some landscapes roll away to distant misted horizons more Bali than Africa. Other landscapes look so bucolic that it reminds some of the downs and vales of the English Lake Country. But there are too many people for that. Demographers tell us the boom will ease, even reverse. But between here and there, who knows what ache will wrack the countryside? In the middle of the twentieth century we numbered about two million, and were packed at that. Before the middle of this century, we will number fifty million. The apt picture isn't England's lake country, but the lovely green vales of nineteenth-century Ireland, just before the landed gentry began shipping a catastrophic abundance of tenant families off into misery, and those barbarous Molly Maguires began fighting back.

LIKE A DOG WITH EYES

ABOVE GISENYI, MONDAY, APRIL 4, MORNING. Great monsoons blow from this part of Africa. They blow northeast across the Indian Ocean to Yemen and Hadhramaut and on to the Malabar Coast, bearing dhows heavy—at times listing—with ivory, horn, incense, skins. Then they blow back, bringing India, Persia, and Arabia to Africa. It's a world of its own, this world of the monsoon, with nabobs who have long been avid falconers. My president, *mon général,* is not of princely lineage, but he's a man of distinct military bearing, and he has a bird that can soar with the best; nay, better. It was a gift of French president François Mitterrand—that twin jet Dassault Falcon 50, complete with its three French pilots, Colonel Jean-Pierre Minaberry, Major Jacky Héraud, and Chief Adjutant Jean-Marie Perrine.

This morning (as on the backside of midnight I forever dial, and dial), their craft climbs up and out of Gisenyi, banking steeply in a broad arc toward the east. Beneath them as they cant toward the Indian Ocean, the pilots can see the brilliant jade ledge that is Rwanda perched high above the endless dun savannah of East Africa. They keep on banking, gradually bringing the Falcon all the way round, then level off—headed almost due west, toward the Atlantic.

All about looms Africa's rocky spine. Just ahead, out of sight in mist, sinks the spreading wet welter of the Congo basin. On the far side of the basin are Gbadolite and Mobutu Sese Seko.

Who knows what's on Habyarimana's mind as he flies west out of Rwanda, Mobutu-bound? It could be more than Mobutu. One of the few things we know for sure about this safari is that Mobutu summoned Habyarimana. Habyarimana did not ask to see Mobutu, and he may have more to preoccupy him than big brother M. For random instance, two women, both named Agathe.

The first is his wife, Agathe Kanziga, "Queen Agathe." At fifty-four she remains a woman with all the graces of lineage. She wears her princely Hutu ancestors like emeralds. Once that conceit belonged mostly to us minority Batutsi. No longer. Now Hutu aristos stand front and center. Habyarimana knows too well how distressed she is that the masses, the Bahutu, *her* people, are about to see democracy critically compromised. The accords he's signed with the enemy call for guaranteed posts for minority people— people who most likely couldn't win those posts in a general election. Under these circumstances she must certainly tell her husband he must do whatever he can to stay such a calamity, such a blow to democracy.

She knows, of course, that the Mobutu model for hanging on has been tarnished in recent years, but aren't the French rehabilitating his reputation? And more to the point, desperate times call for desperate measures: Look what Mobutu does when he's pressed. Stall. Then agree to talk. Stall again. Bargain. Forever. Strike an agreement. Stall signing. Sign. Stall compliance. Agree to comply, and . . . And then what?

This is where her husband is now stuck. This is the pretty pass to which he's brought their Rwanda. He can't comply. He knows he can't comply. He's made it clear that he and his outfit resent ever having had to sign the deal. For the Habyarimanas, for both of them, the question is simple. Isn't democracy, majority rule, supposed to be the standard by which the free world measures African states?

Ever since coffee prices began collapsing nearly a decade ago, times have been getting worse. With less to go around, everybody wants more, more. Even Batutsi want more. Which of course gets the Hutu masses mad as the devil. What can the Habyarimanas and their crowd do but marshal the masses to go to work and hit back? Indeed, in the last few years they've made *work* a word larger than itself, a word now pregnant with larger meaning, the kindest of which is "hitting back." But no sooner do they stand up against Tutsi greed than the bankers get embarrassed, and the cash drawer slams shut.

As his Agathe sees matters, only France and Zaire have stood firmly behind the *rubanda nyamwinshi,* the majority folk. And not just the Socialist regime of François Mitterrand, but the old-school French military establishment. Right enough, they insist that "the work" embarrasses them. Their recent counsel does hint that matters cannot go on as they have. But there's no question in Agathe H's mind that the French are committed to majority rule, to her *rubanda nyamwinshi*, to what she insistently sees as democracy.

But then again, what about him, Habyarimana? Just how committed are the French to him?

As for Mobutu, he's long been Habyarimana's mentor and patron, and he's especially fond of Agathe. "Kanziga Agathe," he says at times in the Rwandese manner, reversing names. Habyarimana's canny Agathe sees Mobutu playing the French like a harpsichord. The French are resurrecting Mobutu's famously tarnished reputation; they know how to handle the bankers.

Mobutu and the French. The French and Mobutu. Habyarimana has reason to hope that they will tell him how to handle this impasse. It's in their interest. Or is it? Will they help? Or will Mobutu again fix him with that blank stare, like a dog with eyes.

And how committed is his wife to him?

Quite aside from her distinctly personal distress with the parleys that threaten to ruin so much, she positively despises, personally despises, the other Agathe.

Would that the other Agathe were one of Habyarimana's mistresses. She is not; his headache is not nearly that simple. She's the prime minister. She's the redoubtable Uwilingiyimana Agathe. Like Habyarimana and his wife, Kanziga Agathe, Prime Minister Agathe is a child of the majority Bahutu. Indeed, she's an energetic advocate of the Bahutu of the south—of Nduga country. The president and his wife are from the northwest, from Akazu country, and as the Akazu sees matters, this Agathe from Nduga country is all too willing to live with Batutsi. Habyarimana despises her nearly as much as his wife does. She won't be bribed or bullied. As education minister, she enforced a regime of honest entrance exams that robbed the presidency of patronage. She's an upstart with no redeeming dignity, an unreconstructed marplot. She's everything his wife is not.

Habyarimana owes his career to his wife. He'd been nothing. She was something; her family was something. But husbands and wives can have their differences, their problems. . . .

BACKGROUND MUSIC

MONDAY NOON. Kigali-ville is a town becoming a city in spite of itself. The Germans threw it up because a colony needs a capital, and the royal family wanted to keep the taboos of the court at Nyanza, several miles south and west. Much of Nyanza's magic lay in its spare pastoral elegance, its giant *rondavels*—windowless round houses with high-pitched walls and thatch roofs—sprawling easily over the almost treeless green hills of what looked like nothing so much as a world without end, an ever-rolling deer park peopled by tonsured nobles in tunics, attendants, ever-busy servants. There was no room in this idyll for anything less than idyllic—at least by royal lights.

Like Zambia's Lusaka and Zimbabwe's Harare (né Salisbury), most of the ville went up in the fifties and early sixties; most of its buildings have the bland indifference of those years, but unlike those places, it's not a prairie town laid out in neat grids. It doesn't look like it belongs more in Nebraska than Africa. It's hilly, graced at every turn with flowering trees. It looks like it belongs in Africa.

Especially peasant suburbs like Masaka Hill. As almost everywhere in Africa, towns are ballooning with landless peasants, but with all of Kigali's gospel missions, diplomatic missions, banks, shipping agents, shops, and hotels, enough petty cash bubbles in the Kigali of 1994 to keep good numbers of the poor working. Masaka Hill is a quarter that shows how Rwanda's poor fare when left to their own devices, with scant help, in a threadbare economy. It's wedged against one side of the airfield and one side of the Presidential Guard's Camp Kanombe. Most of its shops and houses are mud brick, with corrugated roofs. Their owners have built them. There's little plumbing, but it isn't a scene of squalor. It doesn't yet have the congestion of a slum. It's deep green with family banana plantations. The bulk of its people can't read; they're almost all Hutu.

Down by the high road, you see the matchbox shops called "bodegas" in Latin America and "dukas" from Burundi to Bangladesh. Here, on a footpath with no name, you see a shop selling used hardware. In such a hamlet once, on a nameless, unpaved road, I saw a bakery with a hand-painted sign: baguettes crossed like sabers on a coat of arms, and in neat letters:

BOULANGERIE

AUTOMATIQUE

From this building, ghosts periodically emerged, black men powdered white from head to foot, stooped with work. But the mood wasn't—isn't—gloomy. The music is Congolese or Rwandese in the lively Congolese manner. The welcome is friendly.

In most of Rwanda, its footpaths and red clay roads go nameless. Ask directions and you're liable to hear something like: "Look for the dentist sign, the one with the big bloody tooth. Turn left there. Then look for a bicycle repair place on the right. There's usually a bloke out front roasting corn. You'll smell the corn. Turn right there and . . ."

On yet another byway with no name, two barefoot kids kick a limp football in front of a duka. A picture, of course, that you're likely to see anywhere, from Burundi to Bangladesh. The inclination is to picture the quarter facelessly, from behind, just the backs of heads, just to remind us that there are, in fact, people out there in the backdrop. But the mind resists. If there are people out there, they are people with faces. You strain to see, even if the bike you're pedaling never stops, even if you're forever in danger of getting run into a ditch by a lorry dieseling by. Just there: two kids, both barefoot, with a ball made of banana leaves. One of them is eight or nine and good. With a bare foot and his knee he keeps it going forever. People walking, people on bicycles, keep passing in a blur, obscuring the two. The bigger kid seems to indulge the little one; the bigger one seems adolescent, awkward, shaped like a bowling pin.

A flatbed rattles up. Somebody throws another lad a copse of little bananas. The weight of the copse and the force of the toss knock him over. Bananas fly. He scrambles to get up, slips on one, falls back, squashes another. An old lady waddles out, waving a broom. Sheepishly, he puts on his shoes.

If he's among those who have shoes.

Let's just arbitrarily say he is. There was someone back there putting on shoes—shoes with a shine. Before he put on each shoe, he breathed on it and polished. He wore no socks.

MALICE IN WONDERLAND

EARLY EVENING. Mobutu Sese Seko's palace in Gbadolite stands silent, bodyguards and chauffeurs in Ray-Bans standing idly about, grim ladies-in-waiting. Gbadolite lies on the south bank of the Ubangi, celebrated by enthusiasts of the bizarre as the river along which a tribe can be found whose women distort their lips into virtual platypus bills by forcing into them progressively larger dinner plates. The Ubangi flows in a broad arc west and south, emptying into the Congo. Just south of Gbadolite, the River Ebola, of viral infamy, flows in a muddy arc that mimics the Ubangi, likewise finding, and dovetailing into, the Congo. The Ubangi rises in the River Uele, which is fed by the River Bomokandi, which runs west through the Ituri Forest, whose expanse yawns forever on.

North and west of the Ituri are the Ruwenzori hills, also called the Mountains of the Moon. They rise just north of Rwanda. With imperfect but nonetheless canny intuition, Herodotus posited them as the source of the Nile. More than three millennia later, nineteenth-century explorers were finding as much fault with each other as with ancient Herodotus in locating the Nile's headwaters. The first was a rogue orientalist, Sir Richard Burton, who raised a modest fortune, then hired a priggish subaltern in the Indian Army, John Haning Speke, to set out with him from Zanzibar in search of the source.

The two wrote fevered field notes in which they conjured fearsome supermen out of mostly secondhand tales of Batutsi—tales of dread spun for them by imaginative Arab dragomans. Thus began the practice of racial myth-brewing that has plagued us; tracking its progress to race hate and racial murder in twentieth-century Rwanda dazzles and bewilders me. This celebrity-hungry pair made many claims in the realm of physical geography, most flawed, many dead wrong. But it was their big ideas about race that were perhaps their greatest legacy, their gift of dread and mass hysteria.

MOBUTU IS FINISHED WITH OUR PRESIDENT. THE AUDIENCE IS OVER. HABYARIMANA AND his party are back on the tarmac, boarding his Falcon 50. The day now fading has been hot, the air-conditioning frigid, the generators loud; right now the night air is heavy, still, sweet. What was said? There are versions, but no one knows for sure. Should I wonder? Speculation can be a hazard to your health.

The drone of cicadas is replaced by the drone of Dassault engines . . . and that's all we know for sure, that and what the pilots see beneath them as they fly Habyarimana back to Kigali: the endless basin, the storied Ituri, and then at last black mountains against an electric dusk and the shimmering black depths of Lake Kivu beneath smoking Nyiragongo.

It's safe to say that Habyarimana has more on his mind than scenery. Even if he's looking at it, he's looking through it. Some will remember him walking from meeting to meeting in Dar as if he were in a daze.

Crystalline to the eye but too poisonous—naturally poisonous—for the crocodile, Kivu is necklaced by deep volcanic fjords. Its frigid depths hide so much methane and carbon dioxide that it is among just two or three lakes in the world that are in literal danger of blowing up. Odorless, tasteless fumes leak from vents hidden around its periphery, where they lurk in hollows, ready to asphyxiate leopard, parrot, and rat with impartial malice.

Habyarimana's job, by contrast, deals with some highly partial malice, but even a decade from now it won't be easy sorting it out. Within a few days that malice will send whole communities of bloated human beings (bloated children in shorts and pinafores, bloated grandmothers, mothers, toddlers blown up round as balloons in a circus parade) tumbling and bobbing down the rapids of the Akagera River as it winds out from the heart of Rwanda down into the endless blue expanse of Lake Victoria.

OF COWBOYS AND COWARDS IN THE
WILDS OF OFFICE POLITICS

AFTER DARK. *"Salut!"* Today is not only Easter Monday, it's the national day of Senegal, and a day for *la gloire* it is. Stella Artois all around and Dom Perignon for the ladies. Pearl of what the French call their *"pré carré,"* their own backyard in Africa, land of giraffe and camel, Senegal may not have the wealth of the Ivory Coast or Gabon, but it has the horizon, and it has the Senegalese, it has *le désert du beau geste* and the riverine homes of great artists in wood and metal. Not to speak of that cookery, worthy of *French* recognition.

"Salut!" someone shouts, and a grin creases the beefy face of Théoneste Bagosora. The retired colonel's substantial presence, ample but not corpulent, his clinking glass, his laugh, command attention. *"Salut!"* he chuckles, and grabs a chuckling diplomat by the elbow.

It hardly matters that Bagosora is not Senegalese. He's Rwandese, and we're in Kigali, half a continent away from Senegal. Tonight bottles pop. Tall black men have donned fezzes and red cummerbunds, manned the bars, and waded out among the diplomats and officers, trays of goodies on high.

The crusty baguettes these Africans have baked for the evening may just miss the measure of Lyon or Brussels, but they're better than most of what I find passing for baguettes in Washington. Just ask Colonel Marchal over there. He should know. He's both Belgian and an intelligence officer. Or for that matter, ask the man to whom Marchal is grunting in French, his boss, Roméo Dallaire.

Dallaire is a major general in Canada's army. The first time I saw him was four months ago, at the Christmas celebration in the garden that hosted yesterday's Easter affair. At Christmastime he was a happier man. Just a couple months earlier, he'd assumed command of one of the decade's smaller UN peacekeeping forces. Its mission was monitoring Arusha, the peace deal struck last August between Habyarimana's crew, their political opponents, and the Inkotanyi gang from Uganda. Back then it looked like a gratifying challenge for a young general on his way up, refereeing such an important peace.

Dallaire's boss is a fellow Canadian and fellow general, Maurice Baril, commander of the UN's Department of Peacekeeping Operations in New York. Baril gripes that his man Dallaire is a cowboy. He should know. The two went to school together. But then again there is equal evidence that Baril and his New York crowd are cowards, which tends to color his characterization of Dallaire. In fact, there may be more going on here than some bad blood in the officer corps. Legally, the UN is in Rwanda to referee the peace deal, and as Baril and New York see matters, the only question is how aggressively they referee. As they see matters, Dallaire is too aggressive. But in one troubling respect, Dallaire may be the less ambitious party. Parsing legal documents to win office arguments is not how he spends his day. By now, his only ambition is to save lives. He spends his days trying to scrounge the food, fuel, and spare parts to do it.

In at least one legal sense, the functionaries in New York and Washington are correct. The UN is not in Rwanda to save lives. It's there to "facilitate the accords," whatever such diplo-speak means, and heaven forefend it should mean doing something. The rub is what New York and Washington can't see: That when history judges, the UN's own convention against genocide will carry more weight—more legal weight—than the casebook niceties of dyspeptic functionaries looking for excuses not to act and thereby put their careers in jeopardy. The rub for Dallaire is that he's a soldier, not a lawyer.

His looks don't help the cowboy problem. He's forty-seven, his hair and moustache are blond turning gray, his concrete jaw is cleft at the chin as if by a jackhammer. Pencil out a front tooth and he could pass for an enforcer on the Québec Nordiques, who as of 1994 still held their franchise with the National Hockey League. Only his voice seems out of character; it scratches, sometimes even squeaks. As the diplomatic swim washes about him, Dallaire shows Nelson Mandela's ability to stand straight as a rake without looking stiff, and with an eye-dancing grin to boot.

Still, however much Dallaire is addressed as *"mon général,"* he is in fact just a gendarme, and not a very substantial one at that, a gendarme with neither baton nor leaded cape. On the roads at this moment, his men are patrolling in their white Land Rovers, the color having been chosen years ago for UN peacekeepers because it's less intimidating than anything dark; less than a kilometer off, jeers, then rocks, fly at them. Some of Dallaire's men, maddened, have taken to throwing rocks back. Every day brings word of yet another murder. He was supposed to be collecting arms the peace deal outlaws inside a so-called Kigali weapons-free zone. Little more than a month ago, his deputy Marchal reported in an official aide-mémoire that after 320 foot patrols, 924 mobile patrols, and the establishment of 306 checkpoints, they'd collected exactly nine weapons.

Locked away in Dallaire's safe are official government death lists targeting temperate members of the compromise government—and peace pivots on this handful of figures, not one of whom has an armed constituency. The UN wants them to remain at their posts. Only Dallaire can protect them. But there are diplomats here tonight with more guns at their disposal than Dallaire, and everyone knows it. The responsibilities of these diplomats, at least comparatively, are slight. In the event of emergency, which the big powers have every reason to expect, there is vastly more armed force at hand to protect diplomatic house pets than Dallaire has at hand to protect the compromise government's Hutu prime minister, the Akazu's unreconstructed nemesis, Agathe Uwilingiyimana. The amply protected diplomats politely patronize him. For the past few weeks, it hasn't been easy mustering the Dallaire grin.

Tonight, though, he's not alone. Bottles pop not so much with relief as with nervous energy. The town is on edge. Every few minutes, if for just a nanosecond, Bagosora himself tenses, and a certain static intrudes on his bonhomie.

Dallaire's job was supposed to have been a cakewalk. The two warring parties had signed a cease-fire and an agreement-in-principle for a broader peace. A broad-based temporary government was in place. They just needed the UN on site to referee, and back in August when he showed up for a few weeks to look things over, every party to the dispute said they wanted the UN. Back in August, Dallaire used to talk about what a wonderland this is. "How can you lose?" he used to say.

Tonight, fear is being served up with the canapés.

Things got especially bleak in October. In Burundi, our twin to the south, the minority Batutsi had never yielded power to the majority Bahutu. Some Batutsi simply felt entitled; more were afraid of what would happen should they yield power to a tyranny of the majority on the Rwandese model. Finally, in 1993, Burundi's Tutsi president opted for reform, scheduling elections he knew he'd likely lose—and did lose. In June, he yielded the presidency on schedule to an engineer from the majority Bahutu. For four months, the new president managed to negotiate a treacherous course. Unfortunately, that involved exciting expectations among the Bahutu, which in turn excited fears among Batutsi. Then in October, disaster struck. Hotheaded officers in the army, still controlled by Batutsi, assassinated the president. Outraged Bahutu began killing ordinary Batutsi; the Tutsi-led army cracked a whip that sent thousands of Batutsi-hating Bahutu upcountry into Rwanda, and a new wave of pogroms began blistering Rwanda's hills. Straightaway, the Akazu found its propaganda campaign fueled by big new constituencies of Bahutu frightened that Batutsi would seize power in Rwanda. It hardly matters that the Tutsi officers who killed the Hutu president had to flee the country, and that by now, a Muhutu is again Burundi's president.

DALLAIRE'S MAN MARCHAL ISN'T HERE TO PARTY. A TANNED AND SALLOW COUNTERPOINT to the tanned and ruddy Dallaire, Luc Marchal has eyes behind which either sorrow or craft seem to rule the soul, but you can't tell which. Landing at Kigali in November, at an airfield washed by the aroma of wild lavender,

Marchal found a crime scene worse than reported. It's not so much that the killings are worse than reported, though they are. What troubles Marchal is a distinct sense that something is wrong with the picture.

Marchal has understood from the beginning that Rwanda is and has long been a cruel place. He knows the Akazu didn't invent Rwandese cruelty. He also knows that lawlessness, chaos, and random killings have never been part of that cruel picture—and it's hard for him to believe that they have become so overnight, that brittle bonds of civil order have snapped and the natives have gone wild. He knows the bonds aren't brittle, that Hutu, and Tutsi, and Twa (the pygmies of Rwanda) have been schooled by centuries of rigidly regimented rule to obey. When the sign says KEEP TO THE WALK, we keep to the walk. People he trusts tell him Rwanda is as regimented as ever. This has never been the sort of place where you've had to worry much about locking your car, and despite an uptick in theft, it still isn't that sort of place.

Your life, though, is something else. At least now it is.

The partiers whoop. They shout. The shouts drift outside, there to meld with the murmurs of drivers chatting as they dust their big black Chevrolets, Peugeots, and Range Rovers. By and by, the din of insects overcomes the shouts—insects, the song of night birds, and an alternating lilt and squawk coming from the car radios of drivers who wait behind the wheel. Here and there, *askaris* (troopers, in Swahili) lean over car hoods, listening to transistor radios. Besides the usual shortwave stations, the BBC, the Saint Siège's Radio Vatican, they have just four choices: Radio Bukavu, broadcasting from just over the frontier in Zaire; Radio Rwanda, the staid voice of the government; Radio Muhabura, the staid voice of the Inkotanyi rebels; and a private station, financed by an astute elite, Radio des Mille Collines. It's breezy. It's engaging. It's the runaway favorite. Its owners hire and cultivate professional pop singers, producers, directors, audiotape editors, talk-show meisters. They premeditate seeming banter. They pretend they're Batutsi who hate Bahutu.

"So tell us, just what is it you find most disgusting about these Bahutu?" asks a supposedly Tutsi interviewer of a supposedly Tutsi honorable, who waxes disdainful so convincingly that you'd never suspect he's no Mututsi at all, but a fake in a fake interview. To the same end, the station fakes news, invents fake bulletins. *This just in and just for you, Mama Rwanda. . . .*

Even those fingered for murder on its airwaves listen in stupefied fascination. RTLM, Radio/Télévision Libre des Mille Collines, the free voice of the thousand hills, broadcasts breezy talk, veiled threats, and infectious Congolese music in a campaign worthy of the developed world's savviest marketers, and right here in the middle of Africa, thousands of miles from the nearest African imitation of a freeway. Recording artists themselves show up live on-air to shill a public eruption against the hated ones, the "*inyenzi*," the cockroaches, us Batutsi.

"The hour is near, the time is here!" shouts a DJ as he eases the volume on his last cut. "Five before the hour. Time to *teach*. Time to *reach*!" Then in a hoarse whisper: "For the top of the house, *now*! Let's listen to the sweet tones of Simon . . . *Bikin*deee."

For Scots of a certain era, *reach for the top of the house* would translate as "grab for the thatch." The thatch at the top of the house is where we Banyarwanda, like the Scots of Robert the Bruce, keep our weapons, especially blades, and for Banyarwanda that means the machetes East Africa calls pangas. It's where our father kept his. The chief manufacturer of pangas is a British outfit, Chillington; reports are about that its Kigali rep took delivery of more pangas in February 1994 alone than in all of 1993. For what?

Almost every day, the station broadcasts pointed threats on Dallaire's life and on the lives of moderate ministers in the bridge government called for by Arusha. "Set your Seikos, we're coming up fast on the hour. But first this. A bulletin just in. From: the people. To: a certain Muzungu, and you know who, our Canadian fool in a jeep with no fuel. Are you ready, Quebecker? The blade works fast, my friend. It's ten. Now the news."

Every time Dallaire's ability to act is restricted by New York, the goons, most of whom can't read, somehow find out. Probing to see just how weak Dallaire is, they get a little bolder every day, challenging Dallaire's patrols, killing members of the opposition one by one, killing Batutsi at group discount rates. There's no longer any question in Marchal's mind that these groups are controlled, as RTLM is controlled, from the top.

THE NETWORK INTRODUCES ITS FINAL
SOLUTION TO POLITE SOCIETY

In the old days, we were the top—a caste of warrior giants known for their long years devoted to martial instruction and for an exquisitely developed capacity for self-punishment. Not to speak of an exquisitely developed capacity for cruelty. As Habyarimana is wont to note, our war drum, the *kalinga*, was indeed tasseled with the testicles of our enemies, and we performed leaping war dances that tended to capture the imagination. Shooting *King Solomon's Mines* on location in the fifties, Hollywood was so hypnotized that it shot far more footage of our leaping giants than the script could ever use, and it was high-cost footage, shot on deep location with big studio cameras by a high-cost cinematographer; the man won an Academy Award for his work on the movie. But he shot so much footage that entire reels ended up on the cutting-room floor, where someone sagely collected them, archived them, and rented them out to be spliced into a string of cheapo jungle movies produced for boys six to twelve—at just about the time Roméo Dallaire and Luc Marchal were boys six to twelve.

This impressive footage kept showing up in unimpressive movies, until at last came 1961, when the Vibrations, an R&B group from Los Angeles, cut a single with moves unabashedly lifted from these B movies. Suddenly, in the wake of the twist and the slide, American kids were doing their take on an African war dance.

> *Shimmy your shoulders*
> *Slop with your feet*
> *And wiggle your hips*
> *In _time_ with the beat.*
> *Do the bow and arrow.*

Then came the Philly sound. The Delphonics. Al Gorman's barely pubescent falsetto—"Hey there . . . lonely girl." Within a year of the LA hit, a Philly group called the Orlons cut their take on the rage, and it went to number two on the charts for seventeen weeks. The first hit was "The Watusi," the second, "The Wah Watusi" ("Waaah, oowaatusi . . ."). Yes, for what it's worth, this is the Africa of those brief icons of American pop, the Watusi, since fashioned Tutsi by fastidious editors; among the coarse (especially among the coarse who looked on these new black dances as coarse), *watusi* briefly became a racial epithet, replacing *jungle bunny*.

In Rwanda, the epithet *cockroach* (*inyenzi* in Kinyarwanda) began its life somewhat earlier, as a sobriquet for Tutsi outlaws who sallied forth by night with World War I Enfields and Mausers, in quixotic attempts to restore the monarchy. Now it's used to describe all Batutsi, while today's Tutsi night prowlers, the lads from Uganda, are generally described by friends and enemies alike either as "deserters from the Ugandan Army," or "Inkotanyi." After four years of on-again, off-again attacks, the Inkotanyi occupy only a chunk of real estate on the Ugandan frontier, plus an unused new national assembly building in Kigali in which they have negotiated the right to expose themselves to disaster. They garrison six hundred men in the building—which incidentally is the same number that charged to their deaths with the light brigade at Balaklava.

The UN doesn't allow Dallaire an intelligence operation, even though his outfit is officially designated an "observer" force. Some Belgian troops under his command have nonetheless patched together the semblance of an intelligence unit, with a roster of informants that probably ranks about fifth in size behind the French, Belgian, German, and U.S. payrolls. This state of affairs might not be so squalid if these diplomatic ladies and gentlemen—all of whom supposedly look to Dallaire as the top cop of the cease-fire—were ever of a mind to share what they know. They aren't, and they don't. Maybe it's just bureaucratic proprietorship. Maybe it's every careerist's instinct that whatever he does either advances his career or endangers it, and heaven knows his career is more important than the mortality stats of some African backwater. Either way, the big powers almost always deny any knowledge of what Dallaire most critically needs to know. "We're pretty much in the dark," they tell Marchal.

"You can't tell me those bastards don't have a lot of information," says Dallaire.

They do. In a few years, investigators will document that by this date—Easter 1994—the big powers have better evidence of a looming genocide than the free world had before the Nazis began their final solution.

Zoologists tell us the quick, vicious shake a cat gives a mouse so stuns the little beast that it falls into a waking, painless trance. David Livingstone said that's how it felt when a lion clamped its jaws on him and shook. That's what it will be like for me when I someday learn what the big powers know this Easter of 1994. Nor will I be the only one thus struck numb. The "revolution" Belgium choreographed in 1959 sent Batutsi fleeing Rwanda in a diaspora that spread over Africa, Europe, and America. Nurses, engineers, cabbies, accountants, pilots; many of us did well in our adopted worlds. We cherished our new worlds. We were fond of its leaders. When we learn what these Zungu chiefs knew but wouldn't tell, most of us will react with that flat Tutsi gaze. Happily prosperous in our new roosts, newly confident and trusting, many of us will stubbornly ignore what we hear.

Now and then, though, an insistent question will intrude on us, warriors become doves in our cotes: Why would these wise men of the West refuse even to issue an alert, a wink, a nod, anything at all, discreet or indiscreet, politic or impolitic, tipping us off that furlongs beyond the perils of war and unrest and even pogroms, the Akazu was putting final touches on a comprehensive plan for mass murder? What profound paternal wisdom could possibly underpin such silence? And why would the West ignore its own lesser, better, voices—Vaclav Havel's Czech Republic, New Zealand, Spain? As the Akazu state begins killing the helpless in just a few days, these nations will demand that the UN at least deny the Akazu the rotating seat that Rwanda is scheduled, at just this moment, to assume on the UN Security Council. Why will it be allowed to take that seat? Why won't it be expelled altogether? Is protocol that greatly to be treasured? By what logic can the world's Great White Fathers allow mass murder in Givenchy serge to remain seated, snug and smug, among civilized nations?

Trying to sort this out will send me rummaging back to my father's days and on past him, back three lifetimes to the first days of the first white men to climb our heights. Like some hapless sister searching for her missing in morgue after morgue, I'll slink from source to source, scavenging for answers. In every stray comment, I will look for clues. I'll ponder pursuing a degree in advanced knot theory.

As I write in a new century, I feel the dead weight of fact still building, the endless detail of what the big powers do in fact know this first week of April 1994. Randomly:

They know that back on December 3, 1993, senior officers in the Akazu army, unsettled by what was afoot, wrote to Dallaire revealing that the massacres of the past few months were officially planned and that they were rehearsals to train and condition the population to join in an action aimed at exterminating all political opposition and all Batutsi.

They know that during the night of January 10, 1994, a chief of the largest militia, a man code-named Jean-Pierre, made his way to Dallaire's headquarters, where he met with Luc Marchal and spilled it all: How he thought at first he'd be training recruits to defend Kigali against the Inkotanyi; then how it hit him that his lads weren't being trained to fight Inkotanyi at all. They were being trained to kill the helpless, with the stress on volume. A thousand every twenty minutes. Jean-Pierre offered hard copies of the plans he detailed, plans set to kick off on coded orders. The big powers know he wasn't asking for money. All he wanted was safe passage for himself and his family. They know that he told Marchal where to find a cache of illegal weapons earmarked for the killing machine. They know Dallaire sent troops to check out the story. They know . . .

DIDN'T I TELL YOU THIS WOULD BE TRICKY? STICKING TO WHAT WE THE IGNORANT MIGHT witness during the last six days of Juvenal H? Let me get back on track.

This April 4 evening, as usual, Dallaire and Marchal learn little. Except once, near the end of the sad *soirée sénégalaise*.

Bagosora holds no cabinet post. He's not even an active-duty colonel. He's retired from the military. His title now is director of services in the Defense Ministry. But Bagosora intrigues Marchal. Bagosora will lose his ministry job if Habyarimana ever complies with the accords. More important, he represents a cadre of retired officers, all from Habyarimana's privileged home region, who have already lost their jobs to the peace process and are getting naught but scraps from the cash-strapped presidency. Bagosora's brother is Pasteur Musabe, a bank director who was among the power crowd that harangued Booh-Booh in Gisenyi. Bagosora himself has been on vacation in Gisenyi since the end of March, but now he has suddenly and unexpectedly returned to Kigali.

Belgian officers on Dallaire's staff call Bagosora *"un dur,"* a hard case. Reports say he's shown up at every bargaining session in Arusha, at each of which he has remained as silent as Kilimanjaro looming above. But he would take careful notes. They say he has a memory that won't let go. Perhaps it's the cognac, perhaps it's coldly intentional, but tonight he's a bit more talkative.

In earshot of Marchal and Dallaire, he expresses himself on what he calls "the only plausible solution" to the Tutsi problem. Surrounded by UN officers, he says, "The Batutsi must be eliminated."

· 5 ·

Day Four: The Game Is Up

TUESDAY, APRIL 5. It's the morning after his night flight back from Gbadolite. Our president has decided to stop resisting the accords. He'll make it official at the parley tomorrow in Dar.

We know all this because that's the message from his secretary, Enoch Ruhigira, to the UN. Ruhigira rings up Booh-Booh's staff to report the news—news that flies in the face of what UN nuncio Booh-Booh got from Habyarimana and his crowd in Gisenyi, just three days ago. Dallaire's aide, Luc Marchal, meets with Habyarimana's aide, Elie Sagatwa. Elie Sagatwa is an elegant, soft-spoken man, one of Queen Agathe's cousins. *Radio Trottoir*—that is, gossip heard along the track—says this stately fixer is closer to the president than anyone else; but one must parse sidewalk gossip carefully—close to the president doesn't necessarily mean close to his cousin, the president's wife. Among other things, Elie Sagatwa is in charge of presidential security. He goes over the details of assuring a smooth and secure transfer of power.

AFTERNOON. It's the season of short rains. A short rain walks over the airfield and then it walks across Masaka Hill. It's one of those rains that fall while in another part of the sky the sun shines. People don't bother to run. They walk faster, along with the walking rain. Over here, a girl crossing the road seems to bring sunshine with her. Off in the distance, by a duka in the purple shadow of cloud, it rains harder. In front of the duka, a lad tries awkwardly to hold an umbrella over a pretty young woman in the color-bright costume we call a *mushanana*. She seems distressed by his attention.

Surely he's not the same lad who got knocked over by that big copse of little bananas the other day, the lad with freshly shined shoes. Regardless, bananas strew the road, and what with the bananas, and the rain, and all his attention focused on the young woman, it's only a matter of time before this already awkward, already stumbling young man falls down. But he doesn't.

She does. She's up in a huff and off, her beautiful mushanana soiled. He stands in the rain, staring after her, abashed, then turns back to the duka. With a memorial shudder I remember him wiping each handsomely shod foot on the back of a trouser leg.

Masaka Hill isn't oblivious. As on most of Rwanda's many hills, some of the people hate Batutsi; some don't. Some are political; most aren't. Every resident of Masaka Hill senses something coming. Some sense it keenly. But they have no idea what, or when, and so they carry on, as does Rwanda beyond Masaka Hill. As I write I review the settings of those close to me this Tuesday before the apocalypse:

On Kicukiro Hill, my sister, Anne-Marie, is wrapped up in the business of her children's eyes. Tomorrow she's driving down to Butare to see an eye doctor. In a scene without sound, I picture her collecting this and that for their safari south.

On Kimihurura Hill, Mama, brother Lando, his wife, Hélène, their kids, Malaika and Patrick, their young cousin Rudasingwa, are watching a video at small *c* chez Lando, Lando's rented bungalow where they're all staying, safe behind locked gates and two different squads of armed guards.

Further out of town on Karuruma Hill, brother Karangwa's most pressing concern is his twelve-year-old son, Nyarugabo. Karangwa was long our scapegrace, the family jester, impossibly bright but just as impossibly provocative and thus destined for trouble, which caused never spoken but ever evident disappointment for Mama and Papa. Shortest of all the boys and such a clown with his elephant ears, Karangwa now has a son tall and handsome, everything (Karangwa seems now to hope) that he has not been, the proper scholar, the upright son. Except that he's just as provocative as his father, just as much the troublemaker, and today, young Nyarugabo's troubles at school are more on brother Karangwa's mind than presidential flight plans. In a scene likewise without sound, I picture him (Karangwa, who otherwise never lectures) lecturing his chastened son as his two daughters, sixteen-year-old Chantal and fourteen-year-old Sandrine look on.

In Kisangani on the Congo River, my eldest brother, Nepo, works as a librarian for the French; he's the picture of our late father, long dead of the croup picked up draining swamps.

On Remera Hill, near Chez Lando, brother Gaetan, the family athlete and Chez Lando's comanager, is getting ready for work; at Chez Lando, business is heaviest during this last half of the day.

Back in our home hamlet of Kabuye, lanky brother Wellars, my closest sibling, is at his desk in the supply office of the sugar mill. Fear has already prompted Wellars and his wife, Annonciata, to move into Chez Lando with their baby girl, Madudu—companion, they hope, to a baby girl named Kadadu, if ever she's born. Chez Lando is close to the security of Dallaire's headquarters.

On the road south from Kigali, brother Muzungu is driving visiting Canadian officials to the town of Bujumbura on Lake Tanganyika in Burundi. Fear has likewise prompted Muzungu to move into Chez Lando with his wife, Tabu, and their baby son, Boss.

I can't hear a word that any of them are saying.

6

DAY FIVE: DISTANT KEENING

WEDNESDAY, APRIL 6, MORNING. Uneventfully, Habyarimana's Falcon 50 has taken off on a bearing east from Kigali's grandly titled Kayibanda International Airport—a single strip known familiarly as Kanombe for the Presidential Guard's adjacent Kanombe barracks. The flight lands at Dar. Habyarimana goes about the scheduled meetings with neighbors, all of whom have long pressed him to stop resisting the accords, all of whom press him once again.

Well before the meetings in Dar have ended, in fact while it's still morning, he sends a new coded message to his secretary, Enoch Ruhigira, back at the presidency in Kigali. He instructs his man to schedule the actual power transfer for Friday, just two days from now.

The parleys have worn out Burundi's president. He's Hutu, as was the man he has succeeded, Burundi's first president and one of the first and few honestly elected presidents in Africa. But Burundi is as troubled as Rwanda. In Rwanda, induced fear has enabled a tyranny of the majority. Real fear that Rwanda's fate will be theirs has driven Burundi's Batutsi into the arms of a tyranny of the minority. I've heard it said that fear and greed take wild turns driving the pursuit of wealth in the world's capital markets. In Rwanda and Burundi, fear and hate take turns driving the pursuit of power.

Before Burundi's two Hutu presidents won their elections, the country's Tutsi-led military resisted every effort by Belgians, missionaries, and Hutu politicos to get them to give up any power at all. As we were getting cut out of the school system in Rwanda, Burundi's Hutu masses were just starting to get some education. Then the military at last loosened up, allowed elections, and Burundi was plunged into a period of wild Hutu expectations that with or without education they would replace nearly every Tutsi civil servant—which in turn drove the Batutsi mad with fear. Tutsi hotheads in the army assassinated the Hutu president. The military's Tutsi leadership didn't let the plotters seize power; in fact, they had to flee the country, and Burundi again has a Hutu president, but it's not a happy place. At this moment a tired Hutu president who doesn't relish a flight home in his mere propeller-driven craft is asking Habyarimana for a lift. Habyarimana says of course. This means there's not enough room for everybody on the Dassault. Several officials, including Rwanda's interior minister, must stay behind.

WEDNESDAY, ABOUT 8:15 P.M. Habyarimana's Falcon begins its descent. It's about to land. It's dark. Two Russian SAM 16 ground-to-air missiles, somewhat sophisticated but easily available on world arms markets, race skyward. Most evidence has them leaping from just outside the airport perimeter but inside Camp Kanombe's razor-wired and closely patrolled security zone. The aircraft explodes, plummets, crashes through the wall and into the garden of the president's own palace. Habyarimana's head rolls out. With him in death are Burundi's Hutu president and two Akazu ducs close to Habyarimana—armed forces chief Déogratias Nsabimana and that stately fixer, Agathe's cousin Elie Sagatwa.

8:30 P.M. Lando's place on Kimihurura Hill is well away from the crash, behind high walls and a metal gate. Just as yesterday, Mama is there, along with Lando's wife, Hélène, and the three young people—their son, Patrick, fifteen, their daughter, Malaika, seventeen, and cousin Rudasingwa, twenty-two. In the front garden inside the walls, the two squads are camped in two command tents. One is a five-man squad of enlisted Rwandese gendarmes. The other is a UN squad of eight Ghanaian soldiers. Both units are here to protect the family. Both are equipped with automatic rifles and radios. They can't do much against a determined attack by a determined and organized unit, but in the midst of chaos, these two official and organized units can easily discourage bloody play of the sort that defines chaos, especially given the inclination of thugs to beat up on the helpless.

The scene is nearly still. The Ghanaians carry on in routine murmur; likewise, separately, the Rwandese gendarmes murmur. The two units have no common language, neither European nor African. Patrick is outside with the gendarmes and the gardener, Tharcisse. Lando, Hélène, Malaika, Rudasingwa, and Mama are inside watching a video. Patrick and Tharcisse hear distant small-arms fire. They turn on the radio. RTLM, of course. First comes sprightly DJ Kantano Habimana, introducing pop star Simon Bikindi "singing it out, singing for you."

He breaks into his latest hit, "I Hate the Hutu," two fake Batutsi in concocted rap:

> *Getting it off my chest,*
> *gonna do my best*
> *to say the hate*
> *'cause hate I do,*
> *their Hutu-itude*
> *makes 'em fuss*
> *like they think they're us.*
>
> *Here, here, okay.*
> *I hear what you say.*

RTLM breaks in with another of their "hot bulletins," except that this time it's authentic news: The president's plane has crashed. Patrick goes inside to tell his father, returns outside.

IT'S DARK, BUT PUT YOURSELF ON A HILL NEAR MASAKA HILL AND YOU CAN MAKE OUT movement. In the foreground, figures dart furtively from doorways, then back. Someone grabs someone and yanks him back. Gunfire, light and sporadic, *thacks* nearby. Again, figures quickstep back into doorways. Light gunfire is walking across Masaka Hill the way the short rain did yesterday.

It's just small arms. From a distance, the *thack, thack* sounds a little like corn beginning to pop. Some of it you can't even hear. You just see random muzzle-flashes, like tiny bulbs randomly flashing on a Christmas tree in a darkened room.

The gunmen are Presidential Guards. Some of them are in jeeps. On this corner, a squad patrols, but it's not a real squad composed of real soldiers. It's just a squad of silhouettes, out there in the distance. At another corner a Panhard jeep slams to a halt. Silhouettes jump out, and now they seem more flesh and blood and less silhouette. They bang on doors with the butts of their Egyptian-made AK-47s; the ones they call AKMs. From five hundred yards off, their banging sounds like polite raps. Troops disappear into huts, dukas, drag people out. There's no way to make out what they're saying. Folks seem to be shouting in fear, doubtless protesting their loyalty. They are, after all, virtually all majority people, Bahutu, gunmen and victims alike.

Downtown it sometimes seems Batutsi must be something more than 15 percent of the population, certainly more than the 9 percent figure the state favors. But that's because downtown is where Batutsi tend to show up,

Batutsi in business, Batutsi working for foreign agencies. Batutsi live amid Bahutu everywhere, but downtown the proportion is higher. Downtown, you see the Tutsi wives and mistresses of Europeans. On Masaka Hill, you see the *rubanda nyamwinshi,* the Hutu masses.

The darting is now more frantic than furtive, and for onlookers on nearby hills, a series of shadow-box tableaux, fragmented and barely visible, begins to unfold over on Masaka Hill. The bent shape of a stout old woman waves a broom. Here and there, a few silhouettes just stand about, as if dumbfounded. The form of a trooper, rifle at port, rushes by the silhouette of a boy almost grown. The silhouetted lad briefly waves his arms, perhaps in dumbfounded exclamation. Maybe the trooper stepped on his foot. The boy's silhouette turns away. The trooper's silhouette takes the rifle in two hands by the barrel, comes up behind the boy, and just like that he swats the lad's head broadside with the flat of the stock. The silhouette falls to its knees, then on its face, into the mercifully invisible dark. Another form unslings his weapon, fires point-blank. At that distant all onlookers can see is a muzzle-flash, nearly silent.

Distant keening, and the *thack, thack* of small arms goes on for a couple of endless minutes. Then there's an enveloping silence. Where silhouetted forms had been running, there is now no movement. Bodies, like puddles after a shower, lie everywhere.

BACK IN DAR, WHERE HE'D STAYED BECAUSE THERE WAS NO ROOM ON THE PLANE, Rwanda's interior minister hears the news. "Rwanda is finished," he says, and drops all plans to return.

Back in Lando's garden, more "hot bulletins" crack over RTLM. In the Ghanaians' UN tent, a bad walkie-talkie cracks with static-ripped military bulletins. The Ghanaians carry on as if nothing special is up. The Rwandese gendarmes are listening to RTLM, which is coming through clear as can be. The gendarmes hunker by their transistor radio, stunned—and so they will sit through the night, well past the hour when only a single watch would ordinarily be awake. The Ghanaians snore.

The killing is on, genocide has begun, and the first victims are ordinary Bahutu, the *rubanda nyamwinshi* on Masaka Hill. Are they getting killed in a search for those who fired the missiles? That's what the killers think, but is that what their bosses think? Or have their bosses dispatched them to Masaka Hill to get rid of witnesses? The truth is as hard to see as the killings.

7

DAY SIX: OUR POOR CAGED BIRD

THE FIRST TWO HOURS OF THURSDAY, APRIL 7. Those awake in the eastern reaches of greater Kigali prefecture—and that's most everyone—hear the muted *thack* of gunfire creep beyond Masaka Hill. To the ear, its progress seems almost desultory.

Now the Presidential Guard is working from prepared lists.

BAGOSORA SEIZES COMMAND OF THE MILITARY. DALLAIRE TELLS HIM THAT HE'S LEGALLY obliged to serve the prime minister, Agathe Uwilingiyimana. Bagosora says no. He calls the prime minister and delivers the same message.

In the glass palace of the Hotel des Mille Collines in Kigali-ville, correspondents bang out reports. Some, gripped by a prepainted picture of tribal warfare, report that the "ruling Hutu tribe" has gone to war with "the Tutsi tribe—known here as 'Inkotanyi.' That's the local word for 'cockroach.'" (The word for *cockroach*, you may remember, is *inyenzi*.) Other correspondents assume that because Prime Minister Agathe opposes Habyarimana, she must be Tutsi. Many cabinet ministers oppose Habyarimana; Lando is the only Mututsi.

Dallaire shouts at Bagosora; it does no good. He speeds back to Force HQ, dodging checkpoints thrown up by goons. As he hits the office door, he hears the phone ring. It's the prime minister. She's been trying to get through to him. She still refuses to yield to the putschists. She wants to get to the radio station so that she can speak to the nation and try to restore some calm and civil control. Dallaire agrees to have his troops drive her there at daybreak. Daybreak is when Radio Rwanda goes on the air and everyone is listening.

At Lando's place, everyone save a lone sentry has at last gone to bed.

5:10 A.M. A UN officer at Force HQ rings up the Akazu army unit at Radio Rwanda again, this time to tell them that the prime minister *will* be coming to broadcast. The duty officer tells him flatly, "The prime minister isn't working anymore."

5:30 A.M. In four jeeps, a squad of Belgian paratroopers under UN command speeds off to secure Prime Minister Agathe at her official residence. Another unit speeds off in four jeeps to secure the radio station. Just short of the station, they're stopped by bursts of small-arms fire. None are hurt, but they're marooned. Whichever way they try to move, fire pins them down. They call for help and wait. Soon the reinforced squad sent to secure the prime minister is confronted by a unit of Presidential Guards. They call for help and wait.

AND THEY WILL CONTINUE TO WAIT. OVER THE NEXT HUNDRED DAYS, NEARLY TWO MIL-lion souls will wait, and wait, for some sort of relief, any sort, as they face the blunt and imminent prospect of extermination. These people in jeopardy include not just Rwanda's million-and-a-half Batutsi, but scores of thousands of Bahutu.

The propaganda machine likes to call these targeted Bahutu *ibyitso,* "accomplices," by which it means accomplices of the Inkotanyi. In fact, precious few of the Bahutu opposed to the Akazu are accomplices of the Inkotanyi. Bahutu genuinely in league with the Inkotanyi are a small, distinct group drawn largely from Rwandese Bahutu long living in Uganda. Finding themselves caught in the terror of Uganda during the sixties and seventies, they made common cause with refugee Batutsi caught in the same Ugandan horror—a tale for later. The tale for now is ordinary literate Bahutu living in Rwanda who now face death. Some don't even like Batutsi. They are Hutu teachers, nurses, mayors, judges, policemen, who for any number of reasons, from dumb luck to scruples, find their interests up against the interests of the Akazu, which wants them dead and so labels them accomplices of the Inkotanyi.

For months, the Akazu has been ignoring a UN arms embargo on Rwanda, smuggling weapons in by the container-load, but its most valuable weapon doesn't show up on shipping manifests. Its most valuable weapon is the ingenuity of its own educated cadre. These young men and women have put together an artful propaganda apparatus, and now they're using it to enlist hundreds of thousands of ordinary people to kill hundreds of thousands of other ordinary people. Meantime the sideshow of just who shot down that

Falcon 50 will become one of the great whodunits of fin de siècle African politics.

In this cordite fog is lost the story of one man at the very top of the killing machine. Not the hapless Jean-Pierre, not simply a militia commander, but a senior influence peddler with a strong, armed constituency, who for whatever reason (quite possibly, a self-serving reason) may have been ready to help stop the killing had he not been ignored at every turn by the UN and the big powers. Along with hundreds of thousands of his fellow Banyarwanda, he disappears, his story untold and likely untellable, one thin clue for which to scavenge as the years ahead unfold. I blink myopically at the search ahead.

SUNRISE. Roosters. Dew. Troops sweat in the chill. Breath drifts visibly from mouths like cigarette smoke. All across Kigali, people are waking up, trying to wish the dawn away, afraid to face the day.

Outside the walls of the prime minister's house, the UN troops who came to secure her are still pinned down.

6:00 A.M. A Hutu master corporal commands the gendarmerie squad assigned to Lando's place. Right now, he's routinely relieving one of his gendarmes. The chap sets off for home. His comrades are awake, but still in a stunned state, and groggy. My picture of them is likewise groggy, a fuzzy interlude that cranks erratically through my head.

It's bright, so bright that all color has been leached from the scene, leaving nothing but harsh morning light casting long black shadows from a sun still low in the east, backlighting the picture. The off-duty gendarme trudges home. I see him trudging along a track so harsh with morning light it looks as artificial as a stage set. He looks up. Stark black against a bright eastern horizon, another trooper is coming his way, waving with the erratic movement of still photographs flashed in succession. Black-and-white photographs, overexposed.

"*Waramutse*," mouths the oncoming comrade, for these pictures that run through my head are as silent as my pictures of Anne-Marie during these same hours, and my pictures of Karangwa and of Karangwa's young Nyarugabo. From household accounts, I know more of this particular interlude than I do of most others, but no matter how much I know, my picture of it is artificial. I can never bring it to life with sound. "*Waramutse*," mouths the oncoming comrade. "Good morning."

"*Waramutse*," mimes our gendarme, homeward bound.

His Hutu comrade then mouths something provocative—or so I imagine. What I know is that the young Hutu homeward bound now dodges back by a shortcut and arouses his Hutu squadmates. After a rush of chatter, they charge the house. They bang on the door. They peer in; they bang on the windows. From inside they must look ghoulish, their faces pressed against the glass. They are all over the house, and they are all Bahutu. The UN troops do nothing. They watch.

"Lando!" the Hutu gendarmes shout, and these words I can read clearly on their lips.

"Up! Out! Hide!" This I do know. They've come to warn him.

HALF THE GLOBE AWAY, IT'S HALF A DAY AWAY, A LONG NIGHT JUST BEGINNING. "HAVE you heard?" a disembodied voice calls to ask. Try as I might I can't get through to Kigali. At one point I get a helpful operator, but she's never had to deal with an entire country entirely cut off. She's confused, and I conflate her confusion with so much other confusion about Rwanda, right down to all those confused efforts to get our names straight. I pace the flat, portable phone in hand. I talk to the walls. Maybe we should change our names to something simple, maybe then the world could get it straight. At the Nyundo mission school the nuns thought it at best impolite to use the words *Hutu* or *Tutsi*, so we called each other Hippies and Tourists. So just think of me as a Tourist, that Tourist Louise, or if you prefer, Loulou the Tourist. Mind you, though, I don't much like Loulou, and in any case, Louise isn't my real name.

Nobody knows my real name. My real name is hiding as a family name, Mushikiwabo, which is not, in fact, a family name at all. It's my name, my real name, my Rwandese name. I don't have a family name. Nowadays many Rwandese families do, but not us, not our family, and that's a story in itself, a story of bloodlines that ends with my mother forcing back sobs from the stomach up as she scours Kabuye parish in search of a priest willing to baptize me. Maybe that's where I should go if I want to get to the bottom of things.

PART II

IN THE CRÈCHE OF THE GREAT RIVER

Revisiting the Scene of the Crime
1959–1990

"Who among mortal men are you, good friend?
. . . come closer, the sooner to meet your appointed destruction."
Then in turn did the shining son of Hippolochos answer:

. . . .

"There's a city, Corinth, in the corner of horse-pasturing Argos;
there lived Sisyphus, and he had a son named Glaucus,
and Glaucus in turn sired Bellerophon the blameless [who]
. . . had him kill the Chimæra, snorting fire . . .

. . . .

"At that Bellerophon became proud, and for that the immortals hated him.
From then he wandered alone, eating his heart out,
while Ares . . . killed his son Isandros in close combat . . .

. . . .

"But [his second son] Hippolochos begot me, and I claim he's my father;
he enjoined me to be brave, to hold my head above others,
not shaming the bloodline of my fathers, who were
the greatest men in Corinth and again in wide Lycia.
Such is my generation, and the blood from which I claim birth."

—*The Iliad*, BOOK VI

· 8 ·

Mama Marries the Seducer

*A Boy's World, a Man's World, and the World According to
Little Chief Elizabeti; 1916–1978*

Providence, in her encompassing grace, knows that my mother's frantic search for a priest willing to baptize me wasn't my father's fault, but it's nonetheless a story that starts with him, and with stubborn memory.

Pretending that the name you get when you're born is a family name begins early in the century just past, even before my father's day, but in his day—he was born in 1916—people still see the pretence clearly for what it is, a pretence, not the inevitable march of Christendom. At home, they give you a name, an African name, in my case Mushikiwabo, and then at the mission they give you a Christian name, in my case Louise, or more exactly, Marie-Louise. Put them together and it sounds so gentile, either Mushikiwabo Louise (as we Rwandese are yet wont to frame our monikers) or Louise Mushikiwabo. But everyone knows that's just to make the White Fathers happy, and unless they're fools, they know it too. Both names, African name and mission name, are given names; neither is a family name, and everyone knows it.

THE BOY'S WORLD

The infant, the *toto,* who will be my father is Bitsindinkumi, and that's it. No Christian name. No family name.

You might suspect this to indicate weak families, even casual spawning. Certainly the church fathers do. First there were the half-dozen Lutheran pastors who came as the century turned, fulminating in German, the first of the white men to grab for souls in this, the last of uncolonized, for them uncivilized, Africa. Then the Kaiser, despite his bristling mustaches, lost the Great War, and Belgians came to our rolling downs, Walloons and

Flemings fulminating about sin in red-faced French and Flemish. The White Fathers insisted, and still insist (for their success has not been total), that our African names, given to us at birth, become family names, and that each man and woman, boy and girl, take on as a new given name what they call a Christian name. The missions refuse to baptize any soul so careless of salvation that he or she doesn't bear a proper Christian name, or at least a proper name. Pagan names, like Fleur, Cynthia, Cuthbert, are acceptable. Just no African names.

By and by, and strictly for the mission, Father does get a Christian name to hook up with Bitsindinkumi, as if Bitsindinkumi were a family name, but who would have the heart to address a child as Frodwald? Few do. In formal documents banged out on Africa-battered Olivettis, he is Frodwald Bitsindinkumi, but only the last half of that moniker means anything, the name his mama and papa picked just for him, a name that brings smiles either sly or affectionate or both to the faces of those introduced to the quiet child who stares down at his bare feet as he tells them his name, "Bit-sin-dink-umi." The name is not unique, but it is unusual. It means "he who seduces young women." Colonial authorities who don't know any better are heard calling for "Frodwald who seduces young women." The snickers nonplus them; African insolence.

If anything, the Frodwald business tends, as the years pass, to confirm him in his real name, for if his parents had not made that Frodwald gesture for the priests, he might have felt obliged at some point in adulthood to take on an auspiciously royal name like Baudoin, as so many do. Likewise might his father have been dubbed, oh so royally, Leopold Nyarugabo, and so might Nyarugabo's Bismarck-era father have been Fritz Kanyamuhungu, or maybe Wilhelm, doubtless to be known as Kaiser Bill Kanyamuhungu, at least until the armistice, at which point he could have become Woodrow Wilson Kanyamuhungu.

But such is not to be. Not in his family. To most people, and most especially to this proud family with no family name, he is and will remain until the croup overtakes him in 1972, simply Bitsindinkumi, The Seducer.

Is the mission right? Does this refusal to take family names indicate weak families? Well-born black belles of old families giggle at arriviste black belles who insist on parading Christian names—Immaculée is a favorite—names that make them sound so made-in-Belgium "you'd think they were Godiva chocolates." There are at times mass conversions, mass baptisms. Decades later, ladies of the parish with names like Immaculée will be elbow-deep in the blood of mass killing.

Still, what strength does it show to reject upstarts out of hand? And they do tend to be stiff-necked, these families that won't use a family name. They claim it makes for strong individuals. They say it's no good to have a child running about parading his—or her—family's name. They say it's not good for the child.

One morning when he's perhaps five, and playing beanbag football in a dusty yard of orange clay, Bitsindinkumi looks up and sees a pair of bony knees. He looks farther up, much farther up, and sees a man he's never seen before, at least as tall as his seven-foot father, giant Nyarugabo. For Bazungu, Nyarugabo is just another of our tongue twisters. But to our ears, it has such stomach, such authority, Nee-YAHRoo-gahbo.

"Who's your father, child?" the man asks. The man doesn't say, "What's your name?" He says, "Who's your father?"

The boy knows what to say. He says, "I'm Bitsindinkumi, son of Nee-YAHRoo-gahbo, son of Kanyamuhungu, son of Sekabote, son of Garuka, son of . . ."

It's the first of many such recitations over the years.

Is this stress on bloodlines, on what we call *inzu,* at odds with the individuality valued by a world that refuses to give its children family names? It is. Crosscurrents cut through our rushing rivers from bank to boulder. In a world so taken with questions of pride, many a stranger will tell you more than you want to hear about this man, this lion killer, this leopard slayer, this owner of many cows, of whom he is the son of the son of the son . . . and all this he will tell you in meter.

Bitsindinkumi's world has also a tradition of heroic ballads, metered renderings of real battles. The heroic ballad, however, is a form distinct from the metered reeling of ancestral names. For ancestor reeling, the form is *ibyivugo.* It can be rendered seriously—it *should* be rendered seriously—but even then there is almost inevitably some embellishment of the truth, at which point the lyric becomes self-satiric, intentionally or not. The prouder and more serious the tone with which you boast of your exploits, or those of your father, or of your father's father, the more delighted the listeners, who are not beyond hooting.

Which to the quiet lad Bitsindinkumi, and later to the lad becoming a man, means that he may well be the son of Nyarugabo, son of Kanyamuhungu, son of Sekabote, son of Garuka and must strive to be worthy of them ("Be strong," his father often admonishes him), but their names are not his name. He's simply (and perhaps magnificently, it's up to him) Bitsindinkumi. He can't lean on these names he reels off. He must live up to them. *Ibyivugo* is not to be our father's favorite form. He will avoid it like the pox.

One day, a day long distant in years far ahead, a grown and thoroughly sober Bitsindinkumi will pass on Nyarugabo's lessons to his own many *totos,* of whom I will be the last. In particular he will pass them on to a son who will be perhaps the brightest and decidedly the most irrepressible of us, our nonstop brother Karangwa. Karangwa will take such delight in life and in danger that he must forever play either the provocateur or the fool or both. Almost from the moment he's born, in 1948, our hill will regale itself with tales of how this brother of ours slipped from the womb looking for all the world like a little bat-eared fox, those tiniest of vulpines with the most enormous of ears. The name Bitsindinkumi will fit Karangwa far better than it ever did our father, for Karangwa will be quite the seducer, and so what if his ears make everyone laugh. Girls love it when you make them laugh. Even as he chases the lovelies, he will carry those ears, nay, wiggle them with pride, as proud an emblem as Cyrano's nose. Of all Bitsindinkumi's sons yet to be born, Karangwa especially will need old Nyarugabo's sober lessons.

Alas, brother Karangwa will never be one for such lessons, but in time he will have his own son, and name him Nyarugabo, after sober grandfather Nyarugabo. Fully aware of himself as our father's bane, Karangwa will see his son, Nyarugabo, as his redemption . . . and what a *toto* this new Nyarugabo will be! No, he won't be blessed with his father's ears. He will be as lovely as any girl. To his father, Karangwa, he will be as handsome as any hero. But alack, he will also be as irrepressible as his father. Karangwa will look on his son, and for the first time ever he will talk sober sense, which we Banyarwanda call *kwitonda* . . . and which is a story in itself, and one we can't ignore, not if we don't want Bitsindinkumi glaring at us from the beyond.

Kwitonda is a solemn reserve in which we Batutsi find great dignity. You could also describe it as a Tutsi hauteur in which our brother and sister Bahutu find great humor. Now and then, it's a hauteur that makes them look at us and laugh out loud. Just as often, it makes Batutsi look at one another and laugh out loud. (*En Picardie on dit*, *"Ils pétent haut que ses têtes,"* which sounds better in French than in English: "They fart up over their heads.") Asleep, Karangwa's son, Nyarugabo, will look like Tutsi *kwitonda* itself, an infant iteration of the gospel according to old Nyarugabo. Asleep.

And then there's the other reason old folk have for not giving a child a family name: This is a dangerous world. People carry grudges. Families carry grudges. You may not want to be known by a family name.

THE MAN'S WORLD

Bitsindinkumi is a man born to struggle. Born to the Batutsi, a people distinctively tall and patrician, Bitsindinkumi as a man is distinctively tall but more austere than patrician. A certain austerity of bearing is an aristocratic feature in the lake kingdoms—*kwitonda* after all—but Bitsindinkumi's austerity is too raw, his hands too callused.

His clan, the Batsobe, are traditionally the keepers of the closely guarded rituals of the court, what anthropology dotes on as Rwanda's *code esotérique*. Among other things, Batsobe are the rhapsodists of Rwanda, the *abiru*, those whose responsibility is learning and telling the ancient epics, a heavy responsibility and not so easy in an illiterate world, as difficult as it was for Hesiod and for Homer. Every king has to include some of these clansmen in his court. But the Batsobe are not close to the court, and besides, Bitsindinkumi is more representative of another avocation associated with his clan. He's a farmer. Bazungu routinely, almost reflexively, picture Batutsi as herdsmen and Bahutu as farmers. But as they say in Uganda, that's a load of old codswallop. Bitsindinkumi is a farmer, and all around him is land that seems to sing of richness. Beneath young mountains thrown straight up among the clouds are rolling green foothills and valleys of rich earth, black volcanic earth on the high slopes, red earth in the downs and vales that roll amid and away from the mountains. But farmers are not much taken by montane beauty. They know how little hillsides yield, and how hard they are to work. Bottomland is what they cherish, and they don't have to calculate how squeezed bottomland tends to be in hill country.

In such country, Bitsindinkumi is a farmer doubly burdened. He works his own plot, as does his first wife, and in time their two children, and he manages coffee plantations for white men. He organizes plantation work, keeps the books, and either collects a portion of the crops for the white owners or collects a portion of the cash proceeds, in effect a tax on the proceeds.

Some call this work tax farming, and nowhere is it either easy or pleasant. The lord of the land sets the taxes according to his wants. The peasant must yield regardless of his family's need. The tax farmer, caught in the middle, must collect according to his ability, and God forbid his ability fall short of what the landlord—or the market—demands. A decent colon who eases his demands does not find the market going easy on him. Many are getting rich; many go broke.

Meantime, here in the middle of the most thinly peopled continent on earth, this is one of the most densely peopled nations on earth. It has been so for a millennium, from the time that slowly migrating tribes of farmers from the west, then herders from either the northeast or the east, displaced the local forest people (aboriginal pygmies long since reduced to tiny bands of hunters, potters, jesters) and began calling the country Rwanda, "the big world." To those early people, in their ancient time, it doubtless was the big world. For Bitsindinkumi, it's the hard world.

Aside from the difficulty of farming anywhere, at any time, Bitsindinkumi is a farmer from the wrong people.

Oh yes, some white men, Bazungu of the old school, still prate of Tutsi glory. "Watusi," they call his people, or "Watussi," or "Watutsi," the minority people who conquered the nation and installed their line of kings at about the same time the Normans from France were imposing their kings on England. In the late nineteenth century a French missionary, one Monsignor Le Roy, describes the Batutsi in a way Bitsindinkumi will often hear his people described: "Their intelligent and delicate appearance, their love of money, their capacity to adapt to any situation seem to indicate a Semitic origin." A Semitic love of money indeed; whatever grotesquely distorted shred of truth there is in the good monsignor's observation, by my father's day, the *Wunderdoktoren* of the Western world have spun it into fully fledged, poisonously invidious reality. The Batutsi now supply the much resented educated class that acts as middleman between white man and peasant.

After his awkward fashion, Bitsindinkumi speaks four languages, some German, French, his native Kinyarwanda (native to all Rwanda's people), and Kiswahili. This last is the language of East Africa's Swahili coast, and long the lingua franca of traders plying the interior. Rwanda's European colons, Bazungu, prefer Kiswahili, finding it easier than Kinyarwanda.

Bitsindinkumi, this raw-boned farmer whose bare legs forever stick out from some white man's cast-off woolen overcoat, doesn't speak Kiswahili because he's a member of an educated class; he's had no more than a few years of school. He speaks it because he's a driven man, and because of a happy circumstance—both Swahili and his native Kinyarwanda are Bantu languages. In particular, they are both "inflected"; that is, they work by sticking prefixes and suffixes onto root words. It's easy for Bitsindinkumi to see that *Ki*swahili is the language of the Swahili people in the same way that *Ki*nyarwanda is the language of Rwanda's people, and more usefully, that *ki* is a shared prefix meaning "language." The confused white man (the *Mu*zungu, *mu* being the prefix for one person) likes to flatter him with palaver about how his people, "the *Wa*tusi," are known as brave warriors. Then in the same sentence, the man talks about "those *Ba*hutu." But Bitsindinkumi's people don't call themselves *Wa*tusi. They call themselves *Ba*tutsi, just as the peasants call themselves *Ba*hutu. It isn't hard to figure out that Kiswahili uses *wa* the same way Kinyarwanda uses *ba* to mean "people" . . . and that saying *Ba*hutu and *Wa*tusi in the same breath is a white man's barbarism.

Of course, Rwanda's white landlords could figure this out just as easily and speak a respectful modicum of Kinyarwanda with their peasants, but precious few bother. (At least one writes a book about Rwanda in which Hutu people are Bahutu in the same happy sentences that Tutsi people are Watutsi.) And who is Bitsindinkumi to quarrel with that? It makes him, and his effort to learn Kiswahili, all the more valuable. He lets them prattle on.

During the years that see Adolf Hitler rise to power, years during which racial humbug is popular well beyond Germany, most of Rwanda's colons fawn over Bitsindinkumi's "Watusi," holding that they aren't Bantu, like the Bahutu, but Hamitic—descendents of the biblical Ham (whence Ethiopians), Shem (whence Semites), and Jephet (whence Aryans). It's the heyday of what scholars now call "the Hamitic myth," the notion that Batutsi couldn't possibly be Bantu. Indeed, many see us as more likely Nordic than Bantu. (One resident—as the Belgians call their governor here—argues in bound print that he can connect us with our Icelandic cousins.) But Kinyarwanda is a *Bantu* language. For a millennium, at least, the celebrated poets of the supposedly "superior non-Bantus" have been composing our courtly lyrics in the Bantu language of our serfs, knowing no other.

By and by, racial notions that blithely ignore such facts begin to look shopworn, especially after the race-crazy Axis collapses. With majority rule in the wind everywhere, Rwanda's European colons hitch their fortunes to the majority Bahutu. They handpick among the Bahutu, train the handpicked, and by the late fifties, begin yielding to them, one by one, year by year, the instruments of state power.

By the late fifties, independence is sweeping Africa. Royalist assassins among the Batutsi are at work killing Hutu politicians anointed by Belgium, and Belgium wants out. What Bitsindinkumi sees is a young king hopelessly out of his depth. What he hears are reports of attacks against his people. What he knows is that in this man's world, faded glory doesn't grow crops. Only work and grim determination do that.

Even then the result isn't always success. His wife works. His children work. And before he knows it, the wife he hardly sees for all his work in the fields is dead of disease, and here he is: an awkward, taciturn, some would say humorless yeoman, old enough to show wear but too young not to long for another wife.

THE WORLD ACCORDING TO
LITTLE CHIEF ELIZABETI

Kabenga, all six foot eight of him, is a white-robed patrician of the old Tutsi order. He's a poet. He's a warrior of whom song has been composed. He was an official chronicler in the court of the deposed king of Rwanda, an adviser to the king, and a boon companion on royal hunts when such there were. He is rich in land, rich in cows, rich in wit, a grandee. Kabenga and his family, uncles and aunts, nieces, nephews, sons and daughters, lead lives swimming in spirited talk, which might at first seem yet another aspect of highborn inheritance, and in some ways it is. The stuff of their educations, both Tutsi and Belgian, is often the stuff of their jokes and their arguments.

But Batutsi are not a lively bunch. The liveliness is something this family has adopted altogether unconsciously from their Hutu neighbors.

Kabenga dotes in particular on his daughter Bibiane, in whom he sees almond eyes and all the treasured qualities; to him his little girl is long and lithe and lovely. But Bibiane no longer lives in her father's house. Her mother has died, Kabenga has remarried, and after some tension between new wife and favored daughter, Kabenga has sagely decided that his young bride is no better for daughter Bibiane than Bibiane is for his young bride. So he's sent Bibiane to live with his sister, Elizabeti, who has a family of her own, plus several other nieces and nephews in her care. In all it's a household of seven children, which means that while Kabenga is the man of the world, the poet, the hunter, the statesman, Auntie Elizabeti takes care of all the little things . . . like actually ruling Kabenga's large and substantial extended family.

Among her long, lithe relatives, Auntie stands out, and not because she is longer and lither. She's not. She's of average height, built solidly. It's in other respects that her Tutsi attributes are distinctly apparent, especially those famously hard-nosed attributes that are those of defunct German East Africa. In the world according to Little Chief Elizabeti, and in the world according to her look-alike little sister, Stefania, someday to be our Kommandante Stefania, the buses run on time.

Is it time to bathe? Amid shouting and laughter, she barks orders (as someday Kommandante Stefania will bark orders) and instantly a queue forms—with consequences for the laggard. Is it time for supper? The same. To study? The same.

The household bubbles with jokes and debate. The lane outside sees an endless progression of games. Beyond that, though, the world threatens quietly; sometimes, not so quietly.

Only the order imposed by Elizabeti stands between them, and that.

So perhaps it is not so surprising that as Bibiane turns fifteen, the man she dreams of is not a swashbuckling young poet but someone who can secure a household the way Little Chief Elizabeti can.

Do not leap to the conclusion that when she meets Bitsindinkumi, she chooses him, nor even that after meeting, he chooses her. In this world, it's the head of a girl's family who finds a likely groom. Before a potential pair even meet, he negotiates with the man, and upon agreement, pledges his daughter to him.

Which means that it's Kabenga's job to arrange a marriage. Which means that it's Auntie Elizabeti who does the actual arranging, who picks out Bitsindinkumi, who negotiates with him, before Bibiane ever lays eyes on him; it's Elizabeti who pledges her. It takes the girl a day or so to adjust, but she's bright. She soon sees the strength in him that Elizabeti sees.

Not so her brothers and sisters, cousins, and friends, who have less at stake. What does she see in this man? This tongue-tied farmer, bent beneath a long woolen overcoat he seems never to remove? It's not as if she were a homely stepchild of the family. She basks in her family's embrace. It shows in her self-confidence. She's a beauty, twenty years younger than this Bitsindinkumi. This "Seducer."

The *ibyivugo* custom of ancestor reeling can have fun with itself, which is another way of saying that the name you give your child can have fun with your child. A child born to short parents might well be named "too tall" in the hope that he will be, but if he turns out short, he might well rue the name, for he'll be called "too tall," with pointed insistence, for the rest of his life.

Thus is the widower Bitsindinkumi, this awkward bumpkin, now forever called "The Seducer."

And Kabenga doesn't even know what's up. But he isn't, after all, exactly immaterial. He's a man of substance in the world of affairs, and this is his family. Will he give his blessing?

He will not. He dotes on Bibiane. No. He will not give his approval.

But Little Chief Elizabeti will not back down.

There are three weeks of silence, and then he announces that he has an announcement. He blesses Bibiane's union to this "self-made man."

"As long as this Bitsindinkumi doesn't insist that she plow. That I will not abide. I will not abide it."

Bitsindinkumi's future, however, is far from assured. His is never to be the story of a climber. He's proud of his independence, and that's never good for a climber. And then come the troubles, the *muyaga,* "the winds," full of insanity and unpredictable gusts.

By and by, the Belgians set 1959 as the year they will begin turning power over to their handpicked Bahutu. The Bahutu call it their "revolution." Nobody is sure when the revolution happens. They just remember a scheduled transfer of power by the Belgians to their Hutu clients, accompanied by several assassinations of Hutu politicos by Tutsi hotheads, and then the pogroms, Hutu mobs sicked on Batutsi of convenience. It begins with Belgian appointees organizing a vote against a king with no experience and no army. It ends on a bridge.

It's a bridge in the mountains, rapids through a defile far below.

In the clouds above, the mountain gorilla gambols. Lavender-breasted rollers flutter and chirp. At one end of the bridge stands a mob. Some wield pangas. Some wield pangas already wet. Near the middle of the bridge, above rapids far below, stand a clutch of Tutsi mothers with infants swaddled to their backs. They jump.

Barely a decade has passed since Bitsindinkumi began his new family.

His *rugo,* his house and household, is already large, seven children, and he has carved out a farm large enough to support them. They lose it all. One morning his son Nepo, backlit by the morning sun, whistles to him from atop a hill that Bitsindinkumi spent five years terracing. Sorghum is nearing harvest. Nepo is their eldest, twelve, more than six feet tall. He raises his arm to the northwest: wisps of smoke. Ten-year-old Lando is a few meters up the slope from his father, a question on his face. Early next morning a Hutu neighbor is at the door. Hushed talk over tea steaming in the chill. "What's wrong," young Lando wants to know, shifting his weight nervously from good leg to bad.

"Nothing's wrong," says Bitsindinkumi.

"Nothing," says Bibiane.

"We're going on a little trip," says Nepo.

Outside is a small flatbed truck used to haul coffee. Whatever they can load onto it in a half hour is loaded, the rest abandoned. Everyone is rushing out with boxes and sacks. Then Mama and Papa are in the cab, the kids are hanging on the back, and they're rattling off as fast as they can for the safety of Kabenga's rugo. "The cash," says Papa. "The cash in the cash box in the—" He never finishes the sentence. They never look back. Tens of thousands of Tutsi homesteads will burn, tens of thousands of Batutsi will die, one hundred thirty thousand will be driven out of the country.

Bibiane's uncle, a man with some land, gives several hectares to The Seducer as a grubstake. He's starting all over, at his age, grimly determined. With his own hands, he builds a new house. It's smaller than the one he lost, and another child is coming. There will be nine, in all. New latrine, new well, new banana plantations are dug, rice fields laid out and irrigated, pipes laid. All around him the wit of his highborn in-laws pops like firecrackers, but he never has a moment to relax, absorb, become one of them. As we grow, excelling at school, immersed in games, he tries to play Little Chief Elizabeti, ordering us outside until we can contain our laughter . . . which, duly obedient, we do, and we won't come back in until we are genuinely certain we have settled down. Half the time, though, we come back in, take one look at Papa's oh so stern face, and break up all over again. At last we fall quiet, there's silence, and we gather the courage to meet Papa's gaze. Before us we see that flat, impassive stare meant to convey menace.

We struggle not to laugh. In a way it's worse than if we just laughed and went our way. "Keep laughing like that," he says flatly, "and someday your brains are going to shoot out your mouth." We run out the door, struggling to contain ourselves lest our brains shoot out our mouths.

9

THE BOULEVARD BITSINDINKUMI

Indépendance, Cha, Cha, Cha; 1959–1965

We Banyarwanda do favor our drink, and we likewise have a fondness, nay, an overfondness, for propriety. If you have trouble picturing two such antagonistic affections married under one national roof, just talk to the Catholic Church about it, or the Poles, or the Irish. Indeed, it's often hard to tell us Banyarwanda apart from the Poles and the Irish.

Progress, mind you, is fine. Nobody should stand in the way of progress. But first comes propriety, and then a drink. Or maybe, it's a drink and then . . .

Progress smacks our Munyarwanda in the eye. First he looks stunned, then he starts swinging. Progress smacks him again, and he's like the drunk who doesn't know the donnybrook is over. He's bloodied. His right eye is swollen shut. He can't breathe through his nose. He's spitting teeth. The saloon is empty. He keeps on swinging at the tables and chairs.

All in defense of propriety, of course, the right and proper way of things, right down to the small things. Take the way we build our family compounds. Years after circumstance (progress, if you will) forces us to stop building those graceful old rondavels of bamboo and reed, we won't stop laying out our compounds, our *rugos*, just so, just as we have for lo the many ages, and everlasting shame on him who doesn't. Everything has its assigned spot. Outbuildings, lanes, high fences, everything placed just so. Nothing graceful about it now. No reeds. Not much raffia. Less bamboo. Mostly mud bricks and corrugated metal. But everything placed just so. Proper.

WHEN THE BROOD BITSINDINKUMI LOST THEIR FARM, IT WAS UNCLE KAREKEZI WHO stepped in. When that wind hit them and they were alone on the road, running away to who knew where, Uncle Karekezi "picked them up."

I try to picture what must have happened. Uncle Karekezi is a cautious man, somehow made to deal with stiff winds. I know because this is what I hear people say. I also know what people mean when they say "the Chevrolet." They mean the big black fantailed crow of a sedan that carries Karekezi about. It's a Chevrolet—and just like a crow, it has yellow eyes and swept-back fantail wings. I even know the year—1959. I know because that's the year my family lost everything—a year just made for big brothers to singsong tales to baby sister about Uncle Karekezi, and how he's out one night in that fine '59 (with HydraMatic Drive and wings all streamline) when *clap!* a gale blows up. He shifts to a creep, crawls along, and after a way he makes out a pile of rags by the road, nearly invisible in the storm, nearly blown away, soaked. There Karekezi stops "and picks us up."

Which is more or less what happened, though Uncle's '59 Impala had nothing to do with it, nor did a literal storm, nor did he pick us up on the road. What Karekezi did was give Papa some hectares to farm by a hamlet called Kabuye, the seat of Kabuye parish, an hour by truck north of the town of Kigali. What he did was give Papa a new start.

Way uphill from Papa's new place are the estates of our great white hunter, the Count de Borchgrave. Even farther up lives Granny Mariya. Her compound is Grandpa Kabenga's old rugo. Granny is Mama's stepmother, Kabenga's second wife. Mama was the first of only two children Grandpa Kabenga had with his first wife. When his first wife died, he married Granny Mariya, and now he's dead too, and all his children by Granny are off in Burundi.

OUR HAMLET IS DOWNSLOPE AND FARTHER OFF FROM TOWN—FROM KIGALI—THAN Granny and de Borchgrave. Kabuye's clinic—Dr. Zitoni's "surgery"—is on the side down toward Kigali. Just the name, *surgery,* is enough to put the fear of Kabenga in any child, but not so here, not so for me, for just behind the surgery is Dr. Zitoni's compound, a rugo hiding shyly amid bamboo, a bungalow full of books. It's become a virtual lending library for the hill, and not just books grace this bungalow, but daughters, *playmates.* Here I am mothered by their mother, Adele, a woman so far up there, so assuring.

At times I'm fathered by the good doctor himself, so spare, so tall, and at home so gentle, so dreamy, nodding off in his hammock, his glasses falling off, an open book on his half-pint belly, nothing at all like Dr. Zitoni at the clinic. There he's so doctorly in his crisp white jacket so starched and clean and pressed just so, one hardly need know that he is not, in fact, a doctor.

Then comes the mission—church and school, our very own École Primaire Saint Alexis; behind it sits the grand manor (grand by our measure; a

bungalow) of Uncle Alexis Karekezi, Papa's benefactor, the school's benefactor. (How adeptly the White Fathers have named it Saint Alexis.), At last,
yet farther out, comes our place. On his new hectares, Papa has planted bananas, terraced for sorghum and maize and haricots, drained bottoms for
rice, plowed new furrows, built a kraal for his dozen head of great long-
horned Ankole cattle. And of course, he's built his family compound, his
rugo, just so. They tell me it's more modest than the rugo he built and lost
in Ruli, but everything is here: eighteen-foot-square family quarters plus
two sheds, surrounded by a wattle palisade ten feet high.

Kabuye hamlet hangs on the eastern flank of Mount Kigali, which rises
from a rutted track that starts in Kigali-ville. The track runs all the way up
to the Uganda frontier. This quiet, rutted road is Rwanda's major north-
south artery. To get to our place, you catch a bus in Kigali-ville and ask the
driver to let you off at the Kabuye stop on the Uganda Road, which he
won't understand unless you call it the Byumba Road; Byumba is in
Rwanda.

The Kabuye stop isn't the hamlet, it's just a marker on the open road, but
it's as close as you can get. After that, you walk north a few hundred meters.
Somewhere on the left, you see what looks like a dry wash running down
off the mountain, and if it's raining, it will be spilling mud and water right
out on the road, but it's not a creek, it's the track that climbs up through
the bush to the hamlet. Start climbing the track through the bush and the
trees. By-and-by, you see a long grassy lane veering off to the right. About a
hundred meters off, the lane ends at a palisade with a squeaky metal gate
dead center. The lane is barely wide enough for a pickup. There's no place to
turn around. If you drive in, the only way out is by backing up the length
of a football pitch, and then you're back on the track, and there's no place
to turn around there either.

This is our lane; we call it our boulevard. We've planted it on either side
with red flowering trees, spaced just so. (We. These trees were planted before I was born.)

Squeak through the gate. Now you're in the courtyard, and the palisade
reveals itself as a half circle, with our cottage. Outside the palisade, the lane
is all grass, but the courtyard is pounded earth. Papa has graded it, but all
the same, when it rains, it's mud. Outside the palisade, trees rise all about;
this is green country. But here in the earthen courtyard there's no shade.
It's a bald place, like Papa's pate. When the sun shines, it shines hard. It's
hot and it's dusty. A half circle of rusty tins lines the inside base of the palisade, each tin spaced just so, compassing the courtyard: First comes a
cooking-oil tin labeled with a bright blue elephant with trifling tusks and
garish red lips and lots of front legs to flourish as he sits up like a mahara-
jah. Big brother Karangwa, such a scoundrel, says it's a Hendi elephant.

Wagging his head Hendi-like, Karangwa singsongs, "That's how tuskas be back in Mutha Inja." Then comes a motor oil tin from Agip, labeled with Agip's fire-breathing wolf; then Lait Nido with its cow. We have an entire tin menagerie, tin elephants, tin wolves, tin cows, from which lovely bright flowers grow, plants watched and tended, watered and pruned, by Mama.

Our place is built of big mud tiles, muddy red; the roof is corrugated and a similar rusty red. Two squeaky metal chairs sit in the courtyard. Like the courtyard, the front door is unshaded. The raffia roofs of the old rondavels would extend out over the entrance in a graceful, precisely trimmed scallop, providing shade, and our place tries awkwardly to follow suit. The unshaded front door hangs open. Beyond it is a three-foot-wide passageway. Three feet in, a reed curtain spans the passage. This three-by-three-foot area just inside the front door is meant to mimic the scalloped portico of a rondavel.

A covered porch spans the entire back. It's about four feet deep, or perhaps I should say four feet shallow. On it is a rickety wooden chair on which Papa sits and begins teaching us to read as each in our turn we turn three—though at three, that's hardly how I see things. As I see things at three, it's me alone he teaches, and the strange languages he teaches me are ours alone, his and mine, our own secret languages to be shared with no greedy brothers. In one or another of our secret languages, I ask him questions. "Papa, do you get to plant rice in heaven?"

Mostly he teaches in Kinyarwanda, the language in which I am Mushikiwabo. When his blood is up he uses Swahili, and when he laughs, he laughs in Swahili. It's not right for Batutsi to show vexation, so he never gets vexed, nor does he laugh, in Kinyarwanda. He gets vexed in Swahili. When the subject is homework, he uses French. When Mama's blood is up, she says, oh so evenly, "I'm not going to tell you a thing. Nothing." Then silence, followed by, "All I'm going to tell you is . . ." But she doesn't always break her silence, and nothing can be worse than that, Mama cutting it off right there, biting her lip and turning away; your marrow chills with guilt. Sometimes after lessons, Papa sings to me. "I've got to sing," he smiles. "I get burned up; I've got to sing."

The first to get lessons, way back in Ruli, which they tell me had such a fine back porch, a big one, was Nepo, the firstborn, whose towels are blue. He's the image of Father, tall, shy, fastidious, bespectacled, broad shouldered, polite to a fault, never a teller of jokes but a rapt devotee of others' jokes, especially brother Lando's, and he's most especially a devotee of the deadpan canards regularly offered by that scoundrel Karangwa. "Tell us that one again, Karangwa. Tell us again."

Just after Nepo came Vincent, who has no towel here because the White Fathers have spirited him off. Taller even than Nepo, but slight, without

Nepo's shoulders; the priests said he was "gifted" and took him away to a seminary somewhere off in the Congo, someplace called Albertville. They won't bring him home. They don't want Tutsi priests in Rwanda anymore. Just like that he's gone, in another world.

Next, Karangwa, our knave, our beloved scapegrace, he of the elephant ears, short for a Mututsi, the one Grandfather Kabenga called "my Mutwa," because the Twa are pygmies—and court jesters. Karangwa serves as jester to the Court Bitsindinkumi, our "Bwana Rigolo," our coconut. Karangwa's towels are yellow. Karangwa: big ears, big head, big joker, kicked out of boarding school in Nyanza for playing an off-limits spinet and snacking on the Holy Eucharist; in big trouble with Bitsindinkumi. In that huge head he can store anything and does so with indiscriminate and altogether impractical abandon: Swahili epithets, French epithets, even, when he truly wants to annoy you, Latin epithets; choice jokes, stale jokes, the arcane stratagems of a complex game called *igisoro*. He has all the old epics down cold, and he's so good at *igisoro* that outraged opponents forever accuse him of cheating. In fact, he doesn't cheat, but he does nothing to disabuse them, just gives them that delighted sidelong leer and a wiggle of the ears.

Next Lando, the *tempered* scholar, the brother with legs that don't match. His towels are green. I don't see him as a brother, I see him as a changeling dropped into the family to be my friend. My brothers take me for granted. Lando makes me feel good. No, he makes me feel super; he's super. Whenever I look at him he's smiling. For me, he's the flavor of chocolate, all comfort.

His leg scares me, though. Everyone wears shorts. Everyone but Lando. Lando never wears shorts. What's under there? I don't want to know, and I don't want to know how it happened. I'm afraid to ask Mama, would never ask Papa; finally, at five, I blurt the question to Lando.

"An accident," he says. "Fell off a bike." From then on bikes frighten me—and his story wasn't even true. It was a lie. Years later Mama will tell me the truth: at four, a shot with a bad needle.

Then Gaetan, somehow, like his name, handsome and swarthy, the athlete, with the flavor of coffee, as tall as Nepo but even more muscular. White towels. No head for letters. The natural and mechanical sciences are his domain; he's forever fixing radios or monkeying with motors. At the Collège Saint André they call him Cassius Clay, not for his fists, for his looks. Gaetan is our *beau morceau*.

Then the first of just two girls in this brood of nine: Anne-Marie. Powder blue towels. With all these brothers, a tomboy, of course; always wearing boy's shorts, tall and skinny. Her flavor is mango. Tough with everything but food. The slightest thing wrong with a dish makes her gag, which she tries desperately to hide. Before I came, Mama despaired. "My only girl . . ." No interest in cooking, cleaning, or even eating, eats books for breakfast, lunch, and supper. "How are you going to get a husband?"

Then Muzungu, which means white man, because just after he was born, still without a name, the neighborhood kids rushed in to see him, took one look, and began chirping "Muzungu, Muzungu," unaware that African newborns often look white right after they're born, when they're still ugly. Regardless, he is thus named Muzungu. The more he grows, the less he looks like a Muzungu, but the name sticks. He is big, black, big-boned, placid; for me, his flavor is butterscotch. His fingers are long but sturdy; he's impossible to beat at marbles. He always sports a buzz cut. He has the cast of Bitsindinkumi and Nepo, big nose, big forehead, big laugh— a laugh that inspires the Bitsindinkumi glare. "You're waking the neighbors." Red towels going pink.

Then Wellars, too tall, fine boned, full of nervous energy; they say he's as tall as Vincent, that skinny stalk of asparagus off in Albertville. Turquoise towels. A personality like fresh lemon. He has a Somali cast to him, and like Gaetan, a head more for math than for words. He's popular, and a troublemaker. Always fighting at the mission school, always fighting with me—until Lando scolds him, tells him that I'm *bucura*, the youngest, and he should look after me, which delights Wellars because it gives him an excuse to fight at the mission. "Hey, that's my sister."

And finally, me, Mushikiwabo, Marie-Louise, Louise, Louisa, Loulou, last in this brood, this *ribambelle de gosses,* flock of kids. Pink towels. Spoiled. A girl from the beginning. Pinafores with carefully pressed pleats. *Bucura,* the youngest, the smallest. A big problem for Wellars.

Papa Bitsindinkumi's back-porch lessons begin when he gets back from the fields and washes up. When he finishes teaching, he stares out over the hills and says to no one in particular, "*Ibihe n'ibindi.*" Things are different now. Times are changing. It's become his own private rosary, a quietly chanted call to arms, rallying the household against a future he hears groaning like timber in a gale.

Behind and to one side of the house is a seven-foot-square cooking shed with a tin roof and a dirt floor, swept just so, without a brush mark. There is no running water. We draw water from a hand pump at a well Papa and the boys dug a couple hundred meters off, in the banana groves, where he dug it because that's where it's most needed. A long wooden shelf runs one length of the cooking shed. On it are big galvanized washtubs, plastic buckets of every color, scrub brushes, handmade short-handled brooms, twig brooms for outside, soft brooms for inside, a detergent called Omo, a cleanser called Vim. Passion fruit and bunches of tiny bananas dangle from nasty big hooks that hang from the rafters. In one corner is a brick oven with a wattle-and-daub chimney. Neatly bundled faggots stand stacked to one side.

Farther back in the yard is a freestanding bathhouse, six feet square. Grass mats cover a dirt floor graded so that water running through the mats runs outside into a drainage ditch. Every morning either Mama or Anne-Marie pulls the mats out, cleans them, and hangs them to dry on a line in the sun. Laid out on two shelves on the wall of the bathhouse are bars of fragrant, bright-white Savon Lux, and all those color-coded, threadbare towels, one for each child. The shelves are too high for me; I jump and jump again, all to no avail. "Okay, who's the boss?" asks Wellars. He's not joking.

"You."

"And who's going to listen to her big brother all day?" asks Wellars.

"Me."

I get my Savon Lux and barely absorbent towel.

Behind the bathhouse is a privy; a mud brick wall surrounds a Turkish toilet over a trench Papa and the boys dug fifteen feet deep into hard clay. Farther back still, and downslope, is a kraal made of stout tree limbs for Papa's dozen or so head of cattle. A pair of farmhands keeps them sleek, their coats shining. They milk them every day at dusk and at dawn.

The "big house" (all eighteen square feet of it) has a shiny concrete deck, washed every day with Omo, rinsed, and rinsed again. In addition to no running water, there is no electricity. Mama and Anne-Marie lug wash water bucket by bucket. A sitting room cum dining room is off the passageway, to the immediate left of the front door. It's furnished with a bandy-legged table, wooden chairs, smelly Coleman lamps that cast flickering light, and two plastic radios—even though there is only one station, Radio Bukavu, broadcasting mostly Congolese music from somewhere out there across the lake in the west. Right now, Africa is belatedly enjoying the cha-cha and freshly won independence. The radio crackles,

> *Indé-pen-dance*
> *cha cha cha*
> *Indé-pen-dance*

Talk fills the parlor more than radio. Karangwa of the elephant ears, Lando, Wellars, and Anne-Marie (she's still not fully grown) are the talkers, and so am I. The best talker of all, when he's there (a lot), is *Tonton*, Uncle, virtually our only uncle because all the others are off somewhere. Everywhere except our place, Tonton is a listener. He's always asking people questions, and then just listening and listening. What an article! He even pulls out a pad and takes notes. But here with family he talks—and what notes he must take because what stories he tells! His proper name is Kagame, and he's a priest.

Papa, Nepo, Gaetan, Muzungu, and Alexis Karekezi (when he visits) are the listeners, the rapt listeners, as quiet and as rapt with the talkers (except me and Wellars, of course) as we are when Uncle has a story. Mama is a listener, too, but she isn't there in the parlor listening; she's across the passage listening. When man-guests are about, grown women quarter themselves across the passage. Even Mama's Auntie Stefania (she's also Uncle Kagame's auntie) sits across the passage, and she's the greatest talker and commander of them all. You'd never know it, taking off your shoes and walking into a household thus marshaled by sex, but when Auntie Stefania is over, everybody marches to *her* cadence-call. Not Papa's. Not Uncle Kagame's. Not Lando's. Certainly not Mama's. Even sitting over there in the ladies' quarters while the men deliberate the fate of the world, Auntie Stefania calls the family cadence. She even calls it when she isn't here. She never shuts the front door without leaving marching orders, and the angels weep for the sorry soul who she decides, upon her return, hasn't measured up.

The ladies' visiting room is also the big boys' bedroom. This week Nepo, Lando, and Karangwa are home, somehow squeezed in. Next is the little boys' room. It's on the same side of the passage. Wellars shares it with Muzungu. It's where Wellars hides his *Tintin* comic books. On the same side and at the very end is the girls' room. Anne-Marie's store-bought bed lies along the outside wall, a tiny window above. My pallet is on the inside wall. Under it hides my one and lonely *Tintin*—the one where Capitaine Haddock sneezes so hard it takes two bubbles to capture the full grandeur and mayhem. I've got three pegs and two painted shelves for clothes. Anne-Marie has a treasure I eye jealously—a fiberboard portmanteau with its own tiny lock and key.

Opposite our room is the big bedroom with its centerpiece bedstead, deeply carved mahogany draped with a swooping mosquito net, a giant bed in a tiny room. Gracing it also are two heavily studded Zanzibar chests, plus a bookshelf with a few volumes in Swahili and German, and above all, Mama's little "secrets" basket. It's the Rwandese way—or at least the way for literate Rwandese. No one goes into that tightly woven, tightly held basket. No one except Papa. In public with her husband, a Rwandese wife never disagrees. She keeps her peace. But she doesn't quite keep quiet. Alone, she scratches her exception on a scrap of paper and drops the note in her secrets basket. A good and literate husband never fails to check it nightly. A good husband gets the memo.

A raffia rug covers the polished concrete floor. A shelf features Papa's one indulgence (if saving his own sweat-stained hats over the years can be called an indulgence), a collection of trappers' hats. Oh those sweat-stained chapeaux, oh those *bitos*; they all have high, narrow crowns and broad, flat brims, the sort of hat worn by the man in the book who's always chasing Curious George.

Finally, Mama's room, an extra room, just four by seven. It's squeezed between the "big" bedroom and the parlor. In the passage just outside it is a carved armoire filled with tea, sugar, and provisions for guests. The room itself is Mama's private chamber, really a large cupboard. It features a Singer sewing machine (nonelectric, of course), a trunk full of sewing gear, a trifling stand where she can make tea with milk on a small charcoal brazier, and an ironing table, padded with old blankets and complete with charcoal-fired irons.

The room's public centerpiece is Mama's *Lives of the Saints*, gargantuan, with selected plates in color. A volume not to be trifled with by a child's dirty hands; inside lies mystery, inside lies a splendor of vivid illustrations, revealing worlds of which you could never dream. In bits of this, bits of that, I hear of "the line," meaning uncles, grandfathers, grandsires. I want so to know about them. I ask. No one hears. Perhaps they lurk within the redolent leather that binds Mama's *Lives of the Saints*. "They do not," Mama assures me, and I wonder, is there a companion volume titled *The Lives of the Wicked*? Holy Mother of God, could *that* be where our line is to be found? Wisdom deeply inborn tells me not to broach the matter with Mama.

But I'll make you a wager: Hidden away somewhere, tucked away more securely even than Mama's *Lives of the Saints*, there *is* such a volume. What it must be to fold it open and gaze! The wicked queen Kanjogera, about whom we children whisper; surely she hides there, and some choice Bazungu too, but just who? Relish grips me, then fear. My strategy, should ever I come upon the volume and open it and read something terrible, is to slam it shut and run.

Tucked preciously within the *Saints* is an eight-by-ten black-and-white photo of Grandpa Kabenga. White hair, white beard, long white pipe; he's seated in a big carved chair, all six foot eight of him, wearing a sparkling white mushanana. A big black umbrella leans casually against one knee, half-grasped by one huge hand as if it were a prize fountain pen. I ask about him; Mama, grand mistress of secrecy, says nothing. Except when she wants to stamp her foot without stamping her foot. Then she says, "By Kabenga!"

So who was this Kabenga? And who was his father? His grandfather?

"Never mind. Clean your room."

The secret centerpiece of the chamber, hidden away in a trunk, is Mama's collection of tiny pipes. Don't tell anyone. It's not proper for a Tutsi lady. But at the end of a long workday, in the privacy of the back porch, she can sit for hours, drawing on one of her tiny pipes, looking out over the hills, her eyes wide but distant.

10

ALONE IN AFRICA

Where Even the Lives of the Saints Offer Scant Comfort; 1965

The tin-roofed bungalow at the end of the Boulevard Bitsindinkumi is the place where I am forever four. It's when I'm four that Mama abandons me for two or three months, leaves me all alone in the silent dust of this rugo.

The morning she leaves, she rises as usual just before dawn; I know because I'm up too, but with just one eye, listening to Mama pad down the passage and out the back. As the hired hand goes off to milk the cows in their kraal, Mama goes off on her morning walk, tracing the property line, up the hill, across the hill, down the road, alone. What could be running through her head?

Time to wake Doll Baby, the gift of a Spanish nun. Doll Baby has some problems. She has only one arm, and worse, her hair is lank and yellow. I'm baffled by the stuff hanging limp from her head, the color of elephant grass. Somebody said something about "that's Bazungu for you," but they say that about almost everything that's wrong. Besides, I know some Bazungu. A couple White Fathers—no hair there—and the nuns—and everybody knows nuns don't have any hair either.

Once Doll Baby had two arms; I cried for days when she lost her arm, perhaps in the dust of the yard, the banana groves, the rice fields, the verges of the marsh. I must confess that as names for dolls go, Doll Baby isn't especially imaginative. I hope I don't further disappoint you by confessing that I have no imaginary friends.

Mama returns from her morning walk. The house fills with the aroma of green coffee roasting, then roasted coffee brewing, then the laughing and squawking of kids. There's a mass movement to the back porch. Set before me, on the cement deck of the porch, is a monster cup of café au lait, mostly lait, fresh from the cows. We breakfast on mangoes and passion fruit, and just like that the bustle is over. The kids are out and away. It's silent. Mama begins changing her clothes, putting on a pretty mushanana. "Mama. Why are you getting dressed up?"

"Never mind, Loulou."

I feel edgy. I don't know why. "Why, Mama?"

"Clean up your room, Loulou."

I retreat. I find a corner where I think Mama can't hear me. I begin scolding Doll Baby. "Clean up your room. Don't pick the flowers. Never mind."

Mama is dressed, leaving her bedroom. "Never mind," Mama said, and so of course I can now do nothing but mind, tagging after Mama, dragging precious Doll Baby by the hair. This close to the equator, the sun sets and rises with little twilight; Mama is walking out the front door into the bright morning light of the yard. I quickstep after her, Doll Baby in tow.

"You're not coming, Loulou. Go back."

"Not coming where, Mama?"

"To the mission, toto. Just for a while."

"Let me come with you, Mama. Don't leave me, Mama. Please."

"Loulou. *Louise.* Please. You're not coming. Go back." I don't go back. I grab Mama's skirts. I tug. Mama picks me up and puts me down inside the front door.

"I'll be right back. Go look at a book. Go open the *'Saints.'*"

"Mama."

"The pictures are so beautiful." Mama is at the gate now, squeaking it open, starting down the boulevard, down to the Uganda Road. I run after her.

"Louise, back! The *'Saints!*

Sharp words from Mama Gentille. I'm chastened into hasty retreat, all the way back to Mama's private chamber and up on to the bench. I pick up the *'Saints.* It's so heavy. It falls open. A dragon, green and ferocious, rears over Saint George. Saint George slays the dragon. Saint Peter is crucified, upside down. Saint Anthony is beset by temptation.

Today his predicament does not seem so tempting. No matter how faithfully I page and page through the volume, the lives of the saints seem not so lively. Hours pass in empty silence. I look at the door. The door looks back. I look at the book. Door to book. Book to door.

I tease up the nerve to slide off the bench, scoot into the parlor, push a chair to the front window, climb up, peer out. The yard is empty. The world is empty. No people. No sound. The wind blows the gate, *squeak.* It's the only sound in the world. *Squeak.* I peer, and peer again, then shuffle to the open front door, cling to the doorframe, peek out with a single eye; the yard is still empty. I wait another two, perhaps three hours. Forever.

At last I begin to walk hesitantly across the yard, conscious of every footprint I lay in the dust, expecting at any moment to be stopped dead by a clap of lightning. Just as hesitantly I open the gate, *squeak*, close it, start slowly down the boulevard. Suddenly I break into a run, and just as suddenly halt at an invisible line in the dust, the forbidden point where the property line meets the Uganda Road, onto which I am never to venture alone. Here, again, I wait. And wait.

I hide in a clump of wildflowers, white and yellow frangipani, my body so rigid that my jumpy soul leaps out my mouth and I look back at myself. For one chill nanosecond I can actually see myself: a tiny dark face set with two wide white eyes in deep shadow behind brilliantly lit white and yellow frangipani. I can't let Otto see me.

Otto der Flaschenkorker.

Otto, as much a menace to young children as polio and dengue fever. Otto, whose wife is the gentle and short Mututsi, Felicita, long-suffering Felicita. Otto, the half-caste troll whose father was German and left him this fragrant plantation that spreads out beside me and away from me, hillock after hillock of fragrant oranges. Otto, who always wears a pith helmet, a starched shooting jacket, and khaki shorts, who forever plays Wagner on a scratchy Victrola. He runs on bandy legs, rocking side to side as he speed-waddles ahead, waving a swagger stick with a big knot at one end, bearing down on any child who should give in to temptation and steal over his fence for one of those perfect oranges. "*Raus! Raus!*"

"Loulou, you don't want Otto to examine your case, do you?" says Wellars. "Okay, so help me find my composition book."

I can smell Otto's oranges.

On the road, encompassing quiet, broken only by the occasional jing-jinging of a bicycle picking up perilous speed downhill toward town, and once a sudden dusty roar as a lorry barrels out of nowhere, turning my black hair, black cheeks and rosy-cheeked Doll Baby all indiscriminately powder-red. Then quiet again, save the murmur of people walking single file on the other side of the road, the sound of mothers:

> *ceceka, toto*
> *quiet, baby*
> *icecekere, Mama*
> *hush baby girl*

Forever. Hours. At last I drowse as the day slowly closes.

Slow day in; now slow day out. One entire day and tomorrow another. Here Doll Baby and I will wait, and wait, hiding in thorn behind frangipani, and all the more frightened because these days seem never to be punctuated by night, only by the occasional jinging of bicycle bells.

"Why does it get dark?" a four-year-old once asked her mother.

"Because days have to end," the mother had answered. "If it doesn't get dark, it won't get light."

Her easy assurance had felt so good. Assurance that as surely as the sun sets, it also rises. Can mothers be wrong? Is that possible? I begin to tremble. Perhaps mothers can be wrong. Indeed, maybe they can betray, even abandon. I tremble as if it were a stone-cold well I'm in, not the African sun. These long days, after all, have come and gone without night ever once intervening. I begin to quake.

By and by, this woman who calls herself mother comes home, gathers me up in her long enfolding arms, and insists, "Loulou, Mama hasn't been gone more than fifteen minutes," but what can you trust in a world where big tom leopards lurk and Otto the troll runs amok?

"*Ibihe n'ibindi,*" says Papa. Times are different now. Things are changing.

11

BAILIFF SEGAHEMBE

And the Four Scooters of the Apocalypse; 1966–1967

Guess what: My brother is brave. I know because that's what he tells me. "I'm brave," he says. He also tells me I'm not. "I'm brave and you're not." He's not trying to make me feel bad. I'm sure. He's just protecting me. It's just rained and he's climbing straight up a power pylon clearly posted:

ATTENTION
DANGER DE MORT

I scamper up and he stops me. "Stop! Can't you read?"

I can. I'm going on five. I can't read much, but I can read that. I can and I stop. Wouldn't it be awful? Imagine how Mama would feel. Her silly daughter climbs the pylon, she gets electrocuted to death, and we don't even get electric where we live. It just hums on by, *hummm,* hoping to trap little girls who can't read.

Wellars just goes on climbing. That's because he's brave and because he wears magic mary janes on his feet. Yellow plastic mary janes, store-bought from the Bata shop in town.

"*Insulation,*" he says.

Now do you believe me?

Wellars may be braver than me, but someday I'm going to write books. It's easy. All you have to do is climb way up to the top of the little scarp above the Uganda Road, close your eyes, and stare at the sun from behind your lids. I've already started my first book, *The Mousebirds of Owlet Island.* I'd like to tell you more, but you always start with your title, and that's as far as I am.

There's no bugs in our house. Except mosquitoes. They're bad, and boy mosquitoes aren't nice to girl mosquitoes. Papa says I should make them shake hands, but I just take my own hands and *smash*.

"*IBIHE N'IBINDI*," SAYS PAPA. HE SAYS IT ALL THE TIME. TO HIMSELF. "THINGS ARE CHANG-ing." What I want to know is, what's so wrong about things changing?

NOW I'M FIVE. NOT JUST GOING ON FIVE. FIVE. NOW I SIT WITH THE LADIES, IN THE ladies' quarters, listening to the men across the passage in the men's quar-ters (when it's time to eat, there's that bandy-legged table). Now I can do ladies' work. Work starts when I get up. It ends at the worst time you can imagine, when the sun's way up, and kids are playing, and Mama says, "It's two, Loulou." That's when I have to nap. I have a little plastic bucket. A red one. I help draw water. I help make breakfast. I splash clean water on the floor. I help sweep. I help rake the yard. In town once I saw a Zungu lady raking. Herself. No gardener; just her. That's what I do. I rake, myself. The only difference is, Bazungu rake the grass and we rake the dirt. The floor in the cooking shed is dirt. I help broom it. Every day. And every day I help pull the grass mats out of the bathhouse. Then we wash them and lay them out in the sun or up on the line. Then I help scrub the china. The china is tin and it's chipped. Not the tin, but this freckled stuff that covers the tin. It chips off. I help scrub all that stuff.

So you see what I mean. The sort of stuff a four-year-old could never do. The sort of stuff that means you're five.

Like going to the store. The only thing is, I have to go with Wellars. Wellars says it's not much of a store, but we call it our duka anyway, be-cause if it's a proper store, that's what you call it. A duka. That's what Anne-Marie says and she knows everything. She says you call them dukas because that's what Hendis call them, and they're the experts when it comes to stores, even little Hendi women in little Hendi saris. They run all the stores. Except ours. Ours is too small.

So what. It's got ads covering the walls to keep out the dust. It's got or-ange soda. It's got Lait Nido. It's got cigarette papers made for just where we live, on the Nile. It's got Vim, Omo, Savon Lux, kerosene, rosewater, homemade cigars, stale biscuits from Egypt, dead matches from China, vile tonics from Mombassa, Eveready for the radio, and guess what else: Bazooka. Inside Bazooka there's something I like. Little wax-paper funnies.

Wellars is horrid. He hangs on to the Bazooka all the way home. No matter how much you fight, it doesn't help. I fight with him right through the front door. "*Wellars*," says Mama.

This is when Wellars makes sure Mama and Papa are watching. This is when he finally lets me have my Bazooka. And this is how he does it: like he's the Kaiser, or the king of the Belgians, or even worse, like he's the king of *Rwanda*. So he can show off like some Big Bwana Somebody handing out sweets to all the poor children; this is when he finally lets me have my Bazooka. But what about the funnies! He keeps the funnies! "*Wellars!*"

"*Louisa*," says Mama.

"*Papa!*" I cry.

"*Ibihe n'ibindi*," says Papa.

NOW I'M GOING ON SIX. NOW I GO TO SCHOOL AT THE MISSION, AND WHAT I WANT TO know is this: If Wellars can have a little sister, why can't I have a little brother? If I had a little brother, he'd know full well what's right and proper. Because if he didn't, he'd hear from me. I'd let him know that come Saint Tidbit's Eve, there'd be a special reckoning just for him. And then I'd watch him grow up; every day I'd watch for a truly cross look on his face as he came huffing home from school, a look that would tell me that he'd been to the nuns and they'd told him there is no Saint Tidbit. Ha, ha, I'd laugh, and run away.

I don't think I'll ever have a little brother. Mama says I'm the last; not the youngest, the last.

Someday soon I'm going to read chapter books.

PEOPLE ARE ALWAYS REMARKING HOW FAST CHILDREN GROW, BUT IT'S DREADFUL HOW slow we grow. How long must I be "going on six"?

I like to draw. My sister calls me an artist in black and white, and she's not just being nice. She says there are Bazungu with full boxes of pastels, grown-up Bazungu, who just draw in black and white. Whenever I draw, I show it to Anne-Marie and ask her what she'd call it. I say, "I call it good," and she says, "I call it a first-rate *study*."

Anne-Marie also helps me read Astérix, the little red-haired Gallic warrior in her comic book. She points to a blown-up frame depicting a dilapidated settlement: a timber stockade at the center; what look like African *shambas*, thatch huts, all around; a muddy river rolling by the town, by kitchen gardens; smoke rising from dozens of kitchen fires; and beneath the frame a comic legend saying something about the place, "Lutetia." She tests me. "How do you say that?" I have no idea. "Paris," she says.

. . .

THEY'RE A STUDY IN BLACK AND WHITE, THE TWO OF THEM UP THERE ON THE STAGE, ALL black and white and straight as rakes. Behind them is a shining white movie screen. They stand in front of the screen, foursquare, not moving even a hair, both of them skinny, both of them so tall. On the left is Anne-Marie. She's fourteen now, more than six feet tall, no flesh, all bones, and perfectly upright in her starched white dress, stage lights shining off her black skin. On the right is pale white Abbé Massion, stage lights shining off his big blue nose as he stands rigid in a black cassock so that his skinny six feet plus make him almost as tall as Anne-Marie.

She makes me so proud. First it was Mama; Mama was Grandpa Kabenga's favorite. (Grandpa Kabenga, who left before I got here.) Then big sister Anne-Marie became his favorite. Now here she is. Before everyone else, she gets to know what the movie is about.

And here I am: six. Someday I'll be seven, and I wonder: Did Grandpa Kabenga have about him the dignity of Abbé Massion? The abbé's raw bones speak dedication. He came to our Kabuye mission, and he took on as his very own life's work the building of this structure in which we now sit, this entire thirty-foot-square clay block edifice (if *édifice* is the word for something thirty by thirty), this Centre Culturel de Kabuye. It became his *mission civilatrice,* his calling to bring civilization to our raw end of the earth, where even the best off have no running water, no lights, no electric, where buzzards hover and heathen notions haunt the marshes. Peering out from above wire-rimmed reading glasses, the abbé lectures solemnly on the motion picture to come. Now here is a priest! The sound of his crisply precise French is far more fascinating than what he's saying. I have no idea what he's saying.

Her head straight ahead, big sister uses her sidewise eyes to show she is listening to him (as we all know we should), then on cue she shifts her eyes back to the audience, or more accurately, to the back wall. Without turning his head, the priest stops speaking and shifts his eyes to Anne-Marie, who begins translating his impeccable French into impeccable Kinyarwanda. She stops, the abbé begins again, he stops, she picks up, black girl in stark white, white man in stark black, until at last they both fall quiet, the lights go out, they disappear, and a hand-me-down sixteen-millimeter projector clatters on, throwing onto the screen flickering images in black and white. Titles flash up in some strange lingo. Grand orchestral music taxes both sound track and speakers. Grandly sweeping orchestral cacophony blows up the little thirty-by-thirty-foot building like a brick balloon. Twisting around backward in the first row, all I can see in the black is the brilliant white circle of the projector lens and the wide white eyeballs of fifty children staring straight ahead.

The sound of galloping hooves yanks my head back around. Horses kick up shining white dust. It overwhelms the first row. I wave my hand and squint to see. The dust clears and I see the strangest of all landscapes, a desert, sand and rocks, rocky mountains, and all those Bazungu on horses, firing pistols like the ones brandished by the comic-book cowboy Dangerous Danny, who brother Wellars says is really him, Wellars, dressed up to look white. Not too long ago, I believed quite firmly that the world's only white men were priests. Now I'm quite disabused of that notion. Now, after all, I'm six. But I'm certain that plenty of these poor benighted children who are my neighbors, especially these strange rough boys, still suffer from the same delusion. If nothing else, this movie should at least demonstrate that somewhere out there beyond this Kabuye mission there are white men who are not priests.

But then again, these are actors. Maybe these are just priests, acting. Maybe priests *are* the world's only white men. I turn around with a question mark on my face for Wellars in the second row. A pistol cracks and yanks my head back to the screen.

The swagger of a big white man in a big white hat slowly fills the screen, walking right into my face, his broad shoulders pitched forward, his eyes narrowed. So menacing. Surely this man is a priest. He fires off another round, right in front of all these children, and the entire front row ducks for cover, not just me but everybody, even those two sour brothers, Ernest and Théoneste.

"Jeanwayyyne," whispers Wellars, clearly impressed.

When at last my heart stops thumping, I struggle to make sense of it. It's impossible. Anne-Marie had just explained, but I wasn't *listening,* I was just *watching,* watching old Kabenga's favorite, gazing proudly up at big sister. There are subtitles in French, but the subtitles are either white, fading into the white of the screen, or they're black, fading into the black of the screen. And anyway, what's this Africa-bound six-year-old to comprehend of the U.S. Cavalry and its battalion commander Owen Thursday and his sergeant Victor McLaglen? Or is Owen Thursday the actor-priest that Abbé Massion calls *Henri Fonda*? He looks at times like such a nice man, but mostly he's as grim as any priest, and makes as many dumb mistakes, not the least of which is blundering into an Indian ambush. I cheer as the *peaux-rouges* massacre the priests. All the children cheer.

On the way home, through the dark, Dr. Zitoni's daughters are especially alert. Little Miriam is younger than me, but (thank goodness) her big sister, Mimi, is along, and Mimi knows how to deal with dangers that lurk on nights like these. (The Zitoni girls call their father "the sheriff.") For surely there are hostiles about, lying *en ambuscade* behind trees—and not just in my imagination. It's good that I'm walking with Anne-Marie and Mimi. Ahead lurks a huge eucalyptus. Behind it lurks . . .

"*Bouge pas!*" shouts a dark form as it jumps into the middle of the track, squarely blocking our way. It's Wellars, aiming squarely at us. "*Haut les mains!*"

All up and down the track the sounds of ambush rage. "Pow! Pow! Hands up! Don't budge!" Every child in Kabuye is either John Wayne riding out from Fort Apache, or about to be the victim of John Wayne riding out from Fort Apache (aka Le Centre Culturel de Kabuye).

SAME TRACK, SAME SPOT, SEVEN-THIRTY THE NEXT MORNING, AND WHAT A CHANGE. People walking with the peaceful gait of angels. Down the Uganda Road, and it's the same. As far as a child can see, and in both directions, down toward Kigali and up toward Uganda, all is quiet. Mama, wearing a lovely long mushanana, is striding down toward Dr. Zitoni's surgery, and I'm quickstepping behind her to keep up, under one arm a sun-bleached copy of *Tintin en Amérique,* its hard cover featuring young Tintin roped to a pole by a redskin. Never mind gunfire; not even a backfire disturbs the silence. I think: All this quiet. This lonely road, all rutted. This place called Africa. Not nearly as thrilling as the Wild West.

Finally, a speck shows up on the horizon. It's coming at us from town. Now it's larger, accompanied by a faint mechanical whine and a cloud of red dust from the red clay of the Uganda Road. Now larger still. A car? A lorry? Now larger still. A motorcycle?

A scooter.

Now yet larger. A banged-up blue Vespa. For a shadow of a second, blind terror crosses Mama's face, as if it weren't a banged-up two-stroke Vespa closing on us, but a man on horseback, and not just one man on horseback, but four, and not just any four, but the Four Horsemen of the Apocalypse. Now you can see the scooter bounce every time it hits a rut. Now you can see it swerve to miss the ruts, its motor whining in complaint, a sewing machine motor sent to do a scooter's work. A man in a dusty suit and tie is riding it. His briefcase, tied by its handle to the saddle, flaps like the wing of a wounded bird. Now the whine is a mosquito in your ear and the cloud of dust fills the sky. The dust covers us. The scooter bangs just past us. I squint to follow it. Suddenly the clerkish man on the seat squeezes his brakes, the little front wheel pivots, and the man nearly bounces over the handlebars. "Bibiane!" He's grinning.

"Bailiff Segahembe," says Mama. She's not grinning.

"Bibiane!" he grins.

"Segahembe," she says.

"Fine morning, Bibiane."

"That it is, Bailiff."

"And how might the husband be? How's . . . *Bitsindinkumi*!"

"Best of health, Bailiff. Best."

"Still—ha!—The *Seducer*?"

"Still *my* seducer," says Mama.

"The Missus, too," he says. "Best of health."

Silence.

"And Mama Mariya," he says. "And Abbé Kagame. How's he? And Alexis Karekezi. How's Karekezi? How's Elizabeti?"

"Gone," says Mama. "Been gone a good few years now."

"May the holy father grant her rest."

Silence. Awkward silence.

"She wasn't much one for rest, was she," he says, and forces a laugh. "The others?"

"Best of health."

"Stefania? Nepo? Lando?"

"The best."

"Karangwa? What a scoundrel. How's the little scoundrel?"

"Still little."

"Gaetan? Anne-Marie?"

"All the best."

"And *this*. Just who might this be?"

"Louise. This is Louise."

"*Louise*."

"Louise."

"And what a lady. Just the size of Sixbert, she is. Bibiane, you've never seen little Sixbert. Such a fine healthy lad. You should see the lad."

Silence.

"Such a scamp . . ."

Mama takes my hand. "Well . . ." says the clerkish little man. For the first time, a faint, stiff smile crosses Mama's face. "Well . . ." she says.

"Been running late all the morning," he says.

"Good fortune to you, Bailiff," says Mama.

"And good fortune to you, Bibiane! And to all the family Kabenga! I mean all the family Bitsindinkumi. I mean . . . Good fortune to you then!" With that he's off, on up the road in the direction of Uganda, as I stand staring after him.

By the time I turn around, Mama is half a football pitch down the road toward town. I have to run to catch her up.

"Mama!" I yell after her, panting.

"In your good time," says Mama.

"Who—" I pant. "Why—"

"Segahembe," says Mama.

"Who's Segahembe?" I ask.

"The bailiff. A bailiff."

"What's a bailiff?"

"A bailiff works for the court."

"The court?"

"The court. The prison. He's the bailiff. Bailiff Sega—"

"Mama, why were you so rude?"

"Your mother wasn't rude. Was your mother rude?"

"You didn't seem very . . ."

"It's been years. He's from the old hill. We don't have anything to talk about anymore."

That's good enough for me, secure in anticipation of a new Tintin to read. Tintin in America. Tintin with the redskins. It will be years before I reflect on how easily a child accepts a mother's word. Had nothing to talk about? Hadn't seen him for years? All the more you'd think they'd have to talk about. All that catching up to do.

MOTHER HAS SUCH STRANGE, MYSTERIOUS RULES GOVERNING WHERE WE SIT ON A BUS. Rules she never spells out. We're headed for town, headed for a visit with Mama's friend Marguerite, who's good to visit because she has two children always ready to play. I'm in the window seat, my nose to the window, letting the shoulder rush by in a blur. If I focus just a bit farther out, the shoulder comes into better focus; I see rivulets of sewage lacing it. The shoulder tumbles away, becoming a hillside patched with banana groves, kitchen gardens, and helter-skelter yards in which Africans try to make something of the white man's refuse: scrap-metal yards lit by blowtorches burning hot in the dust of yards already hot enough; an alfresco machine shop graced by Egyptian vultures atop a chain-draped block and tackle; yards in which ragged men with giant upholstery needles stitch shut wounds in discarded truck tires; acrid black smoke rising from tires even they can't rescue. The bus hisses to a stop for a solitary passenger. Just behind the stop yawns the dark cavern of an open shop. From within its gaping maw, I hear the saw-saw sound of the carpenter. Gears groan, the bus moves, again the verge blurs, and suddenly a huge, endless frog of a building, a massive building of dark red brick, looms up. It too is on the slope downhill, rising from beneath us, but it's so big it looms nonetheless, backlit by the sun, covering the sun. "What's that?"

"Time to sit on this side." Mama crosses herself and lurches to the other side of the bus, drops down by an open window. Grit hits us face on.

"Why?"

"Time."

I'm peeved, filled with questions, suspecting connections. I twist around to look back at the place. A broad dirt yard spreads out in front. On the far side of the yard, a broad brick arch spans a wide iron gate. In the yard, men in coveralls stoop, policing bits of garbage, attended by men in crisp khaki bearing rifles. Set in the bricks above the gate is a tile molded with a number. Our houses don't have numbers.

1930

"Is that where Bailiff Segahembe lives?"

"No."

"Is that where he works?"

"No. And just who are you, little lady? The Inspector General?"

"What goes on there, Mama?"

Silence.

"What, Mama?"

Silence.

"And Bailiff Segahembe. What *does* he do?"

"He works for the—"

"I know that. You told me that. What does he *do* for the court?"

"He summons people."

"Any people we know?"

"No. Yes."

"Who?"

"Never mind."

"With a rifle? He summons them with a rifle?"

"No."

"And people listen? To *him*?"

"Yes."

"What does he *say*?"

"He asks them their name."

"Even if he already knows their name?"

"That's the law."

Silence now from me.

"He says . . ." she says.

Again I twist around to look at that mass of bricks called 1930, then turn back to Mama. She's staring out the window in the other direction, facing down the grit. She's talking into the grit. Her voice gets swallowed in the wind. "He says, 'Elder Kabenga: Are you Elder Kabenga?'"

"And what does Grandpa say?"

"By Kabenga, he says that he is. 'That I am,' he says."

"Even though Segahembe already knows who—"

"Even though."

"And then what?"

"Serves him with the bans is what. Serves him with the paperwork."

"The paperwork?"

"The summons."

"To court?"

"No. To prison."

"No court?"

"No court. Prison."

"For how long?"

"Forever."

"Forever?"

"For three weeks. Forever plus three weeks. He went in, and three weeks later he was dead. There."

He was seventy, and as Mama's Instamatic caught him (in snapshots that would someday vanish in a heap of refuse left by genocide), still trim. Six foot eight with a white beard and a long white mushanana. Of course, I can know none of this as now we rumble on to visit Marguerite, and even if I did know, it's doubtful I could make much of it. But I do find myself, as the bus rumbles on, toying with my mother's favorite interjection. "By Kabenga!" she likes to say. Will we be on time to school? "By Kabenga!" I practice saying it this way. I practice saying it that way. It's now my favorite interjection. By Kabenga!

12

MELODY RANCH

*All Things Come to Her Who Waits Above the
Uganda Road; 1967–1968*

Again the study in black and white, and why is it that some stray notion always gets in the way between me and them, between me down here in the first row and the black-on-white pair up there on the platform trying to tell us about the movie coming up? As Anne-Marie stands silent beside him, Abbé Massion begins his dry lecture, and again what my ear hears is not what he's in tedious fact saying but his style, the austere impeccability of his French. This time I've slipped into reverie with especial ease. Lando is home from university, rehearsing his part in "a dramatical presentation," and listening now to Abbé Massion begs a dreamy question: How is it that Lando and the Abbé Massion can speak such equally impeccable French with such different results? Abbé Massion, so dry and lean; Lando, such a joker, so deep-throated, even at nineteen.

Why can't he be as dignified as Abbé Massion?

Now it's Anne-Marie's turn. She's translating the abbé's words into Kinyarwanda, and as ever, I'm just watching, not really listening. Anne-Marie gets to help Lando rehearse. She reads a female character, Magdelon (how's that for an odd name), to his Gorgibus (how's that for even odder)—a couple articles from way back in the Zungu way-backs. I could do that. After all, I'm going on seven. In fact you could say I *am* seven. Doesn't Lando know how well I read now? He should ask Abbé Massion. "*Ma petite fille, ton français est* impeccable," says Abbé Massion.

His compliment makes such an impression on me. Even sitting here waiting for the movie, and apropos of absolutely nothing, he inclines his head in my direction and, right in front of everybody, he says, "*Ma petite fille, ton français est* impeccable." Of course, what he actually says is nothing of the sort. What he actually says is "Hush," then shifts his glare to the back wall as Anne-Marie renders his summary of the movie into Kinyarwanda.

She so neatly mimics his dry presentation, right down to its very dryness. Her impersonation so tickles me that I wonder how any of these kids could be paying attention to her words, but they must be, because the instant her translation makes it clear that cowboys will yet again be agallop in Kabuye, the children are unable to contain themselves. "Yahoo!" comes a shout from the right. "Pow! Pow!" from the left. Abbé Massion signals the projectionists (two tiny beadles, devoted deputies of the abbé) to restore order. "*Crack,*" goes a sapling on the back of an empty chair, and from each of the two tiny men in squeaky succession, "Silence!"

"Silence!"

Silence.

From the priest, nothing but the glare for which this grave Walloon is known to every child in the parish of Kabuye. At last the lights drop and the projector clatters on. It's now the chamber's sole source of sound and light. Flickers in a black, African silence. Then . . .

"Ah'm baaaack in the saaddle agin. . . ."

"Yahoo!" (In a whisper.)

"Back whar a maaaan . . . is a maaan. . . ."

"Pow!" (Louder some.)

Twice the abbé's beadles have to stop the film to restore order, but no matter. No fan of Gene Autry (or his horse, Champion), Abbé Massion is long gone.

"Yahoo!"

No struggle here to follow the story. This silk shirt cowboy with an easy, dreamy smile rides with you into reverie. School holiday. The short rains. Haricots in season. Lando home on holiday, rehearsing.

"Yahoo!"

I don't even bother following the story. I just watch and ponder Lando and how he's rehearsing. But pow! What's this he's rehearsing? *Les précieuses ridicules*? By Kabenga, I know that Lando is more than capable of acting ridiculous. You could even call him an expert at ridiculous. But *précieux*? People? Isn't that a word for things like emeralds? Rubies? Diamonds?

"Holy smoke, Curley. Not sure ah catch yer drift."

"*Bouge pas,* Slim."

And just like that, to the strains of "The Bells of Capistrano" (or some such): "FINIS," it's all over, and we're "On the Trail to San Antone," headed home.

Plenty of "pows!" on the road this time too, but without the heart-stopping menace of those Fort Apache "pows." These are silk shirt "pows." Instead of pretending their index finger is the barrel of a six-shooter, the boys are strumming their belly buttons, striking chords on make-believe guitars. Up and down the track, boys in school shorts and ragged hand-me-downs are slowly swiveling their bottoms as if they were astride ambling cow ponies, a brief parade of African children, juvenile silhouettes, so small against the shadows of trees so tall and the overarching blue-black of the sky, crooning falsetto to flamingos asleep in the African night, every lad in Kabuye, even those sour two, the handsome brothers Ernest and Théoneste. "Ah'm baack in the saaddle agin. . . ."

CONTROVERSY. WITH LANDO HOME, MAMA WANTS HIM AND KARANGWA TO COME along with her tomorrow to visit Granny Mariya, old Kabenga's widow. Mama says they never visit Mama Mariya. They say they do, and with all the time back and forth on the bus, it will be an all-day affair. Meantime, Lando has to rehearse his Gorgibus, and Anne-Marie, who visits Granny aplenty, has asked a chum on a distant hill to come visit. With no phone to break the invitation, she has to stay put. She can't come along to help Lando rehearse. Karangwa ("*D'ac, d'ac*, I'll come") can't help Lando because if he's coming, he has to bring along some papers from Hatton & Cookson where he works now as an accountant. Karangwa an accountant! Naturally, he's been larking about at work and has to catch up. You can tell Mama is vexed, but ever the Mututsi, she won't show it. Lando, ever the Muhutu at heart, is having fun with her . . . and Karangwa (Mama can't tell, but *I* can) is conspiring with him. They've got Mama convinced she's put each of them in a pickle and both of them in a pickle with each other. Karangwa huffs at the pickle she's put him in, them in. I can't help it. I laugh.

"*Louise!*" says Mama.

"What do you want from me?" Karangwa asks Lando, as if he's actually at odds with Lando, pretending to provoke Lando just as he knows Lando wants to be provoked. "Help you rehearse. Where am I going to find the time?"

From Lando, an exasperated puff.

"Sure, and aren't you just the Tutsi gent," says Karangwa. "Never let them see your feathers mussed."

Now Lando can shift into true high dudgeon: a puff, a half roll of the eyes, a hand half-raised to the heavens . . . at least he can delight a seven-year-old. I laugh out loud. "*Louisa!*" says Mama.

"But I bet *Louise* can help you," says Karangwa, gazing upward in mock innocence.

Perfect.

Karangwa and Lando extend hands and shake like the successful conspirators they are. I giggle, only vaguely aware that my glee was the real object of their conspiracy. Imagine: I'm going to help Lando rehearse.

. . .

JUST DOWNHILL FROM OUR PLACE, DOWNHILL THROUGH THE GROVES AND OVER PAPA'S
roughly terraced fields for sorghum and carrots and leeks, just beyond
some thorns, there's that short, stony scarp overlooking the road. You
hunker there long enough and sometimes you can spy lorries with
strange registration plates. For hours, there's nothing down there but that
quiet parade of trudgers and cyclers that Bazungu here and there will
someday tell me seems so distinctly African to them, so common that it
can seem one single loose procession that starts at one far end of our continent, wends and winds its way to the other far end, and then switches
back, through every African nation you can imagine, a loosely spaced loop
of people ever in endless single file motion. And more than just people:
fat-tailed African sheep, an occasional calf, here and there a man in a
dusty coat and tie dragging a goat by its ear to market, all of them, goats
and folks, trudging single file along that one single, narrow track next to
the road, or up a dry wash, or across a meadow, or through eye-high
bushveld (there to amuse hidden cats), or through a gravel pit, or a junk-
yard, forever and ever, amen. Women with loads on their heads, so artfully
balanced on such strong necks and backs. Schoolmasters with books under
their arms. Uniformed schoolchildren with books on straps. Mothers with
totos swathed tight on their backs. Mechanics struggling under the weight
of a short block engine suspended from a litter of eucalyptus poles. After a
while you might not be surprised to spy a mincing flamingo innocuously
inserted in the train. Armed guerrillas from warring factions could be filing
along, separated by a dozen or so irregularly spread trudgers. This is what I
gaze at from my scarp, this ragged parade wending on, the quiet barely
broken until at last a sleek sedan speeds out from Kigali-ville, headlong for
Uganda.

Somewhere there must be a lorry, another sedan. As ever, I'm on the
lookout for strange plates. Pretty soon here comes a flatbed with soldiers
hanging on to the rails, their rifles on slings over their shoulders, their rifles
flapping and banging with the ruts in the road. "Sure hope they have their
safeties on," I say aloud to myself, repeating what I have heard Muzungu say
when he sees this. Then another long stretch, an especially long stretch, and
out of the north comes a rumble, a big one, an oil tanker with Uganda,
Uganda plates.

Often I hunker on the edge of that scarp and wait for nothing. Often I
just hunker and stare. So often that once a month or so when Mama and I
catch the bus and our bus passes underneath this spot, I look up and I see
myself looking down on myself.

It's a good place for homework. It's an even better place for comic books.

Dangerous Danny. Lucky Luke. It's a good place to go over your scripts. Of course, this is the first script I've ever gone over in my life, and it's not really mine, I'm only helping Lando. But let's forget about that. It's a good place to go over your scripts. Of course, you've got to ignore the way the wind blows these thin carbon sheets. The way you have to run after them when they get loose. The way, whoa, they're now blowing out over the road, way down there. You've got to ignore the way your fingers smudge oily carbon as at the last moment you grab pages from the wind.

This "dramatical" business is hard to grasp. Lando, patient Lando, has actually tried, has actually taken some precious time to take the words that this man Molière composed for seventeenth-century France and tried to render them into something that makes sense to a twentieth-century child of the African interior. "French from way back, Loulou. What he's saying is . . ." But still, it's hard. Almost as hard as figuring out Henri Fonda in *Fort Apache*. Fortunately, Papa did all right, teaching me to sound words out even when I have no idea what I'm saying. Which in this script is all the time.

DAWN OF THE NEXT DAY, AND WE FELLOW TRAVELERS ARE OFF, MAMA, KARANGWA, Lando, and I. I'm bringing up the rear, and smartly if I say so myself. Tucked under one arm is my own smudged carbon of the script, and I sport a fancy dress with crinolines, thrown on frantically at the last minute ("Let's go, Louise. We're leaving without you, Louise") so I can really get into my seventeenth-century part, my *rôle*.

First we trudge to the bus stop, joining all those trudgers and cyclers in that forever procession that wends on and on until at last you're at the stop, and then we wait for the bus. Forever. There's hardly a vehicle on the road, hardly any of them are busses, and of the two that are, neither is the right bus. Tiny Speke's weavers squeak about in brilliant yellow abandon.

Frustrated glances, until at last Lando flips open his script with one hand:

Lando as Gorgibus: "*Quel diable de jargon entends-je ici? Voici bien du haut style.*"

Me (with a flash of my fan) as his niece Cathos: "*En effet, mon oncle . . .*" No sound on the road. Not a lot of wind. Yet in the enormous emptiness, my seven-year-old voice is lost, muffled by an immensity of sky, hills, the open and empty road. My script flaps in the breeze. I raise my voice. "*. . . mon oncle . . .*"

"What's that?" says Mama. "*Ngw'iki?*" She sounds like one of the squeaking weavers. "*Ngw'iki?*"

As Cathos, I repeat (with another flash of my fan): "*En effet, mon oncle . . .*"

"No, Loulou, not you," says Mama. "*Lando.* What's *he* saying? What kind of French does he think he's speaking?"

Lando (directing his remark off-stage, in a stage whisper): "Hey, boss, how can I develop my art with these shots from the cheap seats?"

"French from way back, Mama," I explain. "You see, what he's saying is, is . . ."

All three are looking at me. Down at me. Three tall question marks loom above me. Lando's eyebrows are cocked at the same angle as his cripple-crooked waist.

"Is, is . . . well, his daughter, his daughter in the dramatical—"

"*You?*"

"No Mama, not me. I'm playing his *niece.* Lando doesn't have anybody playing his daughter right now. But anyway, he has a daughter and he's trying to get her married off, and just before this, she was chewing his ear off about . . ."

They're still staring down at me.

". . . about what she expects from an article who comes courting, about how she expects him to drip with all this high-style rubbish, and he says, Lando says, the father, Gorgibus, says, 'What rubbish! You call this rubbish *style?*' "

"Bravo!" shouts Lando.

"Bravissimo!" shouts Karangwa, and he bows like a cartoon chevalier, presenting me with a hastily plucked spray of road-shocked weeds, in the midst of which, *en bouquet,* is one single pink wildflower.

From the Uganda horizon come a couple squeaks pitched just beneath Speke's Weavers, then a puff of dust from which rise wisps of burning diesel fuel. Now come three more squeaks, pathetic imitations of proper honks, our bus. Out of its own self-generated cloud it appears, a gift and creation of the nation of Japan, a huge, fat, lime-green Godzilla of a bus with a claxon pitched at top tenor.

No, not a Godzilla. A sumo wrestler is more the inspiration for this vehicle. Puffing dust and diesel fumes, it barrels toward us like a sumo wrestler with a squeaky voice. We climb aboard. We pass beneath my roosting spot above the road. I wave up at myself looking down at myself from the scarp above the Uganda Road.

TIME HAS PAINTED GRANNY MARIYA, *NYOGOKURU* MARIYA, WITH A GRACEFUL BRUSH. More than seventy, she still stands tall, trim, erect. In defiance of fashion, she wears her graying hair cropped close to her head.

I've always presumed that she's our real granny. How is it that I'm beginning now to sense that Mama Mariya is not a blood relative? Years of snatched bits of conversation? Mama still has not told me.

Mama is embracing her Mama Mariya. Karangwa and Lando are embracing Mama Mariya. I see treats in the parlor. When Mama and I visit Mama Mariya alone, I sit politely as long as I can, then wander out to play. But now my big brothers are along, and besides, I'm wearing a dress. If the talk can engage them, it can engage me. I stay put, fidgeting. Pretty soon Lando and Karangwa aren't talking much, just listening to Mama and Mama Mariya's small talk, and pretty soon I can't sit still anymore. I wander out. Right behind me, like overgrown kids, Karangwa and Lando wander out too.

From the front porch where we sit (Lando and I rehearsing, Karangwa with his eyes reluctantly buried in his accounts) we can hear the women murmuring through the open window of the parlor. Whenever Karangwa opens his mouth, Lando physically shoves his head back down in Hatton & Cookson.

Lando has also to cope with me. For example:

Lando as Gorgibus: "Do you really have to use so much—"

Me as me: "Lando, when's Tonton coming?"

Lando as Gorgibus: "Do you really have—"

"When?"

"Tonton's busy. You know that."

"I know he's a priest. Does that make him so busy he can't—"

"We're rehearsing, Loulou."

Karangwa: "You do know, child, that he writes books."

Lando: "You do know, brother, that you've got books of your own at hand." Shove.

Books? Tonton Kagame? Tonton who plays with us and otherwise marches to Auntie Stefania's cadence just like the rest of us, even Papa. I wonder aloud, "Tonton?"

Karangwa: "The same."

Me: "Kids' books?"

They must be kids' books. What else could a man like our playful Tonton write? One matter I do know is that a long time ago, when we still had a king and the king had chiefs—austere Tutsi chiefs—Tonton wrote a scandalous story in verse for kids. But that wasn't *a book*. That was just a story about a clutch of typically austere chiefs getting together for a parley, and when they get there, the aroma of roasting pork assaults them straightaway. Roasting *pork*—a vile animal by Rwandese lights, and especially vile to these famously high-cockalorum chiefs. But by and by the lovely aroma drives them so mad they end up in a food fight over who gets the biggest portion. And recalling that, I recall as well that Uncle dearly enjoys good food. And good banana beer. And Scotch.

"No. Not kids' books," says Lando.

"What then?"

Lando as Gorgibus: "Do you really have to use so much—"

"What then?"

"Secrets," says Lando. "Now back to—"

"*Le code esotérique*," says Karangwa. "Went to school in the Vatican, he did."

"Are you two up to something?"

Lando: "Read your part, Loulou."

The Vatican? Our Tonton? Books like that?

Maybe they aren't up to something. Maybe he really does write books like that . . . in which case I shouldn't be so surprised. I'm in the know. I help Lando rehearse. But surprised I am. Even more surprised than I will be in a year or so when I learn that this uncle we call variously "Tonton," "Uncle," and "Abbé" is, and has been for all my years, a bishop. Or to be more exact, a six-foot-five, three-hundred-pound bishop.

LANDO AS GORGIBUS TO HIS DAUGHTER (WHOSE ROLE, YOU MAY RECALL, IS UNATtended; I'm reading her cousin): "Do you really have to use so much lard to rouge your lips?"

Mama, unseen, from the parlor: "*Ngwi'ki?* What was that?"

Lando as Lando: "The days of Louis Quatorze, Mama. Louis Quinze. Louis something. The ladies used lard for lipstick."

"*Ngwi'ki?*"

Lando as Gorgibus, to his daughter: "Tell me what you said to get those boys mad. Can't you receive them as men worthy of marrying you? Men *I've* chosen."

Me, as cousin Cathos sticking up for the daughter: "A reasonable young woman could never stand for that."

Granny Mariya as Granny Mariya, unseen, from the parlor: "Indeed. What daughter *could* stand for that? Cozying up to a suitor just because your father has picked him out. I'm with the girls."

Lando as Gorgibus, again to his daughter: "They're ready to *marry* you. Why doesn't this make you as happy as it makes me? Is there anything more important?"

Granny Mariya, from the parlor: "*Ngwi'ki?*"

Lando as Lando: "A *muterambabazi,* Granny." A *muterambabazi* is a spoiled lady—or young lady—of the virtually vanished Tutsi beau monde; a highborn female who'd never rouge or jewel herself like Mae West, but nonetheless sashays just like her, and can just as cavalierly command, "Beulah, peel me a grape."

Granny Mariya, every bit an old-school aristocrat herself, and now as cool as a cantaloupe: "Bibiane, did I hear somebody call somebody a *muterambabazi*?"

Now it's time for me to switch from playing the niece to playing the daughter, Magdelon. I go into a soliloquy about how I expect to be courted—Magdelon's rules of *bonne gallanterie*: "It's gross making love while you're signing the marriage contract. . . . Nothing could be more *commercial*."

Granny Mariya: "Indeed." Pause, then: "Bibiane, about the sorghum. When did you say Stefania is coming to help dry the sorghum."

As the widow of Stefania's brother Kabenga (if you insist, her half brother Kabenga) Granny Mariya is Stefania's generational equal, but if there's anyone who isn't a *muterambabazi*, it's no-nonsense Stefania. Just the woman, at just such a moment, with whom to associate oneself, and in a characteristically no-nonsense manner—drying the season's sorghum.

AS WE REHEARSE, LANDO AND I BECOME AWARE, AFTER A WHILE, OF HESITATIONS THAT interrupt the gossip in the parlor, and so does Karangwa. He looks up silently from his accounts. It's not like Karangwa to look up silently from anything. Then we hear snatches, noms de guerre half-whispered in the darkened parlor, the boys in Burundi, our uncles, Mama Mariya's sons, Mama's brothers . . . or if you knew the whole story, her half brothers. Blindé, Commandant, Uncle Mpunga, Uncle Mutemura. Uncle Mutemura is the namesake of old Mutemura of the Batemura, our grandsire five generations distant. This young Mutemura seems a man who liked women and collected them in all sizes and colors, and for some reason altogether unclear is now spoken of in the past tense.

Quixotes all, and altogether beyond my young ken. Lando can tap a child's grasp of phonetics to teach me lines, and a driving desire to be included gives me the patience to learn some of what Molière has going on in his play, which in any case is not so subtle. But of Don Quixote and his Rwandese ilk I know nothing, and Lando doesn't even try to explain. All I know is that I have some relations we don't talk about, perhaps because they're insects. Tutsi insects, to be sure, but insects nonetheless. They live "underground" and they're called *inyenzi*, "cockroaches." They even call themselves cockroaches. Go explain that to a seven-year-old.

I'm not sure I can explain it now, all these many years later. Let's just say that during these years when we visit Mama Mariya, a first generation of

Hutu apparatchiks, with their own quixotic flair, are calling themselves "The Revolution of 1959." Right enough, there had been a revolution in 1959. By the time I was born, in 1961, Batutsi were earning nearly as little as Bahutu, and that was a considerable revolution. But the actual makers of this revolution weren't Bahutu. They were Bazungu, social engineers financed by Christian Democrats in Belgium.

Years later I will read of such matters, and this picture of a revolution stage-managed by white men will seem a flight of Tutsi rhetoric. In a way I will almost *want* to see it as a flight of Tutsi rhetoric, perhaps so that I can pull myself above the squalid fray, distance myself, assume the voice of moderation in a world that so sorely needs it. But it's hard to argue with a commonplace, especially when it's abundant in the record, Belgium unabashedly assigning an army colonel, Guy Logiest, to transfer the reins of state to handpicked Bahutu and call it a revolution.

So there you have it, in all its nose-backward glory: Tutsi revolutionaries backed by the Communist bloc tilt quixotically at administratively proclaimed Hutu revolutionaries. Mama and Mariya huddle, and as they murmur, Tutsi patricians train in Communist China. Don't even try to sort this out. Blood is the argument. A game of words played with lives. Our cockroach uncles deploy their ambushes, and too often it's ordinary Hutu peasants, not soldiers, who fall into their traps. And too often, ordinary Batutsi pay the price. Up and down the tracks and across the hills, Bahutu and Batutsi alike call the period another of our *muyaga,* another period of troubling, unpredictable winds.

These men of whom Mama and Mariya whisper are scooting back and forth across the Burundi frontier armed with ancient Mausers, jousting with Hutu regiments armed and organized, in the first instance, by faceless nomenclatura in Brussels, and when Brussels won't do it anymore, by grim war-gamers silently at work at the Élysée in Paris. For a decade now, Grandfather Kabenga's sons, Mama's half brothers, have been jerry-rigging bombs from cassava roots to challenge Logiest's Hutu army, now under the wing of the French presidency's Deuxième Bureau—its secret police. Our Tutsi Quixotes compose impossibly romantic songs about the thousand hills, about the lovely green roll of those hills and how they are ready to lay down their lives. *Oh Rwanda, ma patrie!* You'd think they'd write in Kinyarwanda, indeed in Kinyarwanda alone, since it is of Rwanda they sing, but after all, these are knights, the well-born and French-speaking sons of Rwanda, and so they rhapsodize,

Je ne crains pas la mort
C'est ma destinée

Je ne reculerai jamais
Devant l'ennemi

Only one of Grandmother Mariya's sons, Ntukanyagwe, can live in Rwanda anymore. Of the rest:

Étienne Sayinzoga has fled to Burundi. He's the one known in the underground as "Commandant."

Uncle Mpunga, a trained agronomist, has also fled to Burundi, where he too is a cockroach.

Likewise Uncle Ngirunkunda, also known as Blindé (tiny Blindé, whose nom de guerre means "armored car"); he too has run off to Burundi to join the cockroaches.

Likewise Uncle Mutemura, namesake of Kabenga's great-grandfather Mutemura, founder of Mama's Temura subclan of the Singa people; likewise has he run off, and would still be among the renegades were it not for events reported in a letter that arrived almost exactly three years ago from Blindé, telling his mother, Mariya, what at this instant I still don't know, that her son Mutemura has fallen in combat. Mutemura's widow, Gatarina, is a beautiful woman. She's returned from Burundi with her children. They visit often but not often enough. Whenever they do, Wellars and I fight for their affection. Wellars, who still hides his *Tintins* from me.

Auntie Gatarina's daughter Mutega is a champion at marbles. One day Wellars and I are getting ready for Auntie Gatarina and her kids to come over, and an elegant lady in a crisply ironed *mushanana* comes from a distant hill to visit Mama. Mama repairs to her armoire to prepare tea and cakes. First comes what I will someday understand are the custom-ridden extended greetings of the Afro-Levant. ("How's your mother?" "Fine. And yours?" "Fine. And your husband?" "Fine. And yours?" "Fine. And your Auntie Stefania?" "Fine. And your Auntie . . .") Not until the kettle whistles does this endless ritual ("And your daughter-in-law's cousin Celestin? How's he?") at last end, and they enter into another ritual conversation of polite society in the Great Lakes, which never says anything bad about anybody. (Business is reserved for impolite society.) Elegant Lady from a Distant Hill glances over at Wellars and me (we're getting out our marbles) and says, "Your children are so beautiful."

"And yours," says Mama.

"And yours are so well-behaved," says Elegant Lady.

"You can't be on Mutega's team," Wellars hoots. "You're not good enough."

To which I shoot back: "And you're too dark."

"They play so nicely," says Elegant Lady, with not a trace of sarcasm.

"And yours," says Mama, also with no such trace, and so does she now carry on with Mama Mariya, though now there are traces of something. What is it? Whatever it is, it's somewhat more profound than sarcasm, something closer to desperation, for now their talk is veering toward Uncle Ntukanyagwe, Mama Mariya's one son who can still live in Rwanda.

Were it not for Uncle Ntukanyagwe, Mama and Mariya might not be talking about our uncles at all. When you're Mututsi and you must hide your feelings, the rule is stay away from topics that threaten to flush feelings from their hiding places. But some topics you just can't dodge, and Uncle Ntukanyagwe is one. Uncle Ntukanyagwe can live in Rwanda because he's in prison in Rwanda.

He's locked up in the Ruhengeri stockade, in the high, cold mountains of the far northwest. In hushed tones, the two women fret. What can they possibly do to breathe life into the wan chance that he might someday come out alive? He can't write home. The family can't write him. All that gets through—perhaps—are bribes, *rushwa,* for his jailers, to ease their tormenting. "Rushwa," we hear Mama whisper in a hush. She seems almost to swallow the word. Karangwa looks up at Lando.

"Rush—" says grandmother Mariya. She never finishes the word. Lando, having apprehended Karangwa's look as I cannot, leaps up. "Run, Faranga, run!" he shouts.

From inside the parlor, nearly in unison: *"Ngwi'ki?"*

Then Karangwa is up and shouting, "Faster, Faranga, faster!"

Just like that, Mama and Mama Mariya are out on the porch, aghast, as Karangwa and Lando shout for some Faranga to run, run. I look about for this Faranga. Nowhere. At last it registers that there's a trick in the air, and I squeal along, "Run, Faranga, run."

Though he's nowhere to be seen this morning, there is in point of sorry fact a real Faranga; indeed, he lives just across the road. Now it just won't do to tell you that *faranga* means "franc," nor even that besides meaning franc, *faranga* can mean legal tender in all its cash forms. I must tell you as well that when your mama and papa name you Faranga, it's the same as naming you Dollar Bill. In the hope, of course, that you will have a way with dollar bills. I'm sure I don't have to explain what it will be like if you turn out to have no way at all with dollar bills. Better to be the baldy called Curly. Alack, such is the fate of cash-strapped Dollar Bill just across the road. Nor is that all: In this country where the husband rules, where traditionally a husband can have as many wives as he can support, Dollar Bill is a victim of husband abuse. He is married to a husband beater; his wife chases him with his own swagger stick. She complains bitterly about how shiftless he is, this man named Dollar Bill.

But now at last the ignoble pair have served a noble purpose. They have given Lando and Karangwa a pretext to divert their mother and grandmother from despair. Who cares if Dollar Bill and his wife are nowhere to be seen or heard? Lando's scene is pure theater, a trick on the ladies, and their blood is up. But they're Batutsi. They can't show that their blood is up.

"Hush, Karangwa," says Mama Mariya. "They'll hear you."

"Who?" asks Karangwa, who is loud when he isn't trying, and now he's trying. "DOLLAR BILL?"

"*Hush.*"

"OR DOLLAR BILL'S WIFE?"

Now Mama is hushing him. "I'm not going to tell you anything. All I'm going to tell you is—"

"Loulou," says Lando, "let me tell you about the time Papa Kabenga got all dressed up. As I recall, he had an audience with somebody way up there. The Right Honorable Somebody."

"No doubt the resident," says Karangwa.

"No doubt the king," says Lando. "Put on a freshly pressed mushanana, all bright white and knotted just so." He mimes the fastidious knotting of a robe over one shoulder. "And there was a driver here for him, a driver with a Peugeot, and Papa Kabenga picks up his umbrella, and his briefcase, and his pipe, and *RAHRR*! Just like that, there's a fearsome roar, and it wasn't the Peugeot, or some tom leopard down in the bog."

"What was it?" I ask. "What, Lando?"

Now Lando takes a pregnant pause, teasing.

I turn to Karangwa. "What, Karangwa? Tell me."

"Dollar Bill's missus, of course," says Karangwa.

"Hush," says Mama Mariya. "They'll hear you."

"And the driver had to sit and wait, and Papa Kabenga had to be late for his audience."

"With the resident," says Lando.

"With the king," says Karangwa.

"Why, Karangwa?"

"So he could adjudicate, of course. So he could settle the case."

"So the hill could have some peace," says Lando.

By now it's hard to tell whether the two ladies are trying to hide their anger or their giggles or their embarrassment, lest the *umusozi,* the hill, hear these outrageous grandchildren carrying on. At least the women are no longer trying to stifle despair.

At last, Granny Mariya takes me by the hand. "Come," she says, "there's corn to pick."

"Rehearsal," says Lando forlornly. "Rehearsal . . ."

There have been seasons of drought over the past ten years; more than just hunger, some people have died of starvation. In thunderous protestation the rains would insist they were on the way, and then they'd break their promise. They wouldn't come. Just lightning, lightning against a purple sky, and with it, a sere wind. But this is not one of those years. The corn is high and green. I love plunging in and looking for the ears. They're fat. I lift my fancy skirts with one hand to hold the ears as I pick with the other, an seventeenth-century demoiselle who's lost her concentration and wandered off into an African cornfield with an aristocratic African lady who also likes to pick corn. I can already smell the ears roasting on charcoal. Mama Mariya hasn't even started the braziers yet; she stands just three rows over, talking to me as if I were five instead of seven, but I can smell the charcoal all the same.

A quiet lane runs through the cornfield. People come and go.

"*Waramutse,* Mama Mariya. Good morning."

"*Waramutse,* Thérèse."

"*Waramutse,* Mama Mariya."

"*Waramutse,* Grégoire."

A middle-aged man made old by toil trudges up the lane.

"*Waramutse,* Mama Mariya."

"*Waramutse,* Papa Mpabuka. We haven't seen you much. Why haven't we seen you?"

"Oh, I'm just fine," says Papa Mpabuka, answering a different question.

"I heard they kept you at the clinic. I heard asthma."

"Look at me," says Papa Mpabuka, grabbing the top of his walking stick with one hand and thumping his chest with it. "Do I look like asthma?"

"You look like all the world, Papa Mpabuka."

"Your fields look like all the world, Mama Mariya. Strong. And who is this I see?" He's spied me in the corn. A shudder shakes me.

"This is Loulou, Papa. Bibiane's daughter." The man is missing a canine and an incisor. The gap gives his speech a lush lisp. He stoops to talk to me, smelling of sweat and tobacco. "Oh dear me," he says.

I look to Mama Mariya for security, but she's ambling back to the house with her corn.

"Bibiansh daughter. Elder Kabengash *grand*daughter. Shuch a wee pretty girl. But I wager he wush gone by the time you . . ."

"No sir."

"Sho you knew your mama'sh Papa Kabenga?"

"No sir. I was a baby when—"

"When he went away. Sho you never knew him. Never shaw him."

Mama Mariya has started the braziers. I smell charcoal. My mind turns to roasting corn.

"Let me tell you shomeshing," old Mpabuka tells me—me who doesn't want to hear a shing just now. His voice is low and conspiratorial, as if someone might overhear him on this empty lane through a vast, empty cornfield. His eyes are rheumy. "He wush one of our eldersh. One of our eldersh at *gacaca*."

I know *gacaca* only as a pleasant stretch of sod where people sit and talk; then I remember it's also what you call a country court, a court that isn't used anymore, shade tree justice—literally justice on the grass in the shadow of a tree. "He wush one of our eldersh and he made *gacaca*. Shettled mattersh that had to be shettled. Didn't shide with this shide or that. You'd like him. You would." Rheumy silence. "I know that for a fact. And I'll tell you shomeshing elsh I know." He pauses forever. His eyes drift off. What can I say? I can only gaze at him, trying hard not to let that wonderful roasting aroma divert my gaze. That would be rude. "I know Loulou hash a fondnesh for corn. Am I right then?"

I nod my head.

"Fresh roashted corn?"

I nod my head.

"Well what are you waiting for, child?"

I'm running for the house, Papa Mpabuka's lush laughter ringing in my ears.

IN THE PAST, WAY IN THE PAST, MATTERS HAD NOT BEEN GOOD BETWEEN MAMA AND Mama Mariya. Before the newly married widower Kabenga had summoned the wisdom to keep two households, his bride, Mariya, began to see how her new husband, Kabenga, doted on his eldest daughter, someday to be our Mama, then just seven herself. Mariya began treating Mama like the stepdaughter of lore. When Mariya began to have children of her own, it was Mama who carried them swathed to her back.

But all that has faded, especially since old Kabenga died, and in time it will fade even more. Eventually, sensing her own looming mortality, Mariya will move to Burundi to be near the sons she misses so, but before she goes, she will summon Mama: "Bibiane, I'm leaving you Kabenga's land."

"Why?"

"I've seen that you're prudent. And fair."

"Come now. Why are you doing this?"

"It's true. The years have shown me. You're prudent, Bibiane. And fair."

"Maybe. But what's the real reason?"

"Before I die, I want to make Kabenga proud of me."

ALL THINGS COME TO HER WHO WAITS ABOVE THE UGANDA ROAD. HIGH MOUNTAINS ARE there, thunderheads, and war. There roam gorillas who speak with fierce canines; and there too the Ruwenzori hills where Big Cousin Karani, once Jean, now John, has been chased with his family, there to pioneer at the sufferance of lions with angry red manes. And if this road leads all the way to the Ruwenzori, might it not lead on yet farther to yet stranger realms, to America, say, or even Ohio, where cowgirls dress in pink silk shirts, all nicely piped with soft white leather?

13

Too Much Love Drives the World Insane

So Laissez les Bons Temps Rouler; 1971–1974

Mr Darcy . . . was too much engrossed in his own thoughts to perceive that Sir William Lucas was his neighbor, till Sir William thus began.

"What a charming amusement for young people this is, Mr Darcy!—There is nothing like dancing after all.—I consider it as one of the first refinements of polished societies."

"Certainly, Sir;—and it has the advantage also of being in vogue amongst the less polished societies of the world.—Every savage can dance."

Sir William only smiled.

—Jane Austen, *Pride and Prejudice*

To the unfamiliar eye, Mother Cécile is a quiet Quebecker with two wildly different daughters. Thérèse, in her unrestrained beauty, is a ballerina who aspires to a life on the stage. Hélène, five years older, is an undergraduate student of library science who aspires to a job. But that says little of Maman Cécile herself. To a somewhat more familiar eye, she's a woman with two wildly different sides to her own personality.

Once rural, from a rural family as old as old Quebec, the child Cécile Rochon was never sheltered from the knocks of earning one's way in the world, and indeed she now works as a quiet practical nurse, more a maid, for a wheelchair-bound physician born and schooled in Rome. These days you could even call her staid, but she grew up wild in a wild tribe; members to be sure of the Holy Roman Church, Catholic and Apostolic, but wild. True Quebeckers, they favored cowboy boots, La La fiddles, and rhythm and blues, heavy on the rhythm. Buddy Holly, Roy Orbeson, Wilson Pickett. Their likes set the tone in a clapboard house full of siblings ever in motion and ever in emotional combat, poor, but well enough off that they could indulge their tempers with fully destructive vitriol.

At twelve or so, Cécile painted a piano seat with glue before her kid brother sat down to perform. It was not a practical joke. It was malice. At eighteen or so, slim and vivacious, she stole away with a wild Russian. In a fearsome temper, she quit her family. Her prudent side must have roared and quailed inside her, but she did it, and after that she tried, indeed they both tried. At first, to the tune of balalaikas and kicking kazatskas, she even tried his church, and when the delightful side of that was overtaken by a gloom of grim black cassocks and grim black beards, her mad Russian showed that he was not altogether without mettle. He accepted grim instruction in the catechism of her church, from the alpha of father-forgive-me to the omega of communion, for in the Quebec of those days not so distant, marriage required some sort of holy sanction. There was no such creature as a civil ceremony.

Alack, "not altogether without mettle" turned out too precise a description of her Russian. Not altogether, but almost. Having fathered two daughters, he abandoned her, and now her prudent side has won out by default. With two daughters to support, her prudent side is all she has left. Alone, truly alone, with cascading years turning her gray, she's become a deeply cautious woman, prudent to a fault, scrubbing walls, helping the good doctor in and out of his bath.

All the same, you wouldn't want to call Cécile's dancing daughter Thérèse a full departure from her mother. Thérèse is simply Mother Cécile's other side, her original side, long locked away, a side right out of the doo-wop lines her boyfriends used to sing:

> *Some like whiskey, some like gin*
> *Some like a girl*
> *Who's tall and thin.*

As for the daughter Hélène, the casually familiar eye sees her as the prudent side of Maman Cécile. She is, after all, an undergraduate student of library science, earnestly pursuing her studies. But do not be deceived. For starters, Hélène provides no homely counterpoint to her sister's beauty. True, her features aren't as precious. She's earthier. She carries herself less like a vulnerable innocent dancing before you on stage, more like a chum walking with you down the road. An attractive chum. And that's just for starters. Mother Cécile grew up singing "Do You Loove Me (now that I can dance)." This was bound to rub off on both her children. Just because young Thérèse is blooming as a ballerina doesn't mean that her older sister can't move. Hélène can move; she carries tall and thin as nicely as that girl who can stand up to whiskey and gin. And for a future librarian, she is exceptionally full of mischief. Nay, for any girl, she is exceptionally full of mischief. Period. Full stop. Save. She looks boys in the eye. She challenges them. Not me against you, that overwrought joust of the sexes, but I'm up to it, are you? Eyes that suggest assignation, eyebrows that playfully suggest deeply personal and private conspiracy. Her skin has the healthy flush of someone who can take her licks on a hockey rink of emotions, with anger and ecstasy caromming like pucks, in encounters full of slap shots, deft little dekes, and crushing checks against the boards.

At Montreal's Expo-69, Hélène works as a hostess with a French expat, Marie-France Roy. To the eye of Marie-France, she's anything but bookish. "It's not that everyone thinks she's a study in scarlet," someone says. "They don't. It's that she doesn't care what everyone thinks."

LANDO FIRST WENT TO MONTREAL IN THE SUMMER OF '71. IT WAS THE FIRST TIME HE'D been out of Africa. It was the first time he'd been beyond the Great Lakes. It was hardly the first time he'd encountered the West, though, Rwanda's mission schools drenched him in the West. In fact, Montreal is more like Lando's first conscious encounter with Africa. Abbé Kagame always insisted that the Great Lakes in general and the Batutsi in particular are part of a larger Bantu world, but it isn't until Lando gets to Montreal that he finds Africa.

It all starts with a paperback bought secondhand in a gray Montreal shop. *L'aventure ambiguë* is a story of ever-gathering African moment, the tale of a Senegalese lad who leaves his family and his village and the bush to join the ever-accelerating, still accelerating, migration to the city. It's about the lad's grand hopes, the bleak reality; it's as if the tale's teller, Hamidou Kane, is right there in Montreal, revealing Africa just for Lando. Then Birago Diop's *Les contes d'Amadou Koumba* draws him in further, and before he knows it, he's drunk. Tales from Senegal, Mali, and Cameroon cascade, Hamidou this, Mamadou that. His head spins like the boom-stunned heads of Tintin's black-bowlered brothers, Dupont after yet another Dupont, BOUM!—stars and exclamation points going off in cartoon bubbles above their heads . . . and now above Lando's head.

Alas, it's never been Lando's nature to sit still and enjoy. His work doesn't calm him, it makes him all the more restless, and it's not just a disquiet of the soul. He has Wellars's physically apparent restlessness. Nor does his bad leg hobble this physically apparent restlessness. It highlights it.

At Butare he had directed plays, and what plays! At Butare a thoroughly Western curriculum had created by default a stage that painted Europe in blackface. Now he laughs at how he had fastened pillows around a skinny Rwandese lad to transform him into *Le bourgeois gentilhomme*. He's got no gripe with the writers Church scholars admit to the canon. He was—still is—so fond of them all: Stendhal, Balzac, Zola. In a way it's a wonder that Zola, that bane of the Church, is there. But Europe in blackface is still Europe in blackface, even, somehow, on the page. It was—is—a canon starkly unrelieved.

Such notions, of course, are hardly his alone in Montreal's community of African students. These kids are boiling with argument. Things begin congenially enough. They down a few, and sing.

> *Veux-tu me laisser tranquill-e!*
> *Je veux te quitter, je vais m'en aller*
> *Je vais recommencer ma vie.*

Then they get drunk and shout. They toss Diop and Flaubert at each other like Zungu fraternity boys in a food fight. Nor am I above the fray, albeit as yet on the timid fringes. I'm growing up, after all. I write letters. Lando answers. Lando, now and then, comes home. And there's this thing called the telephone. At home we never had a phone; the phone lines just buzzed on by, like those uselessly, ominously buzzing power lines. Now I find myself getting into heated and altogether lightweight arguments about Art (Papa: "Can you define that term? *Art?*") over oceans that are anything but lightweight. We're both reading Chinua Achebe and Ngugi wa Thiong'o, both of whom raise and wrestle with a Zungu sort of question: art for art's sake or art for Africa's sake?

"Art's!" laughs Lando.

"Africa's!" squeak I.

Deep? Not yet. But give it a few more years, a lot more beers, some Wittgenstein, some Walter Pater. Lando, Loulou, and all this white witch medicine will sink to some truly profound depths.

THEN EVERYBODY LEAVES

Easter, 1972. Everyone is home again, even Lando, home from all the way up and all the way over in Montreal, even Papa, home from the hospital. Dr. Zitoni still takes care of him. Dr. Zitoni takes care of all of us, looks after everything and anything that ails us. For a few francs, he puts on his starched white jacket and pulls our teeth. But the only way he could fight Papa's asthma was to get him out of the fields, and the only way he could do that was to put him in the hospital. Papa's doctor there does a good job. Papa comes out fit as a flea, or at least much better, and just in time for Easter, or more exactly, just in time for everybody coming home (ever the pagan, Easter means little to Papa), even Lando, home from all the way up and all the way over in Montreal.

So it's quite the glad season. It's never easy to see when Papa is happy, but this Easter you can see. It's plain that Dr. Akingeneye took care of him. It's harder to see what a good job Papa does dealing with whatever the good doctor's craft didn't or couldn't do. Everybody is home, even Lando.

Then everybody leaves.

When Lando touches down in Montreal, somebody from Sabena meets him at the gate. From a message passed on through his old boss Herr Hesse at Deutsche Welle, he learns what Anne-Marie, Karangwa, and Nepo learned when they came to see why Mama sent for them, what Wellars, Muzungu, and I had already learned from Mama, what Mama herself learned when she found Papa: that he'd indeed done a better job than any of us suspected at hiding his extremity, that he was happy because he'd managed to hang on until he got everyone around him one last time (all but spectral Vincent), and that now he could let go, had let go.

Loss is such a fuzzy word. You lose something. You think you may never find it, will likely never find it, but you look anyway, perhaps desperately, for there's at least a desperate chance you may succeed, which you may. Or you lose something, and instantly you know it's gone forever. There should be two different words. Mama is not immune to the forever sort. Bitsindinkumi had been with her for three-quarters of her years on this not-so-friendly planet. But then again, he did have a full life, and in Mama's case this bromide, so often glib, is not so glib. In her life, certain sorts of death are truly to be wished for. In her life, death that comes naturally, after a full life, is by any measure a blessing. Mama's great-grandfather Muganza cheated the masters of torment by taking poison. Even I now know this, though dimly, and there is more that I now know, however dimly, and would that I could know just a trifle more: Mama's grandfather, cornered by the henchmen of an evil queen; he tried and failed to escape; he met death by torment. Then her orphaned father's stepfather was hung for all to see in front of Kigali Central Prison. Then, four decades later, at the age of seventy, her father, Kabenga, twice orphaned, died in that same dank lockup. Papa's asthma? Sweet nature's claim on a body. Come funeral time, we Banyarwanda don't shout the joy some display in anticipation of marching saints, but how we do so want to be in that number, and how now we want to shout.

TWO YOUNG WOMEN AND
THEIR DOO-WOP MAMA

Father dies, and Lando balms himself with study; in the midst of Montreal, he plunges into *La famille africaine,* a play about the extended family, specifically of a family in Cameroon, but it could be an extended family anywhere in Africa, indeed anywhere in the world apart from places like Montreal, in the developed world, where the rule for families, like the isolated three-beauty family of Maman Cécile, has become, as they say, "nuclear."

In the summer of '72, no more than three months after Papa died, Maman Cécile, seventeen-year-old Thérèse, and twenty-two-year-old Hélène get lucky. The Italian physician for whom Mother Cécile has been caring all these years insists that Cécile and her two daughters come along with him on a visit home, on his tab.

How happy can a Roman holiday be? With awkward abandon they spend huge (if not hugely valuable) lira notes that unfurl and inflate like sails, grand billowing spinnakers of fiduciary gusto. They drink sunlight. Intoxicated, they walk until their feet swell. Through a diesel haze they gaze up, way up, at the Victor Emmanuel II monument (rearing stallions, concrete cherubs, a grandiose opera in concrete, boomed basso buffo by Mussolini), then dodge through buzzing scooters and tiny Topolinos imitating Detroit's bulbous giants of the forties. They order meals that consist of one single mushroom that fills the plate. On back streets become courtyards, they sample *finocchio,* crisp and fresh. They sample grappa beneath the gazing moon. Afternoons they share with the beautiful young women of the Italian Renaissance. I can only wonder at the response of these three, two beautiful young women and their doo-wop mama, to the Renaissance conflation of virtue with beauty and beauty with youth, as if they're all three one and the same, as if the way to achieve virtue is to become young, and then beautiful, and then have Botticelli preserve you in tempera on a panel in a palazzo.

Regardless, Rome is all they expect . . . and more. Even on Roman holidays, people take the bus; Hélène and her mother turn, wait, and watch as Thérèse skips between two parked buses to catch them up. They watch as the first bus eases its brakes with a hiss and rolls gently back, slowly crushing Thérèse against the second bus. For an instant you might wonder whether she will ever dance again, then whether she'll walk, then whether she'll live. She doesn't. They see it all.

EYES THAT MEET EYES THAT NEVER
LOOK DEMURELY AWAY

Before long, the balm Lando finds in study finds its way to an itch for action. He's been reading more plays, and now two humors—itch and delight—are mounting. Plot each of them on a single chart, look at the two lines climbing, and you just know they're going to intersect at a point of critical coefficiency where something has to give.

First came *La famille africaine,* which I've already brought up. It's by a

Cameroonian woman, Marie-Charlotte Nbarga-Kouma. A couple newly in love find their privacy shattered within an extended family whose demands they try desperately and altogether inadequately to satisfy. Then he reads I don't know what, then *Trois prétendants, un mari (Three Suitors, One Husband)*. In the woebegone ménage of this play, Lando finds an African father something like the father from Molière he rehearsed with us way back. The father is trying to talk his daughter into marrying a man he's gone and picked out for for her. His choice is fat, old, ugly . . . and rich, of course. Of the other two suitors, one is a threadbare young civil servant whom the bumpkin father is forever trying to assay for moneymaking potential, the third a taxi driver whom the father likes to make the butt of jokes—and whom, of course, his daughter dearly adores. The playwright here (Guillaume Oyono-Mbia; "You've got to read Oyono-Mbia," Lando tells Anne-Marie) has fun with the African practice of extracting bride-price. The father is forever murmuring into the ear of the rich old suitor what a wonderful job he, a truly sterling father, has done raising this wonderful girl whom he, a truly generous man, is now offering for such a wonderful (which is to say, ahem, quite modest) price.

By the time Lando's finished reading it, itch has intersected delight. The critical coefficient has been achieved. He has to direct it. Which means he has to produce it, because most surely no one else will.

He infects others. They tell him about chaps here and there getting this and the other grant. Loose talk. What they don't tell him, what they most likely don't appreciate, is that the writing of proposals for grants is virtually a course of study in itself, indeed a culture in itself. So he plunges in with unbridled, and altogether naïve and unschooled enthusiasm. By 1974, he's written to HydroQuébec for seed money. And that means Jacques Roy, who will someday become his close crony, not just in Quebec but in Rwanda.

But that's another story for later. The story for now is that Jacques has no idea who this Lando is or what to do with the envelope of heroic naïveté that has shown up so abruptly on his desk. At the moment, Jacques himself is a lawyer so green that he's out getting some sea legs before practicing. That's why he's a public affairs officer at HydroQuébec. Lando—that is, Lando on paper—is on his desk because public affairs is where Lando has been told you go if you want to raise corporate money, say for a day care center, or adult education, or a neighborhood watch. So however green he is, Jacques is used to having people come in for sponsorship, which is to say, he does know how to say no.

The watchwords if you want a rare yes from him are *workable, practical, measurable*. Jacques, amused and bemused, can't stop turning the pages of Lando's proposal, which of course contain none of these words, and when Lando lopes in with his gimpy leg, Jacques has to hear just how odd this proposal is going to get before he at last says thanks but no thanks—which means he doesn't give himself a chance to say it until Lando is finished, and by then it's too late. By then Jacques doesn't know what to say.

So Lando lopes out and Jacques calls a colleague.

"I don't know what to say," says the colleague.

"No idea?" says Jacques.

"Sure. Give him whatever he wants."

So that's what HydroQuébec does, and Lando makes sure to send Jacques an invitation for opening night and for the party afterward. Jacques, at this moment, is married to Marie-France, the French expat who'd worked with Hélène at Expo-69. Jacques tells his young wife about the off-the-wall proposal, and the play that has resulted ("This should be good"), and about the party after the play. Marie-France not only goes for it, she says she knows just the kid to bring along to make it a foursome, and so opening night, Hélène shows up with Jacques and Marie-France to watch an African father trying to extract his bride-price. Immediately after the play, Lando offers up a *veillée,* a sampling on stage of individual performances—dancers, drummers, a singing group from South Africa—and at last the lights drop and he recites "Nuit africaine."

> *Et le soir autour du feu*
> *Tous assemblés, écoutons ma grand-mère*
> *Battement de mains*
> *Battement de pieds*
> *Tam Tam*
> *Tam Tam*

At the soirée after the *veillée,* it's "Hélène, I'd like to introduce Mr. Lando from Africa," and Lando's eyes meet the eyes that never turn demurely away.

"The four of us go to a club," says Jacques.

Now comes the La La and the *et la-bàs,* the Clifton Chenier and the Wilson Pickett; the organ, the bachinky-chunk accordion, the boilermakers.

"Well, maybe it was a couple of clubs," says Jacques. "Well, maybe a few. Anyway, we finish the night with breakfast."

And there will be more breakfasts. And lunches. And suppers late at night. Hélène, it turns out, shares Quebec's passion for the kitchen, and Lando discovers the earthly *délices* with which Quebeckers keep the bite of their arctic wind at bay: caramelized ris de veaux, escargots, brains in black butter. Barmaids draw pints of bière blonde, blanche, amber, and brown. Yet for all that, this is not where Lando's girth reaches Falstaff's measure. That must wait for his days running a chophouse in Africa. For now, his delight is Hélène. He is briefly distracted but seduced not at all by Quebec's most flagrant creation, something they call *"poutine,"* great platters of fries dolloped with squeaky cheese and smothered in gravy. He remains, for now, our Tutsi-skinny stork, and Hélène, equally vulnerable to the delights of the kitchen, remains equally slim. The closer to the bone, the sweeter the meat.

I never learn all this, of course, until years later, until I've been myself to this cold place called Quebec, where their Sainte Foy is everywhere remembered in the names of narrow lanes. As I will someday wonder, Lando now wonders at these lanes that for America seem so ancient, echoing days so distant that *foi* was *foy* and there really was such a thing as faith, days so Rwandese, days feudal becoming days medieval, and for us now in the Great Lakes, days getting force-fed into *Modern Times,* so that we are all Chaplin Charlie, Charlot, caught in the gears. (*"Féodo-revanchards,"* the oh so progressive Hutu revolution calls us whenever we *ouch* in protest.)

What might I have thought had I learned of their affair as it happened, eleven-year-old me back in Africa? When Lando flew off to Montreal I pictured an ice palace. When at last I get there, so many years later, I will find a place cold enough, but so industrial, slag heaps and soot, snow, cinders, a skyline of pipes and tubes above freeways iced over, slush, slums, a place whose charms are homely and hidden, lurking with the morning mist after a night in the clubs, the squawk of gulls in the harbor, the African *mmmh* of foghorns.

THE BLOOM IS OFF THE WEST

Hélène has a temper, but for Lando she's sugar in his bowl. From opening night, when it begins, their business picks up by the month. Two years later, it's decision time.

Lando has always known he's headed back to Africa, nor has he kept it a secret, and by 1974 it's all the more clear that he can and should come back. Beneath his enduring affection for Africa, there's now a subtext, as well: His infatuation with the West has taken a few rude turns. He's been working happily toward a degree in literature. The language of instruction is French. He reads Cocteau, Colette, Sacha Guitry, Céline, and enjoys them, sometimes immensely, then learns how they carried on during the war.

Always a crank at heart, Céline shifted into high Fascism. Sacha Guitry came up with the bright idea of publishing an anthology of French heroes titled *From Joan of Arc to Philippe Pétain.* He got Paul Valéry to contribute. Even as Fascist punks threw stink bombs during performances of *Les parents terribles,* Jean Cocteau curried Nazi favor. Even as Josephine Baker repaired to the Maquis, and gypsies burned, the gypsy Django Reinhardt strummed trendy jazz for adoring SS *Offiziere* at Le Hot Club. Even as Colette's Jewish husband ran about occupied France looking for closets in which to hide, she pandered, writing a novel, *Julie de Carneilhan,* which featured stock characters from Nazi propaganda: stalwart old blood; an effeminate liberal financed by a "bottomless pit" of Jewish money; a Jewish baroness fond of diamonds. (Colette puts her own fondness for stones on display in her most famous book, in which she has an old courtesan instruct a young courtesan—Gigi—to disdain all jewelry that draws its charm from mere art.) Colette sold her hateful *Julie* to *Gringoire,* a Fascist periodical, which serialized it to complement screeds that excoriated French Jews for such outrages against common decency as somehow cornering (while hiding? while running?) the market in food intended for hungry French children. Nor was this the end of it. She sold apolitical (Colette was always apolitical) criticism to one journal of Fascist criticism after another.

Is Colette's art (when it is art) any the less? Is the work of any of these writers any the less? Quite likely it isn't; maybe it is. By now Lando has come to see that art is illusion, a confidence game, a magician's sleight of hand, and he's got no problem with that, but by the same measure, what happens when the artist does something to break his own artful spell? What good is art gone cheesy? Cards are falling from the magician's sleeves, cheap wine stains the white tie.

Lando learns that during these war years, much of lovely Quebec read this continental world of arts and letters as no more remarkable than any other world of arts and letters, at any other time. A concert at Theriesenstadt? Scarcely more than an occasion for entertainment. Controversial, to be sure—but isn't controversy simply an aspect of the human tableau? Natterings on the left. Natterings on the right. Squabbles of Whig and Tory. Literate Quebec elects a demi-fascist premier, Maurice Duplessis.

But what happens when you know, or suspect, or find yourself trying not to suspect that the impresario has a gun to the artist's head? Or that the artist is a bigot or a toady or both? At what point will you allow that a ptomaine shrimp can ruin an artful bouillabaisse? Or as they put it in Lando's university world, "to just what extent does context compromise aesthetic quality?" Lando will gladly leave it to Zunguland to count the number of high priests and base aestheticians (or are they beauticians?) who can fandango on the head of this pin. For him, what matters is that even as Africa burns the more brightly, the bloom is off the West.

Even Rwanda is a prospect. As full of fright and banishment as they were for us personally, the 1973 pogroms didn't turn out as badly as others. Kayibanda made scapegoats of us for the usual reasons rulers make scapegoats of people: He knew his popularity with the Hutu public was sliding fast; he wanted to deflect Hutu anger. Before long, Hutu powermongers scrapping with each other used the campaign to settle scores that had nothing to do with Batutsi. Bahutu made victims of Bahutu. Chaos threatened. Kayibanda's defense minister, one Colonel Habyarimana, gathered around him a claque of like-minded and equally powerful colonels, a group he may have patterned on Nasser's colonels. They took the anger Kayibanda was trying to deflect, deflected it back onto Kayibanda, and staged their boom-slang coup. Before you knew it, Kayibanda's hairless tail was sticking out of Habyarimana's mouth as our new president swallowed our old president, who now struggles to stay alive as he slips into retirement in the belly of a snake.

The result, for the nonce, means some relief for Batutsi, but it spells even more trouble for Bahutu out of presidential favor, which is to say the great mass of Bahutu. In Kayibanda, now defunct, the White Fathers had plucked from the missions an earnest bumpkin with bumpkin superstitions and nearly unintelligible French. Kayibanda, as president, drove a VW bug, not out of modesty but out of fear that a big car would provoke the jealousy of dark forces. At the airport, once, he picked up the king of the Belgians in his VW bug. Then he offered a speech in French; afterward, an obtuse member of the royal party thanked him for the speech, and in making small talk remarked how similar the language of the Rwandese is to French. "Indeed, Your Excellency, I'm sure I detected in your presentation some words that sounded just like French."

This new chief Habyarimana may be a boom-slang, but he speaks excellent French . . . and even better deceit. Old chief Kayibanda seems never to have detected that the dark force he really had to fear was his own minister of defense, Juvenal Habyarimana. Kayibanda and Guy Logiest, the Belgian colonel who installed him in 1962, thought they were smart the way they so neatly arranged their "revolution," and after a certain narrow fashion they were, but not nearly as smart as this new man Habyarimana . . . and his wife, Agathe.

Colonel Logiest fancied himself a man of vision. Tunnel vision is more like it. He and Kayibanda and the missions were determined above all to lock out the old Tutsi elite. In the early sixties, when it fell to them to put together a regular army, they went deliberately to that corner of the northwest that had been the most distant from the Tutsi court at Nyanza, the least influenced by Tutsi power. They did this even though Kayibanda did not himself come from this region. They feared that outside the far northwest both the blood and the business of Bahutu were too mixed up with Batutsi. Thus Bahutu from the Habyarimanas' far northwest came to dominate the army, and now, having staged a coup, to dominate Rwanda.

Alas, the Habyarimanas, husband and wife, have their own agenda: the narrow aggrandizement of their Hutu northwest. For this they hardly deserve exclusive blame. The ruling style in the old principalities of the Hutu northwest mirrors the style of the old Tutsi court at Nyanza, and for that matter, of all the old Rwandese kingdoms. It is thoroughly autocratic, thoroughly accustomed to rule with impunity, thoroughly Rwandese. The new man cherishes no notions of democracy.

Indeed, before his fall, Kayibanda himself had begun carrying on in a manner more and more autocratic, or as Bazungu put it, in a manner more and more Tutsi. Now his successor and swallower, Juvenal Habyarimana, is following suit, becoming the traditional Rwandese autocrat, with a traditionally Rwandese agenda, enfranchising his own crowd. Not all Habyarimana's colonels are Akazu. Some come from the south, from Nduga country. (And two of their names—Simba and Rusatira—may be worth remembering.) But this is scarcely more than a footnote. Broadening his base appeals to Habyarimana not at all. The game he plays pivots on a powerful home base, and loyalty to that crew.

Attorneys for the new government prepare a legal brief that deposes ex-chief Kayibanda with real crimes (like organizing the pogroms that forced us to run), then brings him before a kangaroo court-martial that hands down a death sentence—after which it grandly pardons the man, exiling him to his home hills, where first his wife dies mysteriously, and then Kayibanda himself dies mysteriously, both at a young age. It is all part of the process with which the boom-slang slowly devours his prey alive, then kills it with digestive juices.

Soon, similar fates begin to befall Kayibanda holdovers, all Bahutu, mostly from Kayibanda's Nduga south. They are shot, strangled, mangled, tortured, and all this the work of him whose Latin namesake, Juvenal, was a man who sought the life of the mind, whence he loosed literate barbs at brutal Rome. After such deaths, often years afterward, a sentimental Juvenal Habyarimana stages memorial services for his victims and presents their widows with medals, even as the mass of the Bahutu fall under his heel.

Here and there, Zunguland gets testy when such treatment befalls Batutsi, for this falls neatly within the pattern of "tribal conflict" that the world fears and even expects from Africa, an African failing that falls neatly within the white man's *mission civilatrice* to fix. But when Bahutu are the victims of other Bahutu, Zunguland gives them scarcely any attention at all. Indeed, Lando himself hears little of it. These days in Montreal, he's more interested in Birago Diop and Chinua Achebe and even Flaubert than in distasteful Rwandese politics. He's now, oh my, such a man of the world, and not a very political man of the world at that; if it doesn't get into the world press, it neatly evades him. All he knows is that Habyarimana has brought some stability to Rwanda, that it is no longer quite so dangerous to be Tutsi, and that as a student of African letters, he now belongs in Africa— the closer to his roots, the better.

ALONE, SO ALONE

Who knows? In the beginning, back in 1972, Lando's attachment to Africa may have made him all the more attractive to Hélène, all the more impossibly romantic, all the more easy to deal with in the present because their relationship was all the less likely to go somewhere.

But go somewhere it does, and now it threatens to go a lot further, all the way to the far highlands of inland East Africa.

What's Mother Cécile to do? This woman with no husband is about to lose the only child she's got left. I think of her and hear the nasal whine of the Cajun numbers she so loves:

> . . . *got the world in a jug*
> *And the cork in my other hand.*

What's Hélène to do? It's an impossible decision. What rescues it from impossibility is Maman Cécile's passionate side, still there, hidden away, ready to break back out. If she'd simply mope, who knows what Hélène might do? Hélène has a keen sense of her mother's loneliness. Indeed, it may be no more than a testing of the waters when she tells her mother that she may well be going off with Lando to Africa.

But Maman Cécile doesn't mope. That just isn't in her. Instead she explodes. That is in her. She shouts. She demands. Then Hélène, with plenty of emotional plastique of her own packed away, explodes too. It gets painful. Indeed, in later years, Hélène will tell me it gets worse than I can imagine, and what I imagine is not pretty. Piecing this together with that, and having heard how Maman Cécile uses words, I imagine her saying to Hélène, "Jesus, Mary, and dear Saint Joseph. Some black cripple out of nowhere. Why?"

I imagine Hélène: "Because he makes me feel like Somebody. Like I'm Thérèse."

I imagine Maman Cécile: "Thérèse you're not."

This I don't imagine. This I know: Hélène is off for Africa, and Maman Cécile is alone.

· 14 ·

BUJUMBURA SECRETS
1972–1978

Just beyond my eleven-year-old field of vision (beyond because I'm no longer so eager to look beyond) our first president has deployed first-rate sermons, first-rate Kinyarwanda, and remarkably poor French to lose power to one Juvenal Habyarimana. What am I to say of this man who staged a coup? That as defense minister, he ignored a bad leg to play occasional basketball for the army? Especially against the university? I'd soon wander off into tales about our handsome brother Gaetan and how he stars as a university forward, and you'd soon suspect prejudice in my choice of words like *star*.

Besides, before Agathe Kanziga's husband, Juvenal, strides on stage, there are more pogroms, and I can't skip the subject. Not out of hand. I never have to see a pogrom itself, let alone get caught in one, or even think much about what they're like, and thank you Saint Anthony for that. But my sister is gone. The pogroms came and now she's had to run away, leave Rwanda. She's in Bujumbura. They don't tell me just why, and I don't ask. I'm still a pupil at the Kabuye mission school. She'd been teaching there. Now she isn't. Anne-Marie Kantengwa, my best friend and sister, is gone. If I were as strong as I should be, I'd be handling her loss as I should be. I retreat behind a Gabonese mask.

There were murmurs, muffled whispers; I should have paid attention. But I've been forcing myself not to listen. Such wretched talk. I don't want to grow up. I want to be forever just me, secure in a cartoon frame with Tintin, his dog, Milou, and their bilious *copain* Capitaine Haddock, dealing with knotty but soluble mysteries like the case of a shady smuggler or a suspicious *Catastrophe aérienne au Népal*.

CHARGE, YE LADS OF THE AVANT-GARDE

Another six months have passed, and now we're all of us gone. Now it's April 1973, and home is a good-bye-forever place. We can't go back, and forgive me if I don't get deeply into our midnight drive through the mountains to Goma. I can't bear it when my mother's friends come over and go forever on about their surgery, or their bridgework; once I heard a Zungu lady go on about her hemorrhoids. What I'm trying to say is that you really don't want me to go on about that passage from Kabuye to Goma to Bujumbura. Suffice to say, there wasn't a cross word. So you can tell yourself comfortably that you didn't miss much.

We're living in a cold-water flat in Bujumbura. It could be a cell.

I'm unsettled. It's not the new language. Burundi's Kirundi is much like Kinyarwanda, and French is everywhere. Nor is it Swahili, the other language I've got to learn if I'm ever to get along here. Swahili (*Ki*swahili, to be exact) is one of Kinyarwanda's "Bantu" (as I hear my brothers put it) cousins. It's not nearly as close a cousin as Kirundi, but it's close enough. Learning it is hardly unsettling. What's unsettling is other things, under the skin. It's things I barely notice, and don't question; it's the way preachers whose native tongue is Kirundi preach in Swahili to congregations whose native tongue is Kirundi. Why does he use Swahili? Is this the holy tongue of Protestants? Or are the deaf leading the deaf? "Praise the Lord," says the pastor. "Praise the Lord and let's hear celebration."

Does someone, at some point, explain to me that in our day, most of Rwanda has been connected to the outside world by way of Kampala, up-country and over by the port of Bukoba, patched together by a Muzungu I never heard of named Emin Pasha, on the big lake named Victoria. But before Kampala and before Bukoba, Bujumbura was the settlement to which the safaris from the outside, from the Swahili coast, all traveled, and from Bujumbura they reached us. For us, Burundi was just the country down there that we raided. But for Arab and Swahili traders out of Dar and Zanzibar, this settlement they called Usumbura on Lake Tanganyika was the interior, and we were the deep interior. This Bujumbura whose boulevards I now walk is the old settlement, the first settlement. This is the place that echoes, and you hear the echoes whether or not you know what they are, whether or not you can make out the voices of the old Swahili corridor, the old safaris. You hear them whether or not you know that this was the corridor followed by a man you never heard of named Burton and his unheard-of chum Speke, of whom there's a big stone statue right here in Bujumbura. But what does that mean?

Does someone, in fact, at some point, say, "This is what you hear, child." I doubt it, but even if they do, it won't register. Words aren't registering, just sensations, and just now there are so many sensations, so many whispers, so much of which to be ignorant.

ONE DAY WE COME HOME AND MAMA IS SITTING ON HER WORN SETTEE, A LETTER IN HER hand, a blank look in her eyes. "Lando is coming back. And he has a friend. She's coming later."

"*Ngw'iki?*"

By which I mean I need to hear more . . . and see more. There are snapshots. "A *Muzungu?*"

"So. Two Bazungu in the family," says Wellars with his eyebrows and an elbow to Muzungu's ribs. Muzungu thumps him.

"She's just a friend," says Mama.

PASTOR SAYS WE'RE ALL OF US, ALL HUMANITY, JUST CHILDREN WALKING ALONG PATHS whose past and portent we hardly know. But we actual children know so little—and sense so much—and these days in Bujumbura, in Africa, there is still so much more for me to miss and so much more to sense. Time and space are intersecting, and wherever I walk I keep looking back. Even when I'm not out walking, I look back, back along our midnight ride in that rusty estate wagon from Kabuye to Goma, our refugee flight from Goma here. I look back along "the lines." I look back along Papa's Tsobe line: Papa, son of Nyarugabo ("big man" the name means, and that, it seems, he was); son of Sekabote; son of Garuka.

Today Mama assigns me ironing. She's firing up the irons. Bujumbura is hot. Like all the Great Lakes, Tanganyika is high, but Bujumbura is lower than Kabuye, and wetter, and hotter; low enough and hot enough that coconut palms grow everywhere. I look at Mama, firing the coals. Beads of sweat are forming on her forehead. Perhaps because she tells us so little, I look back even more intently along her line than I do along Papa's, along old Nyarugabo's—and now she can't keep matters so neatly secret. Now here we are in Bujumbura with her brothers, my uncles, little Blindé, big Commandant, and stories are bubbling up in the soup that is Bujumbura.

So little is what it has seemed to be. Our granny isn't our granny. My uncles here in Burundi are really my half uncles. I learn about Grandpa Kabenga's siblings. Two brothers. Two sisters. Just four of them. So small for a Rwandese family. What was going on there?

"And truth be told, they weren't exactly brothers and sisters."

Who said that? Who goes there with more that confuses me? The irons are hot. Bujumbura is hot, too hot to recall just who said what, but I recall clearly (I think) the facts as someone tried to explain them to me, and now I try to pin down what he said, lest time and fog again overtake remembrance: He seems to have said that yes, the four did grow up as brothers and sisters—that is, in the same household, and they were close. Also, Grandpa Kabenga, his brother, Bitahurwina, and their sister, Elizabeti, were true siblings. But the fourth sister, Stefania, was only a half sister, and technically not even that. She had a different father and a different mother. Her father was the uncle of the three. When their natural father died, his brother, their uncle, married their mother. Their uncle took on their mother as his second wife, and they joined the uncle's family, becoming elder siblings to the baby Stefania.

To which convoluted news I could only respond, "Come again?"

How often I say that these days! How I now struggle to get matters straight. I cover a board with a blanket, take up an iron, and try to put first things first: Our great-grandfather Rudasumbwa was an officer of the king's guard. This much seems clear. Grandpa Kabenga, his brother, Bitahurwina, and their sister, Elizabeti, were his children, and orphaned young. Also clear. Courtly intrigue had forced their father to poison himself. Clear, as well—though that's not quite how I heard it put the other day. What I heard was "the dowager forced him." To which I responded, "The who?"

"The dowager," someone answered. "The dowager queen."

"The which queen?"

"That's it, Loulou. The witch queen." But then someone else broke in with something very funny and altogether immaterial and that was the end of it, except that now, as I iron, and the coals get me sweating, and I spit on the iron to test it—look, can't I see that I've let it get too cool?—my head is spinning. How can I let it be at that? Forced to poison himself. All I've got straight is the next step, technical details: After the dowager had Rudasumbwa poisoned, his brother married the dead man's widow and took over as the brothers' stepfather.

Coming after the barely told tale of Rudasumbwa and poison, this genealogical bit—whose brother is whose—felt at first like little more than a parlor game, straightening out family puzzles for want of a handy crossword puzzle. But only at first. Getting to the bottom of these four siblings is no parlor game. They loom for us. Even for me, who has known only one. Even for me, here, now, ironing. All of them but Stefania died before I was born, yet all four loom for me as much as they do for my brothers and sisters, and did so even before I got here to Bujumbura where fitfully I'm learning why.

Grandpa Kabenga's first wife had eight girls, including Mama, her first child, and died in her early twenties. But you know all that. You know how he then married the woman who is now our Granny Mariya, a marriage that made for bad blood between Mama and her new stepmother, this Mariya. You know how Grandpa Kabenga's sister, Elizabeti, took pity on Mama and had her move in with her brood, which she marshaled like a drill sergeant. And you know how Elizabeti's "sister," Stefania, stepped into her shoes when Elizabeti died. Here's what you don't know: Now, at last, I'm starting to understand where that war lady Stefania gets it. When she comes over, our entire house marches in lockstep.

Except that we don't have a house anymore, and Stefania is still back in Rwanda, where Kabenga, Elizabeti, and their brother, Bitahurwina, lie buried.

WE ALL PILE INTO COMMANDANT'S PEUGEOT, A RUSTMOBILE AS FULL OF RATTLES AS Quixote's suit of rusty armor. The airfield seems furlongs off, and for every furlong, Commandant's *tacot* judders intently. It will get us there and it does.

A metal monster screams. They wheel a ladder up to a hatch. One by one, two by two, then Lando; his face is oh so grave as he lopes on down. All the way through customs and passport control (at least when our craning necks let us catch glimpses), he's oh so grave. Where's that Lando grin? Even when he hugs us: oh so grave. But then at last he can't help it, the smile comes, eyes water. Lots of talk; Lando must hear more of our escape, details that Mama would never put in a letter lest it upset him. We ask and we hear all about Montreal; everything but Hélène. By and by, it becomes clear. He isn't sure how she will take to Africa. He wants to see how she takes to Africa. She'll be flying in from Paris in a couple weeks, but he doesn't say, "and then maybe we'll get married." He just leaves it at that. Maybe that was why the grave face when he climbed down from the plane. Maybe.

All this uncertainty gives street gossip, our own Radio Trottoir here in Bujumbura's own Little Rwanda, just the chance it relishes to invent the news. We start hearing clucks. "As if there aren't any number of wonderful Rwandese girls who wouldn't jump at a chance for the lad; none of *my* girls, mind you, but any number."

"I'll say. Even with his . . . *leg.*"

Lando wants to go back to Rwanda. "If we can, of course."

From Mama, a silent gasp that everyone can hear.

"Back home?" Mama wonders.

Lando: "Kabuye. Back home to Kabuye."

From Mama, another silent gasp. Moving back; that's what we want, but . . . "Is it smart?" she wonders. What she means isn't "smart." What she means is "safe."

"Mmmh," says Wellars, in his voice-is-changing voice.

"Those days are ending," says Lando. "This new man, Habyarimana Juvenal, and his colonels . . ."

"Mmmh," says Muzungu.

"They know they're not going to get the investment they want," says Lando (as I say to myself, privately, "*Investment*. What an interesting word"). "Not if the same old nonsense goes on. It can't."

"Back in?" says Mama.

"Back home," says Lando.

"Mmmh," say Muzungu and Wellars in imperfect duet.

"I don't know," says Mama. What she means is no.

"Maybe you're right," says Lando.

IT'S DARK. I'M SLEEPY. PEOPLE ARE TALKING ABOUT GRANDPA KABENGA AND HIS brother, Bitahurwina.

"Ah, Bitahurwina," I hear someone say. "What a wife he suffered. What a jealous woman."

"What a nasty woman," says someone else. "So spoiled. Spoiled as a child. Spoiled by her husband."

"Just one child," says yet another voice. "How Bitahurwina loved that nasty woman. How they both doted on that one and only son."

Yet another voice: "That Kagame."

Yet another: "*This* Kagame," and we all laugh, because Abbé Kagame is still most conspicuously this side of Jordan. Even I laugh, though behind my laugh I'm doing a double take. I guess I've known, at least vaguely, that Grandpa Kabenga's brother, Bitahurwina, was Uncle Kagame's papa. But people who loom give you a distorted picture of themselves. For the first time it registers that Uncle isn't a true uncle. He's not Mama's brother; he's her first cousin. Yet another easy certainty gone, yet another uncle who isn't.

Does this mean he's only our uncle the way every African male old enough is every African's uncle? That's absurd. (This is a trick I favor these days: I take the worst, reduce it to the absurd, and it doesn't seem so bad anymore.) He's our uncle. Period. Full stop. We see him (well, we saw him) far more than any other uncle. He was always over, and . . .

And now melancholy overtakes me. Now it registers why we see him, saw him, so often. Full uncle or not, we and his one sister—our Auntie Pascazie—are his closest living relatives. In this Africa where the family enfolds all, he and his sister were the only children, and on top of that, he doesn't have a wife or kids because he's a priest.

Or to be more exact, he's a six-foot-five, three-hundred-pound bishop, with a belly laugh, a taste for whiskey, and no sense of melancholy about him. Would that we were with him back home.

MAMA HAS NAMED LANDO THE FAMILY SCOUT. HE GOES BACK ALONE. IN BUTARE, WHERE Tonton Kagame is teaching, he's overwhelmed, not only welcomed but offered a job.

"Back in?" says Mama.

"Back home," says Lando.

"I don't know," says Mama.

"Maybe you're right," says Lando.

"Back home?" says Mama.

"Mmmh," says Lando.

"Let's do it," says Mama.

"Mmmh," says trifling me. The boys laugh. Mama laughs. The school term will be ending soon, and then nothing will be keeping us here.

IT'S GETTING HARD FOR MAMA TO KEEP MATTERS IN HER SECRETS BASKET. NOW I CAN look back, or at least glimpse back, along her Temura line of the Singa clan: her father, Grandfather Kabenga (by Kabenga!); her uncle, Bitahurwina; their father, Rudasumbwa; their stepfather, Mukeza; their grandfather, Muganza (by Muganza!); and at last, their great-grandfather, the eponymous Mutemura, grandsire. Who *were* they? I peer back, but the tales I'm hearing are still tales half-told, and beyond that, all I see is dust and all I smell is Bujumbura, rotting leaves and diesel fumes and frangipani, and thank goodness. Who knows what else I might sniff if I could? What I might see. Do people still turn to pillars of salt?

BEFORE WE KNOW IT, THIS "HÉLÈNE" IS IN AFRICA, AND WE HERE IN BUJUMBURA haven't even caught a glimpse of her. Before we know it, she's in Rwanda, in Butare, she adores it, and they're engaged. My brains are flying out my ears. Lando has a friend, Cyprien Rugamba. Cyprien is the director of the National Ballet. He insists that the ballet perform at the wedding. It will be a true evening of *son et lumière,* a grand evening on the rolling grounds of the old Musée National near the campus. In its way it will represent the new Rwanda, the Rwanda of this new man, Habyarimana.

Cyprien seems so thoroughly Tutsi. His style is so antique. He even composes antique verse. Lando says there are fools (Tutsi fools, Hutu fools) who think Rwandese dance is Tutsi dance. He says they see Cyprien's manner as an affectation in a man who is in fact thoroughly Hutu. But as Lando sees it, and as Tonton Kagame sees it, the notion of Rwandese art as Tutsi art is itself a malignant conceit. Lando tells us that Cyprien's style is no more or less than frankly Rwandese, perfect for one who leads Rwanda's national troupe, and Rwanda's troupe it is: its members are Hutu, Tutsi, Twa. Hardly conservative, Cyprien is a dynamic conservator, a guide to holding high the ensign of a new, welcoming Rwanda. Looking back from the twenty-first century, I read his lines again and see how easy it is to misread them as prescriptive dogma, lines that simply yearn, as Rwandese are so given to yearning:

> *Charge, ye lads of the avant-garde,*
> *Fly, ye fine formed spirits, soar free from struggling humanity . . .*

But the date they've set for this wedding! Just before examinations.
"Yes, the date," says Mama, and I know just what she means.
"Mama. I've *got* to be there."
"Loulou, you've *got* to pass."
I'm stunned. "If I can't go, I'll do my best to fail."
No response. I cry. No response. Mama has come into her own. She's Stefania. She's Elizabeti. *Cheftaine* Elizabeti. Exams are exams. I miss the wedding. They say it's quite the evening, but I can't bear to listen as they go forever on about that glad evening on the grounds of the old musée, and if you don't mind, I have no inclination, even as I write these lines so many years later, to repeat mere hearsay.

THE WHISPER OF BANANA LEAF
ON BANANA LEAF

Tonton Kagame makes up for it some. After a couple of years in Bujumbura, and the wedding, and exams (no, I don't try to fail) we move back home to Kabuye, and the boys and I are even spared the sight of the old place in sagging disrepair. That it's been, and the victim of some desultory looting, but Lando and Mama get there before us. In no time, Mama has it sparkling like a starched nun, and then I hear that Tonton will be driving me to my new school at the Kansi mission on Rwanda's frontier with Burundi. The short rains are coming, and with them, weeks in which to relish home, then weeks in which to visit and to relish this new place, this college town, Butare.

As for my new school way down at the Kansi mission, there's something more to this step than just a new school, something ominous. . . . But there's so much in sight to keep it out of mind—Butare is so new for me, and for the first time I meet Hélène. Mama and I stay with the newlyweds in their new digs, huge by our tiny standards, a bungalow set in a stand of old-growth eucalyptus; indoor plumbing, a hot water heater, a Buta Gaz stove, everything, you name it. Even Paul. Paul is the cook, and an excellent one, in the Rwandese manner. Forever in a spotless white apron, he's the perfect complement to Hélène in her spotless white apron, a cook in the Québécois manner, which is excellent by definition. The back door is off the kitchen and always open, with a eucalyptus breeze forever easing through, and with it, the whisper of banana leaf on banana leaf. I'm smitten. It's Saturday night that Hélène and Lando generally have people over, and as time goes by, there are more; Saturday nights, chez Lando becomes quite the place to be, with a groaning board set up beneath a large back window, and the drums and saxophones and deep Cameroonian throat of Manu Dibango and his Soul Makossa coming from the brand-new speakers of Lando's stereo as Hélène at the door laughs *"Entrez, entrez"* to guest after guest. One after another, Paul pops bottles of Primus. I don't drink, but the bottles pop with such cheer.

> *Jolie bouteille, sacrée bouteille*
> *Veux-tu me laisser tranquill-e!*
> *Je veux te quitter, je vais m'en aller*
> *Je veux recommencer ma vie. . . .*

> *Pretty bottle, bloody bottle*
> *Won't you please leave me in peace!*
> *I want to go, I'm going to go*
> *I want to restart my life. . . .*

Indeed, they pop with such cheer that I almost forget about . . .

"That's All You Need to Know. You Can't Go"

Our Rumbumptious First Lord of the Rum; 1978–1981

BOARDING SCHOOL. Kansi mission. Now I know what's different about this school: I'm being sent off. Away. For my send-off, Hélène and Paul cook a grand midday meal, and some meal it is, half Rwandese, half Québécois, half French, a true meal and a half, with ample red to go around. (Hélène, I've learned, serves no meal without ample red to go around.) There won't be room in the car for Mama. We'll be riding in Tonton's infamous bug, the battered albino he'll let no one persuade him to sell, no matter how we implore. Just why should he sell, he asks? Because a bishop shouldn't be tooling about in a bug?

Karangwa, who has an answer for everything: "No, Tonton. Because it weighs less than you do. No man should ever drive a car that weighs less than he does." The logic is Cartesian but it does no good. Here he is, as ever, in his battered white bug.

Hélène wants to see more of the bush, but she knows that being chauffeured by the family priest is my treat. She insists on sitting in back. She shoves my weighty bags to one side behind weighty Tonton, behind the wheel in his white cassock. Five-foot-eight Hélène and the bags and the engine weigh down the rear. Six-foot-five, three-hundred-pound Tonton and the bags weigh down the left side, the springs of which have long since lost their spring to his heft. With slight little me in the right front seat, the bug lurches ahead with its right front wheel nearly in the air. My seat slides back, hits Hélène in the shins, Hélène goes "Oof!" and the bug goes *clang* on the first of thousands of Rwandese ruts that lie ahead. We lurch again, *clang* again. "Loulou, your seat; *please*," says Hélène. Fortunately, she won't be awake for the sights she's come to see. I can only guess that good Saint

Antoine helped her plan that meal and a half. Deftly, it puts her into a deep snooze and out of her misery.

What puts me out of this misery, and all thought of going off to school (well, almost all thought) is Tonton. Every bend betrays a landmark that to anyone else would be a dull feature of the landscape but for him is a story, and it hardly matters that some are tales nearly as hoary as Rwanda's hoariest tale, told to and by every visitor, the tale of Kamegeri Rock, big and flat, on the Kigali-Butare Road. As Tonton boils it down: "Once, who knows when, a toady seeking courtly favor got the bright idea of currying to his king's obscene addiction to cruelty. He suggested that his majesty fire the rock white hot and use it to roast his next victim. 'Capital notion,' said the king, and roasted the toady."

Tonton gazes about as he drives. It's clear that for him and for his extrasensory ear, the Nile-feeding gorges through which we now toddle are echo chambers for tales from beyond. Many are of great evil, and in the world of these tales, evil is opposed by no glorious Amazons; men are the only warriors. Beauty, cunning love, and cunning greed are the weapons women deploy.

Kamegeri Rock isn't my first brush with tales that distil from the merely bad the truly evil. Missionary piety thrives on frightening cautionaries. Our mission's problem was Father Fidèle, his eyes forever rolling heavenward; who could take such Zungu piety seriously? The nuns, meantime, raged about an evil that burns with such acid brilliance that you can't bear to look at it—so I didn't. As for Mama and Papa and Auntie Stefania, neither sorcerers nor necromancers they. No-nonsense to the core, they teach the difference between right and wrong, not wrong and evil. I must at some point have whiffed unholy brimstone, but I can't say when. Maybe when the great frog of Kigali Central Prison first loomed before us on the bus.

Whenever it was, it was on pixie feet that Old Scratch, only half-recognized, danced into my head, so that I've tended to deal with him with half measures, with pictures of beautiful queens who overcome him with spellbinding humanity. Listening now to Uncle, it comes to me that maybe the trick is simply knowing who Old Scratch is, learning to pick him out when he's in disguise—to pick him out, and then to raise the alarm. "Beware, just there; our unholy grail!"

Toddling Tonton seems simply to be hearing echoes and repeating what he hears. This old dragoman who spends hour upon bookish hour translating the past, who has apparently written volumes picking apart the past, now simply repeats the nonsense he's hearing: "There," he says, as his bug lugs up the traverse of a sheer defile. *"Huye."*

"Ngwi'ki?"

"*Bisi-bya-Huye*. The cave where Nyagakecuru lives. Surely, child, you know about *Bisi-bya-Huye*. About Nyagakecuru."

Surely, I do not.

"The witch."

"The who?"

"You don't know Nyagakecuru?

"The witch?"

"I'll make you a wager—Medusa you've heard something about."

"Uncle, a lot of people have heard *something* about Medusa."

"A lot of people have heard about Nyagakecuru. And if they have, why not you? She's right here, you know. A woman so hideous, you look at her and the very sight makes hideous events unfold. . . ."

"Like?"

"Never mind. A grand poisoner, she is. Wants every bit of land that joins hers, and poisons to get it. No husband, no children, just her and her land and her greed and her viper. You go over there and her viper gets you. If her looks don't."

"Gets you how?"

"Never mind. Just remember where she is, and if ever you're about in these parts, and you find yourself looking at her, look away as fast as you can."

Is *she* that picture of perfect perfidy? Cabbage-faced Nyagakecuru? I have no idea. High crime has so many faces, not to speak of the many faces of misdemeanor. Who knows what cabbage-faced perfidy hides inside the seemingly commonplace? And where in all this are Mutemura and Muganza and old Nyarugabo; and didn't somebody say something about cool juleps concocted of honey wine and crocodile bile?

AND THE MISSION SCHOOL AT KANSI? JUST HOW HORRID IS *IT*? THE GIRLS ARE VIRTUALLY all Hutu. The headmistress is Hutu. They're lovely. It's lovely. From dictée to exposée, it's an idyll.

IN 1976, AFTER A YEAR OF MARRIAGE, HÉLÈNE AND LANDO HAVE THEIR FIRST CHILD, A girl, Malaika. Hélène has trouble breast-feeding. She goes to the clinic. The nurses can't help, nor the doctor, nor the Holy Ghost, to whom patients are invited to pray. It's painful to watch, not just for Hélène but also for tiny Malaika, so exquisite, struggling so desperately for nourishment. She cries night and day. Meantime Hélène's Maman still won't talk to her. She's unyielding. Hélène writes to her, Lando writes to her, all without result. What few secondhand messages get through are clear and final. "She's dead to me."

But even these bitter episodes have their sweet twist. By and by, Hélène turns to Mama for help, and Mama, who can barely speak French, now becomes close to Hélène. "You hold her head that way. You hold your breast this way. You let her suckle just so." Mama learns some French. Hélène learns Kinyarwanda.

One day, Hélène and I are running errands about Butare. Hélène has something on her mind.

"What is it they say in the military? Never volunteer? Your brother should have been in the military."

"Ngw'iki?"

"Well, it's the kids, the students, so sweet, and always coming in for help with his courses."

"Of course."

"Of course, and I'm putting it all wrong. The kids aren't the problem. The problem is this past year. This past year, they've been coming in for help with other courses."

"And it takes a lot of time?"

"No. I'm still not putting it right. It's not that either. It's what he's been finding out when they come in. A while ago he starts helping these kids with one particular course, a course titled something like one of his own courses. So he asks them where the professor is taking it. They tell him. They even get the curriculum for him. Which he reads, and he says, 'Eh, this is familiar.' It's his curriculum. He looks at their lecture notes. They're his lectures. He talks to the rector. Nothing."

What can I say? I'm fifteen. "Mmmh," I say. And, "Have you heard from Maman Cécile?"

"I'm dead to her."

The plagiarist turns out to be a connected plagiarist. "There's no future for Lando in Butare, Loulou."

So once again the Batutsi climb into their suitcases. For Lando and for Hélène, for now, it's a flat in a Zungu compound near Kigali's foreign missions. The U.S. mission to Rwanda now has (how do you like that?) a cultural attaché, and Lando finds a job as his deputy. For me, it's exams and then on to another girls' school and only the Holy Father knows where.

Before I find out, a glacier in Canada groans and abruptly fractures. Great bergs crash into the cold Atlantic and a tidal wave comes roaring our way. Maman Cécile has had a change of heart.

"She's on her way," says Lando, and here she comes (is that the bachinky-chunk of a Cajun accordion I hear?), aboard a Sabena Fokker that settles on the single strip of our grandly titled Kayibanda International Airport. Hélène has been telling us how Lando used to tease Maman Cécile about how we live in trees. Now here she is climbing down from the Fokker, jet-lagged, overcoated, squinting in the full equatorial sun. On the tarmac she stops, turns slowly, and looks about, full of wonder, but who can say at what? The trees are empty of people.

Amid the trivial pleasantries of first greeting, I marvel at what a daunting beauty Maman Cécile must once have been, and how remarkably Hélène is a less spectacular version of her mother.

The next day, Mama and I come to visit. Maman Cécile's face is all lines, her eyes are all relief. Malaika is asleep in a bedroom. We chat; we laugh; and at last Maman Cécile says, "Come." She takes us to the bedroom door, opens it quietly. Silence as we all gaze. "See," says Maman Cécile, as if she's showing us something neither she nor we have ever seen before, as if she's showing the world something it's never seen before. "How beautiful. How peaceful."

ANOTHER BOARDING SCHOOL, ANOTHER IDYLL—SAVE FOR THE COLD SHOWERS IN THE morning, cold of the mountains. Notre Dame d'Afrique sits high above already high Gisenyi, and there are hardly any Tutsi girls here either. Whenever I run into them, they seem weighted by "the line," their mother's line, their father's line, bloodlines, the thunder vault of ancestors whose unforgiving standard every Tutsi son and daughter, niece and nephew must meet. What a weight to bear. They say that among the hill tribes of southern China, women and girls wear hairpieces as broad as their shoulders, heavy with the long-combed locks of female ancestors.

I'm beginning to thank goodness that Mama—and Papa too—weren't much for faded glories. Thank goodness they didn't put that weight on us. Thank you, Mama, for keeping these matters quiet. And yet . . . is that the only reason they kept things from us? Mama, that grand mistress of secrecy. We know her line, we know the names, Mutemura, Muganza, Rudasumbwa, Mukeza, Kabenga; we know the songs that are sung of them. But anything more than that, still fog most dense.

Just what *does* she keep from us? What does she keep so securely hidden in her *Lives of the Saints*? Does she in fact keep hidden somewhere a *Lives of the Wicked,* in which we would find the evil queen Kanjogera, il Duce, der Führer, Stalin . . . and Mama's line?

OFF BROADWAY
(OR DON'T THROW BOUQUETS AT ME)

For Lando and for Hélène, life, for now, has rewards. Two years after Malaika comes blue-eyed Patrick. Hélène, now, is also at the U.S. mission, cataloging in the library. Lando knows he can't stick with this post any more than he could look forward to lecturing in Butare; he knows there's nowhere to go for a local working for the U.S. government. And in the event, this dreamer's mind is never still. He loves teaching more than most anything. All he loves more is acting. So if he can't do what he likes more than most anything, why not go for what he likes most? Before we know it, he has an itinerant troupe working Rwanda, town to town, wherever there's something they can jerry-rig as a stage upon which Africans will come and watch Africans performing French plays . . . and by and by, once he's made a local name, where Africans will come and watch Africans performing African plays.

This last is not an easy sell. Lando's great successes are Zungu scripts, in particular a traveling production of Marcel Pagnol's *Topaze,* in which the playwright has fun with a grande dame of the haute bourgeoisie who refuses to believe that a son of hers, *hers,* could be as thick as he is. The role of grande dame is so rich, I must play it. I plead with Lando. He knows, does he not, how I love to mimic Gallic hauteur. He must; I've seen him tickled by it.

He hesitates.

I pout. The production will coincide precisely with school holiday. He must give me the role.

At last he gives in; he's such a pushover for little sister. Far too young, far too skinny, but shhh! I play the grande dame.

I walk on stage in a satin *jupon*—a big fluffy skirt—flashing a fan beneath a lace mantilla, and what do I hear? Whistles. Whistles that everywhere but in America are the same as hoots. Also, hoots. As a Zungu grand dame, I am simply not accepted.

What a gaffe and a blunder. In my way, I've acted out one of Tonton Kagame's popular misadventures, *Matabaro Goes to Europe,* all about the escapades of an innocent Munyarwanda blundering abroad. And I haven't even been abroad yet! Such humiliation; from now on, I will play as cast, no questions asked.

WHO ARE THESE RWANDESE WHO SHOW UP, NAY, EVEN PAY GOOD MONEY, TO WATCH African men and women play the roles of dated French men and women? Who even pay, now and then, to watch African theater? As a nation, we are as illiterate as you imagine, perhaps even more so. This is, after all, Africa's deep interior. Those ragged schoolchildren you see in documentary films, kids at school in palm-thatched shelters with no walls, no desks, and dirt floors, are the lucky ones; most have no school. Some of us yet walk about with assegais. The bureaucratically structured genocide bearing down on us will be more modern than backward and African, with greater clerks directing lesser clerks in how to administer mass murder. Yet backward Africa will lend its touch. Those greater clerks will admonish those lesser clerks, in mimeographed memoranda, that firearms may be in short supply, so "citizens" (by which they will mean designated agents of mass murder) should have at the ready their spears and bows. The Congo is said, famously, to have had only one university graduate when Belgium cut it loose in 1961, the year I was born.

Still, that's just one side of the story. The missions have made an abbreviated few of us literate with a vengeance. At first we were almost entirely Batutsi, then both Bahutu and Batutsi, now mostly Bahutu. We speak Kiswahili, Kinyarwanda, and French, including a drilled familiarity with Hatier's *Bescherelle* (*"La conjugaison pour tous; les verbes, les tableaux-types, les règles d'accord, les règles d'emploi"*), plus Robert's complete volume of irregular verbs in all their irregular conjugations. Some of us (though not me, and thank you, Saint Anthony for that) know Latin, even Greek. After all, committed priests, priests dedicated to delivering us from the darkness that is Africa, have been our teachers. The church even sends a few of us to Paris, where snide cabbies in black Citroëns ask us, in some thick patois of Parisian French and who knows what, why we don't speak to them in English instead of what they call our *"petit nègre."*

Do I sound defensive? Let's just say that for several millennia now we have had illiterate storytellers the likes of the illiterate Homer and the illiterate Hesiod telling us tales that are just as much things of words, and now for a couple of generations we in Rwanda have had a few souls, Hutu, Zungu, Tutsi, and even Twa, enlightening a few more of us with the words of Saint Anthony, Saint-Simon, Hugo, Achebe, Ngugi. Indeed, who but their grown pupils would now be showing up for Lando's "dramatical" (as an English lady once gushed) productions? Who else would there be to enjoy Lando's earnest young actors as they try to wring every last nuance out of Molière's comedy?

IT HARDLY MATTERS THAT MOST OF MOLIÈRE'S COMEDY (TO ME, ANYWAY) SEEMS TOO delightfully broad for much nuance. Lando is nonetheless a detail-driven taskmaster. He nonetheless barks *"Zut alors!"* if they don't get their lines just right.

His *"Zut!"* is worse than his bite. His earnest actors draw audiences and the audiences pay; not much, but they pay. They may be dreadfully few in number, but Hutu, Tutsi, and Twa alike, the literate of Rwanda are dedicated theatergoers.

And there's something else I must tell you: Lando has competition. While we were away (was it while I was in Bujumbura? Or at the Kansi mission?), yet another modern wonder visited itself on Kigali-ville—a down-town picture palace. Its name, grandly spelled out in colored bulbs right on the road next to the big Hendi duka, is Cinema La Sierra. Having gone there only twice, I concluded that Indian actors in India were more person-able than Indian traders in Kigali. And now here comes another movie joint, the even more popular and louder Chez Mayaka with its own colored bulbs in the Muslim quarter. Both palaces feature scratchy old black-and-white cartoons, jumping with impish invention, and Harold Lloyd, and B-movie zombies, and the Marx brothers, cloud-borne Harpo counterpoint-ing Groucho, with his predatory leer. ("What are you going to believe? Me or your own two eyes?")

Nor is that all. From Hollywood, from Bombay's Bollywood, especially from Bollywood, we get grand productions. Bollywood: Who needs some-thing so prosaic as a kiss when eye-lock results in thunder? When a hero-ine's abashed eyes cast up and away in falsetto song? Even from Egypt we get these productions. Especially from Egypt. With dependable regularity, the Cecil B. DeMilles of Alexandria and Cairo ship slick potboilers up the Nile and across the Arab and Muslim world. For its part, Hollywood now is downright spendthrift with the formula safari thriller of the thirties and forties. In the old formula thrillers, we meet our leading man as a Great White Hunter rudely camped and ready for adventure in some remote spot in the deep interior, which is to say a studio set in Burbank, where canni-bals grunt with an Alabama drawl. How different the new ones! Techni-color! Stereophonic sound! And that's just for starters. During these flush postwar years, Hollywood has been shipping out for Tanganyika and Kenya, for honest-to-gosh Africa. Now we *abafana* (we fan people) meet our Great White Hunter in Cinemascope, at a base camp on the honest-to-gosh East African savannah. No more studio sets intercut with stock footage of an elephant trumpeting. ("Gwendolyn, did you hear that!") Now, in the open air, real Masai leap, the horizon opens up, and now, here in Kigali-ville, we can sit and gaze across the Great Rift to a far horizon for which Deborah Kerr and Stewart Granger set off to find diamonds and "Watusi" in *King Solomon's Mines*. It comes to us years after its release in Zunguland, and the worse for years of projection, but what does that matter?

Home on holiday from Our Lady of Africa, I go to the picture shows. I find Rwandese kids sitting with mouths agape at African wonders. They seem barely aware that the distant and magical realm up on the screen is the realm in which they're living. I, of course, am no silly child. I'm older now; I know these movies are about Africa, indeed about East Africa, of which we are a part. At last they're making movies for us, and when *King Solomon's Mines* comes to town, this is an occasion. "Mama, do you hear that? The Mututsi up there—he's actually speaking Kinyarwanda!"

Cut to Lando, something of a showman himself, on location in this same African yonder. No gay gouache here of chemical color. Lando's hills, if he could but shoot them, would be sixteen-millimeter and black and white, shot on some grainy stock, with the leg of some African insect flickering in the lens.

Even this he can but fantasy as he leads his troupe from stage to makeshift stage, competing with the moguls of Hollywood, Bollywood, and Cairo. Our brother is now a vagabond, a Mututsi in a suitcase even in these, his native hills. Wearing a rumpled suit, a *litron*—a liter as he'd say—of warm beer in one hand, a spotted script in the other, he sits reading in the backseat of a battered sedan in a brief convoy of battered sedans.

Through chill mist they toddle—up hills that do their best to send them back down, through dales thick with rats and rat-roasting peasants. Over bridges ready to fall they rattle, all the while luring fellow traveler after fellow traveler. At one bend, a goggled pygmy on a motorcycle joins them; at another, a pair of gendarmes on bicycles. At the sound of their approach, porcupines set their quills abristle, and checkpoints of snoozing troops do the same with their rifles. Through hamlets gridlocked by long-horned cattle, they thus bump, and all to the tune of someone's marimba, or someone else's static-addled boom box tooting something Congolese, or a lusty leading man in a stained necktie appealing to the encompassing quiet of Africa with his tenor, or an auto-stopping Swahili plucking an oud, the twang of our Afro-Levant.

When Lando left Butare, he was already working into production that play by Nbarga-Kouma that had entranced him in Montreal, *La famille africaine*. By early 1978 he has it bumping across Rwanda. Later the same year, the union of French-speaking nations in Africa—Organisation Internationale de la Francophonie, or for short, la Francophonie—meets in Rwanda, and the Habyarimanas need something to show off.

"Well, there *is* that troupe out there," someone says.

They perform. This is big. Lando calls me down from Our Lady of Africa. France's president these days is Valéry Giscard d'Estaing, so elegant, and he's going to be there. At the soirée afterward, Giscard asks to meet the producer and invites Lando and troupe to perform in France, on the Élysée's tab. Habyarimana beams. He hugs Lando. Gabon's president Omar Bongo, who's been making eyes at one of Lando's actresses, chimes in with an invitation to Libreville, on the Gabonese tab.

Alas, Lando has a family and a job. He takes the missed chance philosophically at a cave called La Cave. In fact, he enjoys La Cave so much, hangs out there so much, that when the patron announces he's moving, a lightbulb clicks on in the cartoon bubble that appears betimes above our brother's head. The premises are rented, including all the fixtures, all the kitchen gear. All he has to do is raise cash for a few improvements and make the rent. Before long, he's got his own saloon, La Fringale, "that hint of hunger." It has a circular bar. It even has an oven handcrafted of native brick, like the brick oven in Mama's Kabuye cooking shed. Into its depths, where you can see hardwood coals glowing blue, Lando slides a great wooden paddle, and out comes fresh pizza, as popular and as thoroughly Rwandese as those cowpokes Lucky Luke and Dangerous Danny. The pies come to the table with bottles of various commercial condiments, bottles long since emptied and refilled daily with the fire of Africa. By my sixteen-year-old lights, La Fringale, with Hélène at the door and Lando behind the bar, is the most sensational restaurant-bar in the world.

You never know who's going to show up; the rowdy (*"jolie bouteille, sacrée bouteille . . ."*) mix with the louche ("trust me") mix with the con-sular ("a toast!"), both Zungu ("here here") and Rwandese (*"garçon, encore du Napoléon"*), and of these latter, many are secret police, *barbouze* ("mmmh"). For the most part, the spooks come to drink but expense it as a place to spy, a craft they actually attempt to ply, and with all the panache of Tintin in action.

Everybody knows them on sight, everybody but Hélène, for whom Lando adopts a code. *"Chérie,"* he calls from behind the bar, and tugs on an earlobe. Not quite the last word in sophistication, but even then Hélène of-ten fails to pick up on it. This lady born wild in a wild tribe is simply not cut out to be the sly and subtle spy. And so Lando, with toothy grimace and rigid index finger, digs madly for an imaginary beetle in his ear. This, at last, she gets. You can tell because she telegraphs her recognition with an undisguised "Aha!"

The *barbouzes* come in, sit four to a table, and lean in unison to eaves-drop on the next table, where eyeballs in unison take note, eyebrows in unison rise, and conversation turns to tennis, or better yet, to the menu. Regardless, they keep coming in, both spies and their subjects; in fact, the one drag on business is Lando himself. One day, the spooks come in, seat themselves four to a table, lean to listen, and Lando sees that one has cot-ton in his ears. He can't resist. From behind the bar, our rumbustious First Lord of the Rum (Purveyor to Her Majesty, Rwanda) roars: "Eh, Celestin, what's the trouble? I see you're at work, but the office door is shut." There goes the *barbouze* trade for a good month.

Karangwa, as La Fringale's occasional promoter, does not care for this. This is not good for business. Should someone bring up Celestin the *bar-bouze* in a manner anything less than respectful, Karangwa tells him to cut it out. "I've got it on good authority that Celestin is a dedicated caseworker. 'Systematic,' they say."

"How's that?"

"He takes every case one bottle at a time." As everybody but Karangwa laughs, he leans over and whispers in my ear: "Picked up that one at Chez Mayaka."

For Lando and for Hélène, La Fringale becomes all their hours awake. The smell of *frites* gets into their clothes. There's a flat above the bar. They move in. Now the smell doesn't just get into their clothes. Now it gets in and it won't come out. Scrub and scrub again around and behind their prized Fry-O-Lators, dripping grease in the heat. Scrub the kitchen. The flat smells like *frites*. Scrub the flat. No good. They ignore it. It's business. La Fringale is packed. "Eh, Jean," Lando growls at a regular seated with some new customers. "That's not your gin, is it? What happened to the twelve-step program?"

Business booms. The next thing I know, Lando and Hélène want to build a lodge out of town, and Lando is going from bank to nasty bank. To listen to them, you'd think it will never get off the ground, but next thing I know, it's built.

At the heart of Chez Lando's many-flowered grounds ("This bloom's a mimosa," I proudly point out, "and that one's a . . .") spreads the beer garden, a wide circle of booths under thatch. The thatch covers only the booths, the bar, and in a far corner, the pool table. At its center, the great circle opens to the sky, which is all that covers the dance floor. But Chez Lando's most salient feature is its business plan, which comes down to *auberge sans tralala*. Nothing is budgeted for gloss. No mod. No mood. No Louis Farouk. It's African, with tables and chairs hand carved by Rwandese and dressed by Rwandese in the skins of game animals. The walls are brick, naked and native; look up and you see rough-cut rafters laid over with raffia. The capital's other hotels sink in wallpaper and imported furniture, they put into upkeep, which is to say labor.

With all this, Lando finds time to prime me for next steps, and the one I fix on is said to be Africa's best school for journalists, on Gorée Island, the old slave entrepôt in Senegal. I picture Senegal and the Sahara beyond, the millennial desert libraries of Timbuktu and Jenne packed tight with knowledge, including Western knowledge carelessly lost by Christendom.

La Francophonie underwrites full stipends for high scores on competitive exams. Eight of us compete, two of us girls. Two stipends are set aside for Rwanda. I leave the exam holding my head.

The other girl's name is Floriane, and she's a beauty. One day she gets word to me that we should get together. We meet for tea in the lounge of the Hotel des Diplomates. "The two of us, we're the two!" she says. "Senegal, here we come!"

Now my head is full of Senegal. I wash dishes full of Senegal. I sweep the floor full of Senegal. Exhausted, I canter through postpandrial naps atop a Senegalese camel, and in full beau geste. *"En avant, ma belle sabreuse!"* shouts Tintin into the teeth of the wind.

A month or so passes. The director of Radio Rwanda summons us to his office. We're sent to a room full of stereos and earphones and asked to wait. At last a man comes in, seats himself behind a metal desk with wires going nobody knows where, and says, "Girls." We approach. He says, "The program with Senegal. It's off. Called off."

"By . . . ?" asks Floriane.

"By La Francophonie?" I ask. "By the Senegalese?"

"By the ministry."

"Whose ministry?"

"By your ministry. You are Rwandese, aren't you?"

"But the ministry doesn't pay for it. La Francophonie—"

"That's all I've got to tell you. That's all you need to know. It's off. You can't go."

· 16 ·

RECONSTRUCTING THE LARGER CRIME

My Unholy Grail; 1983–1989

Floriane and I leave, stunned, to go our separate ways and into our separate rages. My rage lasts into what should be my first year at university. At last Lando settles me, gets me to go to a school of languages that the Akazu is building in the furthest heights of Akazu land, in the frontier town of Ruhengeri, gorilla country. There, in the name of patronage, the Akazu is bringing concrete to our most distant precincts. Down here our mountain meadows are sunlit. Up there they have moors, high and cold, rocky saddles between crags. On the way there, they've built Ruhengeri Prison; more than just a lockup, it's the Akazu keep for political prisoners. When you get sent to Ruhengeri, that's it, no one expects to see you again, which I know because that's where Uncle Ntukanyagwe, Granny Mariya's Ntukanyagwe, is locked up. He's been locked up there so long, people forget what he looks like, and no one has heard from him since he went in. "At least I can try to see Uncle," I say.

"No you can't," says Mama. Mama is Uncle Ntukanyagwe's half sister, and in Africa, where second cousins are counted brothers and sisters, that makes him her brother. "No you can't," she repeats. "No you can't."

THE CAMPUS IS NEW, RAW. MUCH OF THE TIME THERE'S NO WATER. WE HAVE TO ASK the villagers, Please, can we have some? We trudge back with plastic buckets.

Try as I might to find fault with my classes, I can't, and there are other compensations. At times we can sit about over thé au lait, tinned lait; we talk, I learn.

"The Nile rises in Rwanda," says a Rwandese lad, and a Burundian answers back, "Burundi."

Oh sweet Jesus. Burundians and Rwandese can't stop bickering over which of us nurses the one true source of the Nile. As if that dribbling rivulet, wherever it is, were the one true God. And all this business about which Muzungu won the race to find the one true dribble. I hope they don't go on.

I hope in vain.

"Rwanda" says young Mr. Munyarwanda.

"Burundi," says young Mr. Murundi.

Which means it's time for young Mr. Valentine, passing through with his shock of sandy hair, his plummy vowels, and his erudition: "Don't mean to be a bore, but the Nile rises in Lake Victoria. Victoria Nyanza."

"*Des clous!* What are you talking about? That's Speke's Nile and Speke was a fool." I'm not sure who says this. I'm not even sure it's exactly what he says. "It was Burton," he declares. "Richard Burton."

"*Richard Burton?*" I wonder aloud.

"Richard Burton," says young Mr. Murundi. "Talk about getting it wrong."

Now this is intriguing. Just what was it that Richard Burton got wrong? Marrying Elizabeth Taylor? And what a jarring shift of subject.

"Burton didn't get a thing wrong. Don't you recall? They staged a debate on the question. Now that was theater."

Mmmh. Richard Burton. Theater. As offhand as I can, and so the others can't hear, I ask young Mr. Valentine: "I don't suppose it's *Sir* Richard Burton we're about?"

"The same. *Sir* Richard Burton."

"Mmmh," I offer.

"Moody sort, wasn't he? Did you know? He had a scar across his cheek."

"That you could see?"

"Quite. From a saber. Abyssinia, as I recall."

"Abyssinia?"

"Abyssinia. You know, at times it strikes me that the other Sir Richard Burton, the film star, when he wasn't playing some role or other, he was playing the Victorian Sir Richard. Pity Sir Richard the film star never got a crack at playing Sir Richard the *beau sabreur*. Smoking opium. Hell-bent through Tanganyika in search of the Nile. Then finding it. No, Speke found it. Or was it Burton? Blast."

"And Speke?"

"For the love of Mike, how can you ask me about Speke? I can't get Burton straight. My impression is that Speke was another Leon Mugesera."

"A man with no ballast," says young Mr. Munyarwanda.

"Quite. A chap with no ballast."

HERE IN RUHENGERI, WE CAN PICK UP AND TUCK AWAY SUCH PRECIOUS KNOWLEDGE AS the difference a century makes in English popular letters—the difference, say, between Rider Haggard's *She* and Oliver Goldsmith's earlier *She Stoops to Conquer*. No, we can't buy tickets for a stage production of *She Stoops,* but we can read all about high times at The Three Jolly Pigeons. How like Lando's La Fringale it seems, and how alien I find Haggard's *She,* even though it's a hundred years more modern.

Alien but fun. I grew up with my nose in *Astérix*. The She of *She* (aka "She-who-must-be-obeyed") fits right into my galaxy of comic-book stars. This star is a near-immortal priestess of Isis, beautiful despite her years— her several thousand years. She's an ancient Egyptian ancestor of the adventure's posh hero, fresh from Cambridge. (Ah, but blood does out.) Our Cambridge blue pursues this beauty up the Nile and into the African heights of what I'm told (I've seen the movie but I've yet to read the book) was Haggard's first bestseller, *King Solomon's Mines*. Haggard's landscape smolders with volcanoes—and, hello, put Haggard down for just a minute. Look about. Just which ones might She be wandering among? Sabyinyo and Gahinga and Muhabura just there to the north? Or Bisoke and Karisimbi just there to the west? No matter. Here amid a race of superhuman Africans (mmmh), She passes through the fire of life, which at last consumes Her.

Decoding the subtext of all this (superhumans indeed) must wait for a later day; for now it's just entertaining, not to say funny.

WORD COMES THAT TONTON KAGAME IS ON HIS WAY TO RUHENGERI, AND NOT JUST TO visit. He's coming to teach. He'll be living in the bishopric, and he's invited me to live there too. These have not been happy days for Uncle. Every day his battles with the mission hierarchy become more strained. Reason, over the years, has become his confession, and reason is something with which the missions do not much bother themselves. For years he's been asking why they so insist that Rwandese abandon their Bantu names if they want to get baptized. Now he's nearing his eighties, and now at last it's sinking in how this business is more than silliness among the fastidiously sacerdotal. He's learning it has nothing to do with Christian names. Everywhere the church baptizes children with pagan names: Linda, Lucinda, Chlöe, Alexandre, even Perceval. It's not pagan names that repel them—it's African names. Africa, after all, is the dark hell from which the churchly are intent on rescuing us forsaken souls. To this noble end, many have dedicated their lives. They cannot possibly baptize a child with a Bantu name, black with the curse of Africa.

Is it to this that Uncle has professed his life? Is this all his books on our Bantu past amount to?

I do not feel his pain. He's coming to live in Ruhengeri. What else can matter?

Fats Waller plays stride piano as I contemplate this glad turn. He will be teaching here. I will be living in the bishopric. Tonton has stopped over to see Mama in Kabuye, then it's on to the hospital in Nairobi to see about some swelling in the limbs, and then—on to Ruhengeri!

I'M SITTING IN MY ROOM. I'M STUDYING. CRACKLY FROM KIGALI, RADIO RWANDA IS rasping the news. Cracks, pops, static. *The government of Rwanda is sad to announce the untimely death of Bishop Alexis Kagame at hospital in Nairobi.*

My quarters are small. My soul feels smaller. Tonton, once so lively, now just dead, slowly shrivels in a casket. My spirit shrivels at warp speed. The one redeeming feature of this bolt-hole of a room is that it's high up, with a window looking out over the treetops of something rare: the jungle where it's cold. Out there the mountain gorilla, all the more rare, beats his chest, and when he does, it's "the beat beat beat of the tom-tom / When the jungle shadows fall." Here I crouch in my own jungle nest, looking out over this jungle of blue shadow, so deep. The camera paints it in such jolly color, just right for gorillas like Paddington Bear. How the camera lies. It's gray up here where Tonton was headed, and grayer up there where other gargantuans bellow in rage, and grin with fear—gray, gray-green, and bruise blue. It's forever raining, and the rain doesn't fall, it drives. *National Geographic*? More "a range of gaunt thorns all stretching their limbs one way, as if craving alms of the sun." More "a misanthropist's heaven." More *Wuthering Heights*.

Would I nonetheless like to fly from my sill, fly out, up, and into that tangle? At this cold moment, most emphatically yes. I'd also like to climb astride a camel and canter across Senegalese dunes in a burnoose, as beside me white-cassocked Uncle bounces in his battered VW bug. These are the years in which a bold Muzungu is in point of chill fact living up there in that darkness, a cranky crone named Dian Fossey who pioneers and chainsmokes amid smoky peaks. When the jungle shadows fall and her body is found (Was it poachers? Her own research assistant? Someone else?), it's all to the beat beat beat of the tom-toms.

When she's buried up there, the U.S. mission sends Lando to say some words because he'd known her, her zeal and her hacking smoker's cough. For me, her realm up there is stranger than America.

The Leon Mugesera first alluded to as "the chap with no ballast" deepens my gloom. He professes a hard Akazu line everywhere on campus, intimidating all opposition into frightened silence.

PROFESSOR RWASUBUTARE SEES ME THROUGH. HE'S HARDLY MY CONFESSOR. HE'S NOT that close to anybody, not even his wife. He scares the deuce out of students, and I think he also sees students as mini-Mugeseras, and thus they frighten him—which is why he frightens them. He presents such a forbidding image, a professor of English literature (li-ter-a-tyoure) with standards so high and courses so grueling that only fools and masochists sign up; I'm not sure which category I fall into.

But by and by he becomes so engaging that he diverts you with the antics of squads of scribblers whose names, as often as not, we reverse in the Rwandese manner, everyone from Jonson Ben to Carlyle Thomas to Melville Herman to Blake (William! William! burning bright / In the forests of the night). He diverts me from my Tonton-induced gloom. Even if you can't follow what he's talking about, there's bound to be something he says that provokes. For random instance, he's lecturing about a difference of scholarly opinion over a line by a modern American storyteller, how some argue this, others argue that. In the brilliance of the line, the arguments become ether: "The past is never dead. It isn't even past." So maybe Mama's attempts to get us to forget, and Papa's too, won't turn out as successfully as they hoped. So maybe there's more out there, alive, now, for us to deal with.

GRADUATION. I'M WAITING TABLES AT LA FRINGALE, SENDING OUT APPLICATIONS FOR this and that, teaching part time at a lycée, where I make a friend. Judith is *très jolie,* a pretty secretary with a pretty demeanor. She joins the crowd that gathers at Mama's place, the parade without end that has included so many.

One day our box at the post yields a letter stamped Newark, Del. Inside is the offer of a stipend from the University of Delaware, a place so strangely distant that the word I see on paper is *Delawhere.* Then comes that magical letter from the U.S. mission, their letter of intent to grant a visa. Then comes the antimagical letter from our Education Ministry, telling me I can't leave the country. This is when all six foot three of Anne-Marie marches into the passport agency as if she has six legs with which to march, and somehow gets a passport for me from dear Constance. I'm not sure whether Anne-Marie steps in because she's as cross as I am, or whether she just can't bear seeing me through another fit of pique.

Mama's got the melancholy, and I can tell. She won't show it, of course. "I'm not going to tell you a thing. Nothing." Silence. "All I'm going to tell you is, when you pack your bags, leave out the foolish notions."

Full of expectation, I pack my bags. I board the flight. Destination: Newark, Delawhere. Sabena to Brussels, then Sabena nonstop to Newark. How serendipitous: My flight lands right there, in Newark. Full of expectation, I land. Such a vast airport! So busy! "How do I get to university," I ask in my best Ruhengeri English.

"Which university?"

"The University of Delawhere."

"Where?"

"Delawhere."

"Delawho?"

"Not who, sir. Where, sir. Here. In Newark."

"Noork?"

"Delawhere."

"Sweediepie, this is Joisey."

BACK IN RWANDA, IT'S THE LONG RAINS OF 1987. FOR LANDO AND FOR HÉLÈNE, MEETING payrolls and raising kids becomes all-consuming. I hear from them less. Lando writes,

> *Those with low morals will tell you that shame doesn't kill. Alas, it does, especially when you get caught in the vicious cycle of putting off a letter. Even as I battle Shame to write, he's grabbing my pen. How can I explain why you haven't heard from me when you so needed to, when you needed moral support in the oh so welcoming yet treacherous America. . . .*

About shame, of course, he's wrong; shame hardly kills, though it certainly gets some eloquent hand-wringing out of Lando. The woes suffered by your faithful narrator are strictly low grade, and before long, Advent is nigh, Christmas comes, and I get letters from the kids, on pages torn from composition books.

> *Dear Louise.*
>
> *Hello Louise. How are you? I now announce to you my news. I had a great Christmas. We went to Chez Lando. The food was so good. On New Year's Eve we went again. We had méchoui. It's delicious! I'm ten now. I had my birthday at grandma's house in Kabuye. My two grannies and the whole family had a marvelous time. Now I must announce to you some bad news. I had a boil. They had to lance it. No matter*

what you say, it's terrible! And you. How are you? How about some news about your friends? Girl friends. Boy friends? Please let me know what's going on. Was your trimester successful?

Big kisses, Malaika

I reply that my trimester was successful. I'm getting all the essentials of an American liberal education, right down to its Existential (uppercase *E*) details. In Rwanda, French money, jealous of the English language, ended up teaching me English. Here in America, Professor Thibault, of Lyon (or is it Caen?) teaches us Sartre; Sartre, walleyed and myopic in his Coke-bottle glasses. "*L'enfer, c'est les autres.*"

How can I explain to Big Kisses what a different world I now inhabit? Such different foods. I'm invited out. At the next table, a diner orders "Eggs Benedict; hold the eggs." Here's a dish Americans can order, ask the waiter to cancel the eggs, and still gobble more animal fat and protein than many Rwandese get in three full days. In Bujumbura, we have uncles who are credentialed *agronomes,* which means they spend their days telling farmers how to farm, and we all think, how progressive. In America, agronomists spend their days bending the bloodlines of cattle to produce flank steaks cheap, fast, and in enormous quantity. In America, agronomists get cattle doing their bloody best to make sure people get fed. In Rwanda, it's just the opposite. Tradition gets people doing their bloody best to make sure cattle get fed. Eat the beasts? What indulgence! Making a meal of something you work so hard to keep alive? The only bovine flanks we care about are flanks that quiver with life in the morning light of mountain pasture.

FROM ANNE-MARIE AND FROM KARANGWA I HEAR THAT LANDO AND HÉLÈNE HAVE TIME for nothing but the business, the kids, and Mama, and that business is taking its toll, that both Lando and Hélène are showing wear. Hélène, the beauty who studied library science, is now the librarian who looks like a librarian. She wears glasses on a chain. Both of them are getting hefty.

On the phone, I try to gauge Lando's fatigue. The line's all crackly. I can barely hear. Beneath the fatigue, beneath the crackle, I hear him relishing the struggle. I hear a voice seduced by the lure of building something, no matter what, the voice of a man among men so allied to Byron's "Unto the savage love of enterprise, / That they will seek for peril as a pleasure." (Professor, what have you done to me?)

How he enjoys the lads who drop in for a litron of Primus and wander over from the bar or from the pool table and collect around him as he sits with his gimpy leg on the two-foot wall he designed around the central circle of the beer garden where it's open to the night sky. Here he is, himself at last. Here he belongs. This big circular kerb of his mimics the short walls that ran around the courtyards of the old rondavels, then as now an informal place to sit for a minute, minutes that carry forever on as others stop by. I can tell how he enjoys that laughter, and I so enjoy this state he has achieved, this gimpy brother who would never wear shorts, who lied to me that an accident on a *vélo* did the damage when in fact it was a bad needle. And now here he is. On the phone, Mama says, "Such a stride in his step," and now on the phone I can hear him, crackly, in all his fatigued victory. Transatlantic cable, please don't go out on us.

"How about stage productions?" I ask. Doesn't he miss it?

"Productions? What say you, Bottom?"

I say "Mmmh." I'm learning not to indulge my brother.

He tells me, "Running a saloon is like barbering. Everybody you talk to wants to talk to you about everything, and everybody's an expert on everything. Everything apart from matters of stagecraft. Then everyone defers . . ."

"To my humble brother."

"To your most humble brother. The other day a young French couple came in, newlyweds, a couple of these nongovernment government types. . . ."

"NGO types."

"*Exactement.* And they're both sharing the same job. Fascinating. I want to hear all about it. I want to hear all about them. And then maybe we can talk about Imelda Marcos and all those shoes she just lost. But he's been in town awhile, he really wants to get into our big Rwanda, and all he wants to talk to me about is 'the stage.' Her too. 'You're really in the footlights here,' she says, and he says, 'Limelight, *chérie*, limelight,' and then he starts in on books, starts telling me how he so appreciates all the levels of meaning at work in *The Spy Who Came In from the Heat.*" At this, the phone line starts to break up in earnest.

"*La culture*," I say.

"*La culture*," he says through the crackle. "*C'est comme la confiture.* It's like jam. The less you've got, the more you spread it around." Now the line is just about gone, and is he laughing at his own crack? Karangwa, the professional, the master of the Tutsi deadpan, never laughs at his own remarks, never has, but Lando, otherwise the more disciplined of the two, can't help it, can't hide it, never could, is all out there. Just barely, I make out his voice, accelerated by fatigue, but I can't make out what he's saying. Exit static. Exit manic. "*A suivre*, Lando. *Je t'embrasse.* And tell Mama, 'soon.'"

Come June of '89, I collect my degree and get a job working in Washington, DC, for a French-speaking republic girded by the Sahara. With my Congolese girlfriend Mauwa, I scour the city's greenbelt for something we can afford. Soon enough, thoroughly modern Loulou finds a thoroughly modern dream, a one-bedroom flat in a tower block. It has sliding glass doors that open on a balcony overlooking the vast park system that Depression labor and Franklin Roosevelt gave this my new home, my city (at least for now) on a hill. We've moved just inside DC's "beltway," that highway that American myth seems so to resent as a moat girding American privilege, and that New York myth represents as a moat girding a glorified small town "where a supermarket can advertise 'Open all night,' close at ten, and nobody's the wiser."

Come now. Zungu DC may not have the flair of Zungu New York or for that matter Baltimore, but this is Duke Ellington's hometown, and besides, I'm a country girl myself. I could do worse, and meantime there are so many subcommunities of people like me, moved in like me. Some number fewer than five thousand. Many thrive in the tens of thousands, not just hustling Vietnamese but hustling Cambodians; not just hustling Ethiopians but hustling Eritreans. Not to speak of Ivorians, Gabonese, Senegalese, Somalis. I even hear of a community from a country I never heard of before. Lahbi. "Real hustlers," my friend tells me, and how is it I've never heard of them?

"About who? About Lahbians?"

"No, not Lahbians. Lahbi-*ists*."

Or more exactly, lobbyists. And to be still more exact, this thriving subcommunity numbers some twenty-five thousand. All hustlers, all from somewhere else.

COME JULY, IT'S HOTTER INSIDE THE BELTWAY THAN IT IS IN RWANDA. IN RWANDA IT'S cool, and the talk of the tables is a Hutu woman from the neglected south, from Nduga country. She's a member of the national assembly—Félicula (now take a deep breath) Nyiramutarambirwa. As you might guess, anyone who will hold to a handle like that is going to be tough to deal with, and she has been. She doesn't like how the Akazu is shortchanging Nduga Bahutu. She's filed suit against the regime for putting in the fix on road-building contracts.

July wears on. DC gets hotter. News comes of Félicula. "She's been in an accident."

"Accident?"

"Road accident. A lorry. It ran her down."

Dead On Arrival. In Rwanda, this is what we mean by a road contract. By October a Hutu priest who doubles as a crusading reporter becomes another victim of a road contract.

No hero and no martyr, Lando looks about and doesn't see public life as the arena for him. Once in a while, he's had an ache for show business, but with Chez Lando, he's lunging ahead into uncharted territory. In the past, the family has known social and military success; Karekezi (now four years dead) even knew financial success. But Karekezi was a skinflint, and be-sides, in those days, few had the means to build much of an enterprise. Shipping costs to Central Africa are still enormous, but at least now, with a prudent business plan and prudent management, it's not impossible to deal with headaches. Now, if Lando can keep paying down Chez Lando's debt, he's on the verge of homegrown success.

The decade is closing. Life for Batutsi is dodgy, but my umbilical cord to Africa (AT&T, MCI, Sprint) tells me Chez Lando is doing handsomely. It tells me also that the jealous are at work spreading rumors that our brother is about to go under, that he can't pay his help, that he can't pay his suppliers, that his books are all bollixed. At every turn, competitors with Akazu uncles and cousins use government to thwart him. There's as much simple jealousy at work here as racial politics, and he deals with it, and after he deals with it, he has no time or energy for teasing the politics from the simple jealousy.

My interest in public affairs is just as scant. My fascination now is with our roots, my days off are at the library. I even read my mail at the library. A letter from Lando:

> There was a story about a bomb planted at Remera Stadium by Chez Lando! Ru-mors of my imprisonment followed by hourly visits to our house to check it out. I think it's beginning to affect the kids. The funny thing is, business is in pretty good shape. The grill brings in the best profits, followed by the rooms, followed by the nightclub (good music), and last of all the restaurant (competition, slow help). This year's revenues were fifty million Rwandese francs, way above the bank's fifteen mil-lion franc projections.

I picture Papa sitting in his wooden chair, balancing the farm's books, and I half gasp. Sweet Jesus, family accounts the subject of public talk.

Such a proper Rwandese concern, and so wan in such an enormous arena, like a gladiatrix wondering, even as crowds roar and bulls snort, whether her slip is showing.

Lando gets a bright idea: From Mombasa he orders fresh oysters on ice. Costly, thus risky; but the Zungu trade will love it. The competition gets wind of his bright idea and signs on thieves to pick up the shipment at the airfield. Switch off the bright idea.

RWANDA STRUGGLES. LIFE IS ROUGH FOR MOST BATUTSI. LIFE IS ROUGHER FOR BAHUTU who resist. Life is good for Lando. He almost forgets that politics exist. Then comes June of 1990, and France draws our attention—even Lando's attention—to public life. French president François Mitterrand invites the heads of Africa's French-speaking states to the cool Atlantic coast and tells them that they had best make way for democracy. Habyarimana says *d'ac-cord*. But a month or so passes and little has changed, so some thirty Rwandese intellectuals begin working up a formal statement declaring that Habyarimana's vague *d'ac* is too vague.

Lando doesn't sign. The heroic life is not for him. His life now is all business, and business is booming. Every night the car park is full.

EVERY WEEK I'M LESS ABLE TO RESIST THE LIBRARY. AS IF THIS IS WHERE YOU GO TO GET to the bottom of a crime—which comes to me as I write, not at the time. At the time, 1989, I just feel compelled to dig, and this day, July 28, I'm digging into accounts of "proto-Ethiopian" farmers who chased off East Africa's aborigines thousands of years ago, and of the ancient and apparently Nilotic "Chwezi." "Nilotic." Could they be millennial Batutsi? I board a clacking train for Manhattan and its storied public library, its people's palace of learning, flanked by lions. Intrepid huntress that I am, I brave them and plunge into the card catalogs. "Chwezi." I learn they were ancient herders who ruled the upper Great Lakes until some shattering defeat. "Chwezi." I learn they live on in our songs.

Under aliases, these Chwezi may live on in our songs, but what do we know of them? They're as abstract to me as abstract art, and it's not abstract art that I'm driven to get to the bottom of. I'm not an intellectual, nor do I intend to be. An invisible flurry of gnatlike demons, gremlins, biting angels, has been buzzing about my head, and they're neither abstract nor ancient. They're real: war chiefs barely a century or so dead; craven slavers; witch doctors black as basalt; witch doctors waxy white. They've made such sport of us, and so recently, that their ghosts are still with us, as real as gnats. I can fairly hear them whining in my ears, feel them biting my eyelids. It's time to take care of this.

It's time to stop digging and sort out what I've dug up. Not that way-back Chwezi business but the likes of Mutemura, Burton. Mutemura was the grandfather of our mother's grandfather. Let's just say he was our grandsire, and if I'm truly Rwandese, the very mention of a grandsire should now launch me into the *inzu* business of glorious bloodlines, the many songs they sing of Mutemura, what a brood he spawned, what battles he won, the lions he slew, the leopards. Karangwa was so good at that business. He had it all down. He could reel off so much, and so dramatically. "Bottle the theatrics," Papa told him. "Learn the story behind it." The story: Mutemura was a cattle thief. He stole cattle, and he stole people too. And Burton? I now know how disagreeable he was. No charming curmudgeon he. Acid boiled there. Hated everyone but Arabs—his fellow Brits, Jews. Despised black Africans, despised our blood.

These are the cases I've got to get down to. Most every morning on the bus, a picture comes to me of Mutemura in his storied but (as Lando says) not so distant day—General Custer's day, in fact. Just a few years before swashbuckling George Custer headed for the Little Big Horn, those two Bazungu, Burton and Speke, fired by the same notions of manifest Zungu destiny, headed for grandsire.

When our father died he left Mama the rugo, and all of us a millennium of heritage recorded in the heads of his clan's *abiru*. He left us more than we can possibly grasp.

Would that I could grasp it all! Neither my imagination nor my reading reach back much more than those years so recently past that saw the white man come, and we began a struggle still unfinished, groping and grappling like Jacob twisted up with his angel. And even this I can't grasp. Would that I could coolly probate what's come down to us from family ghosts, what's come down to us from Rwanda's ghosts, what's come down to us from white ghosts, and just how their black-on-white minuet became a dance of death.

The melancholy of it! Not so much the dance, so plainly evident in its poisonous progress, but the background music, our whispering inheritance, which seems at first to come through our father's line. It's his clan that's Tsobe, the keepers of tradition. It's his line that has the chiefs, his cousin Chief Rwanyindo and Rwanyindo's son Ngunga. You find few chiefs in our mother's line. But the chiefs on our father's side were chiefs you find in the bush. True, they were Batsobe, keepers of the *code esotérique*. But in a world so full of shadow, these courtly skills did not mean they were at all close to the court.

Our mother's line, for all its lack of chiefs, was close indeed to the court. Through the years, her line was immediately at hand to execute royal assignments and to suffer royal cruelty. And so, as I go back, I go back through her line, which yields at least some of the melancholy. The burden of inheritance that comes down to us through our Tsobe father, we somehow find not in his line but in our mother's. Hers is the line with players who act. And now it's time to watch them act.

PART III

ORIGINAL SIN

The Weight of Inheritance, Probated in Black and White

. . . worst of all: amortization of heart and soul.

—VLADIMIR MAYAKOVSKY,
Conversation with a Tax Collector About Poetry

BLACK MAN, WHITE MAN, BRIGAND, FOOL

The Plagues of Indenture

Here's how it starts:

I grab the remote. I click "power." Up comes Jimmy Cagney, *Yankee Doodle*-ing. Brilliant, but all the same I hit "mute." I gaze at nowhere. A nowhere minute passes, and just like that, I'm shooting all those miles back across the Atlantic, the Sahara, the Ituri, the Ruwenzori, and alakazam, here I am.

Home. But not stopping. As a muted Cagney *Yankee Doodles* in bright-eyed pantomime, sheer momentum shoots me not just back in place but back in time, back a decade, back five, back another five, until at last, in a hiss of air brakes, I halt. Here it is, the world a century and a half back, in the days of Mutemura, Mututsi of the Singa clan and of our mother's line. I'm someplace green and cool, certainly greener and cooler than down there. Down there is Mutemura himself. I catch glimpses of him amid the heat of a sprawling parade ground. I hear song. What are they singing? I've got to tumble down from my purchase (a ledge, it seems) to the sun-bitten dust of that parade ground.

But first, quick, before I get into this and can't get out, I hit the remote again and shoot hundreds of miles east, same time, same latitude, lower altitude—an island, once Persian, once Shirazi, now Arabian, off the Swahili coast. And just there, those two Bazungu, the boss, "loose-balanced" and swarthy, and his number two, parson-stiff and tall. My overactive imagination stalks them. It seems they're provisioning for a safari, and it's headed straight for Mutemura. Silent as smoke, I slink behind them as they squeeze through narrow stone alleys more like outdoor corridors, ever-winding hallways in shadow beneath stone tenements, rock coral godowns, public baths, private seraglios. Merchants squat in cubbyholes a meter or so above paving stones, huge stones and ancient, sunk deep, swept clean. The businessmen are Hendi, Sindi, Omani. Hadhramauti, Swahili, Persian. Water sellers bent beneath big-belled bottles call "*Maji, maji*" in Kiswahili, then "*Maya*" in Arabic. "*Yaala, yaala,*" boys shout. They run behind trotting donkeys, hitting their rumps with switches. "*Yaala, Yehudi. Nenda.*" ("Get going, Jew. Get going.") Far to the west, our Mutemura drills his warriors. Here in these alleys Richard Burton and John Haning Speke make ready to sail the twenty sweat-drenched miles from this overripe island to our great empty beaches.

It floats near the edge of the world, this Zanzibar, this place beyond which some maps yet warn, "There be dragons." Even now Britain deals with it as an outpost of already distant Bombay, from which colonial command the pair has sailed. As Britain sees the world, Zanzibar is a far outpost of already far Malabar, a hothouse take on Rome's "ultimate north," their Ultima Thule. For Britain, Zanzibar is icy distance become fire in a looking glass, prefiguring Alice's wonderland, a place graced, for all its watery distance, with villas, with skinny wazirs and pudgy pashas in tarbooshes hubbly-bubbling on water pipes, with lofty pilafs, with doves served crisp and fragrant, with groves of citrus and clove, with mosques of graceful line, with comely concubines. Night falls and the two Bazungu retire to gray coral chambers randomly scattered with ottomans and tribal rugs and languid men in burnooses. Burton, dark-eyed, drags on a hookah, languishing on rugs on cool stone, as flat-footed Speke cools his impatient heels, unable to make out a word of the strange and sibilant lingo his boss seems so to enjoy over Turkish coffee with Arab sheiks.

It stinks with slaving, this Shangri-La and its scrubbed alleys. What we see at dawn is the Shirazi place Isak Dinesen saw and must have had in mind when she described man as "a minutely set, ingenious machine for turning . . . the red wine of Shiraz into urine." What we see at dawn is what Dr. Livingstone said we'd see, humans in chains—families, children. They stand atop a rough-sawn platform framed out with mangrove poles, and "all who have grown up seem ashamed at being hawked about."

Narrative of an Expedition to the Zambezi, the good doctor titled the notes of his own approach to Africa by way of Zanzibar, and why didn't I read him more closely? "The teeth are examined, the cloth lifted to examine the lower limbs, and a stick thrown for a slave to bring, and thus exhibit his paces."

It stinks of urine, of disease. Just now, it's the beach we smell, a public privy. Hand-pegged dhows and pirogues and graceful feluccas float in the harbor, and there's more afloat—just there, a corpse—an ass—its black belly swollen. Just there, another—a human—its black belly swollen. A new stench. Rot? Or dengue fever?

They say dengue fever gives the gas of living humans the stink of a recrudescent corpse, a thick, sweet, warm stink that seems physically to knock you back and muscle you away—as it now does.

Go ahead. Look the locals in the eye. Trachoma makes one soul after another look back at you walleyed. Burton consorts with Arabs who know the place, and beyond that, he fancies himself an amateur physician. A learned man, this Burton. He uses words like *hydrocele* and *sarcocele*. He guesses that three-quarters of the people suffer from genital or urinary tract infections. He says syphilis is common. So is elephantiasis. Here and there, coolies scurry with sacks hanging from beneath loincloths. Burton tells Speke that the hanging sacks are swollen scrota. Speke feigns disinterest. Often the distended cods hang to the knees.

OUR WORLDS ON A COLLISION COURSE

Mutemura, Burton, Speke. All three are soldiers. More to the point, all three are foot soldiers. From what I've come to know of them, even if just in chronicles, I don't envy them, and most especially I don't look forward to the agony of following them. For all three, crossing great African distances afoot is the compelling test to which their lives are now inescapably indentured. (As a matter of fact, if I'm going to follow them, I better make myself a fellow traveler who can clearly do no more than gambol along in sheerest fancy—a water fly, say, or if you prefer, a water sprite.) In these days, two trade routes are opening through the wilderness of East Africa, clearing the way for the likes of Burton and Speke as they close on the likes of our Mutemura. One route starts at Cairo's Bab Zuweila, its southern gate to inner Africa. The other starts on the Indian Ocean. Plot their courses on a map, and they look destined to cross Remingtons where we live.

Out of Zanzibar, Afro-Arab, Afro-Shirazi merchants are pushing a Swahili corridor (or more properly, a loose network of corridors) west into the empty unknown. Out of Cairo, the Ottomans who rule Egypt are pushing a corridor that runs south up the Nile toward the river's unknown source, whose discovery, just now, is Speke's passion, and Burton's as well—though if you ask, Burton will deny it, the better to deny, should he fail, that he has failed. (The Nile? What Nile? I was just out documenting some new languages.)

However blasé Burton might like to appear on the topic of the Nile, Britain is not. Britain now is passionate about the Nile. One after another, the world's uncharted places are being charted—charted, fixed, and plotted—and whenever they are, the popular press chatters the more about the Nile's "coy fountains," still undiscovered and so named by the ancients for their hide-and-seek allure. Ancient Greeks and Egyptians alternately pined and searched for them. As the Greeks saw matters, Phaëton, in his fire-trailing chariot, so blistered the heights of heat-blistered Africa that he drove the source of "Egypt's mother" into hiding. Alexander dispatched a mission to find it; his men were confounded by cataracts, bogs, sickness, and warlike tribes. Caesar dispatched a mission; his men were likewise confounded. Caesar said he'd desert his troops for a chance to glimpse the Nile's birthplace. The Ptolemy who was a mathematician and geographer records that in the first century A.D. a Greek trader named Diogenes somehow reached hills he called, as they are yet called, the Mountains of the Moon, whence the fabled source.

Now the river is similarly confounding one Zungu expedition after another as it brings the wealth and industry of the industrializing West to bear on the same challenge, hacking upriver to the Nile's coyly hidden source. One after another, the river keeps throwing them back. Burton's plan is to sneak up on it from behind.

FOR ALL THE ROMANCE WITH WHICH THE VICTORIAN PRESS DRAPES OUR RIVER, THESE merchant corridors are fly-bitten realms, and merciless. They push through an Africa seized up with disease and knotted in thorn and thicket, haunts fit for neither girl nor woman—but where girls and women often hold fast at the center of life. And at times there's even ease enough for that amusement men so enjoy, and enjoy even more to claim that only women enjoy: gossip. Gossip of evil queens; of Great Lakes kings with great harems; of dangerous glances from behind veils; of the treacheries of courtly love; of dowager empresses; of fortunes in ivory; of slavers deep in dry forest who serve you Turkish coffee, Turkish delights, even (how in the world?) sherbet.

Salt spray whips Burton and Speke full in the face as they stand on the quarterdeck of the Sultan Majid's personal corvette, the eighteen-gun *Artémise*, Africa-bound.

Sad-eyed about Burton and Speke is a third Muzungu, a feeble man. He must be Hamerton. He's Britain's "agent" in Zanzibar, an Irish colonel fifteen years on station and fast approaching the end of the slow death that Zanzibar imposes on those who survive its swifter executions. Hamerton sails today to see the two men off. He's at once impressed and troubled by their brave gamble, that sneaking up on the Nile from behind is a better bet than following the river up its forbidding course. They worry him. He should be worried about himself. He shouldn't be here. He doesn't look good.

Burton couldn't look more fit, just the figure who infatuated Swinburne, who pictures him as a "wider soul," a man who rides "life's lists as a god might ride." Burton's brilliance dazzles. Certainly it dazzles his biographers. They read his vitriol as indulgently as Swinburne does. They say he despises everyone—Brits, Africans, Jews. Burton insists it's not all Jews he dislikes, just moneylenders.

Is it? Near the end of his life, this surpassing scholar, this authentic lover of scholarly discipline, will pen an anti-Semitic screed in which he will list one blood libel after another, with no documentation save their repetition over the ages by one anti-Semite after another. The same vitriol infuses Burton's disdain for Africans. He is nonetheless a man of surpassing scholarship.

The beach is in view. Where Zanzibar is soft and stinky, the beach is harsh, sea-breezed, broad; at low tide it's especially broad. It's ruled by an emptiness relieved here and there by vagrant palms and a few scattered huts of mud and wattle. The sun is unremitting. Thorny beach stretches endlessly in either direction, an eternity ruled by mangy lions scavenging dead fish. Beyond the beach, scrub stretches to the horizon, broken here and there by clumps of baobabs, big, thick, oafish, ancient, to all appearances growing upside down, with limbs that look like roots. A solitary coral mosque (thirteenth century, Burton is told) sits derelict. With no harbor about, they beach at high tide, which is to say they wash in with the crabs, the dead fish, and the driftwood. Slaves carry them ashore on palanquins. At low tide, slaves return to unload. Here and about, stuck in the sand, soar mangrove poles capped by human skulls.

Beneath these onlookers starts a process that carries on forever. Much bustling, much bickering, much waving of arms. Not enough labor for sale; they buy asses instead. At last, with platoons of porters, askaris, guides, and camp followers (wives, concubines, children, chickens), they set out upcountry to an oceanside village and slave entrepôt called Bagamoyo, which translated means "bury here your heart."

Try to forget its name. To the eye, at least, Bagamoyo is a grace note, flanked by flamboyants ablaze in oranges and reds against the thorny dun of the scrub. Here they bivouac, provision some more, and one day before dawn they begin walking west toward Africa's unmapped interior, in search of the headwaters of the Nile. It's June 16, 1857, on which date our Mutemura is living at their destination.

BURTON'S DARK EYES, THEY SAY, BETRAY A CERTAIN LANGUOR, A QUALITY BETRAYED EVEN more by my picture of our Mutemura at the other end of the trail. Mutemura's languor shows in his eyes and in his pace. In 1857 as in the year 2000, our highlands may be notably organized, but our people don't step as lively as other Africans. Patricians in particular walk and talk with reserved deliberation, and Mutemura is no exception. He is, as well, a laconic man.

He is taller even than Speke, and muscular. He wears a white, waist-cinched mushanana knotted over the left shoulder. It's made from cloth beaten from bark. Zanzibar is trading its African produce (among the plethora: cloves, ivory, beeswax, ambergris) for "merikani," cotton bolts from America. Some of it, traded from Shirazi Persian to Omani Arab to Swahili African to tribal African, may well have fetched up just the other day in the salt market near Mutemura's rugo, his sprawling homestead near the royal court. (It seems the West's trade goods are more skilled than the West's explorers at finding the world's hidden places. By all accounts, Western goods turn up centuries before the West in the flesh.) But Rwandese count merikani crude. Homespun—cloth beaten from bark—is better. Mutemura's wives most likely pass it up with the impassive glance characteristic of Batutsi, a manner a later day will call arrogant.

Their husband's gaze can have the same blank impassivity. It's deliberate, but it doesn't have the impudence of authentic arrogance. It's more a poker face, cultivated for a world in which it's useful to have a poker face. He's dark, and has a hairline goatee, carefully shaved. His hair is cropped close on the sides and high on top, with a distinct tonsured groove carved into it like an offhand notch on a Borsolino, or some such fashionable hat.

On this afternoon, he stands sweating in the dust of that parade ground. It's roughly one hundred meters square. Bees and finchlike little bee-eaters dart amid clouds of orange dust rising from the beat of three hundred pairs of feet. Next come little lavender-breasted rollers, then pygmy kingfishers. Mutemura carries no weapon save a six-foot staff resting horizontally behind his neck and across his shoulders. He's draped his wrists over either end of the staff, in a relaxed posture that pulls his shoulders back. All around him, men and boys, Hutu and Tutsi, drill in platoon formation to the steady, slow beat of drummers. Some platoons exercise purely military drills. Others dance: They dip low, as if stalking a leopard, spring, dip again, then leap; spring, dip, then leap, spears aloft. The beat is one that achieves its grandeur from synchrony—many drums, many feet as one—but here today there are only flashes of synchrony. Each platoon is drilling separately. The only synchrony is what they achieve as individual platoons, and what many achieve is not impressive. The total effect, with each platoon drilling to its own drummer, is one of cacophony, and with the sun and the dust and the heat, it is migraine-inducing.

None of which seems to bother Mutemura. He seems to be doing it deliberately, trying to throw the lads off, conditioning them to endure distracting stress. Are you barely able to follow your own drummer for all the dust and heat and glare and insistent drumming by the wrong drums? You must condition mind and body to focus on the lethal synchrony of your own distinct unit and its assigned mission.

IT'S INESCAPABLE. FOR MUTEMURA AND FOR ALL RWANDA, CACOPHONY IN THE AIR IS becoming as common as thorn in the bush. Clearly, this is a time of abrasive change—and this has nothing to do with the modern world, in the persons just now of Burton and Speke, closing relentlessly on their African fastness. They know nothing of the West. What it has to do with are wrenching changes that this restlessly evolving, isolated, and unknown world is inflicting upon itself. Our songs hint at a headlong, self-generating momentum, with growth generating yet more growth. In a land without coinage, let alone banks, growth means ever more cows due to ever more organized war-making, and ever more land (banks, really) for the cows, ever more intensive farming to feed the tenders of cattle, ever more central power; in short, ever more. To me, Mutemura's languor looks more apparent than real, a mask behind which he holds turmoil in check.

Explorers will soon write with some rapture about how complexly and thoroughly life is structured in these parts. This highly structured way of life, they'll insist, is the key feature distinguishing what they'll call the Great Lakes' "aristocratic tribes" from its "vassal tribes" and from all the outside tribes surrounding us. By the middle of the twentieth century, new generations of scholars, Zungu and Rwandese, Hutu and Tutsi, will begin to treat the notion gingerly—and eventually with outright hostility.

One problem is that neither aristo Batutsi nor vassal Bahutu meet the tests anthropology uses to decide if a group is a tribe. Anthropology tends to hold that tribes are "micronations," usually living at least somewhat apart from other tribes. Bahutu and Batutsi have always lived thoroughly mixed. Tribes most likely speak their own language, or at least their own argot. Batutsi and Bahutu speak the same language, even sharing regional argots; a Mututsi from my hill speaks more like a Muhutu from my hill than she does like a Mututsi from somewhere else. Also, when tribes divide into smaller units, anthropology reckons these subdivisions as tribal clans—which means that if you belong to a clan, you must also belong to the tribe of which the clan is a part. Most of Rwanda's clans include both Bahutu and Batutsi. This can only be, scholars will say, because these aren't tribal clans. They do not exist in a tribal world. Bahutu and Batutsi will be seen less as tribes, more as castes with hazy, often overstated genetic elements.

On top of this, there's no proper evidence that the nomadic ancestors of the Batutsi brought kingships to Rwanda, but there *is* some evidence that migrating Bantu ancestors of the Bahutu did, and that they brought, as well, the ability to smelt iron. For all the overlordship we Batutsi came to wield, the way of life is not Tutsi, it is Rwandese, the result of dynamic flux in the unrecorded past.

Dynamic in the past and especially dynamic in 1857. There is much tradition, but it's forever in flux, and now especially so. Rwanda's king has by now conquered cousin kingdoms in what will become southern Uganda, creating the Rwandese fiefdom of Ndorwa. He's forever mounting raids into Burundi and across the roaring Akagera into the kingdom of Karagwe on what Speke will soon name Lake Victoria.

For Hutu serfs, it has meant yet more sweat, as the ever more powerful court gains power to exact days of *ubuhake*—a form of unpaid labor in the manner of the feudal corvée. Why don't they revolt? They do, now and then. Why not more often? You might as well ask why the serfs of feudal France seldom revolt. The Great Lakes hardly mirror feudal France, but I see no evidence that revolt is any more on the minds of these Rwandese serfs than it was on the minds of so many other serfs in so many other feudal worlds.

In this Rwandese world, nobles protect peasants from invading armies, slavers, bandits. They assure order. Theft is rare; so are rape and local bloodshed. In return the peasant gives himself up as his own man, so that there is nothing left but his identity as a Rwandese peasant, and more specifically, as a Rwandese peasant of a certain hill and a certain clan. The king is Tutsi (which is as meaninglessly evident as saying the king is highborn) but you'd never call him the king of the Batutsi, not any more than French kings are kings of France's nobility. He's the king of all the Banyarwanda, the people of Rwanda, the serfs' king as much as the nobles' king. Meantime, the Muhutu's clan is not a serfs' clan but a clan of both serfs and nobles . . . and if his clan is not as close to the king as other clans, or if his hill is far away or newly absorbed, he and the Batutsi of his hill will chafe together. Every year the king increases his power, and every year the king wrings more sweat from the serf's wracked frame.

What's more, cruelty is a routine feature of courtly life. Beyond days of forced labor, Bahutu may suffer the court's direct, physical, cultivated sadism. But the way the king exacts blood is vastly different from the way he exacts sweat. Sweat is common to life in Rwanda, especially to Hutu life. Cruelty is common mostly to the court, and here Batutsi are as likely to suffer as Bahutu. Because the king is divine, he can indulge whatever whim or passing jealousy seizes him. Did he catch a glimpse of a favored Singa maid casting a glance at a handsome young warrior? Draw and quarter them both! Or how about drawing him and quartering her? In fact, the court is just that fond of wordplay.

Such cruelties in the arena of courtly love can cut close to Mutemura's bone. His clan, the Basinga, is one of the so-called uxorial clans. In 1857, there are roughly two dozen clans in Rwanda. Tradition, as it is evolving, demands that the men of the royal family restrict their brides to Tutsi girls from a limited few of these two dozen clans, primarily the Bega, the Bakono, and Mutemura's Basinga. These are what anthropology calls our "uxorials."

Gratuitous cruelty does extend beyond the court to invade the "thousand hills" upon which ordinary serfs and ordinary gentry live together, but it's enjoyed mostly by the king, for this is how kingship shows serf and gentry alike that the king—pivot of Rwanda's vaunted social order—is divine.

THIS YEAR, 1857, IN THE WORLD OF THE UPPER NILE AND ITS GREAT LAKES, WE ARE A highly regimented people becoming all the more regimented, with the result of great efficiency and great stress. All the while, along the corridor up the Nile from Cairo, and along the separate corridor west from Zanzibar, come human and material emissaries of the West and its close cousin, Islam, themselves in the midst of dynamic change, industrial change.

RUANDA ÜBER ALLES

As Mutemura's weeks of drill roll on, he begins to focus on a mission, drilling his lads for something coming. He's the *mugaba w'ingabo*, commander of the evolving unit. In modern armies, a commanding officer of his rank would have staff officers to dope out tactics and strategy under his direction. In the Great Lakes, command and control of the military are of a piece with command and control of civil society. To control civil society, the court appoints "chiefs of land" and separate "chiefs of people," which they can do because in the Great Lakes chiefs do not inherit their rank, the royal court appoints them, and the court is given to pitting chief against chief in a deep-bush variety of office politics. This tends to sap efficiency, but it inhibits the growth of fiefdoms, which mark kingships at their most primitive, least efficient. By this design, Mutemura has no staff officers to plan tactics and strategy. He has instead an autonomous partner, the *mugaba w'igitero*, the chief of planning.

Every day now, they eat together, paying scant attention to the food. Afterward, they sit together taking contemplative drags on long-stemmed pipes. They dispatch long-range reconnaissance patrols and spies posing as nomadic cowherds, traders, displaced serfs. Often, those entrusted with these dodgy missions are Bahutu. The two dispatch runners across the kingdom, ordering the assembly of subordinate units. Drums begin to talk; drumbeat drifts from hill to hill with the clouds and the bustards. They can't render their words in writing, but they can render them in drumbeat.

Strategy brews, strategy mulls. Just now it's got a roughness that might seem inconsequential, but could spell disaster in action. It has to mellow, and this is done according to rituals that seem even more distant from reality than the rituals of the parade ground. Depending on the style of the men and of the period, the rituals can either fail, tying up the military machine in empty ceremony, or they can succeed, giving ritually refined precision (the West would call it spit-and-polish precision) to the military machine.

First the court summons the *abiru,* the ritualists of the Tsobe clan, our father's clan, my clan. The *abiru* have had nothing so far to do with the mission. They are most likely distant from the cliques and intrigues of the court. They are not wealthy. They are not an uxorial clan. But they know the ways, the *code ésotérique,* and their art is to lay on the steadying hand of tradition. Some are good at their art, some aren't.

Above all, they consult the ancestors to see if victory is ahead, an oracular feat they can perform only because of dizzying feats of memory. Recorded within their heads are hundreds of years of history that they can reel off on notice. Who knows how much of their sessions with the oracle of lore is witch medicine and how much is simply paying heed to communal memory? If the odds look good (and they need only be odds), Mutemura and his troops will move out within days. If they don't, more intelligence will be gathered.

The *abiru* order a vestal fire. It can't die until the campaign is over. Mothers and sisters old enough will tend it. If they let it die, their men will die. The *abiru* then instruct the court to select a fine cow, to have its women lead her to the fire, and to have them calm her with gentle grooming. If the women lose their focus, if the cow becomes restless, or worse, backs off from the flame, so will their men.

At last word comes down, the outlook is good. Drums pick up in steady beat across the hills, ordering units from across the kingdom to set out and assemble at rendezvous points near the Urundi frontier. On the eve of the troop movement, Mutemura approaches the broomed courtyard before the king's chamber within the king's rugo. The king emerges and ties an *icyondi,* a band of monkey skin, around Mutemura's forehead, then an *ishyira,* a band of rabbit fur; within the knot he fixes the red plumes of a rare bird, the *intuku.* A throne crafted of rare, red-blooming mimosa, *umuko,* is brought out for the dowager queen, the king's mother. She's a large woman, with a bilious eye. Borne upon a palanquin to this throne, she ascends, sits, and assumes a rigidly erect posture, staring straight ahead with never a glance left or right, absolutely, rigidly still from evening until dawn, lest her troops lose their focus. Gnats may bite, lizards may cross her unmoving hands to snatch flying beetles from the night; the bile never leaves her eye.

As dawn breaks, the women and girls tending the vestal fire begin singing that perfect, sonorous harmony of Africa, and their words are as purblind an expression of national will as humans have ever composed. Of all the anthems of all the states in the modern state system, there is only one that asserts not just love for the fatherland, but supremacy of the fatherland over all others. In this, the simpleminded chauvinism of these women matches the simpleminded chauvinism of "*Deutschland über Alles*"—dropped by Germany after Hitler's defeat. "Our king," they sing, "is better than your king," and with that the drums pick up, the feet of the troops hit the earth, and the men move out, backlit by the orange light of dawn.

THE KING'S RUGO HAS MANY APARTMENTS, EACH A RONDAVEL OF ITS OWN, ARRANGED along lanes formed by bamboo walls. The king appears before a crowd. Approaching him, petitioners offer a half bow in the Japanese manner, averting their eyes and lightly clapping their hands. The royal family's well-being is an oracle, anticipating the well-being of the land and of the people of the land. Because his divinity embodies Rwanda in human form, the king can't be touched lest the land feel it.

The land is already feeling it. Many Rwandese have suffered. Mutemura, though, is not among them. Or is he? There is no question that he's the king's man. He's close to the court. He's fought in the king's wars and come out of each with greater honors, each time taking command of larger units. But these contests have pushed Tutsi mettle and Hutu muscle and pushed it again, often to near exhaustion of spirit. They are victors, but by now many of them are dead victors, and the living comrades of the dead are much like Prince Hal's forsaken band, sad, bone-weary, condemned, the prince's "happy" few, to whom he can only pledge blood brotherhood.

Now platoons from across the kingdom trot in file toward Urundi. Warthogs scatter at their progress, and so do I. Marabou storks with their squat black bodies, their downcast pelican beaks, flap aside, then look askance with a baleful eye and a brow seemingly arched. By separate, synchronous routes the formations file down past frontier principalities over which the kingdoms of Rwanda and Burundi are fighting. Mostly these statelets are downslope to their east; they collect water from the mountainous west, sending it down to the Akagera, Lake Victoria, Khartoum, Cairo,

Alexandria. Upslope to the west, over a six-thousand-foot spur and down precipitous flanks, the Rusizi River rushes, flowing south into Lake Tanganyika, the Lualaba, the Congo, the Atlantic. The country the troops come from is heavily peopled, intensely farmed, light with game. The higher country they now pass to the west is wilder, elephant meadows and timber harboring peahens, peacocks, the giant bongo, and the scaled-down elephant of the forest. These heights are wet. The lads splash cadence through downpours. Lightning strikes, thunder claps, as feet slap mud. In columns of twos, they ford feeder creeks of the Nile. The sun breaks. They ford another creek, joining otters and lily-trotters (thin little birds, trotting blissfully from lily pad to lily pad), lolling hippos, quarter-ton Nile crocs. The crocs surface from below the lilies, first just their viscous wet eyes, then their nostrils, blowing volleys of bubbles. The crocs rise slowly, but the bubbles do not. The bubbles, dozens upon dozens of them, rise swiftly, fizzing, fissile, fissiparous. Now and again a single white ibis will skip just in front of the warriors and take flight like a scrap of paper on the wind.

Sun bakes the hills dry. The men never stop to sleep, instead breaking cadence by half and going half-asleep afoot, like elephants napping through midday heat, their weight shifting drowsily from flank to flank, elephant troop and human troop, lullabied by the buzz of biting flies. Muscles twitch.

One by one the units snake together. The men are hot, exhausted. Their withers tighten in spasm as they file into the final rendezvous just north of the frontier. A single unit files in from the south, the last of the long-range reconnaissance patrols reporting in from Urundi. On the ground in front of Mutemura and his *mugaba w'igitero,* the patrol leader scratches intelligence into the dirt with a twig. The combined force now numbers some fifteen hundred men, about half the regiment Mutemura commands.

BAD BLOOD, BLOOD BROTHERS, AND SYZYGIES OF THE HYPNOID

Burton's expedition numbers about one hundred thirty, including a dozen askaris, half of them armed slaves, the other half Muslim Baluch from Persia's Afghan frontier with India, rugged men in baggy pantaloons. Each askari carries a German saber, a powder horn, and an ancient muzzle loader; every time the man fires, he must bring his weapon down, reload it with powder from the horn, ram a lead ball down the muzzle with a ramrod, remove the ramrod, and lift the weapon to his shoulder before he's ready to fire again. A couple of Goans serve Burton and Speke as cooks. Most of the rest of the safari are porters. The porters' trail boss is a Swahili, Said the son of Salim. They carry on their heads a command tent, pots, soap, bolts of fabric, Rumanian beads, copper wire, domestic fowl in bamboo cages, even what they call "gummy" (that is, rubber) air pillows for Burton and Speke. Burton and Speke carry a pocket sundial, a telescope, several chronometers, prismatic compasses, sextants.

There are two Swahili gun bearers, Sidi Bombay and Mwingi Mabruki, in charge of four rifles, a couple of shotguns, and three pistols. The Baluch, the Goans, Said, Sidi, and Mwingi; they all snap to and issue a brisk "Salaam, sahib" whenever Burton or Speke approach.

Cocks wake the safari every day at dawn. As the askaris genuflect toward Mecca, Burton and Speke breakfast and the porters fight with each other over who carries what. Inevitably, the smallest carry the heaviest loads. By five thirty, they are moving. By eleven at the latest the heat hits them like a mallet on the nose, halting them there and then. On a proper day they make about ten miles.

Burton's expedition is truly a foot safari, but the two white men—*ajami* to those in the party whose tongue is Arabic, Wazungu to those who speak Kiswahili—don't always walk. At the outset, Burton hangs back, reconnoiters his own safari at a coy distance, then, ever the swashbuckler, swoops down on them astride a camel bounding at full rack. Then the camel dies. Then the two *ajami* get sick and ride donkeys. Then the tsetse fly kills the donkeys. Then Africa begins trying to kill Burton and Speke.

Fever and dysentery lay them low. Ulcers plague Burton's mouth so badly he can barely speak or eat. Speke's eyes are infected. He's nearly blind. They lie on palanquins rigged of mangrove poles resting on the shoulders of porters. No one records how sick the porters are.

It's now a month into the trek: Back in Stone Town, and unknown to either Burton or Speke, Zanzibar has at last claimed Colonel Hamerton. Burton and Speke get sicker by the day. Burton looks with pity on Speke, seven years his junior. Back in England, Burton has a younger brother, Edward, who survived the Indian Mutiny only to come out of it on an express train to insanity, a state that now has him firmly and forever in her grip. Burton was close to Edward. Now Burton looks on Speke as a younger brother and a sick one in need.

I picture them, at night, in fevered sleep, and I get the feeling Burton can see me. I can't imagine any human possibly could, not without some great faith in spirits, and for all his fascination with spirit worlds, crusty Burton has always been above superstition. Even now, at his malarial worst, he resists fevered imaginings. Still, I can't shake the feeling that he can see me, and I'll tell you why:

It begins with Speke waking one night to find a beetle boring into his ear. He can do nothing to get it out and does much, as days drag by, that makes it worse. He digs madly. The bug bores through his eardrum, recrudesces, dies, decays, drives Speke half mad. Now the fevers have him.

One night he wakes to hear his mother—or is it Queen Victoria?—calling him home. Then Burton is seized by a sickness that will render him unable to walk unaided for nearly a year, and now the fevers have him as never before. In fevered dreams he sees himself waking to the spectacle of his men squirming in pain at the firebrand bites of inch-long ants. In another nightmare, he wakes to encounter men whose heads grow from their chests. In yet another, a slave babbles to him about a young girl one of the porters bought in Bagamoyo. Blistered feet brought the girl down, the dream-slave babbles, and rather than abandon her for others, the porter hacked off her head.

Burton and Speke improve some, then fall victim to a peculiar and particular sickness that the Africans warn them will soon yield a fever that will reveal troops of zombies, part flesh, part iron, and conjoined as one like Siamese twins. Do such nightmare fantasies sound rather like slaves chained in train? Nobody ever says so; they just say it takes these particular fevers to see these particular visions. Both men get the fevers; both see the zombies, part iron, part flesh. More than once, Burton dreams of catching his most trusted servant robbing him. More than once, trying to comfort Speke, a fevered Burton daydreams of a little brother who tells big brother Burton how much he despises him. Then at last Burton's fever breaks and he's lucid, at which point he can only sigh that all this has been the stuff of fevers, just fevered imaginings.

How long his relief lasts is hard to say, for soon he's visited by authentic horror. Soon he discovers that his dreams weren't dreams at all. His most trusted servants have in fact been robbing him, and at every turn. Cherished specimens, drugs, sextants, trade goods, gone; he's lost instruments to measure altitude, key to determining which waters feed which. Likewise vanished is the slave girl. The porter who bought her has indeed hacked off her head. And firebrand ants are indeed driving his men mad; at one point, Burton sees them carry off a dead rat. And Speke, with his inhibition disabled by fever, reveals that he does indeed despise Burton. Burton's worst dreams are reality. He must surely wonder whether we Africans are right after all, that dismissing the spirit world is the height of folly and imprudence.

Now, on the question of whether the heads of those men truly grow out of their chests, and whether he can see me . . .

THEY ARE EACH OF THEM ACHILLES

Mutemura's expedition isn't scientific. Booty is its aim. The tools he needs are heavier than sextants: a full complement of knives, war swords, heavy bows, heavy arrows, heavy assegais, and staves; there are only a few bearers.

A bearer could easily be a Mututsi. A warrior, less easily, could be a Muhutu. Their feet pad hard. Many of the lads are as large as Mutemura, and some of these large lads are Bahutu. Few are shorter than six feet three or so, and the weapons they carry are heavy, ironwood and iron. But what they bear above all is the heat, a wet compound through which they must somehow plow and that they must somehow breathe without drowning.

They push on relentlessly. Some know somewhat the Urundi hills they now see ahead, but even these men know them as they know the storied but barely glimpsed features of a strange place, and many of the lads don't know these hills at all. Lads who draw their security from the familiar shapes of their home hills plunge into the unknown, driven on by lockstep faith in leadership.

On a day that Burton's crew makes about five miles, Mutemura and his men make about fifty, uphill and armed. His men's feet pound a steady beat as they snake across the hills in columns that traverse the slope just above the bottoms of the hollows, a slight moving shadow along the shadow of a tree line. There is something of a ticking clock to the wordless beat of their progress, irrigating dry fields with slender trails of sweat and urine.

When they get where they're headed, the kraal of the king's prize cows, Mutemura must put together an ambush without getting caught. Wordlessly, platoons peel off in formation. It looks as formal as something you'd see on parade, but in their disciplined formality, drilled and drilled again, the design is pure function. The kraal and its royal guard located, they silently position widely spread rear guards, specially trained cattle herders, attack columns, a guide to signal attack at Mutemura's command, and then they attack. First the sudden zither hum of arrows everywhere, then the next step, which is neither shriek nor war cry but the deep doleful harmony of war song from a long flank to one side, as from another side another flank bears down in thunder, assegais fixed. They have the advantage of surprise. They have the disadvantage of fatigue.

Iron punctures torsos. Blades slice flesh. Here are men and boys slippery with warm, pumping blood, slicing each other as they might slice meat. The faces of the falling look stunned. Then swift retreat and attack from a third flank: few shrieks but many desperate gulps for air, life sucking out of bodies. Then a strike through the *rugo* in search of choice girls to join Rwandese families. Desperate, cowering girls, seized and carried off. A quick, orderly count to see if Mutemura has enough men left to seize the cattle and drive them back, then the stampede. Suddenly Urundian reserves rush in. The stage is set for heroic combat. The opposing regiments retreat a few meters, then stop.

From both sides, individual warriors step forward. One bears a staff. He's challenged by another with a staff. Then a challenger armed with a lance. Then another with a sword. Some live. Some don't. It's so alien to me, so unspeakable, I can barely sense the sweaty crunch of muscle against muscle, the disciplined parry at fate, the sudden panic of death at hand, the slice of blade through stringy meat. Theirs? Ours? His? Yours? Adrenaline may well hide the truth. At last Mutemura steps forward, and at last I get an inkling of why these Tutsi men take such scant delight in food. They are each of them Achilles. "Food and drink mean nothing to my heart, but blood does, and slaughter, and the groaning of men in the hard work."

Mutemura lives. Men dying are dispatched. Men with limbs sliced by blades or broken by staves are thrown over broad shoulders. Then the drive back; thieves, wounded and exhausted, driving a hundred head a hundred miles home, beating a trail now of blood, sweat, and Urundian cow manure. For Mutemura it is booty of which his clan will sing. The cows he drives are among the finest, the disconsolate girls a beautiful grace note. But the larger purpose is to strike a blow at the divinity, and thereby at the social order, of a rival king. Our king is better than your king.

A NOISY, INSOLENT RACE

Mutemura, Burton, and Speke were born within a decade of each other, between 1809 and 1819. By then Europe's trade in slaves had begun a slow wane, but the trade out of Zanzibar had not yet reached its awful pitch. By 1857 it still hasn't reached that pitch, but it's getting there. All through Tanganyika, civilization is savaging Africans, often reducing them to drunken fatalism. They demand *honga,* bribes, to let Burton's safari through. Mutemura's world is untouched by slavers. From its heights, it looks down all around on the wretched state of savaged tribes. It sees itself living above and apart from the imitations of humanity "down there." The Great Lakes realms seem only to fear each other, certainly not Arabs with a few muzzle loaders.

The Arabs do, however, impress Burton. What an exuberant Arabist he is! He seems forever ready to see the salutary in slavery, consistently mistaking brutalized tribes for brutish ones. For the Arabs, he is forever "Burton Pasha," or as it sounds to my ears, "Boorton basha."

It takes all of five months for the safari to reach Kazeh (today's Taborah) in the heart of Tanganyika. When at last he reaches this Arab settlement, Boorton Basha is struck by the contrast between the Arab and the African, between "the open-handed hospitality and hearty goodwill of this truly noble race, and the niggardness of the savage and selfish African." For all that, it is one of these Africans who pins him with the acuity of a practiced entomologist: "A good man," the African says, "but too angry."

Some argue that the Arab slave trade wasn't nearly what Zungu myth makes it out to be. They say you'll find far more offspring of slaves in America than in the Arab world. There's something to that, but here and now, in Tanganyika with Burton and Speke, the Arabs' trade in slaves looks substantial enough. The Africans they grab carry the ivory they plunder. Wherever I read, there's a tendency to picture Africa of this period—after all, it is the Africa of the great explorers—as "terra incognita," and it would be foolish to shrug off the yawn of its forbidding expanses. It would be rank folly to shrug them off in our day, for all the maps and gimmicks we like to think have tamed these distances. (The driver of a trans-Africa petrol tanker: "Watch your engine blow up with your maps, start walking, run out of water, and hope you don't go ecstatic when you find an old corroded battery, a broken Fanta bottle, an empty sardine tin. The world is *not* just over the next hill.") Still, I can't let myself get carried away with the notion that I'm following these men into the utter unknown. Well before these two Bazungu hack their way into East Africa's interior, Arab merchants have already cast a loose skein of commerce from the Swahili coast west and from Cairo south. However tentatively, these two worlds of Arab commerce send out slender side trails, a fragile few of which meet at a place called Gondokoro near Lake Albert, the most northerly of our Great Lakes. At distant Gondokoro, Cairo links up with Zanzibar.

Much will be made in coming years of Speke, on a second expedition out of Zanzibar, reaching Gondokoro, whence the way is known, if not clear, down to Cairo. But even now in 1857, Arab and Swahili merchants are dispatching runners and even traders back and forth between the two Muslim realms. In the southern Sudan and what is now northern Uganda, there are fifteen thousand Sudanese gunmen in the slave and ivory business. Greek, Armenian, Turkish, even Maltese traders show up here, at times ahead of putative explorers. At one point, a Greek trader coming up from the south will surprise an Egyptian garrison surrounded on Lake Albert by hostile tribes; he'd traveled right through them—and from the south.

The growth of these two Islamic realms coincides almost exactly—and altogether coincidentally—with the growth of the kingdom of Rwanda inside the isolated world of the Great Lakes. But the kingdom of Rwanda's growth is the growth of a small and tightly run state, so small and so tightly run that scarcely a thing happens without the court learning of it—and fast. Its growth is not simply coincidental with Arab growth in East Africa, but of a different order altogether. The kingdom is about the size of Vermont. It's of major moment when it defeats and absorbs a sister kingdom the size of a county in New Hampshire. By contrast, the spread of the Arab across the swath from Cairo to Zanzibar means a holocaust of slave raids, along with outposts here and there of Arab settlement, lonely Islamic atolls in a vasty sea. It is precisely because his control of the Upper Nile is so loose that the Ottoman khedive in Cairo will soon ask a hero of the Royal Engineers, Colonel Charles George Gordon, to take over as governor-general of the Anglo-Egyptian Sudan's southernmost *pashalik,* whose southernmost outpost is on Lake Albert.

Be they ever so loosely cast, these lonely trading posts have nonetheless been established, and they keep in touch. As Burton's safari pulls out of Kazeh headed our way, the guide holds aloft not the Union Jack but the red ensign of the Sultan of Zanzibar, under whose *firman* they travel.

Beyond their settlement here at Kazeh, the Arabs have cobbled posts at Ujiji on Lake Tanganyika and at Mwanza on the southern shore of Lake Nyanza, soon to be known as Lake Victoria. They've beaten safari tracks between these settlements, and keep agents in frontier realms of the Great Lakes—particularly in the kingdom of Karagwe next door to Rwanda. A village might have only ten Arab families. Kazeh at this moment has only twenty-five. They are nonetheless a nexus for a community on the Arab and Islamic model. There are shops—soon to be Indian dukas—along a lane. Each of the Arabs has his own *tembeh,* an ample enough house of sun-bleached mud with quarters for servants, family members, and cooking, all about an enclosed courtyard. They have long since brought in seed stock for vegetables, fruit, and rice that they now grow. Each town has a bazaar where you can buy basics—at prices greatly inflated from Zanzibar's.

Islam is a portable culture. They tell me that in the wastes of our Africa, one often comes upon a simple circle of stones—mosques for the wanderer. These Arab towns, which exist largely for a brutal traffic in slaves, always extend to the traveler, especially the traveler in extremis, the succor the Koran commands. Each town has a simple mosque, and even a small madrasa where the young student, the *talib*—plural, the *taliban,* a word to blaze in Afghan hills of the twenty-first century—is made literate.

In a few years, David Livingstone will set out from Zanzibar on his own search for the Nile, and drop out of sight, seemingly swallowed up by Africa. Knowing where he is, the Arabs will refuse to carry his letters back to Zanzibar, for they know what his letters report of their slaving business, yet they will keep him alive, nurse him, feed him, when all they'd have to do is ignore him and he'd die.

ON FEBRUARY 13, 1858, SLUGGISH WITH THIRST, BURTON'S EXHAUSTED SAFARI GLIMPSES what he at last glimpses himself: a sparkle somewhere out amid the seven-foot papyrus through which his porters hack with pangas. It's Lake

Louise's mother on the back porch of the family home, about 1967. The family had been displaced by the 1959 pogrom.

Louise's brother Karangwa with her sister Anne-Marie's son Safari, her mother *(center)* with Anne-Marie's second son, Shara; and Karangwa's wife, Donatilla, with Lando's daughter, Malaika, at Anne-Marie's house in 1979. All were victims of the 1994 genocide.

AUTRES RENSEIGNEMENTS

1. Police d'assurance No ....
2. Permis de conduire No ....
3. Caisse Sociale No ....
4. Immatriculation ....
5. Groupe sanguin ....

Uzayikoresha binyuranyije n'itegeko azahanwa.
L'usage non autorisé sera puni par la loi.

Itanzwe kuwa ....
Etabli le

Amazina, umukono wa Burgumestri na kashe
Nom, signature du Bourgmestre et cachet

BAIIWFITE Thecele

KARITA YIBIRANGA UMUNTU
CARTE D'IDENTITE

No ..21-975-

Republika y'u Rwanda
République Rwandaise
Ministeri y'Ubutegetsi bw'Igihugu
Ministère de l'Intérieur

Prefegitura KIGALI No A 258752
Préfecture
Komini ya ....Rutongo.......
Commune de
Segiteri ....Jabana.........
Secteur
Amazina ..Mushikiwabo...
Noms et prénoms
Igitsina ...F.
Sexe
Se ...Bitsindinkumi.......
Père
Nyina ..Nyiratulira.......
Mère

Mod. 3

Ubwoko (Hutu, Tutsi, Twa, Naturalisé)
Ethnie
Aho yavukiye ..Jabana....
Lieu de Naissance
Italiki yavutseho ....1961......
Date de Naissance
Umwuga ....Etudiante.......
Profession
Aho atuye ..Jabana.........
Lieu de domicile
Amazina y'uwo bashakanye
Noms du Conjoint ....
No C.I. ...21-975
Umukono cyangwa igikumwe cya nyirayo
Signature ou l'empreinte du titulaire

Amazina y'abana n'igihe bavukiye
Noms, prénoms et date de naissance des enfants.

Amazina Noms et Prénoms	Yavutse kuwa Né le	Igitsina Sexe
1.		
2.		
3.		
4.		
5.		
6.		
7.		
8.		
9.		
10.		
11.		
12.		

Louise's Rwanda identity card, classifying her as Tutsi.

Anne-Marie, her brothers Karangwa *(left)* and Gaetan, in front of the family house in the late sixties.

Newlywed Anne-Marie at her house before a dinner party, 1978.

Anne-Marie's children Shara *(left),* Safari, and Nana, on their baptism day, September 1984.

Louise with her niece Malaika and nephew Patrick at their home in 1982.

Louise's mother, with her brother Mpunga and her friend Adele Zitoni, about 1982.

Anne-Marie with her four children and brother Lando's two children at her home in 1987. Of the children, only her daughter Nana *(back row at right)* is alive today.

Lando and his daughter, Malaika, in Mombasa, Kenya, 1991.

A Mututsi with a traditional
unisex haircut, about 1925.
SMITHSONIAN INSTITUTION

King Musinga *(right)*
and Queen Kankazi.
SMITHSONIAN INSTITUTION

An ordinary Mututsi; most were
not aristocrats. SMITHSONIAN INSTITUTION

Left: Richard Burton's distaste for Africans was exceeded only by distaste for his partner, John Speke, who outdid Burton's racial humbug with his own theory of the conquest of inferior by superior races, developed in his *Journal of the Discovery of the Source of the Nile.* VANITY FAIR PRINT COMPANY **Right:** William Gladstone labored to keep Britain out of East Africa. VANITY FAIR PRINT COMPANY

Left: Ottoman Egypt's Ismail Pasha labored to drag it in and, with its help, pushed the modern world up the Nile. VANITY FAIR PRINT COMPANY **Right:** Ismail's agent, General Charles Gordon, wanted to trade his command at Khartoum for Mombasa, the better to reach the Great Lakes. VANITY FAIR PRINT COMPANY

Left: Humbug-riddled Henry Morton Stanley despised Africans; he tried and failed to march on Rwanda. VANITY FAIR PRINT COMPANY **Middle:** Rider Haggard spun humbug into an adventure novel about a superior race of Great Lakes giants, the bestselling *King Solomon's Mines.* VANITY FAIR PRINT COMPANY **Right:** Film found amid the wreckage of Juvenal Habyarimana's palace. ÉDITIONS KARTHALA AND REPORTERS WITHOUT BORDERS; CINÉ PHOTO, KIGALI

Louise standing in front
of Hotel Chez Lando
bungalows after
the genocide, 1995.

Anne-Marie in 1996 in her office at Hotel Chez Lando, which she has managed since the genocide.

Louise and Anne-Marie in Rwanda at a family dinner announcing Louise's wedding, 1999.

Louise with her husband, Norman, at a friend's house, 1999.

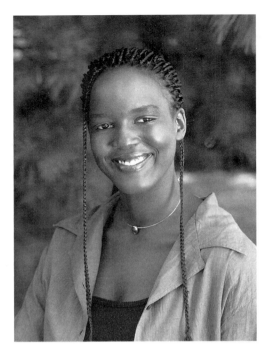

Anne-Marie's daughter, Nana,
in her last year at high school,
six years after the genocide.

© 1999 STONE PHOTOGRAPHY

Louise and Anne-Marie dressed in traditional Rwandese costume, 2001.

Tanganyika, and it's a sight, luminous blue beneath the green hills of Africa and an enormous white sky. He can have no idea that it's the longest fresh-water lake in the world and, aside from Siberia's Baikal, the deepest. He is nonetheless virtually certain that it is the source of the Nile. So intent is he on the Nile that it never occurs to him that it might be, as indeed it is, the greatest lake feeding Africa's other great river, the Congo. Soon he comes on a little Arab port, the port of Ujiji, and straightaway sets about trying to rent pirogues to paddle them north.

He nags one Arab after another to help him make his way up to where, surely, this lake flows north into the Nile. One reason the years have made Burton so fond of the Arab may be that the Arab is so much more patient than the Muzungu, and especially Burton. Just now, Burton is painfully im-patient, so much so, and so reckless is his proposal, that he's scaring the lo-cals. No polite Islamic patience today; whenever this too-intent *ajami* broaches the subject to either Arab or African, the man literally bolts.

The reason is not simply Burton's intensity. At last, the forbidden zone is at hand. For the men of Ujiji, the forbidden zone is quite literally that. They tell him that sooner than paddle north toward this zone, they will cross the lake to country that on Burton's German Mombas Mission Map appears as *Menschenfresser*—cannibal—country. "*Haram, ya Boorton basha,*" they say. "*Forbidden. Haram, haram.*"

Urundi, the Arabs warn him, is so savage, so hostile, that the people of that benighted highland have no need or want for the stuff of civilization, and even less need or want for traders who bring civilization. They simply rope whatever intruder they find in their realm, and bring him to their sul-tan, who executes the man for courtly entertainment. But Burton, to his credit, will not be denied, certain that their horror is but part of the bar-gaining game. He's only partly right. Their palms sufficiently greased, they paddle him north, but with terror that seems ready to turn their black skins white—and yes, as they paddle north, purple clouds do roll out from over the darkening mountains before them. Amid lightning and thunder, they paddle north in frigid rain.

For months Burton has been dismayed at the scabrous inhospitality of the countryside, plagued as it is not just by disease but by heat, thorn, flies, scarce food, scarcer decent food, and Africans who to his angry eye are a lar-cenous, indolent, insolent, and ugly lot. At Ujiji, the prices appalled him. And now they seem headed for something even worse.

At last the rains let up and they drag ashore at a frontier village near this forbidden place called Urundi. The village is in a no-man's-land at the foot of soaring peaks. Like so many of the world's frontier districts, it's lawless and filthy. Stinking human feces cover the spit where their canoes must beach. This and other hamlets they visit are full of nasty types demanding *hongo,* and by now both Burton and Speke are so sick and testy that Burton is able to record—but altogether unable to appreciate—that tomatoes, eggplant, plantains, beans, palm oil, fish (both fresh and cured), fine basketware, and even milk are abundant and cheap, much cheaper than in Ujiji. Since they left Zanzibar, prices have climbed consistently the farther they got from civilization, a straightforward matter of supply running scarce. Meantime, variety and quality have been plunging, a straightforward matter of traveling through country whose farmers grow for themselves and their chief and that's it. Now just the opposite is happening. Quality is improving; variety is increasing; prices are dropping.

Instead of mulling this odd circumstance, Burton's account in *The Lake Regions of Central Africa* simply indulges yet another rant about scabrous, ugly Africans:

> The people of this country are a noisy insolent race, addicted, like all their lakist brethren, to drunkenness, and when drunk, quarrelsome and violent.

Then he drops these throwaway lines:

> At Wafanya, however, they are kept in order by Kanoni, their Mutware or minor chief subject to 'Mwezi', the mwami or sultan of Urundi. The old man appeared . . . followed by a guard of forty or fifty stalwart young warriors.

Still later there's another glancing reference to stalwarts, Burton's last:

> I received a visit from the three stalwart sons of the Sultan Maruta: they were the noblest type of negroid seen near the lake, with symmetrical heads, regular features, and pleasing countenances; their well-made limbs and athletic frames of a shiny jet black, were displayed to advantage by their loose aprons. . . .

Does Burton come ashore in Burundi proper? Certainly he never steps over the crest of the spur that separates the Congo basin from the Nile basin. Regardless, he and Speke have come within fifty or so miles of their grail, the actual headwaters of the Nile. Upon hearing that the River Rusizi at the far north end of Lake Tanganyika flows south into the lake, not north toward the Nile, they turn back for Ujiji. Burton's jaw is so ulcerated he can't chew. He will later recall, "Speke was deaf and almost blind, I was paralytic, and we were both helpless."

Generations of Bazungu will read of this magnificent miss with a sigh. Batutsi aren't given to sighs; I must concede all the same that Burton and Speke do turn back within a heartbeat of their goal, oblivious that just east of the brief Rusizi, in the countryside through which our Mutemura is mounting his raids, the watershed dips north and east, feeding the mighty Akagera—or as Bazungu will soon call it, the Alexandra Nile. It flows into Victoria.

On a second expedition, Speke will reach two Great Lakes kingdoms in modern Uganda, and he will approach them with a view of Africans somewhat less harsh than the one Burton now nourishes. But Speke is simply not equipped for such a human assignment. He will be able to convey little more than the sensational cruelty of the places. Despite his bias, Burton *is* equipped, both emotionally and intellectually. Given the chance, he might see beyond cruelty and begin to decipher mysteries. But a true encounter will never happen.

Amid all this misery—misery that grips not just the discarded slave dying by the track but the Arab slaver as well—only the highland kingdoms remain largely disease-free. Neither syphilis nor rinderpest, nor even much malaria is here—and neither are the Arabs. Arabs surround these kingdoms, but they can't get in. It's not for nothing that they call it the forbidden zone.

Largely because of this lack of Arabs, a reason neither Burton nor Speke will ever quite appreciate, neither of them will ever get where they want to go. In the ultimate headwaters of the Nile, there are no Arab slavers to feed, supply, direct, and nurse them.

THE CELEBRITY-HUNGRY PAIR DO GET PAINFULLY CLOSE TO THE RWANDESE HIGHLANDS whose giants they make myth, but they never quite get there, and when on the way back Burton falls ill, Speke falls out, taking a small party on a side trip north in search of Arab reports of a large lake—which lo, he finds. An immense lake, it is, whose coconut-palmed shores relieve the thorn and stubble of the savannah, a lake "flecked with wings of sails"—lateen sails, the storied sails of Araby, billowing from feluccas. For Speke, it's love at first glimpse. Certain without much evidence that this is the source, he returns to camp, afraid even to raise the subject with Burton. He nonetheless does, and their partnership never recovers.

Burton is appalled at how slim Speke's evidence is, and even more, at the slimness of his scientific acumen. They bicker all the way back to Zanzibar and then Aden, where Burton, a grand dallier, chooses to dally. At last Speke agrees to publish nothing until Burton arrives in England, then decamps straightaway aboard the HMS *Furious* for London, where he delivers a paper before the Royal Geographical Society declaring his lake the source of the Nile. Burton is livid. He doesn't believe that Victoria (as Speke has proudly dubbed the waters) is the source. From his own more informed researches he has his own ideas about that, and he has both the erudition and the persuasive power to make a fool of Speke.

In the fullness of time, Burton will be proved wrong. Where he believes the Nile to spring, it does not. Where Speke claims that Victoria cascades into the Nile, it does indeed.

TWO CONFIDENCE MEN AND A CONFIDENT MAN

Con men get a bad press. Just ask one. He has you see him from the opposite angle of approach, from which vantage he's a prince. Which he is, of sorts. True princes, after all, must also deal in the currency of confidence.

Clearly, Burton, Speke, and our Mutemura all carve their names large. After Speke dies, he goes to Bujumbura and becomes a statue. Burton plants the criminally provocative idea of a master race amid the Great Lakes. Mutemura could be exhibit A to prove the malignant point. Let us now praise famous men.

BOORTON BASHA. Look him over once or twice. Imagine he's prime flesh for sale atop a rough-sawn platform of mangrove poles. Throw a stick for him to catch. Read his swagger. You've already read his words in *Lake Regions,* dividing us into "a noisy, insolent race" on the one hand, and on the other, those who keep the insolent "in order," sultans flanked by "stalwart young warriors." Not until much later in the book does he elaborate, but by then it's all speculation spun from hearsay and laced with humbug about how such lads represent a superior race. Here, where his text offers first-hand observation, he describes his exhibits in such an offhand manner you'd think he was just reminding us of something with which we are already familiar.

What I hear is a fashion-conscious man of that Darwinian day fashionably offering pseudo-science spun from Darwin's careful observations. But Burton always nursed a reputation as a man with little more than contempt for fashion. Do I hear things wrong?

In his first adventure, Burton disguised himself as an Afghan dervish to penetrate the forbidden cities of Mecca and Medina. It was a sensation in the British press, and he handled celebrity with true brio. Instead of going home to fancy-dress balls, he disguised himself as an Arab merchant to penetrate a Muslim realm even more fraught, the forbidden city of Harar in Somaliland. This wasn't simply disdain for publicity; it was a show of disdain that added yet more dash to his public personality. Burton, it turns out, is as much a master of éclat as he is of arcane languages. But he's so flamboyantly and "forever most divinely" in the wrong that it's hard not to suspect he's a showboat.

Leaving Zanzibar for Africa's interior, he advertises his wrong belief that getting malaria early on will "salt" him for later bouts. He wrongly doses himself with something called Warburg's Drops, doubtless a pleasant concoction of quinine, sloes, and opium. At Ujiji, he wrongly identifies Lake Tanganyika as the Nile's source. Back in Kazeh, he wrongly ignores Arab talk of an inland sea to the north, then wrongly conveys this news to sneaky Speke, who's been sitting in Kazeh, unable to grasp Arabic and looking to make a little mischief. Burton wrongly allows Speke to forge north—then wrongly decides not to lead the side trip, the result of which is Speke's discovery of Lake Victoria. Burton uses all the right reasons to dispute, wrongly, that Victoria might be a source of the Nile. In Aden, he wrongly accepts Speke's word that he won't publish his claim until they're both back in England. Back in England, he wrongly convinces himself he was hearing things wrong when he was told that the Rusizi flows into, not out of, Lake Tanganyika, for this contradicts his obstinately wrong conviction that Lake Tanganyika is the source of the Nile.

It wasn't Africa that did this to Burton. As a young man, he left Oxford because he found it too regimented. And where does he go to escape Oxford's regimentation? A regiment in Her Majesty's Indian Army.

When Speke rushes back to London to claim he's discovered the Nile's source, then grandly accepts the world's honors, Burton is deeply offended. He slinks offstage, there to design his own personal coat of arms. But before I tell you about it, let me tell you how I picture him wearing it. First, I picture water-fly me at large in a West End men's club, and there by a French window, I spy this magnificent iconoclast advertising his worth with an icon, that crest, on the left breast of a jaunty blazer. He fits right in.

Burton's device reads "Honour, not Honours." Clever turn of phrase. After all, every graduating class, no matter how uniformly dull, must have its best of a dull lot collecting class honors. But honor, that singular honor that sees a light and pursues it regardless of the crowd—this quality is not dished out so routinely. Still, "Honour, not Honours," there's something to it of a man displaying a prickly weakness for daws to peck at.

THE SHOOTIST. Speke is a loner who wants anxiously to belong, to be one of the chaps, a sportsman. Before joining the army, he strove mightily to become a crack shot, and did, but a sportsman he never becomes. After sticking it to Burton, his boss and intellectual better, he sticks it to his number two, James Grant, the second time around. After months of misery, Grant and Speke at last approach their grail, the north end of Lake Victoria, where they've been told (by the Arab network, of course) that the lake spills into a raging river that cascades north. Witnessing this will confirm that Victoria in fact feeds the Nile. Then, at the last minute, with nothing but an easy march ahead, Speke cooks up some reason for Grant to hang back. Grant complies; he doesn't share the discovery of the Albert Nile.

On his return from this second expedition, Speke gets his. He tells tales of bizarre goings-on in the kingdoms of the Great Lakes, and they inspire London wags to flights of ridicule. What was Speke up to, fooling around in the harem of the king of Buganda when he should have been looking for the Nile? (The king had kept him a captive curiosity for five months—five months as a prig hopelessly at a loss in a harem.) Worse, geographers exploit his scant scientific acumen to question his findings. Burton points out that rivers don't rise in lakes, they rise in highlands. Forget that Burton himself had long touted Lake Tanganyika as the source of the Nile; he has a point: Rivers do rise in highlands, not in lakes. In September 1864, the Royal Geographical Society schedules a debate between the two in Bath, near the Speke country seat. Here Speke grew up, an only child intent on pleasing mater and pater. To this house, still presided over by his parents, he's long dreamed of coming home a hero, a son of the West Country returning triumphant. Instead, he comes home to die, and alone, in what will officially be ruled a shooting accident. Risen suddenly to fame and just as suddenly tarred with infamy, Speke goes off hunting grouse and never comes back. Somehow a charge from his own gun kills the man. There's no debate with Burton.

But he does have those statues, and credit for finding the Nile's source, and his name on a lovely weaver, a bird seen everywhere in East Africa, and there's something immensely important he does do. After Burton breaks racial wind in *Lake Regions,* Speke outdoes him in licentious scholarship. He punches up his *Journal of the Discovery of the Source of the Nile* with a "theory of conquest of inferior by superior races." He can't just solicit celebrity. A desperate man, he must grasp, and the hand with which he does so is the race hand. His book, like Burton's, is a bestseller.

THE RWANDESE WAY OF CELEBRITY. In the Rwanda of this day, it isn't easy to be your own man. This is a regimented place. As in Japan, the thumb that sticks up is the thumb that gets smashed down. But combat command demands initiative, something that makes winning commanders hard to come by. Neither military culture nor Rwandese culture cultivates initiative. Both nonetheless need it in the few, and I can only guess that to the extent he seizes the initiative, Mutemura becomes his own man and is rewarded for it—and inasmuch as he easily enjoys public tribute, he becomes that much less his own man. He's been induced to enjoy approval. For him, honors and honor are all one. Burton's device would mean nothing to him.

Burton dies childless. Speke dies unmarried and childless. Mutemura dies a patriarch. Who knows how many daughters he has? Twelve sons survive infancy. His honors and his progeny oblige Rwandese history, that is, Rwandese song, to count him the founder of a subclan of the Basinga, the Batemura, whose glory will be to serve the royal family with blind faith, and with blind discipline to accept its torment.

One of Mutemura's sons will become a military figure—and cattle thief—in his own right. One of his grandsons will defend his king against regicides—then suffer death by torment at the hands of regicides. Another grandson will be the first man the Belgians hang after they take Rwanda. Among his great-grandsons will be a great black hunter who dies in prison, and a skinflint philanthropist who finds in his confused heart the ability to support both the Belgians and Patrice Lumumba. And among his great-great-grandchildren will be a hard-drinking bishop who mocks not just the monarchy but the chiefs (right up to the day of his murky death), and Bibiane, wife of Bitsindinkumi, Mama.

LOOK THEM OVER: BURTON, SPEKE, AND ALL THE OTHER HIGH-STRUNG BAZUNGU COME to examine our cases, look *us* over, check our limbs, explore us. To an African reading their accounts, they look like nothing so much as white witch doctors conjuring their own spirit world in the deadly precincts of a river that transfixes them. When first I heard of them, at school in Africa, they were simply names recited in class. I had no sense of them as personalities of their Victorian day, and no sense at all of the steam bath of celebrity in which they alternately swooned and squirmed. But look closer and it becomes clear: They're the movie stars of their day, and Burton and Speke are hardly alone.

Squads of these Nile-crazy personalities are about. The first, Sir James Bruce, almost defines the pathology and makes me wonder: Did Zunguland's celebrity game begin with this shy man? By all accounts, he was bright and magnificently brave. As Samuel Johnson was discovering coffeehouse fame in London, Bruce was discovering the source of the Blue Nile in Abyssinia. Blissfully unaware of what awaited him, he returned to a Britain eager for his tales. Alas, the tales he told—all since verified—were so bizarre that they provided nice targets for London wags. So stung was Bruce by the witty ridicule of Dr. Johnson and his coffeehouse crowd that he shrank home to Scotland (terrain famously reviled by Johnson), there to fret for sixteen years before finally publishing his discoveries.

Gordon of the Nile aims above all for our Great Lakes. Like Burton, he never makes it. Lytton Strachey pictures him in *Eminent Victorians* as vastly more taken with the world than with himself—and the price he pays for this power to escape himself is bouts of black despair.

On the same day that Britain learns that Dr. Livingstone has died in Africa, of Africa, for Africa, Gordon accepts a commission from the Khedive Ismail to push Egyptian influence beyond Khartoum to the farthest reaches of the Upper Nile—which means us.

· 18 ·

MUGANZA OF THE PRINCE'S OWN INZIRABWOBA

*The Khedive and His White Witch Doctors Cast Long
Eyes Up the Nile; 1850–1889*

One of Mutemura's twelve sons was Mama's great-grandfather Muganza.
Muganza was a fat man. Exceptionally fat. Nobody knows just how fat because you go back those few generations in Rwanda, and forget about
scales, people don't have numbers. They're innumerate. When they go to
bed at night, they can't count sheep.

How does an illiterate, innumerate world engineer rondavels with ceilings thirty feet high? How does one generation tell the next, this is how
high you can raise the roof beams before they collapse? How does an innumerate brigadier divide and position his brigade? How does he form up a
battalion? How can a battalion consist of five hundred or so men if the
number five hundred doesn't exist? How do elegists apply form? How do
king's ministers plan? How does the chief of the breweries brew to standard? The language has a word for a standard measure; what makes the
measure standard? A bean? "Right, then," you say at the market. "Let me
have five hundred beans' worth of eggplant."

Of course, this is reducing the problem to the absurd. We know how
this sort of encounter most likely works out, and it hints at how more
complex ones might work out: You show the lady a sack of something like
a hundred fava beans and point to her eggplants. She has no numbers
with which to count; nonetheless you can imagine her looking at your
beans and making up her mind whether there's enough there to get you a
small eggplant.

Forget the lack of coinage; these markets often teem with commerce.
Eggplant mongers, banana mongers, carrot, onion, cassava mongers come
with too much of this or that to sell and find themselves bartering
wholesale to mongers who have sold out and need something to do for the

rest of the morning—and that just begins to describe how these floating, once-a-fortnight markets can bustle with deals. Inevitably, they cultivate middlemen (and in Rwanda they can as easily be middlewomen) who, through experience and a certain innate (if indefinite) numeracy, become skilled at arbitrage. These canny ladies buy from mongers whose fear and lack of numeracy are inducing them to sell cheaply. They sell to mongers whose fear and lack of numeracy are inducing them to buy dear. But that still leaves a lot of questions.

Would that Muganza could answer them. By all accounts, these years in the middle of the nineteenth century find him an exacting man. It's an aspect of the austere Tutsi personality: Everything ordered just so, total organization, the sort of personality that drives you mad and saves your backside when you least expect jeopardy. Muganza does drive people mad.

Caught in a storm one day, he runs into a hut belonging to one of his field hands; I come flitting in behind him, thoroughly enjoying the rain. Now it so happens that this field hand has a billy goat, and he's been having a problem with the animal. Billy has a cold, he's been sneezing all morning, and the field hand has him inside with his family to keep warm. He's sneezing when Muganza rushes in. Sure enough, the goat sneezes all over Muganza, and the big man is so disgusted (goat sniffle everywhere!) that he bans goats forever from his rugo. He forbids his family ever to eat goat. Goat becomes taboo for the Batemura. (To the day she dies, Mama won't go near goat. At least not as far as she knows. "Hmm, what's the meat?" she wonders as she picks at a suspiciously gracile bone in an uncertain stirabout at her sixth grandchild's first communion, and her daughter Anne-Marie stares innocently upward.) Muganza's decree may not get him even with the goat, but he does win battles.

I've known from the year dot that he's fat, and that he wins battles, and that he hates goats, because one thing Rwanda is not bereft of is stories. A couple days ago in the king's rugo, I heard court ritualists rattling off twenty-one generations of kings, along with lengthy accounts of each of their reigns. They just can't count to twenty-one.

In a few years, Muganza may gain the sad weight of industrial-age people who get so fat they can't rise, maybe four hundred pounds, maybe five hundred. But even then he'll never be so fat he can't rise, and rise with a vengeance, and if in fact he gets as heavy as five hundred pounds, it's because his frame is huge enough to carry it. Muganza is a big man.

You might well imagine that if an African of this period, in Africa's deep interior, is fat at all, he couldn't be so fat he'd be immobile, that lard to the point of immobility is a luxury for only the richest, most technologically accommodating societies. For African males, this is doubtless true—and for virtually all females. But because the princes and barons of interlacustrine

Africa downright adore fat women, and because sweat and organization have made their worlds rich, they are able to support harems of young women so fat they can't rise. Rwanda is called the land of the lance and the cow, and if the lance represents the courage of Rwandese males, the cow represents the beauty of our women.

Oh, to have the large, dewy eyes of a bovine finely bred, the shimmering flanks—and might there be something piquant in her heft? Perhaps a certain heft is prized because so many of us are so skinny, and kept that way by work and by hunger. One is reminded of the round figures in stone that are humanity's earliest representations of fertility. On Speke's second visit to Central Africa in the eighteen-sixties, he will enter the state of King Rumanyika of Karagwe, our cousin kingdom (Rumanyika is a Rwandese name) between Rwanda and Lake Victoria. Rumanyika, Speke tells us, keeps a harem that he feeds, and betimes force-feeds, with the richest milk from the finest cows. The girls (and that they must be; I can't imagine them achieving womanhood) can't stand. They waddle on their bellies like seals. They suck milk from gourds with long straws.

Muganza, as a young man, a trim young man, wins admission to a regiment of the crown prince's guards, the Inzirabwoba, those who fear nothing. He commands the regiment, then becomes an aide, some say a collaborator, of King Yuhi IV Gahindiro, who sends him off, as his father Mutemura was sent off, to Burundi.

From these campaigns, Muganza returns, as Mutemura returned, with prize cattle, with beautiful Burundian girls, and with warriors bearing tales of his exploits to put to verse. In the Rwandese manner of recording history, the lads compose an epic, *Inyamibwa y'Inzirabwoba ya Rukomerangungizi,* "The Best Among Those Who Fear Nothing, The One Who Defeated . . ." By his side stand stalwart sons, most especially two tall ones, Rudasumbwa and Mukezarugamba, whom we will call Mukeza.

And then he starts getting fat. So fat they have to build a special chair for him, a chair so big it will someday be displayed, along with his shield and his spear, at the museum the missionaries put together at Kabgayi Seminary.

WEST NILE VIRUS

Maybe it's the water. Up and down the watershed, from Rwanda down to Lake Victoria and on down the Nile through the Sudan and Egypt, it seems to be making white men sick and Africans fat.

Since the expeditions of Burton, Speke, and Livingstone through lands mostly east of the river, the bug seems to be biting worst west of the river. In these the days of our fat man Muganza, Nile waters are drawing young

white gents intent on finding out where the river rises, or taming its frontiers, or simply surrendering to its mystique. Sick with the mystique when
they arrive, they're most likely sick as dogs when they leave. After Burton
and Speke, these young Bazungu begin showing up by the dozen in Cairo
(some of them young officers of America's defeated Confederacy), looking
for adventure in the service of the Khedive Ismail Pasha Ayoub. A Turk who
rules Egypt for the Ottomans, the khedive likes to sign on adventurous
(some would say foolish) young white men.

As we call white people Bazungu, Ismail and his world at the other end of
the Nile call them Franks. For the nineteenth-century Levant, right through
the Sudan and Zanzibar, it simply means Bazungu, white people, French or
not. All of which would interest the greed-besotted khedive not one bit. Rubies are his preferred object of contemplation, and he'll take a fool by any
name if the man is ready to help push through to the uppermost reaches of
the Upper Nile. The khedive wants to make the river Egyptian all the way to
the Great Lakes, all of which, save our Lake Kivu, have now been discovered.
Egyptian geese come from our end of the river, and Egypt's papyrus and the
Egyptian heron and Egypt's sacred ibis and the Nile croc; why shouldn't the
land be made Egyptian?

Until now our Great Lakes have been cut off from the commercial, Muslim Nile, and Rwanda is still cut off. Now, however, some Great Lake kingdoms are slipping into the thinly colonized Levantine world that begins at
the massive Bab Zuweila, Cairo's great stone gate to inner Africa. Even with
most commerce plying the river, this monumental arch stands choked with
camels, slaves, sabred bedouin, and rich merchants on scabrous donkeys,
all either arriving from, or headed to, parts south.

South is an unforgiving, often cutthroat world. Given the fly-bitten desolation of these dry expanses, and its disease, you might wonder why the
traffic. But there is wealth to be had up the Nile. The tinkle of piano keys
and the click of billiard balls are attending the burgeoning wealth of the
West; ivory keys, ivory balls, letter openers of ivory. Ostrich feathers are in
vogue, gum arabic is in demand, so is rubber, and even after America's Civil
War, there is still a robust market for slaves. From the Swahili coast west to
our eastern frontier, the Sultan of Zanzibar stakes claim to the turf that
yields up this wealth. From Cairo south to our Great Lakes, the Turkish
Khedive Ismail stakes claim. Both realms are largely without borders, held
in terror by war merchants with their own private armies. Most infamous
out of Zanzibar is Tipoo Tib, a slaver of fabled wealth who knows how to
live like a sultan in the most rotted bog. Most infamous out of Cairo is
Zubeir Pasha, whose compounds in the parched wastes of Darfur and
Bahr el Ghazal are much like those of our kings of Rwanda, though the

structures (as in Rwanda, each serves as a distinct state apartment) are square rather than round, and inside Zubeir's apartments are divans covered with Persian rugs. At the compound gate, he keeps two lions chained. Deep inside, and draped in robes befitting his wealth, is Zubeir himself, offering you Turkish coffee, fine Turkish sweets, and somehow, even in the distant heat of the deep and dry Sudan, that vaunted sherbet, sherbets, really, each flavored with a beguilingly indefinable essence, cardamom, orange flower, rosewater. Years later, a young Winston Churchill will meet a defeated Zubeir in Cairo; even then he will impress Churchill as a man of great wealth and self-assurance.

It's a distinctly Afro-Levantine world, this swath running from Cairo to our Great Lakes and east across to Zanzibar, but often the leading figures pushing and staking claim to its frontiers are neither African, nor Arab, nor Muslim. They are the river's Bazungu, its Franks, men like Leopold's thug in safari duds, Henry Morton Stanley, and most especially like Lytton Strachey's Charles George Gordon, a man full of confused intentions and given to suffering the black despair of victory. It somehow matters not at all that these Bazungu who hold commissions to push the frontiers of commercial Egypt, and of commercial Zanzibar as well, are utterly dependent on Muslims who have already been to these frontiers, and actually live and do business along the way, Muslims who guide them, guard them, and nurse them when they fall sick. These are nonetheless the larger-than-life Franks of the Nile.

And then we have the Nile's larger-than-life Africans. Take the Ottoman khedive himself, Ismail Pasha Ayoub. It's hard calling him African. He's a Turk. But he's ensconced in Africa as the ruler of an African land; being described as an African goes with that territory—and it's not at all hard calling him tubby. Or take Wadelai. By 1845, Wadelai is no longer a person, it's a place that will become one of Gordon's military posts, not that far from us on the Upper Nile. But Wadelai is named for a chief of whom it is said that he was so big-bellied that he'd stride through his tribe with a child standing upright on his glorious great paunch. In later years the precincts of Wadelai will give us Idi Amin Dada, no reed in the breeze himself.

And of course, there's our own Muganza, and King Rumanyika next door in Karagwe. Slim and handsome in youth, already getting chubby, this lover of chubby girls will die nearly as fat as Muganza.

And then there's that other mythic giant of the Nile, the Mahdi.

The Mahdi's life is at first the very stuff of lean asceticism, a pure, burning, desert asceticism. Born to a pious boatbuilder on an island in the Nile one hundred miles our side of Khartoum, the young Muhammed Ahmed bin Abdullah cultivated his self-denial in an island cave where he lived on virtually nothing, and now during these years that see Muganza getting fat, the Mahdi is hardening his austerity to a gemlike brilliance in the heat of the open deserts and dry forests that stretch west of the Nile.

The people of these dry lands are mostly tribal bedouin driving camels, horses, and goats, but in a couple of respects they are somewhat Egyptian. For one, Ottoman Turks (in particular Ismail Pasha) are claiming the Sudan in the name of Ottoman Egypt, making these Sudanese Egyptian subjects. For another, and more to the point, they have a past in ancient Nubia, whose black pharaohs united ancient Egypt and ruled it for centuries, right down to its Mediterranean delta. Into the twenty-first century, they will paint above the doors of their mud brick houses an iconic Egyptian eye, and to this day you can see their ancient pyramids rising in the wastes of the Sudan.

But the Arabic these Sudanese faithful speak is not at all Egyptian Arabic, with its hard *g*s. They don't wear the Egyptian galabeya. They wear a "jelabah," a flowing white robe with a white tarboosh about their heads. And they don't look like most Egyptians. Black African in physiognomy, Muslim and Arab in their ways, Arabian in the classic purity of their Arabic and in the fire of their faith, the tribes of the Sudan chafe at the corruption of Ottoman Turks and Egyptians who muscle what they want with mercenary thugs called *bashi-bazooks*. One after another, Sudanese tribes rally to the Mahdi's green banner, his *jihad*. The banner whips in the desert wind at the head of charging masses of *Ansar*, the faithful, mounted on camels and high-strung Arabian stallions.

The Mahdi is tall. His manner is exceedingly, betimes excessively, polite. His eyes pierce. His beard, as the Koran commands, is untrimmed. His frame is powerful but lean. He is, after all, an ascetic, Osama bin Laden prefigured, a model for the tall, quiet ascetic who a century or so hence will dub his men, as the Mahdi now dubs his, the *Ansar*. To represent their pride in poverty and in the purity of their faith, the black Mahdi's black Arabs wear deliberately patched jelabahs. And then . . .

But before we get to the Mahdi's showdown on the Nile, let's look at how the river has been working its way with a man whose eye is on our Great Lakes, a Briton soon to be the Mahdi's adversary, Gordon of Khartoum.

Under the Khedive Ismail, Egypt is now both a satrapy of the Ottoman Turks and a protectorate of Great Britain. The Sudan, in turn, is a protectorate of Ottoman Egypt. Gordon has already served as Egypt's governor in Equatoria, far south on the Upper Nile where our Great Lakes begin. After that, Ismail appointed him governor-general in Khartoum. In disgust at Ismail's corruption and slave dealing, he quit. During the years he was gone, Egypt's corruption deepened, her creditors chafed, and in 1877 Gordon received an oily imprecation.

*I refuse to believe that, when Gordon has once given his word as a gentleman, any-
thing will ever induce him to go back on his word.*

Your affectionate Ismail

Gordon returns with a flourish, takes the title of viceroy, and just like
that he must resign again after Ismail's creditors depose the tubby little
Turk at great big expense. Egypt and the Sudan should be the better for losing Ismail, but they aren't. His mafia (not his word, but its origins *are* Arabic) simply becomes a mafia without a capo.

Now comes the Mahdi, afire. The Egyptian and Sudanese troops of
Britain's Egyptian protectorate are everywhere on the run, and this time it's
Britain's War Office, with bully cheers from the Fleet Street press, that urges
the return of Gordon to Khartoum. It should be plain that these particular
dogs of war are all bark and no bite. Holding them in leash is William Gladstone, a formidable prime minister. Never one for adventures, he is notably
cautious. At last, Gladstone's cabinet reaches a compromise. Gordon is to
return, but only to negotiate the honorable surrender of the Khartoum garrison to the Mahdi. It will be a conditional surrender, one that allows the
Egyptian garrison to return to Cairo. But what a sorry mission for a Briton
in Africa—negotiating surrender to native warriors; and even with that,
there's no guarantee the Mahdi will buy the conditions, and certainly no
guarantee that Gordon can force him to. He will have no British troops.

On January 18, 1884, the cabinet offers Gordon the commission. By
eight that evening, he's at Charing Cross Station with satchel in hand and
nothing but loose silver in his pocket. He has to borrow traveling money.
Gordon's not poor. He's just a highly distracted man.

He's also, by now, a major general, and in the tradition of Themistocles,
the soldier who saved Athens, he's a thinker. Like Themistocles also, his
veins lack any trace of blue blood. Gordon, presumptive savior of Khartoum (or at least of Khartoum's garrison), is the evangelist son of an austere middle class. His pastimes do not, like Speke's, run to billiards and
shooting grouse. Having grown up something of an ascetic himself, he'd
become all the more ascetic in Equatoria, and then, like the Mahdi, ex-
ploded as an ascetic in the deserts of the Sudan. Through the twentieth
century, a popular notion will linger that Gordon returns to Khartoum on
a British campaign to rescue the Sudan from the Mahdi's corrupt debauchery and to end the slave trade that fed in good part on human flesh from
tribes surrounding our Great Lakes. In reality, the Mahdi has taken the Sudan by ending the corrupt debauchery of Egyptian grandees and by enforcing a moral code. So far from a campaign against slavery, Gordon is
returning to negotiate for an Egyptian officer class that deals in slaves. For
all the bully headlines attending his send-off, Britain in fact has no more

heart for wasting lives and treasure in a dry and distant Africa than Bill Clinton will later have in Mogadishu.

In fact, the Sturm und Drang that is about to unfold on the Nile at Khartoum and on the Thames at London will prefigure debacles that in 1994 will unfold on Manhattan's East River, on the coast of Africa's Horn at Mogadishu—and ultimately in Rwanda where the Nile rises. There will, however, be one difference. As prime minister, Gladstone will be prudent, and he will prevail, but Britain's bully cheers for Gordon at least reflect a popular temperament more open to the larger world than will America's ignorant and insular news business in the last decade of the next century.

Gordon's great ambition has always been opening up our highland kingdoms. In 1875 he wrote, "the only valuable parts of the country are the high lands." To reach and "civilize" them, he was ready to "make my base at Mombaz [Mombasa] and give up Khartoum." He jumps at the chance to go back, even if it is in the service of Britons he dislikes, to rescue Egyptians he dislikes from the righteous wrath of Sudanese he admires. Ostensibly he will be fighting slavery, and that's what he will do. But Gordon is no fool. He knows the khedive doesn't really want to end slavery; all he wants is a cut of the purse. The question is, what does Gordon want, and does he harbor a death wish?

Years later, a French Canadian, a major general named Roméo Dallaire, will show up in Rwanda in the service of the United Nations, and find himself cast in the role of this British major general named Gordon. That's how Dallaire himself will put the matter, and his comparison will have none of the posturing of Henry Kissinger comparing himself to a lone cowboy on a rough frontier. The comparison of Dallaire to Gordon will be catastrophically apt, if not exact, both in its consequences for us, and in its personal consequences for him.

Like Dallaire landing in Rwanda, the minute Gordon is on station in Khartoum, he's left dangling at the quibbling whim of the men who dispatched him to negotiate that honorable surrender. They fuss about this, they fuss about that, and then all of a sudden their fussing becomes moot.

The telegraph line from Cairo to Khartoum goes dead. The Nubian frontier between Egypt and the Sudan has fallen to the Mahdi. Khartoum is cut off and surrounded.

Gordon builds impressive defenses, parapets and a ditch from the White Nile to the Blue. His shipyards maintain a fleet of armed and armored steamers that master the river and could make it down to Egyptian Wadi Halfa were it not for the need to forage for fuel on banks controlled by the Mahdi. His armory turns out forty thousand rounds of ammunition a day. He is forever on the move, inspecting strong point after strong point, rallying his troops.

Which brings us back to the Mahdi, still lean.

He decides to starve Gordon out. Gordon's Egyptian troops get hungry. His defenses begin to look vaguely wistful. The few Franks still with him fret. He sends them packing on an armed steamer, the *Abbas*. Runners have gotten through with word that the lead elements of a British relief column are close enough that the *Abbas* won't need to forage for fuel among hostile tribes. The boat is heavily plated, heavily armed, and as it steams north toward the British force, Gordon's second in command, Colonel J. D. H. Stewart, is aboard with explicit intelligence informing the British rescuers just how desperate matters are in Khartoum, how crucial it is to hurry.

Gordon is now alone in his Palladian palace. Built by the Brits of sandstone, it is bigger than most U.S. county courthouses. The ceilings rise some sixteen feet, and its style is so insistently Georgian that it looks like it belongs in London. Each evening he dines alone—or nearly alone. He takes to allowing a mouse to join him at the table. As he nibbles from his plate (Gordon never had much of an appetite), the mouse nibbles also.

In London, the Nile has the vernacular press in thrall. As the relief column reconnoiters in Upper Egypt, *Punch* runs a full-page cartoon on its cover in which Gordon, standing at the gates of Khartoum, welcomes his rescuers.

The Mahdi drops Gordon a line: "Know that your small steamer, named *Abbas,* which you dispatched with . . . Stewart Pasha . . . has been captured by the will of Allah." He graciously invites Gordon to surrender. His compassion does not extend to Gordon's Egyptian troops. They will not be allowed to surrender. Gordon answers, "I am here like iron." The Mahdi moves his forces up for attack. Gordon's Egyptian troops are now so weak with hunger they can hardly move about; those who can search by night for breakfast rats. The Mahdi sends Gordon a final note: "I've taken pity on some of my men and given them permission to die in order to enter paradise."

As Burton was within a heartbeat of the source of the Nile in Mutemura's Rwanda, Britain's ever-reconnoitering relief column is within a heartbeat of reaching Gordon in time, but by just that margin it is too late. Gordon dies in freshly pressed summer whites, sword in hand. His head is severed, kicked, spat upon, and shoved in the fork of a tree for further abuse.

Back in London, anguish grips the vernacular press and its public. Upon reading the offending telegram in her chambers, Queen Victoria gets a sick look, walks a stunned quarter mile to the cottage of her private secretary, wanders in on his wife, and says vacantly, "Too late!"

"Too late!" laments *Punch.* In her own hand, Victoria writes to Gordon's sister, "*How* shall I write to you or how shall I attempt to express *what I feel* . . . what I do so keenly feel, the *stain* left upon England . . . !"

Just as European air forces will one day fly into Rwanda with strict instructions to rescue no one but European nationals (with the result that a diplomatic dachshund will be brought aboard even as Rwandese children are left to die), the British force had been ordered to confine its rescue to Gordon, no one else, and so, with Gordon dead, the British force retreats. The troops whose surrender he'd come to negotiate are massacred. Their wives and daughters are raped.

The Mahdi's men are ascetic Muslims, and so is the Mahdi, but there is nothing ascetic about a Muslim's vision of paradise, and by all accounts the desert temperament that feeds asceticism can feed feverishly alternating moods. Dream worlds of booty become reality before their eyes—and before mine, for this I can see. I can see the humble man made for a mule riding into Khartoum astride a high-stepping Arabian stallion. Hundreds of the town's women and girls, modest Muslim women and girls, rounded up and stripped for the Mahdi. He dallies among them, taking his pick, and dispatching his pick to his harem.

"*Haram ya Boorton basha, haram,*" the men of Ujiji had warned their Burton Pasha when he wanted to enter our forbidden zone. Here, in a harem, a *haram,* a forbidden place of his very own, the Mahdi, *ya Muhamet basha,* finds life exceptionally pleasant—and gets exceptionally fat.

In a desert instant, asceticism becomes debauchery. Just five months after Gordon dies on the Nile, the Mahdi dies on the Nile, one exceptionally fat corpse.

The Mahdi's faith seems a simple creed of moral men rising against an immoral world, but his death suggests a man as complex as all these other figures infected by our river. As his successor he chooses the Khalifa Abdullah, a man with a face lean and pocked and a lean body, a man who has no inclination to take it easy and let the Mahdi's realm languish. Throughout Islam, through Sumatra, Persia, the Sind, Damascus, in every faithful realm you can imagine, the distinctively Islamic democracy of the bazaar hums with talk of this martyr for political Islam, the Mahdi, much as the bazaar will one day hum with heroic talk of the Ayatollah Khomeini and Osama bin Laden. Britain recoils; by and by, steadier, quieter voices counsel that neither the Mahdi nor the khalifa can pose any real strategic threat, just as the steadier, quieter voices of a later day will counsel that radical Islam can pose no strategic threat, only terror and its attendant horror. But like Khomeini and bin Laden, the khalifa knows that mounting a strategic threat to the Franks is not the point. He knows that the point is people, which is to say, politics. Islam draws no distinction between politics and religion. In Omdurman across the Nile from Khartoum the khalifa builds a great domed monument to the Mahdi, and pilgrims come from throughout the Muslim world.

The Sudan at the beginning of the Mahdi's reign was already vast, a million miles square. Now it's two million, and the khalifa, the caliph, is looking upriver to Emin Pasha, the bespectacled German medical doctor Gordon left behind as governor in Equatoria, nominally a province, in fact just a chain of outposts on the Nile whose southern frontier is the most northerly of the Great Lakes, Lake Albert. Somehow, Emin is still holding out up there, more isolated than Gordon ever was, the one obstacle between the khalifa and what he eyes, our potentially slave-rich, ivory-rich Great Lakes kingdoms.

THE MAN WHO WOULD BE EMIN PASHA WAS BORN EDUARD SCHNITZER IN PRUSSIAN SILE-sia on Germany's Polish border in 1840. He is not physically impressive, he is hardly charismatic, yet the character of his struggle on our doorstep will prompt a few Germans to present a somewhat more decent face in Africa, which will turn out to matter more to us than to other German colonies in Africa. Germany, already the terror of Tanganyika, is soon to claim "Ruanda-Urundi"; if for no other reason, how Germans look at Africans will matter. Emin shows up often in the literature, but seems always to appear as a secondary character in passing. Sent by his sacrificing Lutheran father to an elite gymnasium, this unimposing German grows up happy enough and even self-assured. In short, he belongs. He does well at his studies, and goes on to study medicine at the University of Breslau. He plays Mendelssohn on the piano for his fraternity brothers, downs stein after stein with them, and one day learns that his mother, Pauline, is a Jew, as is his real father, a man unknown. At first the shock is just personal. Then he's rejected by his friends ("The fraternity is particular about its members, Herr Schnitzer"), then barred from standing for examinations. He tries to enter the service of Maximilian in Mexico, there to prove his mettle by fighting Benito Juarez for the Austro-Hungarian Empire. Alas, Maximilian's recruiters aren't looking for Jews; he loses his chance to prove himself on the wrong side of a colonial war. At last he goes off to serve the Ottoman Empire in Bosnia and then Turkey, where a patron pasha brings him to Trebizond, a Black Sea town storied for the grace of its seafront, its mosques, its villas, and above all, for the comeliness of its women. There he falls for a magnetic concubine in the pasha's seraglio, answers Muhammad's call, and becomes Emin, "the faithful one."

The pasha is old; he indulges the affair, even leaves a sum for Emin when he dies. But when Emin goes home to Prussian Silesia and brings his exotic entourage along in tow, his hometown is not so indulgent. Embarrassed, his family seeks out a spa. The neighbors snicker.

At this, Emin leaves his inheritance to his odalisque and disappears once again into the Ottoman world. A thin little man of sallow complexion, he passes easily for a Levantine. They say he has the curly black beard of a Persian satrap, but not the lusty personality to go with it. He has owlish eyes set in a sparrow's face, the heavily bagged gaze of a scholar locked too long in combat with the knots of the Talmud. One day he shows up penniless in Khartoum, where the Mahdi is still but a holy man in a cave, and finds his way to Gordon. Gordon already has a reputation for hiring with fussy discrimination. He mistrusts adventurers. Nonetheless, he is somehow impressed and takes Emin on. Others, later, will be less impressed. They will describe him as irresolute, a temporizer, an equivocator.

Gordon names him staff physician in Equatoria, whose southern frontier is Lake Albert. He adapts well. Shortly after his appointment, Gordon persuades the khedive to title him pasha, and later to name him governor.

Whatever his physical aspect, Emin's restlessness marks him thoroughly as a man of industrializing Europe in the nineteenth century. He is a Jew, but even more, he is a German. Germany made him. He belongs to the crowd that flocks to the Nile looking for something more. Where he differs, it works to his advantage: he speaks decent Arabic, he's a Muslim, he's a medical doctor, he's a proven administrator. And right now, he is surrounded.

BURUNDI IS NOT THE ONLY FIELD UPON WHICH MUGANZA FIGHTS. HIS REPUTE IS SPREADing; within the family, "By Muganza!" becomes an oath often uttered. "By Muganza!" says his son Rudasumbwa to seal a deal with his word. "By Muganza!" says his son Mukeza. Within Rwanda, Muganza battles forces loyal to the brother of King Yuhi IV Gahindiro. Beyond Rwanda, he fights in Karagwe, where King Rumanyika, who is growing fat himself, keeps his waddling wives. All this adds to Muganza's wealth in cows and in power, and his weight grows apace.

Likewise does the weight of the Khedive Ismail grow apace. During these years (he has not yet lost his mob), Ismail Pasha has a weakness for spending his wealth with no compensating knack for losing weight. Even if you include his tall fez, he's a good foot shorter than Muganza, though easily as paunchy. When at last his incontinent spending loses him his throne, Ismail's tubby sister goes on a petulant tear through the Abdine Palace, ripping up all the upholstery on the Louis this and Louis that and smashing more than a hundred windows.

BY THE TIME GORDON DIES IN KHARTOUM, EGYPT'S PLUMP LITTLE KHEDIVE ISMAIL PASHA Ayoub has retired to a grand palace on the Bosporus. But before his fall, he has quite a run, financing not just Gordon and any number of Franks on their adventures up the Nile, but marketing the Suez Canal—a risky venture with which the prudent British will have no truck, though it will soon multiply mightily their power and wealth. During the very days that Great Lake carpenters struggle without numbers to measure a custom-built chair for Muganza, during the very days that Rwanda's younger captains—like Muganza's sons Mukeza and Rudasumbwa—struggle without numbers to plot tactics and strategy, French engineer Ferdinand de Lesseps and Egypt's pudgy Ismail fairly skip with numeric joy at their end of the Nile. With blithe abandon, they toss numbers to the press like cherubs pitching posies in a Boucher tableau:

Two hundred and eighty-seven million! (The number of gold francs raised in France and Turkey by de Lesseps's Compagnie Universelle du Canal Maritime de Suez.)

Six thousand! (The number of big shots they will host to inaugurate the canal. To entertain them, Ismail builds a grand opera house in Cairo and commissions Verdi to compose an inaugural opera, but *infelice*! Verdi is tardy; *Aida* must debut late.)

Five hundred! (The number of French chefs and Italian sous-chefs who will don toques to keep the assembled nicely fed.)

Twenty! (The number of military bands that will oompah.)

One thousand! (The number of European servants hired, lest countless Nubians be insufficient.)

Ten thousand! (The number of lanterns that will light the Port Said evening.)

This gay enumeration doesn't extend to the volume of fireworks collected for the event, but we know it's a lot because the dump blows up and ignites a fire that sends Port Said up in flames, destroying large parts of the facility built expressly for the canal. Regardless, at the appointed hour, hired bedouin on horseback appear amid the char, fire their muskets, and with more than a whiff of grapeshot the inaugural flotilla sets sail, led by the Empress Eugénie's gilded yacht, *Aigle*.

The canal's impact is not comic opera. Shipping time to the Far East is cut in half. Shipping time to India and East Africa is cut by much more than half. Meantime, ever more ships are being launched under steam, using coal rather than cost-free wind. Suez means less coal burned, more profit. *The New York Herald* enthuses, "The . . . canal brings all these late discoveries around the equatorial sources of the Nile of Speke, Grant, Baker, Burton, Livingstone within a convenient distance for English colonization."

Not to speak of Belgian, German, and French colonization. The canal itself is part of an outright effort by the French to elbow the British aside in East Africa, an effort so passionately nationalist that it will be expressed in Rwanda more than a century later. As genocide descends on us, French sensitivity about English-speaking rebels from Uganda will aggravate the crime and then attenuate it. A few years after the Mahdi takes Khartoum from Gordon, the French see their chance to steal a march on the British and secretly underwrite two coordinated expeditions, both military. One will raise a cadre of Senegalese and cross the Sahara west to east, a daunting enterprise in the twenty-first century, let alone the nineteenth. The other will land on Eritrea's Red Sea coast, attempt to conspire with the Abyssinians, and then head west. At a squalid outpost on the Nile called Fashoda, the two French forces will rendezvous and sail north downriver to Khartoum. There they will either strike a deal with the khalifa or grab the Sudan back from him before the timid British can, then claim for France all the Upper Nile, right up to its headwaters in the Great Lakes kingdoms.

It's a venture drenched in the colonial greed that marks the century, but it's also exceptionally bold, worthy of the most fearless *beau sabreur*. Crossing the Sahara west to east, there to battle the formidable khalifa, is not a Renoir lunch on the Seine.

And note well the Germans: "My map of Africa lies in Europe," says Bismarck. German corvettes are poking around Zanzibar, and in Equatoria on the Upper Nile, at the gateway to the Great Lakes, there is that curious, querulous German called Emin Pasha, Gordon's successor as governor of the territory.

With nary another German for company, Emin holds out. To the north, east, and west of him are the desert and scrub and elephant grass controlled by the khalifa. Immediately to the south is terra incognita—southwest, the cannibals of the Congo's Ituri forest, due south, our Great Lakes. In rags, and running out of food and ammunition, his troops, mostly Muslim Sudanese, are sitting on a fortune in ivory. Gordon is dead. Britain has retreated. Emin is cut off and all but forgotten by the rest of the world.

But these are all merely portents. This year, in the kingdom of Rwanda in the farthest reaches of the Nile, neither white man nor Arab has yet set foot, for all the Arabic and Swahili words creeping into Kinyarwanda. To our Batemura, still (By Muganza!) keeping the goat at bay, the name Ferdinand de Lesseps means nothing. All that will soon change.

· 19 ·

MYTHMAKER, MYTHMAKER

Blood Brothers in Penny Press Africa; 1871–1885

> "What are you going to do with your money?"
> "Buy a battleship and rejoin the Navy."
> —Adventurer to adventurer
> in 1937 British production of *King Solomon's Mines*

In 1871, as our Muganza sits resolutely in his fat man's chair, a solitary traveler just nineteen boards a steamship of the Union Castle Line at the English port of Norfolk, headed for latitudes south. All pink cheeks and celluloid collar, well schooled but less than wealthy, young Henry Rider Haggard has won a post as secretary to the governor of Natal. From what I've read, I think it's safe to say that his imagination is fuller with Africa (writ large) than with the bureaucracy of a governor's office in her majesty's imperial service.

I think it's even safer to say that he can have no idea how his boyish imagination will fire other imaginations, and how in time these other imaginations will inspire a crime that will push our understanding of mass perversion—and lay waste the family of Muganza of the Inzirabwoba.

By Rider Haggard's day, it's been better than two centuries since Dutch Calvinists and French Huguenots settled Africa south of what the Dutch called the Orange River. The first of the Boer Wars is over, Shaka Zulu is long since dead, the taste of the place, the cookery, is more Malay than African, and the land isn't just settled, it's big business. Ringling Brothers Circus and Buffalo Bill's Wild West Show steam all the way out here and all the way down here to tap urban markets in apparent need of vicarious excitement. In the four years he's here, Haggard writes a history of the country and two bad novels and listens to one story after another about Africa where it's still Africa, with wonders yet to be found. Beautiful Amazons. Diamonds. Gold. Lost worlds. Black giants of regal mien who drive long-horned cattle like those on Egyptian tombs. Women who wear their hair straight up, like Nefertiti. The riches of Ophir; King Solomon's mines.

COMES NOW A DREAMER

The characters the West sends to the Africa of Haggard's day are a bumptious lot. They thrive on stories coming from unexplored highlands to the north—and so too does young Haggard, who senses cobalt blue humming-birds of truth buzzing amid the malarkey freebooters spin after adventures in the lands up beyond Britain's settled Natal and the Boers' restive Transvaal. He knows that, unlike Moses and Abraham, lost without relic in the haze of millennial antiquity, Solomon sits on the very doorstep of recorded history. Young Haggard may even have heard provocatively blasphemous speculation that behind the legend of the wise man limned in the Book of Kings, there was a real ruler all too human. Scholarly accounts of Solomon's years suggest a man who borrowed beyond his means to build a fleet that sailed down the east coast of Africa to drop anchor by and by in the land that the Bible calls Ophir, where his men either mined gold or traded for it.

One day I run across Josephus. He tells me that the homeport of Solomon's southern fleet wasn't anywhere near where I always supposed, at the southern tip of the Holy Land. He says it was much further south, far down the Red Sea coast. There the Phoenicians with whom he contracted came to build his fleet, and from there his fleet sailed yet further south.

There, in some indistinct, barely explored zone on the far northern frontiers of southern Africa are the far southern frontiers of the classical world. Somewhere north across what Kipling calls "the great, grey-green, greasy Limpopo" ("all set about with fever trees"), somewhere south of the great Zambezi, adventuring yahoos have stumbled on and looted some small ruins, and will soon stumble across a giant one, the Great Zimbabwe (massive walls of intricately fitted stone), near exhausted gold mines. It's a mystery. The yahoos have dug up some relics, but treasure is what they're after. The relics are gold. They melt them down. The mystery endures.

The Great Zimbabwe sits along ancient safari tracks that drag east to a ghost town called Kilwa—the ruin of a Swahili port. It's unlikely Kilwa's Swahili character means much to Haggard's world. Haggard's world seems to look on the Swahili coast as a colony of convenience cobbled by the Persian and Arab worlds to tap Africa's wealth. In the Swahili tongue Haggard's world hears pidgin Arabic laced with Persian. But Kilwa's ancient Swahili character means something to me. Swahili isn't pidgin anything. It's a language of its own, and its architecture is neither Semitic (like Arabic and most languages of Ethiopia) nor Indo-Aryan (like Persian). It's Bantu. It comes, like its native speakers, from Africa's interior.

From antiquity, monsoon winds carried sailing vessels from Arabia, Persia, Oman, even China, to the Swahili coast, there to trade not just in hides, incense, slaves, and ivory but in gold, great quantities of gold, all of it mined in the thoroughly African interior. Against such a backdrop, a Victorian lad doesn't have to be seized by fantasy to daydream about one delicious possibility after another, and in particular to wonder whether the ruins of gold mines turning up near the Great Zimbabwe might be relics of King Solomon's Ophir. Or whether other sites on up the Great Rift as far as Abyssinia might have been a source of Solomon's wealth. After all, the Abyssinians do claim one of Solomon's wives—the Queen of Sheba—as their own, and even if Abyssinia's communal memory is flawed, and ancient Sheba wasn't there but in Arabia's far south, does this erase Africa as a source of wonder? The ancient peoples of southern Arabia and Abyssinia (from *abysha,* Arabic for "mixed," the land of mixed races) were forever moving back and forth across the narrow straits now called the Bab, "the gate," the Levantine sailor's gate to black Africa. Natal's Malay Muslims (the "Slams" of Durban and Capetown), the Swahili, the Persians of Zanzibar, the Persians of Persia, the muftis of Damascus, all know the year of Muhammad's birth as "the year of the elephant," so named because in that year, an army of invading Africans, replete with trained war elephants, besieged the very gates of Mecca, having advanced from Yemen, which Africa then ruled. Arabia Felix, the Romans called Yemen, "Happy Arabia," a green mountain realm distinct from dry Arabia Deserta and everywhere redolent of the vellum that filled its high-rise libraries— tended, well before and well after the year of the elephant, by African librarians. History, once obscure, incites. A young English poet of the early twentieth century, John Masefield, dreams of an ancient mariner rowing home from distant African Ophir,

> . . . *to haven in sunny Palestine,*
> *With a cargo of ivory,*
> *And apes and peacocks,*
> *Sandalwood, cedarwood, and sweet white wine.*

So much of that bracing wonder about Africa seems to reside in boys addicted to adventure . . . even white South African boys. In these days when Latin and Greek are commonly taught, classical scholars cherish the notion that the ancient Greeks represent a clean break from Egypt, an entirely new and different frame of mind that marks the beginning of the West. But many of the lads they teach, fascinated with the adventures of Alexander and the expeditions of Herodotus and Thucydides to lands distant from Greece are by nature more taken by adventure than by the preening *Kulturkampf* of their teachers. I read an Afrikaaner, Laurens van der Post. He recalls growing up in the bushveld of the nineteen-twenties, reading Homer and discovering with awe how the Greeks not only worshiped Egypt but believed that their gods, and Zeus in particular, chose to live where they most found virtue, among those with faces "burnt" by Africa.

On one point, the historians, the "orientalists" (as scholars of the Near East and Africa are in this day designated), even the philosophers are agreed: Whoever built such feats as the Great Zimbabwe, in fact whoever it was who mined Africa for Solomon, they were not Africans. They could not possibly be. Africans were not capable of this. In 1910, and through the thirties, Collier publishes a twenty-five-volume *History of Nations*. Compiled by leading scholars and edited by Henry Cabot Lodge, just one of its twenty-five volumes is titled *Africa*. The tome is devoted entirely to Europe in Africa, and unapologetically so. Africans, Lodge instructs us, are "savages," including the Arabs of Africa. Africans simply have no history, he tells us. In 1902, Richard Meinertzhagen, a young nephew of a familiar Utopian socialist, bright-eyed and adventuresome, writes home from Nairobi:

> Apparently, Charles Eliot, the High Commissioner, learned that Beatrice Webb is my aunt, so he asked me to dine with him this evening. My only clothes were a dirty old shirt and shorts. I explained my predicament, and refused, but he insisted on my coming. He is not my idea of a High Commissioner; he looks more like a university don, or a priest. He is a scholar, a philosopher, and a very able man with great vision. He amazed me with his views on the future of East Africa. He envisaged a thriving colony of thousands of Europeans with their families, the whole country from the Aberdares and Mount Kenya to the German border divided into farms; the whole Rift Valley to [Mount] Elgon . . . under white settlement. He intends to confine the natives to reserves and use them as cheap labour. . . .

No wonder that in Bitsindinkumi's Africa, the White Fathers will insist that Africans who want to go to school must come with Christian, that is, European, names. Hegel, whose dialectic analysis of historical development is to inform Marxism, writes, "Africa is no historical part of the world." Africa, he says, shows "no movement or development." It's a notion that boys addicted to adventure simply can't abide.

With no idea that it's defying the academy, the vernacular press can't abide the notion either. If for no other reason than the cause of vicarious adventure, the vernacular press likes to believe that the history of Africa is not so much nonexistent as it is unknown—and the unknown is irresistible. When he gets back from Africa, Haggard wagers one of his brothers that he can write an adventure as popular as *Treasure Island,* and begins putting down the vague, tantalizing stories he's heard. In 1885, seven years before a real white man is known to have stepped inside Rwanda, he publishes *King Solomon's Mines,* and in no time he is *Sir* Henry Rider Haggard, the most popular author in the British Empire—and hardly obscure beyond. He will write at least a dozen more thrillers, all wildly popular, meantime providing material for a couple of big adventure movies (with Paul Robeson and Cedric Hardwicke in 1937; with Deborah Kerr and Stewart Granger in 1950), plus countless movies with production values as degraded as the racial notions that informed Haggard's day. In *King Solomon's Mines,* Haggard spins the tale of a white hunter, Allan Quatermain. He tells how young Quatermain, at the end of a treacherous trail, discovers a mysterious tribe of black Africans, women of great beauty, seven-foot warriors, a tribe of regal mien and unsurpassed courage high in the mountains of the Great Lakes.

This is innocence, innocence that exalts black Africa even as scholars abuse it. It would be an exaggeration to say it's also an innocence that will lead directly to race hate. But over the years, Haggard's innocence will yield to a creepy romance with race by the same public that buys *King Solomon's Mines,* a romance with race that will hold Christendom in thrall. The victims will be the families of Bitsindinkumi and Mutemura and Muganza and all the Banyarwanda.

20

AMONG PRINCELY DOMAINS

A Highborn Rugo *of 1879–1890*

Like those barons Mutemura and his son Muganza (Mama's great-grandfather Muganza), indeed like our much less than baronial father, the prince of Bushiru is among the highborn of the people who call themselves Banyarwanda. Unlike Papa, he's no threadbare patrician in a frayed overcoat and scuffed shoes with no socks. He's a chief among chiefs, a prince, a *muhinza,* the Muhinza w'Abashiru. His people grow sorghum and bananas, brew banana beer to the exacting standards of eight officers of the court whose single mission is to assure quality. His people breed sleek long-horned cattle like the cattle pictured on Egyptian tombs.

They hunt elephant with spears pounded from the iron they smelt, indeed that their ancestors have been smelting for at least a millennium, having figured out how to do it without ever going through the intermediate step of learning to smelt copper. They stand in living contradiction to the assumption, held through most of the nineteenth and twentieth centuries, that everything Africans have learned has come from outside Africa. They trade in ivory and rare hides. They command ancient salt routes and salt markets.

His royal compound, his rugo, is composed of nearly a dozen high-roofed rondavels, many fifteen feet in diameter, with three-foot-thick thatch roofs extending well over the walls until they nearly touch the ground, at which point they are cropped to a perfect brush edge. Like the rooms of a palace, each rondavel has an assigned purpose: kitchen, princely court (complete with lutes and pygmy jesters), ministerial court, family bedchambers, guests' bedchambers, *muhinza's* bedchamber, princely mother's bedchamber, harem, bathhouses, warehouses, armory. There are courtyards as meticulously broomed as the graveled courtyards of Japan.

An unblemished blond in color, the thatched rondavels spread over and between hillocks of expansive, steeply rolling green farmland, much like a thatched village in the Welsh hills. The farmland rolls on, broken only by hedgerows and here and there a wood, a brook, a rill, the picture of leisurely country life to which Kipling puts astringent homily.

> *Our England is a garden, and such gardens are not made*
> *By singing "Oh, how beautiful!" and sitting in the shade.*

They don't sit. They salt their fields with their sweat.

Not far to the east, over the frontier in Karagwe where the hills do not roll so steeply, the explorer James Grant has discovered a cool sheet of water that seems a sudden vision of the English Lake Country. He names it Windermere.

I like to picture the commonplaces of this realm called Bushiru. For our *muhinza,* our prince, this is a commonplace morning. Dawn has barely broken but already the morning is bright. Morning fog eddies about a hunting party returning to the princely compound. Fog rolls low beneath a brilliantly clear sky, refracting the cold light of the morning sun. The sun hits the party at a sharp angle as they stride along a broad avenue of pounded red earth. The avenue is crowned down the middle so that rainwater runs off. Alongside the *muhinza* stride barkless basenji hunting dogs and the prince's hunting cronies—the chief of the farms, the chief of the militia, the chief of the cows, the poet laureate. Two bearers struggle under the weight of a sitatunga buck. A big marsh antelope, it's trussed by its legs to a pole resting on the shoulders of two bearers. It has already been field dressed, decapitated, and bled. A third bearer, a pygmy, strides naked through the chill. He carries the head, a two-foot horn over each of his shoulders, the head on his back like a pack. The head too has been bled, but it leaks. The blood washes dry mud from the pygmy's back and trickles through the cheeks of his half-pint bottom. Flies swarm.

Neither chill nor flies seem to bother the pygmy at all, nor do they bother the two bearers in banana-leaf loincloths. The *muhinza* and his companions wear white mushananas, cinched at the waist and knotted over one shoulder.

Until about 1890, one feature still sets the princely realms of our Banyarwanda distinctly apart from our cousin kingdoms to the north and east, Bunyoro, Buganda, Ankole, Karagwe. The Arab slaver, the Indian trader, the white explorer haven't bothered us. It's five years since Rider Haggard published *King Solomon's Mines,* and nearly three decades since Burton and Speke came so close to Burundi proper and even to Rwanda. The twentieth century is something like a decade off, and still no European or Arab has ventured into these forbidden lands and come out alive.

All around us, outsiders are poking. Arab slavers have pushed trails around Rwanda and Burundi to both the north and the south. The ill-famed Tipoo Tib of Zanzibar has pushed around us and down into the Congo basin, where he has set up his own private state. Soon he will sell it to Belgium's King Leopold, who will make it *his* own private state. On occasion, Tipoo Tib has brought with him white explorers like Leopold's agent, Henry Morton Stanley.

There's no doubt that Rwanda is fierce in its xenophobia, but Arab avarice has cultivated some of this xenophobia, and Arabs color how the outside world views us, which is to say, how Stanley views us, which is to say, with deadly intent. Like Burton and Speke, Stanley depends on the Arabs for information, and he tries sedulously to outdo the Arabs in monstrous behavior, smugly certain that "the only thing these beasts respect is force." But a few years from now, in 1892, Oscar Baumann, an Austrian missionary with none of Stanley's blood lust, will wander into Rwandese Gisaka for a few days, and his unprepossessing safari will get out alive. Then a couple of years later, an intrepid young adventurer will set off to cross Africa from the Indian Ocean to the Atlantic, with a stop in Rwanda. Clearly neither an ivory poacher nor a slaver nor an avaricious trader, young Count Gustav Adolf von Götzen will in 1894 win entrée to Rwanda for a two-month stay, then enjoy an audience with the king and proceed on past Lake Kivu, not far from this very spot—the domain of the Muhinza w'Abashiru. Von Götzen will record that the experience is more like entering "a centralized European state" than an East African realm.

Before 1890, records show just one Arab safari having been able to enter Rwanda. (Able to enter; it never got out.) Barred from Rwanda, these Arabs must make long, circuitous detours, detours in which every furlong is measured in time and in gold, if not in blood. They have rifles; by now they even have Remington repeaters. They nonetheless give Rwanda a wide berth.

The Arabs call their rifles *bundegeya,* the Swahili, *bunduki,* and we Banyarwanda have a word for them too, a clearly related word, *imbundu,* suggesting that in some ways we are not quite as untouched as written records suggest. Arabic and Kiswahili are creeping into Kinyarwanda. But in other ways, Rwanda and Burundi may be even more untouched than written records suggest. We have a word for rifles, but we still don't use rifles. Knowing this, Tipoo Tib's brother Muhammed will muster six hundred *askaris* wielding six hundred rifles and try to breach the kingdom. He doesn't.

THE PICTURE I IMAGINE OF THE *MUHINZA*'S REALM IS JUST THAT, IMAGINED. OF COURSE, there really is a Bushiru, and it does have a *muhinza,* he does have those royal cronies; and dawn, along with dusk, is when they like to hunt. Likewise all the other details are real. What's imagined is the picture that composes all this, genuine in its details, starkly real in my mind, but imagined nonetheless, genuine commonplaces in pictures fantasied by their collector.

I picture them one way. I picture them another way. I guess you'd say I fuss, mostly because there's one commonplace of life here that I can't make manifest for you no matter how much I compose and recompose. Were it an unimportant commonplace, I'd forget it. But it's important. Indeed, it may surprise a few who think they know us. But it's so seamlessly a part of everyday life that the only way I can tease it out is to picture a scene just a shade more than routine.

I picture one of the little forest people, the pygmy Batwa. This pygmy belongs to the princely court, where he performs the customary roles of court pygmy, storyteller, shaman, and forest tracker. This month, in fact, he was serving as a tracker for one of the prince's warriors, one of his somewhat taller, shier warriors, when the two crossed north into what will someday be known as Uganda and came upon a rugo of their cousins there, the Banyankole. Now they have returned.

It's evening. A chill has returned to Bushiru. Fires are lit to chase the chill. There are songs. Courtiers recite poems; as pygmies do, this pygmy tells a story.

In the Ankole rugo they just visited, he says, was the Swahili agent of an Omani or perhaps an Indian trader. "A Hendi with great dukas in the place Swahili call Zanzibar." With pygmy animation he talks about these traders who are indeed poking closer to us. Then, with a sly smile, the tiny storyteller recounts how the agent from afar had tried and tried again to persuade the laconic warrior to convey a request to his prince, the Muhinza w'Abashiru. The agent wanted the warrior to ask his prince to let the Hendi enter Banyarwanda country with his trade goods.

As my pygmy goes on with his tale, the warrior grins, covers his grin with one hand, and stares fixedly at the ground, his eyes sparkling. One by one, with a straight face, the pygmy repeats slavish praise the agent paid the warrior's "fine Tutsi bearing." I can hear the men roaring.

The warrior is not Tutsi. Nor is the *muhinza*. They are distinctly of the Rwandese world . . . by custom, by religion, by language—by the Kinyarwanda they speak. But they are not Tutsi. Nor do they see themselves as Hutu. Bahutu are what those Batutsi in the foothills call their serfs. So who are these local gentry? Who is the *muhinza*? Who is the warrior? They do not yet see themselves as Bahutu—but they will soon. They are the gentry from which a late-twentieth-century queen, Habyarimana's wife, Agathe, will someday spring. They are the grandsires of the Akazu.

21

LADY MACBETH IN AFRICA

*White Witch Doctors, Black Witch Doctors, and
a Queen Mum; 1886–1896*

Mama and Uncle Kagame were great-grandchildren of the fat man, Muganza. Uncle wasn't as fat as Muganza, but he was at least as tall and fat enough. He and Mama called each other brother and sister. They were in fact first cousins. Such is the extended family in Rwanda, that cousins often brother and sister each other, but there was more to it than that. You know that we were Tonton's closest living relatives. The past bound him to Mama. Their fathers, Mama's father, Kabenga, and Uncle Kagame's father, Bitahurwina, were close. Close in age, they were orphaned early by the death of their young father, Muganza's son Rudasumbwa, and grew up with the same stepfather, Muganza's son Mukeza.

Uncle was also a priest and a teacher. When I was growing up, he was long since a bishop, teaching Bantu history in the early days of Rwanda's first university, a college upgraded by Dominican missionaries in the old colonial capital of Astride, which we have always called Butare. He wore a white cassock the size of a tent. He drove that battered white VW bug. Behind the wheel, he looked like a happy rhino stuffed behind the wheel of a kid's pedal car. It barely contained him. Under his weight it developed its permanent lurch toward the driver's side. His entire left shoulder bulged out the driver's window. In his huge hands, the steering wheel seemed the size of a saucer. Sitting next to him up front was horribly claustrophobic until you got lost in his jokes and his stories.

Uncle was distinguished by his combat with taboo (Tutsi taboo, churchly taboo) and by his loving knowledge of heathen *codes esotériques*. An author of several volumes of Bantu history, he was known by schoolchildren as the author of that long story in verse in which he pictured the chiefs (forever and famously reserved in their Tutsi hauteur) arriving at a feast, becoming transported by the aroma of roasting pork (a vile animal by Tutsi lights), squabbling with each other over the portions, and ending the evening in a food fight.

He even managed, somehow, to offend taboos yet to be formed. In his office, surrounded by students, nieces, and nephews, amid softbound books and a clutter of monographs, he'd mull a tumbler of whiskey and ponder our inheritance, turning analogies over with the ice, using analogy to set our experience against sad humanity's. Given the spark in his eye, I can't help thinking that he had a hunch what was coming, that he was provoking the future as deliberately as he was provoking us.

What was coming was an attitude. African intellectuals were about to start asking in outraged rhetoric what business anyone had using analogies to outside worlds to elucidate Africa. Africa, they would soon be harrumphing, has no need for outside models to win legitimacy. It is uniquely African, valid on its own.

Who would argue with that? Certainly not Uncle. But he didn't use analogy to win legitimacy. He used it out of sheer love for explication, for explaining to the perplexed, and among the perplexed he counted himself. He was trying to understand.

For Uncle, feudal Europe was a useful analogue, but so were others. None have much precision. Some are helpful. And nowhere did he feel that Rwanda needed more elucidation than it does in its darkest and most overwrought episode, these days of Rwabugiri and his queen, Kanjogera.

IGNORE THE PARADOX: THE DAYS OF KING RWABUGIRI AT THE END OF THE NINETEENTH century are incomparably Rwandese and yet beg for comparison. Rwabugiri is Peter the Great; he's Shakespeare's Richard III. Kanjogera is Lady Macbeth. It is an episode of Rwandese history at once defiantly Rwandese and of a piece with that sad humanity against which Uncle defiantly set our history.

The king of Rwanda in 1886, the *mwami*, Kigeri IV Rwabugiri, carries himself with the authority of the greatest Romanov. On Rwanda's much smaller stage, he has been as precocious as Peter, as successful and as ruthless. He is likewise as driven as the most driven of Shakespeare's Richards. Forget that Richard is a fourteenth-century figure shaped by a sixteenth-century playwright, while Rwabugiri is real and proximate, younger than Queen Victoria. Forget the hump on the back of the English king, his pale skin. Forget that Rwabugiri is blacker than Othello, that he towers, that he is the son of a queen whose beauty is the subject of song. England's pale hunchback could rise from the dead, seize Rwabugiri's throne, and no one would be the wiser. He and the Rwandese king are that akin at their spiritual centers, and their spirits are just that dominant over their physical aspects.

Rwanda under Rwabugiri is at a high-water mark. King Rwabugiri's father, Yuhi IV Gahindiro, patron of our fat man, Muganza of the Inzirabwoba, has long since crushed the Tutsi king of Bugesera. There is no chance the Bugesera dynasty will revive. Rwabugiri has brought Bugesera firmly within the Rwandese fold. Like England's Richard, he leads personally in combat.

He has defeated the Tutsi king of Gisaka, and however much its people may chafe at distant tyranny, Rwabugiri's agents, emissaries, and vassals, like Richard's, are everywhere. Gisaka is thoroughly incorporated into the kingdom of Rwanda. Rwabugiri's people rate him—his enemies rate him—a master of warfare. Friends and enemies alike rate him a master politician, reengineering, as he does, the ancient organizational models he inherited to expand the kingdom and to lock it more tightly into the ordered mechanism of the court at Nyanza. Rwanda stretches to Lake Edward, just south of Lake Albert, to which Gordon staked claim for the Anglo-Egyptian Sudan, and just north of which Emin Pasha now holds out.

As for Rwabugiri's judgment in matters beyond the military and the political, matters that a later day would call personal, in his day such matters are called spiritual, at least as far as kings are concerned, and in the forbidden zone you don't take the spiritual measure of your king. The king is divine. You don't discuss a divinity's spiritual perfection. The very idea is redundant.

Thickening, slowing a shade, still vigorous and going off to war . . . but with presentments, Rwabugiri in the last decade of the nineteenth century begins thinking of his legacy, of what will remain after his death. With great political and meager personal acumen, he selects both a successor and a dowager queen to reign after he dies. The queen mother, a powerful figure in the Rwandese court, is generally the king's mother, but in this polygamous kingship, she need not be, and Rwabugiri's genius is adaptation. He is intent on seeing that the order he has developed from a looser system should survive him. He looks hard among his many sons, and finally anoints Rutalindwa, a young man with three sons of his own and a ready sword. But Rutalindwa is young; his mother's clan, the Bakono, is weak; and he needs a strong queen mother behind him, a dowager queen from a strong clan. Ever the strategist, King Rwabugiri ponders this and chooses one of his shrewdest wives, Kanjogera, a member of the powerful Bega clan, to assume the role of queen mother when he dies.

It's natural for a strong chief to fear that once he's gone, his son and successor will be vulnerable; the younger he is, the more he is vulnerable. It is for just such reasons that King Rwabugiri has fixed his purpose on strengthening the already strong control of the Rwandese state system, which means not just expanding the kingdom's borders but, more crucially, improving what will someday be called command and control, creating an order even more tightly regimented than the one he inherited, something that will live on after he dies, an order that pivots not on him as one king, but on royal legitimacy.

Throughout his reign he has been an astute manipulator of tradition. As Swahili from the coast begin inching closer to the Great Lakes in their search for trade and slaves, some kings, like Mutesa in Buganda on Lake Victoria, begin taking slaves themselves. Rwabugiri does not do that, but he takes the existing tradition of occasional forced labor, *ubuhake,* and spins off a new form of labor. It's called *uburetwa,* a word that appears to derive from Swahili. It means those brought to work for a master, and while it's not chattel slavery, and its use is limited, it's about as close to chattel slavery as serfdom can get.

Now in his later years, this agent of overwhelming change becomes not just an astute manipulator of tradition, but a master. However much Rwandese ways may evolve over the centuries, Rwandese order has always pivoted on perceived legitimacy. He knows that the order he will pass on will pivot on the same perceived legitimacy, on the unquestioned belief that the king's person is Rwandese order incarnate, that the king is the structure, stability, security of Rwandese life.

The worm in all this is something that lurks in King Rwabugiri's past, a worm that feeds on legitimacy. For decades, it has hidden asleep, a dormant parasite within the perfect order he has established, and it all begins with Queen Murorunkwere.

Murorunkwere is a woman known in Rwandese song for her beauty, for her humanity, and for her love of her son—Rwabugiri. She was a flower growing in the deceit, the lies, the conspiracies of the royal court. Her son was strong and hated by the powerful. He dealt with them by asserting his even greater power. Knives were drawn. Rwabugiri enlisted counterspies, and did so with an impetuous nature. He was an angry man. He got drunk and raged. While he was drunk, but before he raged, was the time to get his ear, and one evening, as the herons began their *qua-qua,* a vizier muttered a story to him that was as false as the ill-famed dicer's oath: Dowager Queen Murorunkwere, the man mumbled, was pregnant with the child of an old family retainer. Now came the rage: King Rwabugiri searched out the retainer and killed him on the spot. Then he paced to his mother's rondavel and killed her.

If only because he was the king, there was no question that it was his right. Blood is the king's argument. But he woke in rank horror and summoned the informant. "But I said, 'rumor has it,'" the informant insisted. "I said 'rumor has it that your mother—'" On the spot, Rwabugiri beheaded the man, and for the rest of his life was haunted by what he had done. He said the stench never left him.

Not that beautiful Kanjogera, one of King Rwabugiri's wives and now his designate to succeed as dowager queen, need fear beautiful Murorunkwere's fate as dowager queen. She is smart, her own agents are everywhere, and she knows that the royal family harbors no hothead itching to kill her in order to seize the throne from young Prince Rutalindwa, her charge. What bestirs Kanjogera is something quite different, something for which we must wait.

LET US RETURN, FOR THE MOMENT, TO THE STRANGE CASE OF EMIN PASHA, LINGERING yet at our gates. It's now been more than a year since Gordon fell at Khartoum, the Mahdi's *Ansar* are now the khalifa's *Ansar,* and the world seems to have forgotten that Emin may still be up there, surrounded. The Austrian governor of Darfur, Slatin Pasha, has been starved out of his fortress at El Obeid in the dry forests of the west and made a prisoner of the khalifa, chained to a wall like a pet monkey in the khalifa's garden. Frank Lupton, governor of Bahr el Ghazal, has sent a letter to Emin by runner, a letter now several months old and mildewed, telling him he can't hold out much longer. He hasn't been heard from since and he won't be. He 's dead.

Further afield than any of them, on the verge of our Great Lakes, Emin hasn't been heard from at all by the outside world. To the east, north, and west of him are those two million square miles of desert and scrub and elephant grass controlled by the khalifa. Immediately to the south is the deepest interior of Africa, for Emin, *Menschenfresser* country, the realm of Othello's "Cannibals that each other eat / The Anthropophagi, and men whose heads / Do grow beneath their shoulders."

Where men who eat men do not beset this country, it's the forbidden zone of the Great Lakes kingdoms. On the doorstep of this, Emin holds out with about ten thousand mostly substantial Sudanese troops led by a cadre of less than substantial Egyptian officers. They are scattered in garrisons from Lado, near present-day Juba in the Sudan, to Lake Albert. In Europe and in Britain, he is presumed dead. Hardly dead at all, he toots upriver and across the lake in an eighty-five-foot steamer, the *Khedive*. All white and brass-bright, it has an eighteen-foot beam, a complement of forty-two gunners, two cannons, and two engines that Emin keeps greased with tallow and sesame oil.

For me, Emin is more notable for the tone he sets than for what he gets done. The African subjects of German East Africa are in for some bleak days, so bleak it's hard to imagine Emin setting any sort of tone. But he will. In a few years, a flamboyant German novelist, Karl May, will compose for German-speaking lads adventures of the Haggard stripe. They will feature a fictional German scholar, Kara Ben Nemsi, who adventures through Ottoman Africa in tales that reach sales of seventy million, riveting the formative years of Albert Einstein, Franz Werfel, Hermann Hesse, and millions more Germans even today.

What strikes me isn't how May's Ben Nemsi seems modeled on Emin, nor even his racial message; which if anything is more innocent than Haggard's. What strikes me are those numbers. Now there's no doubting the swelling tide of dangerously romantic bathos on which confidence men in all their variety can set their sails—from the cheesy likes of pitchmen like Stanley to grasping prigs like Speke. As the tide buoys them on toward new horizons of celebrity, seventy million siren voices moan on the wind, and faint strains of a ranting Hitler, a ranting Mussolini, a ranting Leon Mugesera whistle between gusts.

WITH HIS COMMAND IN RAGS AND FOREVER SICK FROM BAD WATER, EMIN PASHA, OUR real-life Kara Ben Nemsi, has been dreaming up and then cobbling together a system to filter drinking water from rocky pools above his garrisons. From this high ground, he uses gravel-lined sluices to run the water down through split logs charged with charcoal. Each morning he has a bugler call his ragged troops to crisp formation, where each man must stand for inspection with twelve dead flies in his fist. He digs deep latrines, covers them with rough-cut boards, then sinks separate angled shafts down to the bottom of each pit. Baskets that let light in but trap flies cover the shafts. Inevitably, flies find their way into the latrine. There, the only light they see is through the basket. They fly up and are trapped. Every morning his men burn the fly-choked baskets.

He finds medicinal plants, sources for cascara, castor, arsenic, strychnine, quinine. He formulates therapeutic doses. Against malaria he deploys insecticides that grow wild, *Chrysanthemum coccineum* and pyrethrum, today one of our cash crops.

For the women of his outposts, he opens new worlds. He has his carpenters build them looms, and he teaches them an entirely new vocabulary: shed and countershed, temple, beater-in, heddle, frame and spool, warp and weft. They are now a cottage industry. His troops are no longer ragged. And their boss is sitting on a fortune in ivory, forgotten by his Zungu world, but not by the khalifa.

. . .

EMIN WILL ULTIMATELY SPEND A GOOD DOZEN YEARS—FROM 1874 TO 1886—STRANDED in this spot at our doorstep, years during which King Rwabugiri, engineer of the unified Rwandese state, will be at the height of his power in the Great Lakes kingdoms, and Rwanda will be at the height of her power, stretching into what is today Burundi, Tanzania, and Uganda. Rwabugiri, unifier of those who speak Kinyarwanda, will loom so large in our lives that his reign will become a reference point in every family history.

Certainly King Rwabugiri figures in the history of our family. Late in the life of our Muganza the fat man, in the fattest of his days, he enters the life of one of Rwabugiri's queens, Nyiramavugo. Nyiramavugo has a young son, Prince Nkoronko, whom she loves dearly, a son she believes gifted, but a lad considered no man by his father or the court. She gives him over to Muganza to raise in his rugo with his sons Rudasumbwa and Mukeza. Muganza makes a man of Prince Nkoronko; indeed, he makes of him a prince of some substance, and Queen Nyiramavugo is so happy she cedes the fat man land grants all over the kingdom.

This provokes no end of jealous whispers at court, and for all his grief at killing his mother on a whispered rumor, Rwabugiri remains vulnerable to talk. Muganza, gossips whisper, is up to this. Muganza, they whisper, is up to that. "Don't worry," says King Rwabugiri. "I'll take care of that silo."

Word of the king's oath gets back to Muganza, who knows, as all Rwanda knows, that King Rwabugiri is not given to idle oaths. The fat man has a julep prepared of honey wine and bile cut from the belly of a crocodile. He consumes it, it consumes him, and as he lies dying, Rwabugiri conquers and his wife, Kanjogera, waits for her dowager day.

22

Rwanda at the End of Her Rope

And a German at the End of His, Namely, Emin Pasha; 1878–1908

In 1884, in some Louis Farouk hall in another world, the Germans snatch us on paper. It will be another decade before one of them manages in physical fact to glimpse what they now fancy they own—and when at last they do get out here for a glimpse, it will be just that, a glimpse, no more than two months long, by a single expedition. This may overstate their presumption. Their knowledge of the Great Lakes, and of us in particular, is more than fancy. As early as 1878, Emin Pasha begins a twelve-year stay in the Great Lakes, limning, with addled brilliance and dainty derring-do, the most enlightened aspect of Germany's seldom enlightened face in East Africa. As far as Germany knows, he's dead.

Still unknown to the outside world, some ten thousand souls are still living under Emin, local people, itinerant traders, the wives and families of his troops, and the troops themselves, Sudanese from the north plus local Nilotes. Both groups serve him well. After a battle, Emin writes,

> *If ever I had any doubts about the Negroes, the history of the siege at Amadi would have proved to me that the black race is in valour and courage inferior to no other, while in devotion and self-denial it is superior to many.*

His Egyptian officers are another matter. They are even more duplicitous with him than they were with Gordon. For the Egyptians, this is punishment duty. Emin issues tough orders, but he's constitutionally incapable of enforcing tough orders. He scurries about in thick spectacles, identifying new species, compiling field notes, and collecting specimens, some of which he actually manages to smuggle out by runner to the British Museum.

Thus does the world learn, at long last, that he's alive, his command intact, and the world is agog at this wonder of a man. All of which is unknown to Emin and his Egyptian command. His command simply wonders at his eccentricity. To them this boss aging fast on the Nile is just the old man, with maybe a touch more regard than that. Had Maximilian taken Emin, he might now be *der Alte* for some minor Austrian command. But Maximilian didn't take him, and what he's become instead (quite unknown to him) is a darling of the German press.

A world away and oblivious of all this, his troops follow him loyally down into the evil emerald light of the Ituri wilderness, here to hunt Arab slavers. As if he hasn't enough to do just staying alive, he must hunt Arab slavers. Every step into this world is accompanied by echoing whoops and shrieks and the specter of a people that seem now to be several tribes, especially in the Congo's only majority Muslim province, Maniema. Emin's day uses the word to describe fearsomely incontinent people haunting country east of Lake Tanganyika and to describe similarly incontinent people haunting country east of Lake Albert, an expanse that today is home to hundreds of tribes. It's also likely that the fearsome reputation of peoples living in these parts owes something to dread of the unknown, but that's a bit too pat. Today as well, their turf is fearsome country in which Rwandese have fought Ugandans, and even when outsiders aren't fighting each other, death is served up every day, at times literally, since the locals still eat each other on occasion. In Emin's day, "the Manyuema" owe their power to slavers they serve as kidnappers. Some dress in the Arab manner. Their trademark cry is "*Ya 'asudu Allah!*" "In God's name, exterminate!" But to Emin's eyes (if not to the Muslim eyes of their twenty-first-century descendants), these particular slavers are neither Arabs nor Muslims. They are cannibals. They file their canines and incisors to points.

Emin makes an enemy of a cannibal chief named Kinena, and all the while the khalifa threatens from Khartoum, but Emin doesn't husband his ammunition. He spends it on forays against the slavers, and his treasury swells with confiscated ivory, tempting the khalifa all the more. Meantime, his garrisons swell with freed slaves who don't know where to go. He has work for them, but no coinage for wages. He monetizes cowrie shells; at least implicitly, the shells are backed by a treasury full of ivory.

He plants gardens. He's got beer, bananas, tomatoes, manioc, millet, goats, chickens, eggs, eggplant, freshwater fish, and fresh game aplenty. He's got an officers' mess, complete with insufferable officers. He's even got coffee, direct from adjacent Abyssinia, and a lovely Abyssinian wife, Safaran, along with an Abyssinian daughter upon whom to dote. He's got everything but a rotund little Turk in a toque stuffing grape leaves. Emin begins to wonder whether he wants to be rescued.

At just this juncture, Henry Morton Stanley shows history he's a creature of extrasensory malice. From his London roost, this buzzard's buzzard names himself Emin's rescuer. Others have floated schemes to mount a rescue, but this is the Stanley publicity machine at work. When he decides to play the hero, he gets the cash—and with a vengeance. First he taps British antislavery sentiment and patriotic spirit to raise a fortune in Britain. Then he secretly conspires with Belgium's King Leopold and the slaver Tipoo Tib to mount the rescue from the Atlantic, and thus open the Congo to his— and Leopold's—greed. Unaware of Leopold's clandestine sponsorship, the British are nonplussed. The route from the Indian Ocean looks distinctly less treacherous.

Stanley's story is largely a story of the Congo. The Great Lakes are more a part of East Africa and the Nile. Straight from the Wild West, quick-change artist Stanley slipped out of one swashbuckling outfit and into another. Just like that, he's gone from a would-be George Custer to a would-be Allan Quatermain.

I won't dwell on his cankerous progress through the Congo. Suffice it to say that the Congo's worst horror is Stanley. He orders floggings of three hundred lashes; they kill. His abuse of Africans was already legendary. Now he turns on his white officers. "Goddamned son of a sea cook," he rails as porters watch. Snakes bite, microbes eat at organs, trees shriek, hostiles lurk. No nymphs, no naiads here. Demons lay trails to nowhere, through thickets haunted by pygmies like flying whispers. Unseen, they loose barbs smeared with a pasty poison. He spends almost all his ammunition, almost all of which was intended for Emin. Half his men desert or die. His hair turns white.

When finally it dawns on Stanley how burdened he is by his own stores of luxury goods (a tin tub for bathing, matched sets of shotguns, jams from Fortnum & Mason), he abandons most of his men in the bog with orders to protect his goodies—they will die doing so—then sprints for high country where the air is healthier and dociles more common than hostiles. But even here he gets lost, gets ill, gets into skirmishes with the dociles, gets into spats with his officers. They want to press on. He wants to build a laager and stay put "until the pasha [Emin] makes up his mind to assist in his own relief." He sulks off with his Bible, leafs through it, and lo, he finds a lone and lonely friend in Solomon: "Woe unto him that is alone when he falleth, for he hath not another to help him up."

Would that poor Stanley could rise in beatitude and gaze through the mist to the east! The hills on which he rants at his peers and pouts to God roll eastward to a sheet of sheer blue that is Emin's Lake Albert, first of the Great Lakes. By and by, one of Stanley's officers does press on, and finds Emin. Emin steams south, but these are African distances. When at last the two meet, Stanley is peeved that Emin took so long to get there. Too polite in pressed white cotton drill, Emin invites Stanley aboard the polished *Khedive* for a drink in the evening breezes that riffle the waters.

It's the start of a short relationship. Emin has been twelve years on the Nile, but only part of him wants to leave. He's responsible for the ten thousand souls he governs, and he doesn't trust Stanley, who insists they leave for Zanzibar straight away. Emin temporizes. Stanley bribes. He offers Emin a thousand pounds a year to govern Equatoria—not for Victoria, for Leopold. For once, Emin doesn't temporize. He refuses.

Sadly, Stanley regains his health. I don't mean that he's sad. I mean it's sad that he regains his health. Somewhat like a Boy Scout dragging an old lady across a street she doesn't want to cross, Stanley tries to bully Emin into quitting Equatoria for the Indian Ocean. Emin's eyesight is now so bad he must hold books two inches from his spectacles. His cherished wife, Safaran, has died. Estranged from his Egyptian officers, he has only one close friend, his cherished daughter, Ferida. She is now nearly nine, in need of schooling. Now his Egyptians get rebellious. He consents to leave.

In 1889, Emin, Stanley, and company drop southeast from Lake Albert through Ankole country, then subject to King Rwabugiri's Rwandese court. Along the way, they're attacked. Routinely, Stanley holds his askaris' fire, deploying instead hired cannibals. Emin is appalled, and at this point *der Alte* becomes *der alte Kacker* (the old fart). He spots a cannibal chomping raw meat right after combat and sets to whacking him about the head with his cane. Now Stanley is appalled.

"*Never* disturb a wild animal when it's feeding!"

AT LAST THEY MAKE IT THROUGH TO THE KINGDOM OF KARAGWE ON OUR EASTERN FRONtier, from which they cut further south and east across the killing plain of Tanganyika. At last they drag into the blistered outskirts of Bagamoyo—the coastal town whose name means "bury here your heart," the town that sent Burton into Africa. The news races through the dust. Boys of all colors scamper alongside the straggling procession. *They're here! Emin is alive!* Tanned German planters in khaki shorts begin showing up, first to gawk, then to huzzah.

As they drag their way toward the center of town, they begin hearing female cheers from German ladies in long khaki skirts. Suddenly a band shows up to oompah in accolade; Emin is engulfed in a blaze of adoring affection. He's puzzled, then dazed. *This? For him?* Warships salute with booming volleys.

The Kaiser, the *Kaiser,* sends salutations. (Ah, the marvel of the telegraph!) Champagne bubbles. Late in the evening, there's a banquet. Kudos is heaped on. Nearly blind, the old coot offers not one but two speeches. He offers toasts all around; he imbibes toasts all around; and then he totters out on a balcony, and under the starlit East African sky, he falls fifteen feet, nearly to his death. His skull is cracked.

Some question whether it ever mends. Wooed alternately by the British and the Germans, he at last makes a deal to stake out our Great Lakes for Bismarck. He books passage for his daughter, Ferida, to Germany and he sets off. He's an old fifty, a cataract in one eye, deaf in one ear.

He claims Burton's favored Kazeh, now Taborah, for the Kaiser. Then the pox that scars the khalifa hits his safari. Emin's troops bury comrade after comrade, then watch as hyenas dig them up. Arriving in our cousin kingdom of Karagwe, he organizes on Lake Victoria the port of Bukoba.

The name will mean much to us. Bukoba's rickety tin godowns, its merchants all polyglot, its limping steamers and packet boats and blur of rickshaws and tarbooshes will soon provide our first real link to the outside world. But no sooner does Emin cobble Bukoba together than Bismarck strikes his landmark deal with Britain. Germany gets the lands south of Kilimanjaro and Lake Victoria. Britain gets everything north. Emin gets orders to stop short.

He refuses. His German staff takes reluctant leave—and all the porters. He sets off with four askaris loyal to him since his command in Equatoria. All he cares about now is science. He cuts quickly through vassal states of Rwanda on the northern verge of the forbidden zone, heading intently westward for the maw of the Congo. To Kibonge, chief "of all the Manyuema," he dispatches a request to collect specimens. Orders again arrive from the coast: Return. From Chief Kibonge in the Congo comes a welcoming laisser passer. Emin crosses over our Virungas and down into the Congo. The Congo swallows him.

One day near a village above the River Lindi, he pitches camp. Here that old nemesis, the cannibal chief Kinena, comes to visit him in his tent. With Kinena are two Arab slavers. All three wear white burnooses cinched with broad red cummerbunds over which are buckled greased leather belts. The belts secure long knives of Damascus steel. One of the Arabs carries a rusty revolver for which he has not one bullet. On a folding table in front of Emin lies his own revolver, greased and loaded. Kinena greets Emin warmly. Kinena can't read, but he knows about Chief Kibonge's laisser passer. He smiles indulgently as Emin reads it aloud.

I am your brother, and your friend, and your servant. It is my promise that no harm will come to you. . . .

Kinena, it seems, carries his own message from Chief Kibonge. He draws it from his belt, hands it to Emin. Emin holds it an inch from his spectacles and reads,

> *To my brother, my son, my chief Lieutenant Kinena: It is known that Emin Pasha who was once Governor of Equatoria, and whom we call the White Devil, is in my country. It is my order that you take some men and go to him, and that you kill him by cutting off his head, and that you send me his head in a box so that I may know my orders have been carried out. Do this, Kinena, and you will show me that you are my loyal subject, my brother, and my son, and that you love me even as I love you.*

Emin glances myopically at the table. His revolver is gone. One of the Arabs grabs him. His glasses fall off. He fumbles. The other Arab, Mamba by name, grabs his curly black hair, pulls his head back, and draws Damascus steel. Emin whispers, *"Ferida."* Mamba's blade slices across Emin's throat. Blood shoots in pumping spurts. Slippery with blood, Mamba hacks off Kibonge's trophy and hands it by its hair to Kinena.

Emin's head held high, Kinena strides out. Warriors stand in battle plumage, ivory plugs in their noses, hair pasted back with dung, incisors filed so sharp their mouths bleed. There's brief silence, then spears begin rattling against shields in a steady *clack-clack* that becomes steadily louder. Suddenly they erupt in shrieks that envelope the village and the hills upon which the village stands, until at last their whoops get lost in the endless Ituri wilderness, already enveloped in its own everlasting whoops and shrieks.

IT'S 1890. RWANDA IS STILL A LAND NO GERMAN, NO EUROPEAN, NO ARAB HAS EVER seen and lived to tell about. Stanley had once tried to become the first Muzungu to enter our realm; to that end, he commissioned a report from an Arab. "Over the past eight years," the man reported, "Khamis bin Abdullah, Tipoo Tib, Said bin Habib, and I have often tried to get into Rwanda, never successfully." At Lake Windemere on our frontier with Karagwe, Stanley dropped the effort, later quoting "an old Arab proverb" to the effect that hard as it is to get into Rwanda, it's a deal harder to get out. That was almost two decades ago. By now Rwanda is a German possession, except that no German possesses her. She remains unbreached.

It takes another two years for that exploring missionary Oscar Baumann to penetrate the kingdom. Financed by antislavery societies, he spends four days about six kilometers on the Banyarwanda side of the Burundi frontier. Needless to say, he doesn't free any slaves.

There aren't any slaves to speak of in Rwanda, and Baumann doesn't confuse serfdom with the slave trade that rages outside the Great Lakes kingdoms, and is now beginning to percolate inside some of them. Campaigning against slavery has become big business, as big by now as slaving itself, and soon to be bigger. It's a monumental fund-raiser for churches and their mission societies. When Germans finally begin showing up in Rwanda in modest numbers, German military officers will find themselves in a running feud with both Protestant and Catholic missions. The military men will insist that the forbidden zone never allowed entry to slavers, and still doesn't. The missions will insist the territory is rife with slavers, and please send cash. At least they won't come to blows. In fully medieval *odium theologicum*, neighboring Great Lakes realms have seen Christian missions wage bloody war with rival preachers of Islam.

Two years after Baumann, in May of 1894, comes Count Adolf von Götzen. A young lieutenant in Bismarck's imperial army, he's four months into a landmark trek across Africa from the Indian Ocean to the Atlantic. For old King Rwabugiri, at the peak of his power and raising great armies to invade chiefly states all about Rwanda, von Götzen's modest safari is little more than a curiosity. Rwabugiri is impressed by the white men's *imbunda,* their new repeating rifles, and later he will counsel his chiefs not to resist these "*Zungu imbunda.*" But it's clear enough that the innocent-looking young count is after neither ivory nor slaves. Headed west for Lake Kivu and the Congo, von Götzen presents himself to Rwabugiri at a royal compound, and heartily impressed with Rwanda, the pink-cheeked lad extends his hand to Rwabugiri, or more precisely, up to Rwabugiri. The king, bemused, extends his down to von Götzen. Von Götzen seizes the king's hand and shakes. The court shrinks back in horrified unison. The king is not to be touched. The royal family is not to be touched. The king is Rwanda incarnate. Shake the king and you shake Rwanda. Supremely unaware that he has shaken Rwanda, the German sets off for Kivu, in due course gazes down on the lake, writes grandly in his journal that he has discovered it, and before the end of June, he's gone, on his way to the Atlantic, which has already been discovered.

THE SONS OF A DISGRACED FAMILY

King Rwabugiri owes a good measure of his success to nerve. He's not merely a *mwami* who makes war; he leads in battle. By the time of von Götzen's 1894 visit, he is already aging. His mind wanders across the Rusizi River to the country of the Bushi people in the king of Belgium's Congo Free State. It's doubtful whether he even knows there is such a creature as the Congo Free State. Either way, he rates the country as plump a target as Leopold does, and begins crafting an expeditionary force that he, the king, will lead personally. Yet again, drums beat orders, units across Rwanda form up and set off for rendezvous. At first the trails they beat are like the trails they beat on the raids that Mutemura and Muganza led on Burundi. But in the high mountains of the southwest they cut sharply west, climb the passes of the continental divide, drop down into the valley of the River Rusizi, and cross the river into the Congo.

The Congo swallows them.

The few it spits out return with the king's body. Kigeri IV Rwabugiri is dead. His son Mibambwe IV Rutalindwa is king. In keeping with orders left by Rwabugiri, the court assigns one of the fat man's sons, Mama's grandfather Rudasumbwa, to the guards, the company that will protect the late king's dauphin and son, Prince, now King, Rutalindwa.

Kanjogera is no longer simply a queen, of which there are several. She's the *dowager* queen, virtually the regent for her charge, young King Rutalindwa, and in a matter of weeks there are troubling signs. The signs begin as she starts enhancing the posture of her already powerful Bega clan within the court. Adversaries, especially among the royal Nyiginya clan, Rwanda's only kingly clan, find themselves the victims of maneuvering. Old King Rwabugiri had himself maneuvered to keep his powerful fellow clansmen in check, but by now they are much weakened by all that, and the dowager queen is moving to make them yet weaker, her fellow Bega clansmen yet stronger.

Powerful chiefs who traditionally surround the king, especially powerful chiefs from the royal clan, are dispatched to foreign wars, where their reward may well be death.

NO SOONER DO BAUMANN AND VON GÖTZEN SHOW UP THAN A THIRD GERMAN-SPEAKER comes round. The year is 1895, and by all accounts he's an intelligent, unassuming man, Lieutenant Richard Kandt. No *von*, he's a shy, lone traveler, a medical doctor, a scholar. The same year, Kabenga's older brother, Bitahurwina, goes off to *intore* camp. The *intore* are Rwanda's fighting regiments. The camp Bitahurwina goes off to drills Tutsi patricians on how to be Tutsi patricians and how to lead the *intore*. For the first time in his life, this somewhat dreamy lad, Bitahurwina, is away from the family rugo, and here, undergoing the rites of initiation in cold isolation, he discovers what Rwanda is discovering: What the Dowager Queen Kanjogera is after is the head, literally the head, of her charge, young King Rutalindwa.

Climax comes with a quarrel between children in a courtyard near the royal rugo in Rucunshu, a few miles north of the royal settlement at Nyanza. Mama's grandfather, young Rudasumbwa, is an officer in the king's guard, but he's not on duty; he's one hill over the horizon with his family. In a flash, the quarrel shows itself for what it is, a staged distraction. Suddenly a troop of painted witch doctors appears, assegais fixed, and confusion makes his masterpiece. These painted creatures are *abapfumu,* men from families in which the family business is witch medicine.

There could be none better to administer the bad medicine of regicide. They close on the royal *rugo.* Queen Kanjogera appears. The guard, and young King Rutalindwa himself, rush from the royal *rugo* and close with the would-be regicides in the broad courtyard of pounded clay. Beneath a balmy sky, witch doctors begin falling in pools of mud and blood, and in such numbers that the balance begins to shift against them. Perhaps the resistance is stiffer than the conspirators expected. Or perhaps it's the spectacle of the young king himself resisting, the taboo of defiling a king. Witch doctors, after all, are not immune to witch medicine. Queen Kanjogera scurries in the dust. Is she unsettled at the spectacle of what she's done? Or dissembling? By some accounts she draws a knife, ready for suicide.

Suddenly, from among the witch doctors, her brother Kabare appears with her young son, Musinga. Kabare is huge. He hoists the boy above his head. "Here see the true king!" he shouts. "Rutalindwa usurps!"

The balance slips back to the witch doctors. Inch by inch, guard and king fall back to the royal rugo. Young King Rutalindwa is doomed. Rather than be taken alive, he torches his own rondavel. In the confusion, the notoriously sacred drum, the *kalinga,* vanishes. Draped with the testicles of the king's enemies, it's a closely guarded emblem of the kingdom's strength. It's gone. Half a century later, church-tutored Hutu ideologues will manipulate myth and tradition as deftly as old King Rwabugiri. They will begin routinely describing the *kalinga* as draped with the testicles of the king's enemies, *the Bahutu.* With few exceptions Bahutu are neither the king's enemies nor his trophies. His trophies are nobles in the armies of enemy kingdoms.

Now comes the hour for Mama's grandfather, the fat man's son Rudasumbwa, officer of the king's personal guard. The dead king's personal guard.

The king's killers don't kill Rudasumbwa. They bind his hands and feet, and confine him to his rugo. Every day they lead him out for royal entertainment. They fit his head with the long heavy horns of a bull. He must struggle to keep his head upright. As Queen Kanjogera and her brothers Kabare and Kayondo look on, as Rudasumbwa's brother Mukeza is forced to look on, warriors charge him, assegais aloft, then halt.

The queen's company chants,

> *Rudasumbwa, Rudasumbwa,*
> *Rutalindwa is lonely.*

Again the warriors charge with assegais raised; again they pull up short.

> *Rudasumbwa, Rudasumbwa,*
> *is Rutalindwa the true king?*

"He is."

At this, one man speaks. "Then you must obey him, oh Rudasumbwa. He says he wants you. He's lonely. Let us help you join him." The speaker is the queen's brother, Chief Kayondo. To Chief Kayondo the dowager court has dispensed leadership of the family, Mutemura's Batemura, subclan of the Singa people.

Now the warriors charge again, but this time they don't pull up short. This time they let fly and their aim is perfect. Which means it's always bloody but never lethal. Each spear draws blood. Not one kills. It would be death for any warrior whose spear ruined Chief Kayondo's courtly entertainment. Spears slice his arms, calves, thighs, never his heart, never his throat. Meat hangs off his frame. He's led away bleeding, to be returned the next day, and the next, for the same.

At last someone smuggles him that concoction of honey wine and bile that so consumed his father, Muganza; at last the courtly entertainment is over.

Young King Rutalindwa, young Rudasumbwa, and their brothers in death this season will inspire a later generation of Tutsi men and boys to tilt at windmills in defense of an antique and obsolete monarchy. Likewise, Queen Kanjogera will become the nickname of a highborn woman in a position of silent power.

IT'S SOME YEARS AFTER THE RUCUNSHU REGICIDE THAT KABENGA GOES OFF TO *INTORE* camp, the orphan son of an enemy of the new royal court, about to be initiated into the service of the new court, by drillmasters of the new court.

A few years after the shock of losing his father comes this shock of initiation. Days of running, nights of torment, regimen and regimentation; you fail, you disgrace your father, dead of torment. In the immediate wake of the regicide, his father died for the entertainment of this new court. How will its drillmasters deal with him?

I don't know for sure. Heroic tales are legion in Rwanda, and legion in our family. Battles involving thousands were often resolved as champions from either side stepped forward in heroic combat. But such heroism is of a formal mold. This is not. What faces Kabenga at this moment, and exactly what happens, is destined to be one of those things that our family, true Rwandese, are determined to keep secret.

Just who are these drillmasters who top-rate the son of a disgraced family? Are they old school themselves? Or is it the ever even hand of the professional drillmaster? I've always assumed it's the even hand. In the telling of the stories, there's no suggestion that during his initiation, Kabenga suffered as a result of his father's allegiances. Indeed, there are no tales of his courage at camp, nor of his terror. Regardless, these questions hang in the air, and they are of a piece with the ambiguity enveloping the kingdom. The Dowager Queen Kanjogera and her brother Chief Kabare are ruthless, but they know that they must somehow heal the wounds they've opened, that they can't kill everybody, and all this makes for an unpredictable, unsettling atmosphere.

Javelin hurling, wrestling, and at last, after long weeks, come evenings devoted to the arts of rhetoric, then conversation. What to say, what not to say, what things mean when parsed, how to hide what you feel. Then come days of *intore,* the precisely drilled dance of the regimental warriors, nights of song and composition, which for illiterates means poetry. At fifteen or sixteen, Kabenga, the boy who will be our grandfather, is at last able to sit with men, drink with them, talk and bargain with them. He becomes a *mugabo,* a man. He becomes an eligible bachelor. He is also eligible for the draft.

FLEDGLINGS OF DECEIT

The obligations of the extended family are manifold indeed. When your brother dies, you don't merely take responsibility for his children. You take them into your rugo, your household, they become *your* children. You take his wife.

Mukezarugamba, whose name I remember as Mukeza, is the brother of Kabenga's father, Rudasumbwa, recently dead of torment. They were both sons of the fat man, Muganza of the Inzirabwoba, likewise dead of torment. In 1896 Rudasumbwa is buried, and the arc of Mukeza's life as a responsible son and brother emerges from the routine of courtly life. He marries Rudasumbwa's wife. He adopts her children, Bitahurwina, grandfather to-be Kabenga, and a girl, Mbangara. He's twenty-five.

Even before the 1896 regicide, Mukeza's new stepson Bitahurwina was somewhat shy, and now he has been hit by his father's death. His bones are finer than those of his younger brother, Kabenga. He's lankier than Kabenga, as willowy as he is tall, a warrior for all that (in a few years he will be at war deep in Uganda), but a warrior with his head up there with the finches, where it's destined to remain until he dies of old age. Right up to his final days, Bitahurwina will be composing odes to his wife, a jealous harridan who commands his total devotion.

Mukeza and his first wife have a daughter of their own, Stefania. She is a rampaging toddler; short for the family, she's already intent on making up for her size. Now Stefania has a cousin become sister, Mbangara, sometimes called Elizabeti, a few years older and Stefania's model in all matters female.

Father Rudasumbwa is dead, but the family is alive, feeling his wounds. Young King Rutalindwa is dead, but the kingdom is alive, feeling his wounds. Rwanda's nerves are raw. For a century or more, big speckled eggs of uncertain origin have been incubating in the compost of a nation producing too much compost. Now the vultures have come home to roost. One by one, the fledglings of one hundred years of greed and deceit are hatching. Whom to believe? Whom to trust? The kingdom is exhausted, its self-assurance reaching a nadir.

You could fool the Germans. They are mightily impressed. They seem to understand only superficially what has happened. A coup? Happens everywhere. In the best of families. They seem not to grasp that this is no garden-variety coup, that the manner in which it has shaken the kingdom is what now enables a modest German presence here.

A year or so after the Rucunshu regicide, one Hauptmann H. von Ramsay, a Scot in German service whose swashbuckling has already won him his *von,* shows up in Ruanda-Urundi. Since before the regicide, young Dr. Kandt has been quietly roaming the country. Von Ramsay, far the more flamboyant of the two, gets right down to cases, requesting an audience with the king. This time the court is Kanjogera's, and considerably more suspicious. Amid elaborate ceremony, which duly impresses von Ramsay, they introduce the Teutonic Scot to a double posing as the new king, and the swashbuckler is none the wiser. Von Ramsay then takes off on a tour of the Reich's possession, gloriously unaware of the political turmoil that has enabled his grand tour—and just like that, he too is gone.

Little matter that so few Germans are able to journey to Rwanda. Kanjogera, for all her caution, has left the gates open, if only by sapping the nation's will to keep them closed. For a while, few new outsiders show up. Studious Lieutenant Kandt continues, quietly, to roam the hills. There is no great rush to join him. Rwanda is still months from the East African coast. But then, in flurries, little white butterflies in pith helmets begin fluttering into the forbidden zone, speaking crude Swahili and somehow inducing everyone to address them as *bwana,* "milord," a Swahili term of address we know but have never before used. No one orders either their evisceration or their expulsion. Rwanda has other things on its mind.

The *kalinga,* the sacred drum, is still missing. Gone with it is all the court's self-confidence, just as the kingdom, now larger than ever, needs confident administration more than ever. Instead, suspicion is rife. A few white men showing up with little more than palaver to peddle are of scant concern. It means little that a few Bazungu called Germans try to tell us we're part of their particular corner of that shabby world down where the country is dry and diseased.

Of course, one must keep an eye on them, especially with their propensity for using cheap wonders to turn the heads of the gullible. Even here, though, there's as much opportunity as danger. Given astute management, their cheap wonders might be turned to a certain advantage in rebuilding the court's prestige.

ABER NATÜRLICH, BWANA

All across Tanganyika, on their way to Ruanda-Urundi, the Germans have been throwing their Teutonic weight about, marching into villages in hob-nailed boots and perfect formation, goose-stepping through the dust, eyes right, Mausers at present-arms. One after another, to the oompah harmony of tubas, they have been inducing the Tanganyikan chiefs to put their crosses on treaties the chiefs can't read. German gunboats, sparkling in light opera splendor, lie off the sunny coast of Zanzibar. The Brits have promised Zanzibar's Sultan Bargash: End the slave trade and we'll take care of you. He does. They don't. As German guns appear on the horizon of a brilliant sea, the Brits swallow their dignity, and Bargash, in due course, dies of indignity. (Restrain your sympathy. Asked years earlier what determines succession to the Sultanate, Bargash answered, "The length of one's sword.") Abandoning Gordon to death by the sword at Khartoum has doubly stunned Victorian Britain, first with shame and then with fear, and for now, fear is the ruling emotion.

Just how deep is this yawning pit called Africa? Like Clinton in Somali country barely a century hence, Britons are suffering from Africa malaise. On top of this, the British need Bismarck's help dealing with the French challenge to British hegemony in Egypt and the Sudan, and what Bismarck wants in exchange is for Britain to make nice in Zanzibar and Tanganyika. For some reason, he seems to enjoy writing check after check for gunboats.

Brass ablaze in the sun, brilliant little semaphores aflutter, German warships draw up in a line: *Ethernets, Storch, Gneisenau, Prinz Adalbert* (into the twenty-first century, Rwandese boys will be baptized Adalbert). An admiral with a waxed moustache stands erect on a deck swabbed thrice. In starched white drill, he barks a command, the command is barked down the line, and the vessels correct their guns for range.

Zanzibar has twenty-four hours to yield its East African hegemony to Germany. Britain folds its hand. Gladstone, having replaced Disraeli as prime minister, refers to Tanganyika as that "mountain country behind

Zanzibar with an unrememberable name" (into the twenty-first century, Rwandese boys will be baptized Gladstone).

Already, Bismarck's investment in gunboats is beginning to pay off, and *Herr Reichskanzler* is likewise performing as banker to the carpetbagger of the East African world, Karl Peters. Every fiscal quarter, the accounts of Herr Peters's German East Africa Company bulge ever greater with ivory profit and tribute. Everywhere, hippo hide whips crack and African blood flows. Everywhere, German planters are putting Tanganyikan warriors to the plow and shaping their new protectorate to the ordered German mold.

Rwanda, of course, is already a thoroughly ordered world . . . but is Rwandese order any adequate substitute for German order? Especially with Rwanda in a state of nervous exhaustion? Suffice it to say, the Germans take one look at Rwanda and decide that maybe this is one place they shouldn't throw their weight around. So far, they have little idea of our nervous exhaustion. Why don't you just keep running the place the way you always have? they suggest to the royal court.

Aber natürlich, bwana. But of course.

Forget colonial plunder. This is a distinctly better deal for the king of Rwanda than it is for Germany. Not for Rwanda, mind you, but for the king and his court, for the court of Dowager Queen Kanjogera. As for Kanjogera, she never even deigns to meet the Germans, not one of them, and she never will. She maintains her remote authority in a manner to be matched a century hence by a latter-day queen, herself described on the roads and the tracks as "Kanjogera," a queen born Kanziga Agathe, Habyarimana's wife.

As Kanjogera and her brother have manipulated events, the Germans are here for one purpose, to shore up a hated royal house that the Germans don't even know needs shoring up.

Before a stiff but silent military band, the flag of empire flutters up in the dust. In front of the band, a brindled cur noses about, suspicious. The band strikes up. The dog runs for its life. The band booms *"Deutschland über Alles,"* then Strauss. A ruddy bandmaster straight out of the Katzenjammer Kids pumps his baton before an African band tricked out in every bit of ribbon and braid that the book allows. Bands were simply not meant to play Strauss, but as young Kabenga looks on, I'm sure he's impressed, and he needs the diversion. Different though he is from his shy brother, Bitahurwina, the Rucunshu slaughter preoccupies him. It's the two girls, short and solid, Elizabeti and Stefania, who will keep the siblings on a stable course.

Sweating in starched white drill, and as impressed with Rwanda as young Kabenga is with them, a few pink-cheeked young *Offiziere* try their best to take it all in. They seem barely aware that to the strains of their band tooting Strauss they have waltzed into the forbidden zone and taken it over without firing a shot. At least on paper.

23

CAPTAIN MAX AND HIS RENEGADE BATUTSI
1908–1917

Men's men: gentle or simple, they're much of a muchness.
—GEORGE ELIOT, *Daniel Deronda*

Back in Muganza's day, no one ever came to the fat man and told him to poison himself. Likewise now, in 1908, no one comes to young Kabenga's stepfather, Mukeza, and tells him to take his family, his two wives, his children and his stepchildren, and go away. He simply does what he has to, marshals his Hutu—and Tutsi—servants and their families as porters, puts his and his dead brother's households on the track, gathers his hunting dogs and Ankolehorned herd, and moves out, like the nomadic Batutsi of old.

They stride, wending north, servants in loincloths, the family in mushananas, Mukeza and his sons with stout staves horizontal behind their necks and across their shoulders, stepping out across broad rolling pasture, through thicket, sedge, and bracken, along tree lines, into timber. Much as Mutemura and Muganza once eyed their men at drill, these three, Mukeza and his two stepsons, Bitahurwina and young Kabenga, now eye their cattle for danger. All about them, children scramble, dogs scamper. Behind them, porters labor, bearing clay pots, fine baskets full of goods, finely woven mats in rolls, bearing Mukeza's two wives aloft in palanquins, their faces half-hidden behind veils of bone beads that hang from their foreheads. Gentry and servants, all are leaving the only home they know, leaving mothers, cousins, grandparents, for parts to them unknown and unknowable.

Mukeza is headed for family lands in Kiyanza country, well north of the Germans' new settlement at Kigali on the River Nyabarongo. They near the settlement. Drums begin to talk. Past the drum-talk they push, herding through the middle of this raw settlement, green with the scent of fresh-cut lumber, a settlement soon to become the kaiser's signature outpost in the Rwandese lands of Ruanda-Urundi. In the face of Mukeza's oncoming Ankole horns, Germans on mules rein aside, as bemused at the sight of Mukeza's people as Mukeza's people are at the sight of them, these so-called Germans, these *Abadage*. On through the settlement Mukeza's people push, on the track across Muhima hill, past Kigali's new colonial police post on their right (past destiny on their right), the Mount Kigali valley falling away in lush jungle on their left. Across swales of green pasture they push, they and their cows, across the flanks of Mount Kigali and on toward Uganda.

THE JAVELINEER, THE *HUNDMEISTER*

I used to wonder about those iconic fighting bulls of southern France and Spain, and the frescoes of bull-baiting Cretans at Minos. How like Egypt and its great horned cattle? How like us? How like our cattle cultures, bristling with horns? Not at all. How different. For Europe, since ancient Crete, it is the bull. For us, from antiquity, it is the cow.

It's not simply that we name our cows; that we compose odes to our cows and sing of them; that we see in our cows the soul of womanly charm. More than that: We render your bull an afterthought. The cow's world that we husband beside our human world is a world of feminist fantasy, in which males, which is to say bulls, are kept in a back lot, used for breeding, and done with. Even among our most warlike males, certainly among the Batutsi, it is the cow, never the bull, that is iconic.

For Kabenga and for his brother, Bitahurwina, as for their stepfather and teacher, Mukeza, the cow is all bounty and all wealth. It's not roaring pride; roaring pride they find in dance, and in the hunt, as once they found it in war. It's domestic pride. It's for their cows that they rise before dawn, calling them by name, cuffing the sleepy, calming the colicky. It's to their cows that they pay patient, faithful attention.

Pushing ever northward from Nyanza, Mukeza and his stepsons trace ancient safari tracks, collect their bearings at ancient salt markets. At river fords, pirogues await—for the women, the children, the porters, the goods. For the cows there are of course none, and so there are none for the foreman, nor for Bitahurwina, nor for Kabenga. As Mukeza stands watch from rocks above rapids, they plunge with the cows into the swirling current, and the current sweeps them between thousand-pound beasts who would crush and drown them and not even know it. Even crocs, their maws drooling mucus in anticipation of red meat, hang back from this mass, lurking in hopes of the weak on the periphery. The brothers swim among the cows, herding them, separating them, quieting them, lest they crush and drown each other, or drift too far and fall prey to the beasts that lurk. In Kiyanza country they settle at last.

Germans are almost nowhere to be seen. Here and there, now and then, on safari, you find them, and these rare occasions turn Kabenga's head. The overriding fact of Rwandese life is still Kanjogera and her deceit. But these Germans provide diversion. Occasional displays of German talent divert Rwanda in her funk.

Kabenga is impressed. The Germans haven't been heavy-handed in Rwanda. Rwanda runs itself. Mukeza and Kabenga and Bitahurwina do hear now and then what the Germans can be like down on the hardpan below. Just a few years earlier, that freebooting mogul Karl Peters was hanging mothers as routine communal punishment. Then between 1905 and 1907 came the Maji-Maji rebellions. Wholesale abuse of the *kiboko*, the hippo-hide whip, drove tens of thousands of Africans in the heart of Tanganyika to rise against German rule. The Germans cut down twelve thousand rebels—and learned something of a lesson. Emin Pasha is beginning to strike slightly more of a chord for the Germans, Karl Peters slightly less. The Germans are beginning to put some effort into infrastructure, and even if Africans don't feel indebted for that, they are impressed with German craft.

Mukeza has tutored his dead brother's sons in the skills of the archer, the javelineer, the hound master, and the tracker, and now the age of the Zungu safari, the white man's hunt, has begun. Even at Rwanda's great distance, one or two wealthy Germans (in lederhosen, no less!) manage to bring mules and the latest sporting rifles. In the marshes between the hills, in the Gishwati forest of the far northwest, in the Nyungwe forest of the southwest, and on the far eastern Akagera floodplain between Rwanda and Karagwe, game flourishes.

Thirty or so porters form up, bearing every sort of Zungu gear: camp stoves, canvas sheeting, canvas webbing, mosquito netting, lanterns, Meissen china, starched white table linen, tinned tubs for bathing, folding chairs, folding desks, Shirazi rugs from Zanzibar, brass-studded Zanzibar chests, the dusty treasures of a small wine cellar, all on Hutu heads. On surrounding hills, Bahutu and Batutsi stand and watch—children especially. At the front of the column stand two or three Tutsi askaris. Toward the end, four hearty porters bear a gauze-draped German lady on a palanquin. At the very end of this procession, the pith-helmeted client and his great white hunter sit mounted on mules. A pygmy tracker trots up and down the line, rousing the porters in synchronous, sonorous song, and the column moves out, at which point the children on the hills pick up the song.

These safaris are as methodical as you'd expect a proper German safari to be. On top of this, they're often aimed at something more focused and worthwhile than just a good time; in particular, at science, which the scholarly world back in Germany does not ignore and at times duly recognizes. For instance, in 1902, one Captain Oscar von Beringe organizes a safari aimed at scaling Mount Sabyinyo in the Virungas, a set of jagged crags twelve thousand feet above already high Gisenyi, and never before climbed by a white man.

A worthy goal, if for no other reason than that the peaks are there, but von Beringe never gets anywhere near the top, if for no other reason than that he brings no rope. He has all the trimmings of a full-dress safari, but this would-be mountaineer has no rope.

Tant pis, something's always happening in unexplored wilds, and he tells us all about it in a local paper called *Deutsches Kolonialblatt.* Stopped cold at something like nine thousand feet, forced to camp on little more than a ledge, shivering with the lichens, Hauptmann Oscar and his mates gaze skyward, and another thousand or so feet up, through mist and fast-moving clouds, they spy what looks like primates gamboling on the very peaks that their lack of rope has prevented them from scaling. Genus? Chimps, it would seem, for many range here. They can't be humans. Not that far up. Not without rope. So what to do? Shoot them of course. These would-be mountaineers might have forgotten to bring rope, but they'd never forget their rifles.

They draw their beads, squeeze off their rounds, and two distant forms plummet through a gray-green defile into a deep ravine.

After heroic effort, they recover a body. Mangled as it is by the rocky plummet, it must be hard to make out. Nearly as big as a human. Perhaps this specimen is a record trophy. No hair on chest, face, hands, feet. Otherwise hairy—and mature. Stretched out, it measures almost five feet. Von Beringe sends skin and bones off to Berlin for proper identification.

Berlin's verdict: "immature male."

Immature?

Immature, and no, it's not *Gorilla gorilla gorilla,* Africa's long known (but seldom seen) giant. This immature specimen implies something bigger. Von Beringe has discovered *Gorilla gorilla gorilla*'s somewhat bigger cousin, the mountain gorilla. Or as careful science will soon identify the species, *Gorilla gorilla beringei.*

What I want to know is, on our great continent, with mountain chains thousands of miles long, how is it that this animal turns up first in tiny, remote Rwanda? A rare and fugitive beast indeed, and how it will one day induce distant Bazungu to dote on our backwater.

. . .

ON THE OTHER SIDE OF VICTORIA, IN KENYA COLONY, SAFARIS ARE EVEN GRANDER, OFTEN much grander, with up to a hundred porters, enough to lay down a chain of camps from which independent gangs can come and go, resupplying the hunt from Nairobi or from Mombasa. In 1909, Teddy Roosevelt shows up. His white hunter is a settler named Frederick Courtney Selous, already an accomplished naturalist. After one of many glorious days on safari, Selous's client exclaims in his diary, "A Pleistocene day!" Neolithic is more like it, even Edwardian, but soon enough, any safari's Edwardian grandeur is swallowed up by what the Germans call the *bundu,* the encompassing African bush, and then the day must seem Pleistocene indeed.

ACROSS UGANDA TO FAR JINJA

In 1912, upcountry Rwanda, the very country from which von Beringe snatched his prize, is seized by the great Hutu rebellion. Drums from hills just to the west of Mukeza's *rugo* talk blood. Gazing west, young Kabenga sees smoke rising in wisps. Through most of the past century, the court at Nyanza has been pushing into this largely autonomous country, largely ruled by Hutu princes, but since the regicide the court has been unsteady, and now Hutu princes east of Mukeza's lands seize the uncertain day. The Hutu lineages of the north know full well how the Dowager Queen Kanjogera and her brothers conspired to murder the young king, the legitimate king, anointed by the old king before he was brought back dead from the Congo. Better than the Germans, they know that this regicide weakens her, perhaps fatally. They sense their day, and when they seize it, they do so under the banner of legitimacy, the banner of what is right and proper and ordered. They choose a Tutsi pretender to the Nyanza throne to lead them.

They don't choose him because they feel they need a Tutsi leader, and certainly not because they see Batutsi as inherently superior to them. They choose him because this particular Mututsi has a credible (if uncertain) claim to a throne whose legitimacy is in question. No matter that had he lived, the old king himself, the font of legitimacy, would most likely have moved against these same autonomous Bahutu, just as Dowager Queen Kanjogera's court is now doing. For the Hutu princes, this isn't the point. The point is tradition and legitimacy. Even these frontier Bahutu know that the banner of tradition is up for grabs, and they grab for it.

With German help, the kingdom strikes back. It does not draft Mukeza. All of upcountry Rwanda is in jeopardy. The court needs the family where it is.

In short order, the kingdom crushes the Hutu princes, the *bahinza.* The word *muhinza,* which has long meant "prince," now means "rebel." Now only a few autonomous Hutu realms remain, Bagoyi, Bakonya, Kibari.

The Tutsi pretender flees north into British East Africa, and the Germans, testing British mettle for their own Zungu purposes, put together a war party of "Watusi" to invade British turf.

No Germans go, but Mukeza's stepson Bitahurwina does, and now Bitahurwina's ever-jealous wife, Rosa, has real and immediate cause for jealousy—that cause being Fate, Fate in the person of a Mauser model 71 five-round repeater. And that's just how every drilled rifleman sees his piece—as a person. Long the standard firearm for black troops in the khaki of German East Africa, it's now been remaindered by the Germans as obsolete.

Here, now, is the family's first firearm. It is something of a wonder that the court has the Germans enlist quiet Bitahurwina, not Kabenga. Bitahurwina is the elder of the two brothers, and his wife is pregnant. Kabenga is still unmarried and the picture of Tutsi bravura. Bitahurwina seems happy to dote on his jealous Rosa, who sorely needs the doting. But when it comes to bearing the family's first firearm, it is clear that the powers that be have made the right choice. In the same way that Bitahurwina has for so long been so attentive to Rosa, he is now forever attentive to his obsolete Mauser. Eyes shut, he practices tearing it down and putting it back together. He learns how the slightest damp in the air brings a dusting of barely visible rust to her nicely rifled barrel, and to her action, there to conjure misfires. As Rosa stews in her jealous juices, he strokes his new beauty, polishes her, sights her; never does he grab rudely, and when it comes to her trigger, he never ever yanks, but squeezes, and oh so gently, lest he pull his shot off its mark.

Comes a chill morning, they muster. As the hour approaches to move out, Bitahurwina hides his piece by rolling it into the grass blanket upon which he will sleep when he can. Likewise do all his Tutsi comrades hide their obsolete and carefully tended Mausers. There are a few porters with basic foodstuffs, mostly rice; Bitahurwina carries an Emory cloth, a two-piece ramrod to swab the barrel, a small dry rag, a small rag doused in gun oil, his pipe, some tobacco, a flint, a knife, a canteen, a little tin cup, and ammunition.

Ahead lie hundreds of miles of enemy bush. They set out afoot, Muganza's men, on the track again. All the way to Jinja on the far shore of Lake Victoria they drive, where they find the pretender and kill him. When Bitahurwina returns to Rosa, he finds that he has a son, Kagame.

WATUSI AT LARGE; GERMANS AT WAR

Count Paul von Lettow-Vorbeck and his subordinate, Captain Max Wintgens, are boys of the same school and the same disposition. They are both smart, engaging. Sticklers for detail, right enough; cynics might say they both have a weakness for standing on protocol. All the same, they're both generally at ease. Both are gents disposed by nature to take up the challenge. Close your eyes, imagine only their military personalities, and they are almost eerie doubles, *echte Doppelgänger.* Naturally, they don't get along.

Lettow-Vorbeck sails into Dar es Salaam in January 1913 aboard the SS *Admiral* out of Aden and Mombasa. The day is perfect. Soot belches from the *Admiral* and loses itself in an enormity of sky. The count is erect, fine-boned; he sports a sandy Vandyke. As he descends the gangplank, he wears cotton drill, smartly starched, salty. On his collar is the insignia of a colonel in the German Army, on his chest a few decorations, in particular those for gallantry while suppressing the Boxer Rebellion in China and the Herero and Hottentot rebellions in German South West Africa. Some historians will one day see the Herero business as mankind's first modern genocide, given its focused, planned use of execution, starvation, and war to wipe out a people.

It will be a few weeks before Lettow-Vorbeck falls out with his subordinate, Captain Max. In January 1913, nearly half the continent of Africa separates them. Wintgens is the German military commander for Rwanda, which is now part of—and at the far western end of—German East Africa, whose new military commander is Lettow-Vorbeck. To get to Rwanda from the territory's seat at Dar es Salaam, you first book passage on the passenger wagon that may or may not be coupled to the freight train that runs at Africa's arbitrary convenience on the brave new Nordbahn, their railway, from Dar to the railhead at Ujiji on Lake Tanganyika. If there's room for the wagon, and if there's a seat for you on the wagon, you board and spend uncountable days trying to figure out whether it's better to open the window and get sandblasted or close the window and melt as fast as an Italian ice in a hothouse. For nearly half the span of the continent, you chug uphill behind a locomotive that chugs slowly when it's headed downhill. To kill the tedium, some passengers jump off and stride alongside. At times it seems the milestones must be ten-mile stones. At times it seems that washouts come as frequently as the milestones. At each washout, you must wait forever in the heat as Goan coolies quickstep to the rescue. Inevitably, as you wait, some earnest young settler climbs topside with his pith helmet and his Mauser and plays great white hunter. Apocryphal stories circulate of lions whose diet is coolies.

At the Ujiji railhead at last, you book passage on the lake steamer *Graf von Götzen* to a settlement at the north end of the lake, Usumbura in the kingdom of Urundi, to be known one day as Bujumbura in Burundi. There you search out porters and askaris for hire, you reserve enough Maria Theresa dollars to hire pirogues along the way, you hope you can trust your crew, your crew paddles you north up the Rusizi from Usumbura, and then you walk. Or more exactly, you climb. Depending on which of the few German settlements you're trying to find, it could be a twenty-five-mile climb or a hundred-mile climb. Or more. If you don't like to walk, you might be able to hire a mule, but then again, if you don't like to walk you've probably turned back by now.

Ever on the move with his little band of Tutsi askaris, *Hauptmann* Wintgens is more or less quartered in Kigali, the rough and ready settlement the Germans are still trying to cobble together in these isolated hills north of the court at Nyanza. It's 1913, but the court still refuses to accommodate foreigners anywhere near Nyanza. Hence, Kigali. So far it's just a few thatch huts, some on stilts above the River Nyabarongo, by which means the outpost's few white visitors usually arrive, announced well before they are in sight by Tutsi drums and Hutu song. In all of Rwanda, there are at any given moment forty-some missionaries serving a stint here and another forty or so traders temporarily resident or just passing through—a few Swahili, a few Indians, some Arabs from Oman by way of Zanzibar, the occasional Greek. Wintgens has just one German on his staff, his second in command, Lieutenant Heinrich Naumann.

On maps drawn in Europe, Ruanda-Urundi in 1913 has been part of the German Empire for nearly three decades, and this is the extent to which the outside world has at last penetrated the forbidden zone: After nearly three decades, no settlers, fewer than a hundred outsiders passing through, and a Tutsi constabulary headed by exactly two Germans. At least we can say that outsiders have pierced something of the forbidden mystique, but this is due mostly to the desultory mood induced by the dowager queen, by her brother Chief Kabare, and by their deceit. Explorers are simply incidental beneficiaries.

CAPTAIN WINTGENS IS NOT THE TOP GERMAN IN RWANDA. THE TOP GERMAN IS THE imperial resident. Germany being Germany, the civil servant who fills this civil post is a military man, Captain Richard Kandt. But Kandt's military profession can be deceiving; like Wintgens and his Lieutenant Naumann, Kandt reflects a Germany somewhat less harsh than the empire's recent history on the Tanganyika plain—and in southwest Africa—would suggest. Like Wintgens and Naumann, he knows the hippo-hide whip, but like them also, he knows about Emin Pasha. Like Emin, he's a physician—in his case, a physician in the German Army's medical corps. But there are differences. Wintgens is a junior captain, recently dispatched and bold. Kandt is a senior captain who clearly cares more about where he is and what he's doing than about promotion, and more than that, Kandt has become, at forty-two, a figure in his own right, quite above and beyond his military rank.

Captain Wintgens and Lieutenant Naumann have come strictly as servants of the Reich. Captain Kandt is a genuine explorer, one of the last. Much of what Wintgens and Naumann have learned about Rwanda, they have learned from Kandt. Of course, they'd heard of vaunted Tutsi warriors and what a curiosity Rwanda is, such a structured place so deep in what the Germans call *der bundu,* the deep bush. That sort of palaver is by now becoming the stuff of myth. But whatever Germany has been able to perceive beyond the myth has been perceived largely by this quiet captain, Richard Kandt.

Kandt knows the forbidden zone better than any other outsider. Just after von Götzen's landmark two months in Rwanda in 1894, Kandt came to Africa fresh from medical and military training. Still in his twenties, and before the turn of the century, he spent several years mostly alone in these hills. He's put together his own landmark account, *Caput Nili,* and with the most careful science he could muster—which may be considerable but isn't enough. The White Fathers came to Rwanda with the strategy of converting the people by first converting the chiefs. And proceeding from Speke's "theory of conquest of inferior by superior races," Bazungu simply assume the chiefs are all Tutsi. The chiefs are all appointed by the Tutsi court, but by no stretch are they all Tutsi. By now Kandt knows that, and beyond that, he knows by now that there's a long tradition of Bahutu becoming Tutsi. But when he wrote *Caput Nili,* he was still convinced of what scholars a hundred years from now will call "the Hamitic myth," the corrosively racial notion that "Hamitic" tribes, descended from biblical Ham, rule the Great Lakes. Unlike other Bazungu, Kandt seems to be getting at least somewhat uncomfortable with the way his fellow Bazungu forever talk down Bahutu, and uncomfortable as well with unquestioning German support for the Tutsi court. Captain Wintgens is likewise concerned.

An early alert for the men came just last year, in 1912, when those Hutu princes of the far northwest rebelled against the court at Nyanza. They rebelled, as they shrewdly framed the matter, not because the court was Tutsi but because they knew about the regicide and argued that it rendered the current court illegitimate. To Rwanda's three solitary German Offiziere, this has to have seemed a sophisticated casus belli for supposedly ignorant Bahutu.

All this while, the dowager queen and her brother, Chief Kabare, are rooting out members of the royal Nyiginya clan, lest the Nyiginya launch their own legitimist revolt. The three officers know something about frontier districts like Gisenyi. They know that frontier Batutsi and frontier Bahutu are inclined to chafe at distant rule. To absorb such resentment— and to lock frontier country into the kingdom—old King Rwabugiri had pushed the court to absorb local Hutu notables into the Tutsi aristocracy, to make them Tutsi, and to appoint a few of them chiefs (recall that all Rwandese chiefs are appointed). Bahutu had always married Batutsi, and it was hardly unheard-of for a successful Muhutu to achieve Tutsi status without marrying into a Tutsi family. But King Rwabugiri made Batutsi of Bahutu on a grand scale. Indeed, the purge of the royal clan had begun under Rwabugiri himself; the crafty old politician feared that his fellow Nyiginya clansmen, in their patrician hauteur, would object to so many Bahutu becoming aristocrats, and so he purged his clan before his clansmen had much chance to gripe. Looked at from one angle, this was smart, even enlightened. But making some Bahutu Tutsi, even making good numbers of them Tutsi, hardly helped the great mass who remained Hutu. They were as estranged from the new Batutsi as they were from the old. Meantime, in a nation of clans, the king's bullying of his fellow clansmen defied Solomon's proverbial wisdom (from the Book of Proverbs): "He that troubleth his own house shall inherit the wind."

CONSTABULARY CHIEF WINTGENS WILL SOON WRITE TO THE NEW GOVERNOR OF GERMAN East Africa in Dar, a man named Schnee, telling him that he fears the Reich is aggravating differences between Bahutu and Batutsi. Imperial Resident Kandt admires Batutsi. All the same, he seems to share the concern about aggravating differences—if it doesn't actually begin with him. But Kandt is a man of science. He's no stranger to physical danger, but with people, he may not be as bold as Wintgens. Maybe this is why it's Wintgens who writes to Schnee—almost certainly with Kandt's okay. There's not much literature on Wintgens, but for all his apparent boldness, he's also a military officer soon to be described in an obscure British intelligence report as a "stickler for protocol." For a military man of that stripe, going over Kandt's head would mean some shattering fight with Kandt, and there's no indication of this.

BATUTSI CAN BE MASTER MANIPULATORS. EVEN IN THE MIDST OF THEIR FUNK, THE COURT has held on to power. In much of East Africa, indeed in African colonies generally, colonial power often means chiefs killed, jailed, or exiled. Even when kings and chiefs do hang on, they do so at the pleasure of the Zungu sovereign, and if they know what's good for them, they display this fact demonstratively. In China, from which Lettow-Vorbeck has just arrived, they use the term *kowtow*. Granted, Ruanda-Urundi gets away with a lot because it's so far off, days distant by lake steamer and foot safari from the blistered Ujiji railhead—itself the picture of Africa at its most remote. All the same, it wasn't until 1900 that Rwanda's king even granted an audience to the kaiser's imperial resident. His mother, Kanjogera, never will. And now, in 1913, the hauteur of the court remains unrelieved.

Is this any way to run a colony? Kandt is more an explorer and a man of science than a colonizer, but events have induced him, perhaps seduced him, into seeing himself as at least something of a colonizer. After all, he's been named imperial resident, and why shouldn't he be proud? He's a proud and patriotic German. It's only prudent to worry about whether the Germans are becoming too inclined to look down their noses at the great Rwandese majority, the Bahutu. If things go wrong, what will the fatherland say of the service he's rendered?

Wrapped up and isolated as he's been in Rwanda, and distant as Rwanda is from Ujiji, and Ujiji from Dar, and Dar from Germany, Kandt has not had much chance for home leave. In fact, he hasn't been home since Schnee replaced von Götzen as governor in Dar. Now at last, in 1913, he has a chance for home leave, and he grabs it. Should he talk about Rwanda with the powers that be in Berlin?

When Kandt at last gets to Berlin, he finds the kaiser's ministers preoccupied by a frantic game of "our cartels are better than your cartels," shaking their fists and spoiling for a fight with Belgium, France, and Great Britain, whose roosters crow right back. But Kandt knows that East Africa was always on Bismarck's desk. Bismarck himself is gone from the Wilhelmstrasse, his assertively imperial backside having long since suffered the humiliation of a jackboot from headstrong Kaiser Wilhelm II. But Kaiser Bill is even more imperial than Bismarck. With Germany's population outgrowing its borders, Wilhelm, like Bismarck before him, sees German East Africa as a relief valve.

Many still speak of Deutsch-Ostafrika as the Reich's "pearl"; historian John Keegan will write that in 1913 the protectorate "straddled the Great Lakes Region, the most romantic and potentially productive part of the continent." It's hard to imagine that as he arrives home in Germany, Kandt does not reckon that this is just the moment to visit the Wilhelmstrasse and speak up.

And then the lights go out all over Europe.

AS KANDT'S DELIBERATIVE MIND PONDERS WHAT TO DO ABOUT RWANDA, EUROPE IS stitched with barbed wire. As he reports for duty, his army is ripped by "maxims," which the papers now dub "machine guns," industry's latest gift to humanity. What scant time the Wilhelmstrasse has for East Africa it spends trying to ignore troublesome Schnee, the governor there, who sees the war as insanity and is forever getting in the way of Lettow-Vorbeck, now the protectorate's military chief. All the kaiser needs is more of Schnee from Kandt. Neither tuba-tooting Kaiser Bill nor any of his ministers have time for the subtleties of administering a place that now seems not just far away but long ago.

There is no practical way for Kandt to get back to Africa, nor can he really communicate with Africa. Yes, wireless technology has burst upon the world. The towering beacon pulsing code into the night has become a signature of modern humanity piercing the darkness, but just now it is truly dark out there. With the outbreak of war, Germany's one wireless link with East Africa is a relay beacon in the Cameroons, which in turn broadcasts to a single beacon in Dar.

It's hopeless. Kandt is assigned as a physician to the Army of Bavaria. He has always been an explorer whose life's work, above all, has been Rwanda. At forty-six he is only a captain. Promotion within the army's medical corps has never been the focus of his life. He may be a forty-six-year-old captain, but he's published a book that is the best yet on the Great Lakes. Now his life shoots off on a trajectory that will remove him forever from the Great Lakes.

WHICH BRINGS US BACK TO RWANDA, AND LETTOW-VORBECK'S DOUBLE, YOUNG CAPTAIN Max Wintgens. With Kandt unable to return, the Wilhelmstrasse adds to Wintgens's job as military chief for Rwanda the title of interim imperial resident for Rwanda. At least this man is on station, aware of festering problems and ready to act—provided Germany wins the war. War fever grips East Africa's Bazungu as much as it does Europe itself, and all of Europe is shaking a collective fist at the evil enemy—which, collectively speaking, is Europe itself. One test of the thermostat: Waves of *der Patriotismus, die Vaterlandsliebe,* so overwhelm a German-Jewish linguist (a careful scholar, my periodical suggests, a man named Victor Klemperer) that he writes in his diary, "We, we Germans, are a truly chosen people." Governor Schnee tells Lettow-Vorbeck that he can't go on the attack. On both sides of the Kenya frontier, senior figures try, much as the crowned heads of Europe had earlier tried, to keep their domains out of the war—and on both sides their children are rallying. Hoots and hurrahs rise from the bar at the club. These assembling clutches of young men, German-speaking south of Kilimanjaro, English-speaking north, are much alike, so of course they don't get along at all. They are dead set on going to war with each other. One of them is Lettow-Vorbeck in Dar es Salaam. He defies Schnee. Briefly, he becomes as much a politico as a soldier, recruiting a force of twenty-five hundred African askaris and two hundred Bazungu. Business booms at Nairobi's pubs, clubs, and Indian cafés. Young settlers and white hunters, intent on enlisting, are rolling in from all over British East Africa.

Lettow-Vorbeck is outnumbered. Just over Rwanda's frontier, in the Congo, there are tens of thousands of Belgian troops. There are tens of thousands more, native, settler, Indian, Baluch, just over the border in British East Africa. What German East Africa has are *Schutztruppen,* African askaris led by German officers and some German enlisted men. Lettow-Vorbeck will never command many more than eleven thousand African and three thousand German troops. On August 8, 1914, the guns of the British cruiser *Astraea* rain shells on Dar. Wintgens, in distant Kigali, is as defiant of Schnee as Lettow-Vorbeck is, and it's hard to see what good Wintgens thinks he can do the Reich by going to war. His job is Rwanda, running it and defending it. Rwanda can run itself, but what of his charge to defend this distant place for the Reich? There are all those tens of thousands of enemy troops under Belgian command just over the frontier in the Congo. Wintgens has three hundred and fifty rifles. The term *rifles* is often used hereabouts to designate troops (as in the King's African Rifles), but in this instance the term denotes nothing more than rifles, specifically those Mauser model 71 five-round repeaters discarded by the German Army and carried by Bitahurwina and his comrades into Uganda. At this point, Wintgens doesn't have three hundred and fifty men ready—in Zungu terms—for much more than police duty. From his great distance Wintgens pays attention as best he can to Lettow-Vorbeck. By runner and by the new Nordbahn from Dar to Taborah to Ujiji, Lettow-Vorbeck sketches his strategy and issues orders. Wintgens recruits a force of seven hundred Tutsi warriors. Kanjogera's increasingly active son, King Musinga, commits them to fight the British and the Belgians for Germany.

There aren't enough rifles to go around, but they have a few of those water-cooled machine guns called maxims, and odd-looking Mausers that look like a cross between a rifle and an automatic.

Within days, there's that same old sound of heavy, callused feet pounding the dust in easy cadence. In all but name, the Inzirabwoba (those who fear nothing), the Imbanzamihigo (those who are praised first), and the Abashakamba (they're tough) are once again commissioned for combat, except that this time they will go a lot farther afield than Burundi or Karagwe on Lake Victoria or even Jinja on Victoria's far side.

Less than a week after Britain's *Astraea* shells Dar, Wintgens puts the torch to Goma across from Gisenyi in the Belgian Congo. Young Captain Max now fashions himself Tembasi; it will be his African nom de guerre.

It's a hit-and-run operation. Tembasi, né Wintgens, has no hope of invading and holding Belgian territory. His attack on Goma seems bound to provoke a Belgian attack on Ruanda-Urundi, which isn't going to be easy to defend. But that doesn't matter. Tembasi isn't going to defend Ruanda. He isn't going to defend anything. He's going to vanish into the bundu and, ever on the move, use his "Watusi" to attack, attack.

Nor is it pointless. The point is to draw as many British and Belgian assets into the East African theater as possible, thus denying Britain and Belgium these assets in the European theater.

THE STRATEGY WORKS. FOR EIGHTEEN MONTHS, THE TEMBASI WATUSI RAID THE CONGO from Rwanda. Then a Belgian named Tombeur shows up south of Lake Kivu with ten thousand men in two brigades armed with sixty maxims and twelve field guns, and a Belgian named Molitor shows up north of Lake Kivu with an equivalent force. Tembasi's lads still number about seven hundred. After their eighteen months of hit-and-run from Rwanda, he readies a strategic retreat into Tanganyika. Drums report. Kabenga's Rwanda is rapt.

As the Belgians strike in force, Tembasi's Watusi form up for a forced march, move out, and before they can mark a quarter mile, they hear the dreaded cadence call to double-time. With the command of execution and a single, synchronous grunt, they double-time down onto the heat-cracked hardpan of Tanganyika—and seldom in the direction their pursuers expect.

British pilots flying Belgian seaplanes bomb them with flechettes. Superior Allied forces close in on them from two sides; they slip the trap, and so late in the game that the closing units close on each other before it dawns on them that their prey has escaped.

Lettow-Vorbeck, whatever follies he shares with his coevals, proves a strategist of mettle, and a good tactician. So does Wintgens-Tembasi. Both soldiers are skilled leaders, sharing with their troops every hardship, and leading them, not following them, into battle.

It was not inevitable that this happen. On arriving in Dar, Lettow-Vorbeck heard from one old hand after another how Africans need a rough command. Germany has been mellowing some in East Africa, but there is no tradition of enlightened leadership of native troops. Tradition holds that unless they feel the hippo-hide *chicotte,* they will do nothing but lie and run away. Lettow-Vorbeck's *Schutztruppen* are, after all, the same Africans who so enraged and frustrated Richard Burton. "Spare the rod and spoil the empire." But Lettow-Vorbeck, late of the Herero genocide, doesn't choose the *chicotte,* and he wins both the loyalty and the tenacity of his troops.

Wintgens-Tembasi and Lettow-Vorbeck blunder often enough, and their men suffer for it, but the two share a sense of when and where to attack, when to retreat, when to pursue, and when and how to disappear. Both are faced not just with a shortage of men, but with a shortage of boot leather for the few men they have. Lettow-Vorbeck looks for men who can teach his men to tan the hides of Grant's gazelle. He finds those men, and it matters not at all whether whites are teaching blacks or blacks are teaching whites. For Wintgens and Naumann, at the other end of German East Africa, there are no whites, just the two of them, seven hundred Batutsi, and a few porters and camp followers.

Both Lettow-Vorbeck and Wintgens make certain their men have the awls, the needles, the gut they need. Each man is responsible for his own feet. Every unit has to be self-sufficient. For most of the war, there will be no supply lines. For Germans, this will be especially hard. They must husband what little soap they have. No matter how parched, they can't drink water they haven't boiled. Forget toilet paper. They use old orders, messages, requisition forms, the rare letter from home, or better yet, that last communiqué sent down by some distant headquarters, the bane of troops everywhere.

As Lettow-Vorbeck destroys the barrier between his African *Schutztruppen* and the Germans, he becomes something of a model, and not just for the Europeans. For Africans, and especially for Batutsi serving under his storied command, he becomes a model of imperial Germany at its least odious. In an army and a culture in which rank and status are all-important, and almost half a century before apartheid is ended in the U.S. armed forces, he mixes his men, forcing them to live together in the most uncomfortable of intimacies. In *Out of Africa,* Isak Dinesen writes that the Germans have a much healthier outlook on race than the British in Kenya Colony.

(In other areas of warfare, though, the British aren't so shabby. An enterprising intelligence officer gets vital information on Lettow-Vorbeck's plans by having his men sift through the Germans' "dirty paper"—all those headquarter-dispatched memos, orders, and communiqués that the Germans have been recycling.)

All Kabenga knows is that a great Zungu war is on, and the news he gets still comes by drum, a rumble from within the earth. There really is something big out there beyond their own "big world" (the literal meaning of *Rwanda*), and if you put your ear to the ground you can hear it, or at least feel it, a monumental shift in gravity as these mysterious Titans do battle in their titanic way.

LESS THAN A MONTH AFTER THE BRITISH CRUISER ATTACK ON DAR, GERMANY'S *KÖNIGS-berg* sinks HMS *Pegasus* in the Indian Ocean and, more important, draws three British cruisers away from seas in which they could do real harm to Germany. For more than eight months, the *Königsberg* plays cat-and-mouse with British warships, leading them into the mangrove swamps and vast, serpentine channels of Tanganyika's Rufiji River delta, where Lettow-Vorbeck is operating, and where the Brits at last sink the German ship. The crew joins Lettow-Vorbeck. They dismantle the *Königsberg's* big guns for field service and for the *Graf von Götzen,* flagship of the inland navy that Lettow-Vorbeck plans for the Great Lakes. A lot of steel tonnage, from magazines to heavy naval shells, is about to be lugged up to the center of Africa.

About this time, the Tembasi Watusi join Lettow-Vorbeck's main force. Lettow-Vorbeck does not like to present a big target. His men patrol in loose formation, anywhere from fifteen to fifty feet apart, and his units maintain an even greater tactical distance between each other. But a quarter mile of tactical distance is not the hundreds of miles that once separated Wintgens's Batutsi from the main force. The lads from Rwanda are now operating directly under the command of Lettow-Vorbeck, and there are several officers senior to Tembasi.

HOWEVER MUCH NERVE IT MAY TAKE TO SHOUT "ATTACK," THE WORLD GIVES MORE credit to those whose creed is "Never retreat," and well the world should. There are none braver than those who stand and fight. Tembasi and his chief Lettow-Vorbeck hardly ever stand and fight. They are masters of retreat. They attack and vanish, composing guerrilla doctrine as they go along. But every day and every night, they fight the bundu, from which they can never back off.

This is their real enemy. One German will recall pushing through miles of thatch and thorn, the King's African Rifles in pursuit, when at last his unit reaches its bivouac and everyone collapses. His skin is raw. Barbed thorns bristle from his hide. A black askari, salty sweat doubtless dripping from his forehead into his eyes, looks at the young German, takes off one of his own hand-cobbled boots, takes off a sweat-wet, rotting sock, and with this rank bit of rag, daubs the German's abraded skin. In East Africa's Swahili lingua franca, the African says, *"Barikiwa,"* or *"Hakuna matata,"* or some such. "Don't worry. I don't need the sock."

It's not pleasant. When you're hit, there's no evacuation. Perhaps more important, when you're hit by disease, there's no clinic, and here it's worse for the Germans than for the Africans, for German guts have not adjusted to the bugs that grow in Africa beyond the equator. On both sides, thirty Zungu troops fall victim to disease for every Muzungu fallen in combat.

AS IF LETTOW-VORBECK'S CAMPAIGN WEREN'T SHADED ENOUGH BY A CERTAIN CALLOW romance, color photography gives us a picture of the East African savannah that renders Lettow-Vorbeck all the more romantic. In fact, Africa on camera is often a fiction. The camera wants to denature the bundu. At best it sometimes shows the flies that buzz forever about the lion. Even when it can somehow suggest the heat, catching it rising in oily waves of pretty color, it catches more color than heat. It only hints at the beast that lies rotting alive in thornbush. It can never show how the simple phrase *nimepotea*, "I'm lost," has visual impact when you're surrounded by endless bundu in all directions.

Think of Lettow-Vorbeck's war as a gentleman's duel if you will. At one point, under assault by the Twenty-fifth Royal Fusiliers, his sights catch Roosevelt's white hunter, the celebrated naturalist Frederick Courtney Selous, and for some gentlemanly reason, he declines to squeeze the trigger. But this war is at least equally a contest in which misery-ridden fugitives lead misery-ridden pursuers on a chase deep into the misery of death by disease, and by infection, and let the devil take the weakest gut.

There is something of Mutemura's formations about Lettow-Vorbeck's deftly maneuvering columns. Where Mutemura and Muganza left trails of sweat and urine, Lettow-Vorbeck leaves trails of sweat and dribbling dysentery . . . and yet for all this, something worse is facing Herr Doktor Kandt, late of Ruandese exploration, on the fronts of Europe. Compared with the war in Europe, war on the run in East Africa is a stride down the Champs-Élysées. Well, maybe not a stride, nor for that matter the Champs-Élysées. You've got to be dead for Elysian fields, and it doesn't count if you just feel that way. In any case, at least these lads in East Africa aren't mired in trenches. They're on the move through Africa's tasseled grasses.

AFTER CAPTAIN MAX'S WATUSI LINK UP WITH THE GERMAN MAIN FORCE, HIS IMMEDIATE commander is Lettow-Vorbeck's Major Kraut. I don't know for sure what happens under Kraut, but it isn't good. Do the lads from Rwanda chafe at losing their independence? Do they want to go home? Kraut's troops are good, but their families encumber them, and every effort Lettow-Vorbeck makes to send camp followers home has failed. Marched out of camp, the women just sit down on the track with their pots, pans, and children. Every morning at every bivouac, family cocks crow, threatening to give away their position. Wintgens-Tembasi can't like this any more than Lettow-Vorbeck does.

Or maybe he just doesn't get along with Kraut. After all, some Tutsi families have followed his warriors. Whatever the reason, one day in February 1917, Tembasi forms up his lads from Rwanda and just takes off.

Desertion, you say? So does Lettow-Vorbeck, but not out loud, and he does not go after the errant Tembasi and his errant Watusi.

The British, however, do. Tembasi's Watusi have deserted Kraut's command. They haven't quit the war. They create enough havoc that by May the Allies have set up a special command, EDFORCE, to knock them out. Besides Brits and Belgians, EDFORCE includes at least four hundred Cape Coloured, Baluchi, and a shock unit of Ugandans called *ruga-ruga*.

The Tutsi crew heads south for Rhodesia. EDFORCE pursues. Suddenly the Rwandese swing north, at first eluding then actually pursuing the British unit, and in this, Tembasi does just what Lettow-Vorbeck does on a larger scale. He ties up enormous Allied assets.

To defeat Lettow-Vorbeck, the British call up Jan Smuts, their guerrilla adversary in the Boer War. Smuts now fights for the British, leading forty thousand tough troops, mostly white South Africans, in pursuit of Lettow-Vorbeck's men, now totaling sixteen thousand, and largely black African. Smuts never gets Lettow-Vorbeck, nor does he ever defeat any substantial African unit in outright combat.

ON MAY 23, 1917, TEMBASI SURRENDERS. TEMBASI, NOT HIS LADS FROM RWANDA. Captain Max has typhus, the plague of men living too close together, or more precisely, the plague of men living too close to infected lice. It's marked by delirium, it will be common to the concentration camps of the next war, and Tembasi is not the only victim. His fighting Watusi now number only five hundred; one of every three who left Rwanda has fallen to either combat or disease. But they have not surrendered, nor has Lieutenant Naumann, who is now in command, and drawing as much British blood as Tembasi had.

You will recall that Tembasi's Watusi wheeled at the Rhodesian frontier, turning on their pursuers and chasing them all the way back to Kenya, and now the British find themselves fighting Naumann's Watusi inside Kenya Colony itself.

Naumann and his men know this can't go on forever. At the end of August 1917, they seem cornered between lakes Victoria and Natron in the midst of Kenya Colony. Again they slip the trap, but in little more than a month, they're finished. Combat and disease have reduced their number to one hundred and sixty-five. Amid the foothills of Kilimanjaro, Naumann surrenders.

WHEN LETTOW-VORBECK SAILED FOR DAR IN 1913, HE SAILED ABOARD THE SAME SHIP AS a twenty-four-year-old Dane named Karen Dinesen. As chance would have it, they met and spent some time alone together.

Picture it: Lettow-Vorbeck is a bachelor. Karen Dinesen is bound for

Mombasa and an ill-starred marriage to a Swedish baron, Bror Blixen. She will soon be known in Kenya Colony as the Baroness Blixen, and later to readers as Isak Dinesen. From what little we know of her wistful passage with Lettow-Vorbeck, it's hard to avoid the sense that she is already unsettled about the looming marriage. She spends New Year's Eve 1913 with Lettow-Vorbeck.

Ashore in Kenya Colony and going her way toward romantic and business disaster, she writes home to her mother in Denmark that to her aboard that ship, this fellow Lettow-Vorbeck represented Germany's best. "He belonged to the olden days." In *Out of Africa* she will write that no other German gave her "so strong an impression of what imperial Germany stood for."

Lettow-Vorbeck's force is never defeated. Two weeks after the armistice, a runner shows up in camp with the news that the Reich has surrendered, and he surrenders. He has diverted enormous Allied assets from Europe. His defiance of poor Governor Schnee has succeeded brilliantly, as has his career as a freelance guerrilla operating mostly without orders from Berlin. Hors de combat at last, he condemns Wintgens-Tembasi, and the only reason seems to be that Wintgens's own career as a freelance guerrilla, operating without orders from Lettow-Vorbeck, has also succeeded brilliantly.

Lettow-Vorbeck writes stiffly, "It is to be regretted that [Captain Max's Rwandese force] was of so little use." He never speculates about what use Britain might have made of their EDFORCE if they didn't have to put it together to chase Captain Max and his Watusi back and forth across Tanganyika territory from Rhodesia to deep inside Kenya Colony.

Belgium now claims Ruanda-Urundi. At first, Kabenga barely notices. After his initiation as a *mugabo,* a chief named Rwubusisi, who is one of the king's uncles, begins to notice his talents. Kabenga is flattered, but troubled. The chief is one of Kanjogera's brothers. Family lore is drenched with distaste for Kanjogera. The man who is befriending him is, after all, the brother of the queen who drove Kabenga's natural father to poison, and murdered Kabenga's king. All the same, Chief Rwubusisi and Kabenga become boon companions on the hunt, though just what they hunt I find hard to pick out through the wash of time and stories. The royal family is trying desperately to temporize, and it has much to temporize about. Into the twenty-first century, the exiled royal family itself will despise Kanjogera, the mother of their line. With this much bad blood pumping during the start of the twentieth century, the least of the royal family's worries is a few Belgians who tell them that Rwanda is something they call a colony.

Would that Richard Kandt, the explorer Rwanda calls Kanayoge, could be thus at large in Rwanda in 1917. The author of the fullest account of the Great Lakes before the Great War, the imperial resident who wanted nothing more than to keep up his studies there, who fretted that Germany was giving the Bahutu short shrift, spends 1917 forever treating the stigmata of the trenches, from chilblains to the burning piss of nephritis. Late in the year he is gassed. He refuses evacuation. In his weakened state, tuberculosis invades him. Within months he's dead, a fifty-year-old captain, once an explorer. And what I want to know is, how many of his illusions (Hamitic or otherwise) did he leave behind, and how many did he take to the grave?

24

BELGIUM'S WAGNERIAN SWOON
1918–1922

Some believe the royalty of Banyarwanda country were originally Hutu, and that's plausible. It's unlikely those royals were called Hutu; the root meaning of *Hutu,* like the root meaning of *Boer,* is "peasant." But if we read Hutu simply as Bantu, then in that somewhat contorted sense (contorted because in practice it almost always entails excluding Batutsi from any Bantu past), it's plausible, and melancholy to boot. One by one, the autonomy of Hutu princes is getting snuffed, and their flickering light represents the last glimmer of a royalty so old that it may have spawned what Bazungu call Tutsi royalty.

A melancholy end, and equally an inevitable end: The days of the prince of Bushiru were always numbered. This is not because he was Hutu. It's because he was the prince of an autonomous realm, the inevitable target of an ambitious court at Nyanza that has conquered Tutsi kingdoms far mightier than any mere principality, Hutu or Tutsi.

But neither does the tale end with the long-standing ambition of the court to absorb and consolidate. Now the Zungu Belgians, now the Bazungu, have arrived. Now, thanks to the Bazungu, you're much more awake to your identity as a Muhutu or a Mututsi. "Watusi," the Belgians trill, are a distinct race, a race of born rulers, African supermen.

In this romance with race, our Belgian colons are hardly alone. During these years, the aggressively Teutonic operas of Richard Wagner, full of Nordic valkyries and blond divas booming in horned helmets, are packing in adoring crowds from one end of Zunguland to the other. Mark Twain hears the bombast, ponders Wagner's compensating genius, and offers that his work "is better than it sounds." All of Zunguland is likewise falling into group swoons over a pseudo-discipline that goes by the name of "eugenics."

Eugenics, Webster says, is "the process or means of race improvement, as by restricting mating to superior types suited to each other." The definition could read as easily "a form of mass vanity in which . . ."

Fascination with matters racial is all the rage from Sweden (where if your palate is cleft, they might sterilize you) to Australia (where if your spouse is aborigine and you're not, they'll seize your kids) to America. In America, twenty-two states pass laws against teaching any foreign language (which ipso facto is the lingo of inferior blood), and distinguished professors are offering studies of the inbred Jukes and Kallikaks of Kentucky, then using their questionable studies to extrapolate grand (and self-aggrandizing) notions about superior and inferior races. Almost every American campus offers a course in eugenics. In fact, eugenics, as a notion so named, actually begins in America. From the United States (where Alexander Graham Bell is among its boosters) it spreads to Germany, not the other way around.

But we boosters of the Great Lakes can stake our own claim here. Just as the authentic science of natural selection gets its start with Darwin in the Galapagos, the related pseudo-science of "racial hygiene" (eugenics by another name) gets its start with Richard Burton and John Haning Speke in the Great Lakes. You've already seen how Burton, taking a cue from Darwin—but with none of Darwin's science—waxes racial in *Lake Regions of Central Africa,* and how, in his *Journal of the Discovery of the Source of the Nile,* Speke advances a "Theory of Conquest of Inferior by Superior Races." Rider Haggard then supplies the romance in *King Solomon's Mines.*

Now the Belgians, Tutsi-entranced, are helping Kanjogera's court defeat the remaining Hutu principalities. At this moment, Haggard's name is still linked above all with plain adventure. But something is starting to happen. Early on, there was something gloriously oblivious of academic cant in Haggard's confections, oblivious in the writing and in the reading as well, and much of this seems to carry on through these years. As late as 1937, Paul Robeson stars in the first film rendering of *King Solomon's Mines,* and the movie doesn't get into any nonsense about race. As in the novel, there is also no mention of "Watusi." But elsewhere on the Zungu stage, spinners of racial fantasy have by now had an authentic go at us, and more yet are getting to it.

Gaetano Casati, Samuel Baker, John Roscoe, and Fathers van den Burgt and Gorju have all waxed or are waxing elegiac. In the Batutsi, van den Burgt sees "beautiful Greek profiles," "Semitic and even Jewish features," "Caucasian skulls." These Bazungu deduce, with scant logic, and induce, with scant evidence, that it was the Batutsi who brought kingship to Rwanda, having cultivated it in Abyssinia, whence, they say, we came. And how certain they are of their conclusions! About all that twenty-first-century scholars will say is that it's "unlikely" we brought kingship from Ethiopia. They will tell us it's possible that somewhere in the millennial past we came from there, but the evidence is slender, and what there is has us leaving Ethiopia before Ethiopia itself developed kingships. Come the twenty-first century, they will have found more evidence that it was migrating Bantu ancestors of the Bahutu who brought kingship to the Great Lakes.

But this is not the end of Zungu scholarship in the nineteen-twenties. It's just the beginning. Next comes a Catholic missionary named Pagès, who devotes long hours to trying to prove that we actually come from ancient Egypt. Then we hear from a scholar who tells us we're from, *mirabile dictu*, Asia Minor. No, says another, we're from the Indian subcontinent. The Benedictines, great scholars that they are, produce a friar, Étienne Brosse, who traces us back to the Garden of Eden.

YOU HAVE BEEN JUDGED AND FOUND WANTING

When Haggard wrote, no white man had yet made it into our realms. Haggard had nothing but fanciful tales to go on. Speke himself knew little of us beyond what he heard next door in Karagwe, where his hosts cum captors spun fanciful tales for him of tall, light-skinned, superhuman cannibals in the misty volcanoes to the east. (I'd say we're blacker than the African norm, and we won't eat much red meat, nor any swine, let alone humans. Mama's Batemura won't eat goat.) Indeed, this appeal of the unknown is what enchanted Haggard and his readers. Unlike the makers of the more famous 1950 movie (in which we are not only identified as "Watusi," but actually speak Kinyarwanda), Robeson's director shows no interest in updating Haggard's fantasy with new facts (like our glamour as "Watusi," which in fact is less than factual). More important—and in spite of the race-crazy days when it was produced—the Robeson movie doesn't scratch the sore of racial preening. It's unself-conscious adventure, and a conscious stalwart of justice like Robeson can indulge the adventure unself-consciously. Regardless, under the skin, something's up. It's about this time that the abiding popular appeal of Haggard's tale starts becoming a popular animator of the pseudo-science that began with Burton and Speke.

When Haggard publishes *King Solomon's Mines,* what captures the popular imagination is the discovery of a peculiarly, powerfully developed world deep in Africa, a world altogether African and altogether isolated from the known world. Now, for Rwanda's Belgians, indeed for British planters in Uganda and Kenya and German planters left behind in Tanganyika, attention shifts fractionally but critically; now it's not just the isolation and wonder of these Africans that galvanizes Zungu fans, it's their superiority to the Africans all around them. Carried away by notions of a Tutsi master race, respected academics (among them, the leading Africanist of the day, C. G. Seligman) indulge half-baked or just plain crackpot theories that trace Batutsi not just to ancient Egypt but to Tibet and every other corner of the globe, and Belgian authorities become eager to help Queen Kanjogera's court extend Tutsi rule.

Many Batutsi look Hutu. Many Bahutu look Tutsi. During the 1994 killings, many Bahutu will die because they look Tutsi. Does this suggest to the Belgians that they might want to temper their racial zeal? No. It simply means that they should begin doing what the Nazis have begun doing in Germany—issuing pass cards clearly indicating the holders "race."

FOR THE GERMANS, LETTING THE ROYALS GOVERN WAS LARGELY A PRACTICAL MATTER, and early on in their overlordship, it's much the same for the Belgians. Then comes a muddle. First, the grand old man of the missions waffles. Father Leon Classe came to us in 1907 when there were few Bazungu indeed. In 1922 he's named vicar apostolic, and widely reckoned the sagest of old hands. Bazungu like to say the monsignor speaks fluent Kinyarwanda. He's long counted himself impressed by the Batutsi—but not as breathlessly as those who keel over. More Bazungu are showing up; they jar Classe with their low regard for Bahutu. Meantime, from where Classe sits, King Musinga is hardly turning out a picture of that storied Tutsi statesmanship. He won't be baptized; he insists on keeping his pagan name; and most crucially, he's truly his mother's son.

Superficially he's different. Unlike her, he deigns to let Bazungu lay eyes on him. He even talks to them. But his mother's craft is there, even in his meetings with Bazungu. As more show up, these rendezvous become artfully staged events, pandering to romantic Zungu fantasies about Watusi.

Musinga is much taken with cameras. He senses the camera's power. All about Nyanza, there is now much posing, preening, attention to beads and baubles. We are losing ourselves. If this goes on, we'll become scarcely more than a snapshot of what's going on in Zungu heads. We're consciously pandering to their fantasies, and they're buying it, even taking it beyond what we peddle, neatly fitting us into their Zungu notions about race, swooning over our patricians as a master race, or at least a master tribe, dismissing our peasants as a lowly tribe. (Funny: If patricians and peasants here are tribes, and two distinct ones at that, why don't these Bazungu ever ask to see the chief of—as they put it—the Watusi tribe? The chief of the Wahutu? And if both tribes are too big to have a single chief, then how about a chief of a Tutsi clan? A chief of a Hutu clan? Has there ever been a chief of the Bahutu? Of the Batutsi? No, for the simple reason that only in the Zungu dream world are we a tribe, or two tribes, rather than a single nation with a single language. You won't find any chiefs of Hutu or Tutsi tribes or clans because there aren't any Hutu or Tutsi tribes or clans. The king names the chiefs. He doesn't name many Bahutu, but he names proportionately more Bahutu to high rank than the court of Saint James does working-class Britons, and each time, that Muhutu becomes a chief of both Bahutu and Batutsi.)

Father Classe knows this. For the ears of Hutu-bashing colons, he cautions that in the old days, kings often raised Bahutu to high rank. He suggests that Belgium do the same. But no sooner does he move to moderate Belgian zeal for Batutsi, and in particular for the Tutsi court, than he reverses course. The old man begins to fear he's tilted too far. He warns the Belgians they could err no worse were they "to suppress the Mututsi caste. . . . They are the ones best suited to understand progress."

You see him wrestling with an angel. But why not endorse a neutral hand? Our caste system is becoming a dangerous relic, but what qualifies these Bazungu to dream up solutions for us? The industry that makes them avatars of progress? Their science? This science that even now spawns some witch medicine called eugenics? What ever happened to Hippocrates' first dictum: "First, do no harm"?

Harm is above all what these Zungu witch doctors do. Their mind-bending *codes ésotériques* do so beguile. Zungu motors crank over and pull great loads. Zungu guns kill. Zungu medicine cures. Zungu pie is tasty, and Zungu π computes. And how they adore all this Hutu-Tutsi business, they and their poking cameras, and how they've got us preening for those cameras.

WHEN MALE ARCHETYPE MEETS
MALE ARCHETYPE

As it happens, the ghostliest meetings between white man and servant hear neither the word *Hutu* nor *Tutsi,* nor for that matter, the crack of the hippo-hide *cicotte.* The ghostliest encounters come when male archetype meets male archetype. The day's avatar of white supremacy is the picture of Wagnerian health, tall, young, tanned by sport, smiling, confident, remote. He's a young man given to lusty turns with the wenches, abundant turns with the stein, and tardiness the morning after—and yet able to hold his work to high standard. Obviously, he doesn't exist in such archetypal vainglory, but as a type emulated he's likely everywhere.

In Zungu heads, the Hutu archetype is lazy, and happy in his lassitude. Right enough, Zungu heads are showing their own mental lassitude. It's abundant in these notions about "racial hygiene." But that's not the question at hand. The question is what a Muhutu of this day thinks of himself, and there's no good reason to believe he doesn't share the common human need to win his place. Yes, many colons roundly discourage him from doing so (lest it be evident that he can), but how can he not aspire? All you need is a heart that needs. The rub is that centuries of kingly custom have brought up all Rwandese to obey, to conform, and so at his most assertive, our Hutu lad doesn't rebel. He strives to show his worth in his master's terms. He sweats and spits and polishes and pushes and plows and totes and applies for Zungu grace. He stumbles. He applies again. He tries harder, does better. At last, with remote finality and mild disgust, his Zungu grace responds with a look that says, You have been judged and found wanting.

FORGIVE ME IF I DO NOT SEE THE COLONS OF THIS ERA IN ALL THE NUANCE OF THEIR various personalities. Forgive me if what I see are caricatures, and in fact just two, all of Belgian Rwanda as two caricatures.

I picture these triumphalist years after the Great War as years full of Zungu egos rampant, and especially rampant in colonial Ruanda-Urundi. I picture my first caricature, Waterloo, as a marabou stork. In real life, marabou are already caricatures of storks. Forget the ones you know, all white, all legs and neck and long thin beak. Marabou hardly have a neck. Their trunks are so thick that at times their storky legs seem to disappear into them. Their beaks, while long, are nearly pelican fat, forever drooping on potbellies that should be spotless white but are always spotted with their last meal. For marabou, every meal is an indecently delicious spectacle of maggoty meat. Their little eyes leer to see such sights, and their tail feathers wag in time with their waddle.

A caricature of our Zungu high-lifes, Waterloo waddles that world, a Copacabana world, the early jazz age in East Africa, a period during which Grandfather Kabenga sees more and more Bazungu showing up. It's just right for our Zungu high-lifes, this world in which the eponymously Congolese but distinctly Latin conga becomes all the rage. Waterloo is forever at a tennis club or a shooting club or some such *cercle sportif* where he vaunts and toadies, but in due course, he's joined by Willy, his marabou co-eval, a bull-necked but bright-eyed lunk, my second and final caricature.

Nothing covers Willy's chest but the braces that hold up monster shorts, forever in danger of collapse, just like his finances. A coffee colonial, forever in trouble, he's a master of ingenuity, conjuring winches out of bicycle parts, but his grammar is fractured. He's broke, which is to say he can't cash out of this mess called Ruanda-Urundi, and what happens to him seems fated. He shows up in Africa bright-eyed but scared. It will help if he can render a forbidding Africa in understandable, engagingly romantic terms. All the pseudo-science about super-Watusi finds a willing listener. And then the other shoe drops. By definition, a superior race is not simply superior. It's superior to an inferior race. By now, Willy has beaten back his early fears and needs to deal with the anxiety of actually making the cartoon fortune of his cartoon dreams. His heavily mortgaged coffee patch has to produce more, and cheaper, and the peasants, so shiftless to his eye, are so easy to blame. Now he must do more than simply lionize the Batutsi. Now he must talk down the Bahutu.

Travel to Ruanda-Urundi during this period, work your way up from Dar and up the Rusizi from Usumbura (as Bujumbura is still fashioned), put in at one of the Belgian river stations, and I'll make sure you run into one of these snappy birds. Either a hale Willy or perhaps a hale Waterloo himself will show up in those shorts and get your ear. First he'll offer you a beer, which sounds just right. The Germans had little to offer besides native brew and schnapps. Fresh beer just couldn't make it from the coast. What little came through was heavily dosed with formaldehyde. But now Waterloo and Willy have a Belgian brewery, so you kick back and listen to your newfound friend tell you this and tell you that and tell you oh how cheerful these Bahutu are. Then you'll buy him a beer, and he'll tell you how lazy they are. Another few rounds and you hear how untrustworthy they are—genetically lazy and genetically untrustworthy.

And just like that, the bird will be gone. But trust me. Waterloo and Willy will be back.

THE ART OF CRANKY DISSEMBLING

Before the Germans and the Belgians, the struggles of the Banyarwanda were mostly this: the struggles of outlying princely realms (some ruled by Tutsis, some by Hutus) to preserve their autonomy against attack by the big court at Nyanza. But by the time the Belgians show up, the realms of outlying Tutsi kings and princes are gone, conquered by Nyanza. As the Belgians arrive, outlying realms are few and Hutu; and as the Belgians see things, Rwanda is a Tutsi realm blemished by some stray Hutu principalities. So first they redefine the conflict. It's Hutu versus Tutsi. Then they pick sides.

No longer is the conflict between the big court at Nyanza and outlying realms. Now the conflict, as redefined by the Belgians, is Batutsi against Bahutu, and they're with the Batutsi.

Of course, this has been implicit in the Zungu worldview since Burton and Speke; now it's explicitly executed. Is a prefecture not producing as it should? Then out with the hippo-hide whip and brandish it with all the swagger you read into Darwin, the fittest asserting themselves over the weakest, right on down the food chain. Start with the Tutsi overseer, lay it on until flaps of flesh lie open on his back, and lay it on in front of the Bahutu he governs. You know he'll deal out the same to them. You've told him he must, and sure enough, many of Queen Kanjogera's chiefs do just that.

Kanjogera's court itself doesn't show much appreciation for Belgian help. Rwanda's top Belgians now regularly describe her as a pest. She, her brother Kabare, and now her son, King Musinga, seem ever so cranky about Belgium in Rwanda. In fact, Belgium in Rwanda suits them just fine. If the Belgians will lend the court legitimacy in the wake of the regicide, and help it absorb autonomous principalities like Bushiru, Nyanza is more than ready to indulge Belgian posturing. It's just that centuries of courtly intrigue have made them masters and mistresses of the arts of dissembling, one of which is the art of cranky dissembling.

More than likely, that hugely successful powermonger, Kanjogera's late husband, Rwabugiri, would eventually have swallowed up autonomous realms like Bushiru without help from Zungu colonials. But just as surely, Kanjogera's shaky court could never have crushed these fiefdoms without Belgian help. King Rwabugiri was strong. Thanks to her regicide, Queen Kanjogera's court is weak.

And so the Muhinza w'Abashiru goes down in defeat, as do all the remaining Hutu princes, the Muhinza w'Abagoyi, the Muhinza w'Abakonya. Autonomous Kibari is crushed in 1918, just months after the League of Nations gives Ruanda-Urundi to Belgium and Kanjogera's court gets Belgian endorsement and Belgian help. Princes become peons, and peons become less than low, a base "tribe" with no princes and no redeeming qualities beyond "cheerfulness."

THESE ARE THE MOST PROFOUND VICTIMS OF THIS EPISODE IN OUR HISTORY, BUT THERE are some lesser victims who suffer their own peculiar excruciation, victims closer to the stories with which we siblings Bitsindinkumi spent our childhood.

In some cases, the Tutsi chiefs that the court puts in charge of defeated principalities are simply profiteering warlords, bent on plunder. But not always. Queen Kanjogera and her brother Kabare need desperately to reduce the threat of a legitimist countercoup, and early on they come up with a shrewd plan, patterned on devices old King Rwabugiri favored. Whenever Rwabugiri felt threatened by bumptious Tutsi brigadiers, he'd cook up foreign adventures, then send these fellows off to lead them. At the very least, this kept potential challengers out of the country. At best, these men, so dangerous at home, might get killed on vacation.

Now Kanjogera and her son, King Musinga, are up to something similar. It seems commonly assumed that feudal kings work their will by rewarding their conquering warlords with the rule of conquered realms. But a regent schooled in devious statecraft can put some wicked English on this tactic. He can *punish* a conquering warlord with the rule of a conquered realm. Indeed, he can be so generous with such dubious rewards that you don't even have to be a conquering warlord to win one.

I remember Mama sitting with our Auntie Pascazie in squeaky tin chairs on the back porch one evening after chores. Mama is dragging on one of her tiny pipes—the ones she calls, in delicate euphemism, her "telephones." Auntie is recalling how she fretted about the safety of her husband during the nineteen-fifties when they lived in rebellious Ruhengeri up in gorilla country. As they talk, the breeze is all deceptive peace. Auntie Pascazie is the sister of Uncle Kagame, the professor who likes to make the chiefs into figures of fun, but Auntie has married one anyway, Chief Kabano, and during the fifties he was sent off to govern Ruhengeri, a heavily Hutu prefect in the high mountains, where ambushes are easy to lay. He was sent there during the decade that ended with the pogroms of 1959.

As they chat, an earlier chief becomes their subject. As I listen half-asleep, they meander through his tale, Mama and Auntie suppressing occasional impulses to giggle. I hear unintelligible murmurs, muted mirth amid the breeze off the hills. They speak of this fellow as a well-situated chief, something of a playboy, leading the good life of the court. I see him as the picture of the Bazungu's Tutsi superman, tall, trim, assured, aging elegantly. He cultivates a clipped white beard. Mama and Auntie call him Chief Kamuzinzi; to Kanjogera's jaundiced eye, he must have looked too assured. He must have provoked her suspicion, though his self-assurance did not denote ambition at all; it was no more than the air of entitled privilege with which courtly gents grew up. Indeed, he seems to have enjoyed courtly games and comforts far too much to endure the risks and hardships that ambition might entail. But Kanjogera was in no mood to take chances. She had her son, King Musinga, send Chief Kamuzinzi off to govern recently absorbed, rebellious Bugoyi.

As I fall asleep, the ladies chuckle gently at how this playboy of the Rwandese world chafed in discomfort in Bugoyi.

25

KABENGA'S WAR WITH THE BELGIANS
1920–1938

And his war with the royal court, and his war with the law courts. A hero born to a heroic age and bum-rushed into an antiheroic one, our grandfather-to-be, bereft of warriors to battle, is a hero at war with the world.

Dogs he gets along with. Dogs can be trained to hunt. With Belgians who would hunt, success is hit-and-miss. And picture their alarm were you to pat them on the head. Belgians he does not brook.

He shows more distaste for the Belgians than he does for the king's court. To listen to him, you'd think that all he has against the court is its partnership with the Belgians. But watch as he talks. Watch his long body as it leans with his words. Soon enough, you descry something different. Kabenga knows that the Belgians aren't the authors of the family's woes. Down in the Congo they've been a pox and still are (ten million living human souls slaughtered between 1880 and 1910), and Kabenga knows it. For that matter, the Germans were a pox just over the frontier to the east, in Tanganyika, and Kabenga knows that. But the Germans kept pretty much clear of Rwanda's gentry, and Kabenga is among the Rwandese who keep clear of the Belgians. Misery is the lot of those who won't—or to tell the whole truth, can't. Tutsi overseers on white plantations aren't doing nearly as well as you might think. The mostly Hutu peasants they oversee are doing as badly as you can imagine. But as for us, no shattering family tales of colons abusing family figures, no tales of colons laying open their flesh so that we, in turn, will lay open the flesh of plantation peasants. It goes on, but it's not much a part of our personal family lore. To Kabenga's eye, the Hutu-Tutsi business that so compels the Belgian mind, the fussy regard for race that exaggerates and exacerbates trouble between gentry and peasant—all this is simply of a piece with the impunity with which they go about reordering our nation. One day soon, he will have a distinct and personal reason to dislike the Belgians, but not yet, not now. For now, he just dislikes them.

By contrast, he has good reason to dislike the court, only gradually coming out from under the sway of the Dowager Queen Kanjogera. No sooner did the family, old Mutemura's Batemura, reach its apex with Kabenga's silo-size grandfather Muganza, than the jealous at court sent the Batemura into decline by forcing the fat man to poison himself. Then they forced the same on Muganza's son Rudasumbwa, Kabenga's natural father. Then they forced Muganza's other son, Mukeza—Kabenga's stepfather, Mukeza—to quit the court at Nyanza for lands far distant. Yet for all this, Kabenga never speaks against the court. Only against the Belgians does he speak. For me, it's the great conundrum of these years.

Why won't he show any dislike of the royals who have been hurting our family genuinely, directly? Why does he look with such distaste on the Belgians, who have little direct impact on him at all? It's a wonder I know the answer, but I do: For much the same reason as the Bahutu of the northwest rebelled against the court, Mukeza and his stepsons, Kabenga and Bitahurwina, refuse to rebel against the court. In both cases, the reason is the power of tradition, the tradition of kingship that says the king is divine. You do not attack your king—you cannot attack your king—no more than a true believer can attack God. Yes, Queen Kanjogera and her brother did just that, and just that was the legitimist hook upon which the Bahutu of the northwest hung their revolt. In their eyes they weren't attacking the king, they were attacking an impostor and rallying to the real king. But for Kabenga's Batemura, fate, in the persons of the blaspheming queen and her brothers, has given Rwanda a new king, and for better or worse, he is the king. He is order. He is divine.

Tonton Kagame tells us that Rwandese kingship is thoroughly Bantu, which means it stands for the fundamental order of things. Without it, all things fall apart. Even the natural death of a king is traumatic, but the murder of a king is the poisoning of wells, the looming end of life as it is known. It hardly matters that you may actually dislike your king. You may not like the brackish water from your wells. But to hear that the wells are gone, the kingship is gone, this is pulling the ultimate plug. It's hearing that laws no longer apply. Similarly, a cloud over the legitimacy of your king is as unsettling as a murmured, insidious question about the safety of the water. The king is order, the king is propriety, and propriety isn't some perfunctory social posture, it's as fundamental as the safety of the water.

So there you have it. On the frontier, kingly custom provides good reason for Hutu princes to rebel against the court. The court had usurped tradition. Its new king is illegitimate. In our case, kingly custom forces compliance with the court. However the new king became king, he's now the king, and divine, and you don't kill a divinity. When the rebels flee deep into Uganda, the royal court sends Kabenga's brother, Bitahurwina, deep into Uganda to chase them—and he goes. It's his duty. His divine duty.

And in the event, he hasn't much choice. The old king left his kingdom a message: Don't get into fights you can't win. Of course, old King Rwabugiri himself challenged fate with impunity, forever fighting treacherous battles; he died in the Congo fighting a battle he couldn't win—the end, at last, of *his* impunity. But the message was earnest. It was one reason (the other being the chaos born of regicide) that the court stopped challenging Bazungu. Bazungu had rifles, repeaters, fusils; harbingers of who knows what.

For all this, hostility toward the court abides silently within the family, and in particular hostility abides toward Queen Kanjogera's brother and collaborator, Chief Kabare, and even more does it abide for another royal brother, Chief Kayondo. It was Chief Kayondo, above all, who staged the charade that ended in the death by torment of Kabenga's natural father, Rudasumbwa.

THESE ARE NOT SALUBRIOUS DAYS, NOT WITH THE BAD BREATH OF BELGIANS OVER THEIR shoulders, and courtly deceit ever lurking, even this far upcountry, on the family's new turf. Even dance takes on a certain bitter edge: The Inzirab-woba are no longer a fighting force; the Belgians allow no fighting force led by Rwandese. But the Inzirabwoba are allowed to dance, and Kabenga leads them. Every year, the king calls Kabenga and his brother, Bitahurwina, and their stepfather, Mukeza, back to Nyanza for attendance at court, their annual service. These in particular are days of dance.

Much of what Kabenga knows of dance he has learned from his stepfather, Mukeza, and it's Mukeza who has taught him much of what he knows about cows, and about the hunt. It's with Mukeza that he heads north toward Uganda at nightfall, toward the hunting grounds about Byumba-ville. Dogs yap quietly at their heels. (These largely basenji breeds have considerably more bite than yap; some are nearly mute.) Porters carry assagais, full quivers, blanket rolls of finely woven grass; they carry no firearms.

Sometime during 1922, I'm not sure when, Kabenga, his brother, Bitahurwina, and their stepfather, Mukeza, by now an old man, leave Kiyanza country to perform their annual service at court. There old man Mukeza feels the abiding antagonism of the dowager queen's brother, Chief Kayondo, by now himself an old man, and while they are at court, Mukeza's rugo back upcountry in the Kiyanza hills is seized by an incident.

The land Mukeza and the family settled in Kiyanza country seems to have come down to him from the lands that Queen Nyiramavugo granted

his father, Muganza, after the fat one made a man of her son, Prince Nkoronko. But I've never been sure. Prince Nkoronko grew up with Mukeza, in
that rugo, with Muganza as surrogate father, so it seems likely that the lands
Mukeza settled were the lands the old queen granted Muganza. But then
again, one of the fat man's brothers, Karekezi, had already been settled upcountry when Mukeza and his migrating family got there. Decades later,
one of Karekezi's grandsons, Alexis Karekezi, will be a figure of some stature
in the family and in the Belgian authority. When the pogroms of 1959
chase Mama and Papa from their upcountry farm, Alexis Karekezi will give
them the land that Papa cleared for the farm where I was born. So it may
not have been the old queen who was the source of the lands Mukeza
settled after the century turned. It may have been Alexis Karekezi's grandfather Karekezi, the fat man's brother. In either case, it's been a relief for the
family to be away from the intrigues of the court, and they get along well
with the local gentry. In particular, they get along with gentry like our father's Tsobe clansmen, and with local gentry of the Kono clan. By 1922, old
Mukeza's stepdaughter, Elizabeti, Kabenga's sister, Elizabeti, has already
married a Kono chief, Rubasha. For Hutu family servants, however, the
change has not been so easy. Many local Bahutu have not taken well to
them, and while Mukeza is performing his 1922 service at court in Nyanza,
a Hutu gang back in Kiyanza invades family lands, sets upon one of Mukeza's
senior servants with pangas, and kills him. Within days, the dead man's
family mounts a counterattack, and this time many die.

This is the scene that faces old Mukeza upon his return from the royal
court, and no sooner does he begin to restore order than Belgian officers in
khaki and pith helmets and flanked by askaris in red fezzes show up from
Kigali-ville. What are they here for? They're here to seize Mukeza on
charges of murder. The punishment for capital crime is death by hanging,
but so far, the Belgians have hung no one.

It's not hard for Mukeza to clear himself. He was at court in Nyanza during the battle. No one in Kiyanza country disputes this. Many in Kiyanza
confirm it. Many in Nyanza confirm it. They let him go.

And no sooner does he get back home than the Belgians show up with
yet another warrant for murder—and this time the Belgians will hear no defense. The reason is the dowager's brother Kayondo. Old Kayondo, as the
story goes, has whispered in Belgian ears, "Hang Mukeza. If you don't, he'll
lead a massacre, and what a pity." Who knows if he dislikes Mukeza this intensely, or if he's just bloody-minded?

It's a public hanging, in front of the police post the Germans built on
Muhima hill, just downslope from the open sewer the Belgians have dug at
right angles to the fall line. The family knows the hill well, and in Rwanda
a hill is not just a hill, it's the people of the hill. It's as if the hill is a person.

This is the hill across which the family filed in procession on the big safari that moved them from the court at Nyanza to their new home in Kiyanza country. This is the hill that watched the passage of two-meter Mukeza, striding staff in hand, all in white, as behind him followed servants bearing palanquins on which sat his two wives, all in white, hidden behind bone beads. It's the hill that looked on at Mukeza's trooping servants with all their earthly goods, theirs and Mukeza's, on their heads. It's the hill that witnessed the passage of his stepdaughter, Elizabeti, his young daughter, Stefania, and saw his stepsons, Kabenga and Bitahurwina, driving Mukeza's great horned cattle. It's a hill, rising high in the center of Kigali-ville, on which hyena will prowl well into the nineteen-sixties.

Drilled askaris in red fezzes lead Mukeza to the gallows, roped. Stefania and Elizabeti must surely look on; I cannot picture them refusing him that. Bitahurwina and Kabenga most surely look on. The hill looks on, no longer a Rwandese hill but a town hill: coolies, Hendi duka wallahs in dotis and sandals, Egyptian traders in fezzes, skullcapped Swahili, rickshaw boys, beggars, bootblacks for Belgians in jackboots, drifters who collect at settlements, puzzled pygmies cinched with banana leaves. A drum rolls. The sewer smells. The hangman, hooded, slips a noose of stout Manila hemp about Mukeza's neck. Saber drawn, a Belgian officer in a colonial kepi barks a command to black sergeants in colonial khaki. Sergeants bark commands to askaris at attention. In perfect synchrony, African palms slap European walnut, executing smartly from right-shoulder to parade arms. The hangman slips the noose. The drum falls silent. "In the name of the King of the Belgians and by judgment of the court-martial, the prisoner Mukezarugamba is to be hung by the neck until dead." The hangman pulls a three-foot lever. The trapdoor drops. Mukeza's two-meter frame drops. Rope yanks taut, noose throttles. A light crack snaps the silence; Mukeza twitches, the first man hung by the Belgians in Rwanda. His bowels empty. The crowd roars in appreciation of the spectacle.

SENTIMENT COMES TOO EASILY. THINK OF ALL THE URUNDIANS WHO DIED WHEN Mukeza's father, Muganza, mounted cattle raids against them. People executing people is a rude spectacle, and likely a trespass against God. But so are less spectacular failings—greed, jealousy, simony.

And sanctimony. In Kinyarwanda there's no word for that, but our onlooking Kabenga knows the posture, and too well. All about him the churchly preach and posture and rub raw the scabbed sore of caste. Indeed, impunity and sanctimony are more likely the wrongs that Kabenga feels at play this day. In years just ahead, Zungu sanctimony will pull up its skirts at the barbarity of capital redress. But I can't presume that as he sees his stepfather hung high, Kabenga feels the piety that grips us these days when we witness execution—and how much does this flaw him? If a still noose is your measure of social quality, this year of grace 1922 should see the Belgian nation close to social perfection. No one has been executed there since 1863; popular sentiment finds the practice too barbaric.

As Mukeza hangs in Rwanda, a novella titled *Bambi* enchants popular sentiment in Europe. Meantime, the same readership that snaps up such treacle snaps up the elitist (and equally romantic) weltschmerz of Friedrich Nietzsche, he of *Thus Spake Zarathustra,* who speaks of supermen, of *Übermenschen,* and yearns for the righteous certainty that resides in strength. Now in the late twenties, not just Austria but much of the continent adores them both, Bambi and Nietzsche's Zarathustra, who booms that after the brazen likes of Asa and Ahab and Solomon, defeated Jews "transvalued" evil into good (by which Zarathustra means weakness into good), and passed on this "corrupt" coda, this blessing of the meek, to Christendom. In Germany, there's a beer hall putsch and a Reichstag fire and then a season of triumph.

Since the end of the Great War, everybody has been looking for work. Paul von Lettow-Vorbeck—he of the great egalitarian guerrilla campaign in German East Africa, he who gave Isak Dinesen so strong and positive an impression "of what imperial Germany stood for" (and he of the Herero genocide)—returns to Weimar Germany to indulge one cranky right-wing cause after another. As early as 1920, he's been cashiered, and now he's an old soldier out of work, one of hundreds of desperate thousands.

Which would end the story except that this is real life, and in real life stories don't end. A few months after I've wrapped up Lettow-Vorbeck in my head, watched him drift off with Germany into the Nazi netherworld, I learn that he marched right up to the Nazi threshold and stopped short. When it might really pay to join the party, he says no. To Lettow-Vorbeck, cranky and out of sorts though he is, the Nazis just don't smell right. He listens closer. He speaks out against them. He suffers. Churchill, meantime, is watching. He knows the guts it takes to resist the Nazis, and he knows that Lettow-Vorbeck's battlefield enemies in Kenya Colony hold him in high regard. One day in the Low Countries, he grabs him—to all appearances on the fly—and tries to talk him into assassinating Hitler. Lettow-Vorbeck says it wouldn't do any good. He tells Churchill Germany has to go through something terrible before all this is out of its system.

I'M GETTING CARRIED AWAY. THE WESTERN WORLD OF THE NINETEEN-TWENTIES AND thirties can't be this toxic. Struggling student of the English tongue that France has made me, I sit reading in our Jetson-modern flat in a tower block, circa 1988, letting lines of verse, circa 1924, transport me to an English meadow—more Rwanda than concrete-paved America—and the delights of sloshing "with great big waterproof boots on," just the sort of rubber wellies that men and boys wear all over Rwanda.

> *A lion has a tail and a very fine tail,*
> *And so has an elephant, and so has a whale,*
> *And so has a crocodile, and so has a quail—*
> *They've all got tails but me.*

A footnote says that A. A. Milne wrote the lines because he was fed up with reading versified baby talk to his young son. Papa comes to me; all those cool evenings on his lap on the back porch. He wasn't one for bow-wowing baby talk either. He just talked to me.

And then I read that at one crux of our Afro-Levant, in Palestine, the Honorable Edwin Samuel reads some verses aloud to a meeting of the Jaffa Chamber of Commerce, and "all those Arab merchants took the afternoon off for endless repeats of 'Christopher Robin goes hoppity, hoppity, hop.'"

Thus, I imagine, does the gentler West invade the East.

> *Hoppity, hoppity, hop.*
> *Whenever I tell him*
> *Politely to stop it, he*
> *Says he can't possibly stop.*

THE GOOD SHIP *WATUSSI*

And thus does Christopher Robin—or as he prefers to call himself, BILLY MOON—everywhere invade, and thus does Britain, with its ticks and fashions, invade, as all the while France looks on jealously, France, whose insidiously lovely tongue spreads also through our Rwanda and our Afro-Levant. In Rwanda, Waterloo and Willy are indulging ever more romantic palaver about a Watusi super-race, a race almost as super as their own. Then comes the crash. Across Britain, soup lines form, and across America too, and across America, academics profess that science of racial improvement called eugenics.

Do you recall the Afrikaaner Laurens van der Post? He's the writer who so startled me when I read him describing how, as a child, he pored over a book about the Greeks, and how they looked with awe to black Africa. Somewhere else, van der Post recalls a passage at sea during these Depression years. He's bound for Durban aboard the Hamburg-Afrika line. The ship is immaculate and all you'd expect of the Germans, all clockwork and first-rate fare. He takes immediately to the captain. A chamber orchestra gives concerts "of the first order," then lullabies everyone to bed with Brahms's "Guten Abend, gut nacht," beneath "a sky full of stars on tip-toes."

Then refugees aboard ship tell him the captain isn't really in charge; a Nazi cell—it's made up entirely of enlisted men—wields ultimate power. Waiters, bellboys, and masseurs spy on passengers and crew and secretly order the officers about. For me, the scene mirrors the Belgian and still somewhat German Ruanda-Urundi of these Depression years, Kabenga's years.

The ship's patrician officers are the titled and wish-they-were-titled, men like my marabou Waterloo who come to us looking for something to do with their cash; for those who still have cash, it goes a long way these Depression days. The enlisted men, by contrast, are the restless and desperate who come to us without promise, looking for promise. They're ready to work hard and carve a fortune out of raw Africa. Even if they're not happy lunks like Willy, even if they're nasty drunks with thick necks, they are all, sooner or later, bruised by the brute fact of Africa. They are all struck by how small they are against the immensity of Africa, and that's when they begin balming themselves with racial fantasy, palaver that blames "lazy Bahutu" for their failures, and praises "Watusi" as a master race, palaver whose subtext is their own racial quality as white men, so tested by this Africa and this Depression, in such desperate need of assurance.

I must remind myself that my marabou lunk Willy does try. I must remember that his tales of race and Watusi begin with Waterloo, who's just looking for someplace to speculate, and maybe get in some hunting. (In Kenya Colony, tallyho; there the gentry tricks itself out in hunting pinks and rides to the hounds, and when they chat, palaver about Watusi has an added piquancy, that romance of the safari beyond even Uganda. In 1921, all the talk at the clubs is of Sweden's Prince Wilhelm, lately arrived at Mombasa. He's out there in Rwanda, and he's shot a record fourteen gorillas.) I must remind myself also that there is more to van der Post's tale.

The refugees aboard ship tell him that the vessel's effective captain is a rating, a Nazi party hack installed as the titular captain's steward. They warn van der Post that he's been seen too often with an American aboard, a man named Jim Williamson, who lived for years in Germany and is now emigrating with his wife, Elsie, to Australia. They say Williamson has been too outspoken. Somehow he can't button up his dismay at what the Nazis are doing to Germany.

Some weeks after disembarking at Durban, van der Post hears from Elsie. At Durban, she and Jim had boarded another German liner for Australia. Jim had remained his outspoken self. One evening Elsie went to bed early, woke in the middle of the night in the middle of the ocean, and went looking for her husband. She couldn't find him. She roused the ship. No one

ever did find him. He simply disappeared "on the calmest of nights." "I had
no doubt that the 'real controllers' of the ship had dumped him in the sea,"
recalls van der Post, who then recalls the gloom of the captain of the vessel
he'd shared with Elsie and Jim. "He concentrated more and more on the
pedigree pigs that he bred on rich first-class swill on the highest boat-deck
from which passengers were excluded, and on chamber music after dinner.
I often wondered how he and his officers could endure the humiliation and
did not resign."

Emblazoned on the prow of this pride of the Hamburg-Afrika line was its
name, *The Watussi.*

OF HARDBOILED POACHERS, POTBELLIED
SINGHS, AND RIGHT GENTS

Sometime after the short rains of 1930, Chief Kayondo, the king's uncle
and the family's bane, calls for a contest in which all the old fighting bands,
the Inzirabwoba, the Impamakwica, the Ingangurarugo, the Inkotanyi, will
compete at dancing, with a grand prize for the leader of the winning band.
It will be a high occasion for the Bazungu and their cameras. Under
Kabenga, the Inzirabwoba muster, and practice and practice. The lads wonder why Kabenga punishes them so. Well out of his earshot, they wonder
why they must forever repeat routines already perfect.

The family has been absent from Nyanza for nearly a quarter century.
Muganza and Rudasumbwa and Mukeza are long since dead, all victims of
the court. The court is still weak from the Rucunshu massacre. It is still too
weak to rid itself of all the enemies it imagines behind every termite
mound, but it can punish the enemies it imagines, and it does—or perhaps
it simply enjoys having them around to torment. In either event, we now
see, all these many years after the family left Nyanza, Kabenga leading the
Inzirabwoba in a contest called by the family's old nemesis, Chief Kayondo.
Here is our grandfather to-be, back where he grew up and went to the Germans' School for the Sons of Chiefs.

There are many bands. According to the Belgians, who are great aficiona-
dos of Rwandese dance, they all perform magnificently—and as matters
turn out, this presents Chief Kayondo with a quandary. He's the judge. It's
for him to pick the winner. He can pick whomever he wishes.

Perhaps he has expected, reasonably, that Kabenga, this leader of a faded
subclan, will perform in an average way, or perhaps better than that, but
certainly not so much better that he, Kayondo, will be obliged to declare
Kabenga the winner. And in fact the bands do perform with nearly equal
magnificence. But what Chief Kayondo has failed to account for is the
bands themselves. They are a good part of the audience, and they respond

with such heart to Kabenga and to the Inzirabwoba (who can say why?) that an off-balance Kayondo is forced to declare Kabenga the winner.

Upon a signal from the chief, stewards select Kabenga's prize from among two or three cows, and lead her forward, a magnificent animal, all black. Magnificent, that is, to my eyes, or yours. For Rwandese of the day, no prize could be paltrier. A black cow.

"I do not accept," says Kabenga.

He does not what?

"I do not accept."

He must.

"Is it the king's prize?"

It's Chief Kayondo's prize.

"Then I do not accept. I appeal to the king." And appeal he does, and King Musinga, Kanjogera's son, awards him a magnificent cow. The same year, Kabenga's brother, Bitahurwina, gives his only son to the church; Kagame, now baptized Alexis Kagame, now eighteen, is sent to the seminary, then to yet another seminary, and at last to the Pontifical Gregorian University in the Vatican, all to the end of preparing himself for a career as scholar and teacher.

FOR KABENGA, YEARS OF ANGER YIELD SLOWLY TO YEARS OF CATTLE, DANCE, AND DOGS, which is to say the hunting of big game, which Bazungu would say is the poaching of big game. These are the years in which Belgium's Leopold III, heir to Leopold the Canker, sets up storied reserves on our Congo frontier. More exactly, they are the years in which he reserves millions of hectares upon which only Waterloo and Willy can hunt.

These are also the years during which a landmark American naturalist, Carl Akeley, first comes to our hills in search of the mountain gorilla. Well into this period between the wars, and even somewhat after, swaths of Great Lakes country remain flush with game, despite the best efforts of Zungu trophy chasers and African poachers. Indeed, in the years ahead, hunters will be a distant second in the great depredation of game. The worst enemies of the game, worse even than renegade armies flush with ammo and hungry for bush meat, will be honest farmers in their burgeoning numbers, doing what they must, scratching at stubborn hardpan, seeding, sweating, harvesting.

The high and wild swath whose southern verge Kabenga stalks stretches from Uganda's high Lake Albert, where Emin Pasha patrolled, south along the eastern flanks of the Mountains of the Moon and the Virungas, and at last downslope to the high-plains grit of the Akagera floodplain, still known to Bazungu as the floodplain of the Alexandra Nile. Here, in the dust of the high plateau, rhino root. Here the horizon has an empty Tanganyikan distance to it. Here the word *simba,* "lion," is still an everyday word. Here giraffe lope, elephant grow taller than the trees, and their trains vanish into an endless beyond.

In the West, the rich are losing fortunes and the poor are in soup lines. Kabenga hunts. Leisure it seems, and leisure it is. The Tutsi likes of Kabenga, detail-driven men, are inclined to make work even of leisure, but leisure it nonetheless is; these men are fundamentally cowherds overdeveloped. As they stand about with their staves, composing bad poems and talking worse politics, appointed stewards stand by to hold their pipes when they're not puffing. Puff, then hand the vessel to your vassal. Want another puff? You need not even glance at him. Just extend your hand.

It's a world still possible, even after the great crash of world markets in 1929, because Ruanda-Urundi is still largely free of the world's cash economy. There is still no Rwandese or Burundian coinage, and few francs from cash-strapped Belgium. The few times Kabenga chooses not to barter for his needs, in particular when he sells skins from his hunts, the clerk at Max Klein et Fils in Kigali-ville is as likely as not to count out the Maria Theresa dollars that have been circulating in East Africa for more than a century.

Kabenga and his ilk live by their cows, their lands, their peasants. Their fortunes rise or fall by the discipline, or lack of discipline, with which they manage all this. As for forces beyond their control, neither cash nor credit yet count for much, just rain or its absence, pestilence, and the fickle disposition of the court. The Batemura are still Chief Kayondo's to toy with, but Kiyanza country, where much of the family now lives, is distant from the court. What's more, it's not the bailiwick of either of the king's two most relentless uncles, chiefs Kayundo and Kabare. Instead it's the bailiwick of Chief Rwubusisi, another of Queen Kanjogera's brothers. Chief Rwubusisi likes the cows Kabenga breeds. He likes Kabenga's dogs. He likes Kabenga. In time, old man Rwubusisi becomes Kabenga's hunting crony, as does the Count de Borchgrave, a Belgian who has purchased estates beneath Kabenga's rugo above Kabuye.

Do not let rank and station impress you overmuch. I'm certain that if we could listen in on them, we'd hear Chief Rwubusisi and the Count de Borchgrave admiring Kabenga more for his aim than for his bloodline. To be equally sure, the two may see blood and ability as one and the same, but that would just expose their bias and princely remove from everyday life. If they reckon that Kabenga gets his aim from his blood, it's because they don't really know him, certainly not his habits. Kabenga's habits are something you'll have to go to women and children to learn. It's the women of his rugo who know how almost every day he sets out on his own with his knife and his Zungu to pepper away forever at trees. And it's the children, tagging along, who watch him take his knife and dig spent rounds out of tree trunks, who watch as he bellows up a fire to melt down the lead and pour it into molds, who listen to his tales as he waits for the shot to cool and harden, ready to be fired off again, and again, and again, at hapless trees. It's this relentless practice, not to speak of this hardscrabble frugality, which has him cutting targets dead center.

Kabenga's exacting ways are not unique. There are others with them, and they're a motley bunch.

To begin with, there are the least motley, the right gents, the Bazungu who come to us to hunt. Ruanda-Urundi is becoming a destination, that storied step beyond for bosky Brits in Kenya Colony. From Kenya, a pukka few make their way to our hills, and once here, they set the style, as the English are wont to do in so many matters sporting. If you can get smoked trout and jugged hare in Kenya Colony, then why not in Ruanda-Urundi? And if Waterloo's manservant in Nairobi is "his boy," then by George, that's what he is here. Before Kabenga knows it, the word *umuboyi* has infiltrated Kinyarwanda. Not *umugarçon*. Not *umujunge*. Instead, the English derivative, *umuboyi*. This far beyond Lake Victoria, there still aren't many Bazungu, rich or otherwise. Ruanda-Urundi is becoming a destination, but that's largely a matter of pub talk, daydreams, idle chat on Kenyan links. In practical fact, precious few of the world's hunting Bazungu can afford a Kenyan or Tanganyikan hunt, fewer still a safari here. But all the same, the few Inglezi who come set the style.

More characteristic of the bundu here are subsidiary personalities of the Brits, men like Mr. Bhagat Singh. Presumably a namesake of the Bhagat Singh of Hindu myth, and soon to be a hoary legend himself, our Mr. Bhagat is just now buying his first elephant licenses from colonial authorities on the Ugandan frontier that Kabenga patrols.

He's shorter than most of our pygmies (who aren't that short), something like four feet six. They say he has quite a productive banana patch, quite a dirty tarboosh, a pair of antique binoculars, and a wife whom professional hunters describe for their clients as a Kiga (or Mukiga or Bakiga or Wakiga) tribeswoman.

Tiny Bwana Bhagat also has an on-again, off-again lisp, a potbelly, a distinctive wardrobe (each item of which is ripped and stitched and stained), thick mustaches stained with tobacco, and the sort of firearm that Kabenga has at last begun to carry, a fusil, much abused but true, worn of all bluing, shining with oil—and immaculate. This despite all that oil collecting high-plains grit. But just you try to suggest less oil. Head wagging, Bwana Bhagat squeaks, "Cripes, no, sahib, a wittle gweathe is a blessing in the wet." Bazungu who cross his path dismiss him as a quirk of the scenery, but he and his two Kiga porters are ever ready with hot tea for the tired sojourner in the bundu, where he spends months on end, just him, these two Bakiga, and the fire ants. He's a first-rate tracker. He's a better shot. And thirty years later, he will be at it yet, still pulling his game licenses, this four-foot-six-inch man with his potbelly and his two hillbillies, bringing down bull elephants.

Would that I could tell you just what Kabenga brings down, but poachers don't boast, especially poachers who have seen their kin hung high. Kabenga was a hero of the Batemura as Xenophon was of Athens. But Xenophon left Athens an entire volume, *Hunting with Dogs*. All Kabenga will leave us is the dogs, prancing almost barkless about his Kabenga-bereft rugo. He hunts at times with the king (I must presume that these hunts, at least, are legal), and you can still see the king's trophy room near Nyanza, full of great-maned lions and lowering black buffalo, but it's a Zungu trophy room. The trophies that the Inzirabwoba want for the flourishing manes of their outfits come from something rare, the colobus monkey.

Hardly pukka, these monkey hunters and potbellied little Singhs, but this is the bundu that Kabenga and his cronies beat, only now and then picking up the spoor of Bazungu on the hardpan, so that when they do, it's a curiosity, something to look into.

CRANKCASES AND EGOS; THINGS TEND TO LEAK WHEN THEY HIT HARDPAN. CERTAINLY my Waterloo tends to leak when he hits hardpan.

Let's say that Kabenga has you along, and you run across rusticating Bazungu amid this thorny stuff. You drag over some long bits of deadwood for a long slow fire; high tea without cucumber sandwiches. You filter some water through a rag. You pull out the dented pot. Likely as not, one of the camp's company has reason to wonder whether he's up to this Africa business and its heat, its bugs, its microbes; and if it's me telling the story, Waterloo is going to be the melancholy camper. Marabou are tough birds, but Loo has led a pampered life. No question. He'll be the one you find in every camp, trying bravely to plug the leak in his ego by calling everyone African his boy, his *muboyi*. When he gets in moods like this, everyone just ignores him.

He'll court attention nonetheless, and firearms are this evening's means for calling attention to oneself. These Zungu *bundugu*, these collaborations of hardwood and high-carbon steel, these fusils, do so compel him. Just look at him, my marabou Waterloo, pouting a slow tango about the camp with his *fusil fatal*. His stubby left wing holds her barrel straight out, as with eyes half-shut he cocks his head back and gazes down her barrel. His other wing holds his lovely's stock fast to his breast. His partner in moody tango is a beauty all scribed with roses. Indeed, she's got everything but a wild

Argentine rose locked crosswise in her bolt. He calls her his Doña Pasacantando.

Loo's swirling adagios are inspired, but he might as well be a swirling dust devil for all the attention he gets. Maybe his mates are just too tuckered out to indulge him. Or maybe they aren't able to detect an imaginary caricature at large in their midst. Or maybe he embarrasses them. They all have their own weaknesses for firearms.

It's often hard to read their faces. They seem always to be sitting, as they nurse their tea, or their beer, with their backs to the sun. Squint through one eye, and they look simply full of themselves, these feckless white boys, these Rider Haggard groupies who have ordered and even shaped our lives. Switch to the other eye, and they seem to know they've got a tick for guns so bad it's hanging up their lives. And so stubborn it rubs off on their kids— and their kids' kids, so that we Rwandese get to know them not just from the likes of our boys—"boys" like Kabenga—but through what they call our "bints"—which is to say, females like me. Listen through one ear, and they sound like they're telling you how they know—they really do—that females like you are smarter than anyone ever thought. (So smart you can actually appreciate their blather.) Listen through the other ear, and they sound as if they know how disabling their gun-tick is, and hope, by going on and on, to get rid of it by palming it off on you. I'll become an unwilling repository of their fussy lore.

To begin with, there is the question of firepower. Especially dear to the early hunting crowd—years before the shooting days of Kabenga and Mr. Bhagat Singh—was the double-barreled Jeffrey gun, sometimes called an elephant gun, which is not really a gun—that is, a shotgun, a weapon that fires shells loaded with pellets—but a huge-bore double-barreled rifle—a rifle fires bullets—with tremendous muzzle velocity, tremendous recoil, and cartridges so full of black powder that they have scant accuracy "at range," by which they mean not much distance at all. Lore has it that these were the weapons of the great elephant hunters, men like Karamoja Bell upcountry in Uganda. Bell (who gave his name to Bell Lager, still on tap in Entebbe) would bag dozens of tuskers in a single day, just for the numeric joy of it. But that was then. These days, the one or two white hunters Kabenga knows use modest weapons, leaving the big-bores to the big bores. Bell himself, they say, accomplished his inane slaughter with a small-bore bolt-action rifle. In short, when the smoke clears, the Zungu obsession with firearms emerges as something more deliciously subtle than any dumb lust for powder.

Anything semiautomatic (you squeeze the trigger, it fires once and chambers a new round by itself, ready for you to squeeze again) is considered unsporting. Rifles this quick and easy to load are for askaris enforcing colonial law. Only humans are fair game for semiautomatic weapons. For game, including Africa's big game, a true sport will use only a single-shot weapon. With these firearms, you squeeze off a single round (unless your rifle is double-barreled, in which case you have a second trigger and a second shot), drop the piece from your shoulder, reload the chamber by hand, reposition the weapon in your shoulder, re-aim, squeeze off another single round, and pray, for the beast may be headed your way. (Lest this sound intimidating, consider Kabenga and his mates. Until recently, they've been doing the same thing with a bow; instead of reloading a rifle during the charge, they'd be nocking an arrow on a bowstring.)

And this is where excess enters the picture, for as always, wealth has its ways. You say you don't like reloading? Why not have a boy standing by with a second loaded weapon? If you can afford one sporting rifle, you can afford two, and boys, *ababoyi,* Waterloo can afford by the dozen.

Loaders do not in themselves make Kabenga wonder. In his days as a bow hunter, Kabenga had spear-carriers standing by. Indeed, now that he hunts with firearms, he still has lads standing by. One or two, mongoose-like, stand bolt upright on termite mounds, peering into the dusty distance for prey. ("You know this *musimba,* this lion, he don't go to school. He don't know no German. But he plenty smart, you bet.") Still another lad holds a bamboo monopod upright to steady Kabenga's barrel as he draws his bead. But there is more here for Kabenga to notice than boys who stand by. There are the weapons, the sporting, single-shot weapons with which boys stand by, and here now is Waterloo, showing off a fusil to best all fusils. Its stock gleams with French polish, seemingly untouched by thorn or grit. With a brow cocked just for you, he volunteers it for inspection, and you can't help but notice all that florid engraving.

Kabenga is a famous pain. He's the kind who eyeballs what hides in the fine crevices of the engraving. There amid high shine, almost obscured by shine, he may well spy light dustings of rust, for dustings of rust are always about on the weapons of sports foolish enough to volunteer them for inspection. The Kabenga of these years is not bashful. He's curious. He inspects eagerly, and he doesn't linger on the brightwork. He slips the bolt and peers, and here amid the action, here where it matters, his eye is especially gimlet and unforgiving.

All the while, my Waterloo will be letting the camp know how he comes by such weapons. He'll chuckle. His tail feathers cocked to one side, he'll let us know you can't just walk into a London gunsmith and buy one. "Not even at the best shops," he'll honk with a wink. "Not even W. W. Greener. Or Boss. Or Holland and Holland."

"Mmmh," says Kabenga, uninterested.

Were you to visit one of these shops and ask to see "their best," all you'd get is an arched brow, for you'd have betrayed ignorance of their *code ésotérique*. "Best" is gunsmith-speak for bespoke, which he feels obliged to tell you means custom-made. "The waiting list is six months, then another year to craft the piece."

"Mmmh."

"They're dear, something like—well, never mind—and you never buy just one. You buy a matched pair. First they assign you a smith. Your own. Apart from the bores, he mills all the metal himself. Hand-carves the stock from walnut blanks. From the Dordogne. And he uses an adjustable creature called a 'try gun' to fit everything just so. To complement your style just so."

But what if your style is all wrong? For instance, what if you don't lean sufficiently and keep getting knocked on your tail feathers?

"In that case," Loo honks, "they give you lessons."

Which begs a question: If you shoot so badly that you need lessons, what business have you got buying a matched pair of the most costly firearms that Maria Theresa's dollars can buy?

Not that all such folk are bad shots. Some are good. Word is that Britain's King George V keeps two loaders in the butts tending three matched guns; George, they say, is especially quick, and accurate too, dropping scores of birds out of the sky. Which begs yet another question: Is it more likely that George is simply a born shot, or that to get as good as he is, he must be spending hour upon hour, week upon week, just banging away at the sky?

This is what Kabenga sees as the royalty to which the Belgians would have our king aspire. The difference is, George isn't divinity on earth, and he has a first minister. All we have is our divinity, Kanjogera's son, King Musinga, and a clutch of Belgians telling him he should aspire to the likes of Albert and George and Leopold.

THE BELGIANS ARE BEGINNING TO FIND KING MUSINGA AN INFURIATION. LIKE KABENGA, he refuses to wear Western clothes. He refuses to get baptized. He keeps talismans, fetish clubs, charms, sacred monkeys, all the old witch medicine, and the Bazungu, which is to say, the Church and the Belgian authority, want to impose *their* witch medicine. They claim that he's adulterous, incestuous, a bisexual, you name it. "*N'ishyano*," says Kabenga. "Infamy. Belgian lies." But who knows? With Kanjogera for a mother, it would not be surprising if Musinga had weaknesses for all that and bestiality too.

In 1931, the Belgians depose him, installing instead, and without the traditionally crucial consultation of our Tsobe clan's *abiru*, his son Rudahigwa, a thoroughly Western gent who cuts a fine figure indeed, elegantly tall and thin in bespoke worsteds and silk ties from Hermès. He smokes cigarettes, drives a Hispano-Suiza (or some such), has himself baptized, hunts with proper rifles and guns, and likes to be known, formally, as Charles. He is nonetheless known by the people as either the king of the Bazungu or by his proper kingly name, Mutara Rudahigwa. This is so even for the many Rwandese who themselves now go by Christian names, for Mutara Rudahigwa is not simply his name, it is his kingly name, his divine name. For as long as anyone can remember, from the year dot, Rwandese kings have had two names. One is the name with which they're born. The other, echoing from a past older than Tutsi kings, is the name by which Rwandese see their king as divinity on earth—and how many divinities do you know who go by the name of Charles?

26

LITTLE CHIEF ELIZABETI

The Rugos of 1928–1962

A woman's rank
Lies in the fullness of her womanhood:
Therein alone she is royal.
—GEORGE ELIOT, "Armgart"

Kabenga's sister, Elizabeti, is a wife with a problem. A rhino has rooted his way into the family rondavel, got himself trapped in the sleeping quarters, and it's disgraceful. How she wishes the problem would just go away. Already, neighbors are beginning to stand and wonder at the thrashing. Were the walls not so tightly braided, and the braids not so tightly bound, the entire rondavel would be down by now. Now and then flurries of little ox-peckers and wattle starlings, given to feeding on rhino fleas, come fluttering out in the daylight, then dodge back in, as much confounded as Elizabeti. Elizabeti, who runs such a tight household. Elizabeti, whose first-time guests carry on barely audible subtalk beneath the talk-talk, "Mmmh, spotless, mmmh."

Soon everyone will know about this beast, this *isatura*, and Elizabeti has no idea what to do. It thrashes about madly, its piggy little eyes glistening blood red, the brightest light in the windowless dark of the quarters. Soon it will bring the entire rondavel down, and the world down about Elizabeti's ears. Heavily studded Zanzibar chests lie splintered about. A bolt of Zanzibar's finest gauze is wrapped in confusion about the thrashing big horn, protecting the beast not one bit from mosquitoes.

No, rhinos don't do this (indeed, there have been no *isatura* in Kiyanza country for years), and in fact, Elizabeti's rondavel is in fine fettle, but some problems can be every bit as ruinous as a rhino, and this is a problem bigger and more stubborn than the nastiest *isatura:* In five full years of marriage to Chief Rubasha, Elizabeti has borne him only two, count them, *two* children, two lonely whelps. This is a grave matter. Numbers are the sine qua non of an African family. In numbers there is more than strength, there is bounty, good fortune, protection, the light of the heavens, the reputation of the family, and the glue that binds two families—one of which, in this case, is the stunted brood of her late stepfather, Mukeza, itself just one branch of an extended family with many branches likewise stunted, limbs become sad stumps. When regicides forced their father, Rudasumbwa, to poison himself, they cut short the number of her siblings at just two—her brothers Bitahurwina and Kabenga. Then Uncle Mukeza adopted them, and his family was cut short when the Belgians hanged him. Now it looks as if her brother Bitahurwina will have just two offspring—Pascazie (our Auntie-to-be) and Kagame (our Tonton-to-be). And now on top of this, Elizabeti herself has given Chief Rubasha only two children. Her blood (the blood of a family new to this country, and since Mukeza's hanging, vulnerable) has given the chief just two heirs in five years.

Will the chief be obliged to take an extra wife? Soon the entire hill will know this rhino of a problem, and after that it will spread across all the hills of Kiyanza country and the people will demand it, the chief will have to take a second wife.

The chief cares. His wife is no beauty, but he loves her. They try. No luck.

Elizabeti is not a woman lightly to accept another wife in the household. Even back in Nyanza she hadn't been what you'd call the run of Rwandese womanhood. She'd been, she is, a woman with her own voice, and a keel for a family adrift. ("Mmmh, spotless, mmmh.") Such is Elizabeti's personality that Stefania—Mukeza's one and only daughter of his own—has grown up a copy (a somewhat smaller, somewhat homelier copy) of Elizabeti, learning big sister's (in truth, big stepsister's) every move, right down to polishing the lanterns.

Here in Kiyanza country, Elizabeti has been everyone's big sister, even after moving out of Mukeza's rugo and into the chief's. Her scant brood is her one vulnerability. For her, the sad migration from the court at Nyanza to these Kiyanza hills has meant moving from strength to strength, for here in Kiyanza country this already substantial woman has fallen in with women of the Tsobe clan, themselves known as substantial people, women whose households squeak and sparkle like the surgery ward of the mission clinic, women who as often as not rule their households. A Rwandese man can have as many wives as he can support, and the chief can easily support another wife, but times are changing, and Elizabeti is a proud woman.

Her Tsobe lady-friends sympathize, but they're at a loss. "What can you do?" Little sister Stefania sympathizes, but she's at a loss. "What can you do?"

Finally, Elizabeti has heard enough; at last, in one piquant bundle, the answer comes to her. The chief (bless him) will *not* be just another rich Mututsi with two wives. No.

No? wonders little sister Stefania.

No. If there's to be another wife, she, Elizabeti, will choose the bride, and she will choose someone with whom she can work, someone who can outdo even Stefania as a partner.

Truly? wonders little Stefania.

Truly. In fact, she already has her eye on a more than suitable candidate.

Now there aren't many ways in which little sister differs from big sister. In every way she can, wherever she can, whenever she can, Stefania copies big sister. But she does differ here and there, and one of the ways, both here and there, is in her role as a youngest sibling. Elizabeti has all the self-confidence of an elder sibling. Stefania has all the vinegar of a younger one, scrapping for every bit of attention she can muster, jealously possessive of every bit she does get. So just who is this female out there? This girl big sister thinks can outdo even her, Stefania? Who? *Who?* she asks Elizabeti.

Elizabeti says nothing. She just stares at her homely little sister.

At last it dawns on Stefania. No. Elizabeti can't be serious.

Ah, but she is, and it's a marriage made in Tutsi heaven. Chief Rubasha is content. He was never out to become yet another Tutsi chief with two wives; he's just as happy as a chief whose senior wife shares him with her little sister, her homely, fertile, and equally assertive little sister, a perfect partner who outdoes herself almost every day.

I'VE ALWAYS KNOWN ELIZABETI AS MY MOTHER'S AUNT, BUT I ALSO KNOW HER AS THE woman who raised my mother. Let me give you some idea what a presence she was in the family. I wasn't even born until after she died. I never once laid eyes on her. But even I look back on her as my substitute grandmother. What she left us when she died was so abundant that it included yet another substitute grandmother to take her place, her stepsister, cowife, and doppelgänger, Auntie Stefania.

In 1939, my mother was ten. Her own mother was four or five years dead. I don't know exactly, because that's one of those matters that never gets talked about. Sickness took her, I believe, but mother turns away all questions. I begin to feel uncomfortable asking. I accept it as a painful topic and leave it at that. Slowly I begin to understand that my mother's people all say nice things about one another. So nice that this is their notion of a cutting insult (stop to think of it, it *is* cutting): "You're doing just fine, dearie. Don't you mind what people say."

At home, we children are always making fun of our Mama's people, and Papa's, too, often provoking a guarded smile, at once timid and disapproving, from Mama, even from Papa. Three people, though, are exempt. The siblings Kabenga, Elizabeti, and Stefania.

Stefania I know all too well. Mama brooks no fun at the expense of Stefania, and that's not easy to deal with, because Stefania, a real Kommandante among women, is ripe for fun. Whenever she visits, she rules. Every night before bedtime she insists, religiously, that all us children sit down on mats on the concrete deck of the parlor to say prayers. She is no great believer. "The Eucharist gives me a cold," she says. But from our earliest years it's clear to us that, as an opportunity for discipline, she is exceptionally fond of the Church. The idea is not to fill us with the fear of God. It's to use God to put the fear of elders into us unruly children.

"Our father who art in heaven," she intones, then interrupts her conversation with the Holy Father by shouting out the window, "Sentama! The cows. They're milked, aren't they? *Hallowed be thy name.* Rukinga! You shut the gates? *Thy kingdom come . . .*" By now we're fidgeting. By now we actually want to go to bed. The mat itches. ". . . thy will be done, thy child Sagashya, who stubbed his toe after lunch; *please* make it well. On earth as it is in heaven . . ."

For brother Karangwa, the medium through which we know wit, she's choice material. "Thy child Sagashya," he intones, in just her baritone. But he has to wait for Mama to go out back before he'll start. Mama goes out back, and Karangwa drones on, in just Stefania's voice.

"My child Loulou. You know, do you not, the tale of the hyena, the mama, and the spoiled little girl."

I do not.

"Well, my child, there once was a little girl, and fairly spoiled she was. Forever cawing for one trifle or another. Until one day her mama uttered words I can't bring myself to repeat."

"What?"

"Didn't you hear me, child? I said they were words I can't bring myself to repeat."

"What?"

"Mmmh."

"What?"

"Well, if you insist . . . Do you insist?"

"Mmmh."

"She said, 'If you don't stop that cawing, I'm going to feed you to the hyenas.' "

"Mmmh."

"And do you know what?"

"What?"

"It just so happened a hyena was lurking just outside the rugo, and you know what it said?"

"What?"

"It grinned yellow teeth, and purred (for you know hyenas are closer to cats than dogs), 'What a *niiice mother.*' "

Now Mama returns. We're laughing at Karangwa playing Stefania, and Mama wants to know what we're laughing at. Karangwa, who never laughs at his own routines, says, "You know these kids of yours. . . ."

Stefania was just not someone you had fun with in front of Mama, because Stefania was here in the name of Elizabeti, and with Elizabeti, Mama had a history:

Mama was Kabenga's first child, and the object of some affection. My mother's stepmother, Mariya Kabarere, was beautiful—and jealous. She did everything she could to make life impossible for my mother, right from the age of five. Forty years later the two reconciled in the most extraordinary way, but that's a story you already know. As a small girl my mother was forced to carry her half brothers, big boys, on her back; she was given spoiled milk, and told to go to bed before the younger kids. She rose before dawn for chores that were beyond her. From those early years, my mother learned not to complain, but my grandfather could read her eyes, and when he did, Mama would hear from Mariya the next day. "If your father raises any more questions, you're going to have to deal with me."

"Come here, little one, tell your father what's on your mind," Kabenga would say. Some days what was on her mind was her departed mother. Some days it was her ever-present stepmother. Mama would turn her head sideways and hug her father's long legs.

At last came Elizabeti. Elizabeti Gatukwa. Kabenga knew Mama belonged somewhere else. He sent her to his sister, Elizabeti, and Elizabeti became her mother.

A DESPERATE HUSH

Some say World War II begins when the commander of an aging German battleship drops anchor at Danzig, pays its Polish authorities a courtesy call, steams out of port, and begins shelling the city. Others say it begins when Mussolini marches south from Eritrea, intent on conquering Africa's last independent realm, Haile Selassie's Ethiopia.

Selassie standing before the League of Nations in Geneva, there to deliver his plea, has become an emblem of the League's collapse in the face of

Fascism, so you might well think it would be the event that signals the war for Africa. Not so for francophone Africa. For francophone Africa, the war begins with the incident at Mers el-Kébir. As Elizabeti runs her rugos on the far outskirts of Rwanda's territorial seat, the incident at Mers el-Kébir is what galvanizes Zungu Kigali.

The Nazis have already overrun Belgium and invaded France and established themselves in Paris, but that happened so fast (blitzkrieg, after all) that it was over before Kigali knew much of it, and "the phony war" is what everyone called the run-up to all that, the fall of Poland, the massing of troops on the Western Front. Just as quickly, the Nazis sanctioned Marshal Pétain's Vichy regime in the south, and that was it for France. Horrible, but what could you do? France, and the Low Countries too, were hors de combat.

France and the Low Countries. Not francophone Africa. For francophone Africa, World War II is just about to begin.

As Pétain sleeps with the Axis, de Gaulle allies his Free French forces with Britain, and the French fleet slips out of Marseilles, bound for the Algerian port of Oran. Where are its loyalties? Britain's fleet in the Mediterranean is outclassed by Mussolini's bigger, more modern ships. Churchill needs to know if the French fleet is with the Allies or against them. The French don't answer. He wires them that unless they answer, he'll have to destroy them. They still don't answer. He agonizes. He destroys them. As they sit helplessly at anchor at Mers el-Kébir, his naval guns sink all the capital ships of the French fleet, and right up to and through the genocide in Rwanda, many in France will still remember, still smart, insisting that at the bottom of our troubles in Rwanda is some ill-defined drive by the British to establish English-speaking hegemony over French-speaking Rwanda, and French-speaking Africa.

You'd think that by the time a tormented Churchill sinks the French fleet at Mers el-Kébir, a good deal of the scramble-for-Africa rubbish would have been put to rest, and a good deal has—but land mines of imperial resentment remain buried, and they'll suddenly go off in our midst at the end of the century. At this moment, though—the cordite-stung moment of Mers el-Kébir itself—the mood in Zungu Algiers and Oran and Agadir is not so much one of resentment as of highly charged nerves. All of francophone Africa enters the shadow world of twilit casbahs, and of Dakar and Banjul and Brazzaville, backwaters where no one can know for sure who is on which side, nor on which side it's safe to be. In Ruanda-Urundi, every Muzungu wants to trade assets for cash, and every Muzungu has a little something wrong with his papers. It's a period of moral confusion.

Conservative circles (but not all; we must acknowledge stiff-necked de Gaulle) are ridden with Fascist posturing, and it reaches beyond the rarefied salons where grand strategic alliances shift. In fact, the posturing reaches beyond conservative circles. Liberal circles (with their own exceptions) enfeeble themselves with pacifist sanctimony we now find hard to remember. I find many who know how deftly Charlie Chaplin (our dear Charlot) reduced Hitler to the *Great Dictator* (and the swastika to the double-cross)— but know nothing of Charlot's message: As Stalin cozies up to Hitler, the pacifist Chaplin is trying to persuade the West likewise to appease the Nazis. Near the end of the century, Lando and I will carry on a running dispute, our own floating grudge match, in which he forever insists that art trumps message in any medium, and I forever insist he's wrong. But today I wonder. Maybe Lando is right; maybe art does trump all. Chaplin's message seems mostly forgotten; we remember his art.

The Allies invade North Africa. French troops there, already unhappy with the totalitarian way of life, already restless, begin defecting to the Allies and to de Gaulle's Free French. Before long, their Vichy general, his back against the storied wall, begins dickering with Eisenhower. At last he agrees to deliver his Vichy troops, but he has conditions. He insists on keeping and enforcing Vichy's anti-Semitic laws in North Africa, he will not join de Gaulle's Free French, and Roosevelt (much to the stiff-necked chagrin of the cranky soldier from Saint Cyr by way of Lille) lets him get away with it.

In Rwanda, uttering the name of Hitler becomes a Zungu taboo underwritten by the force of codified law, the same force of law that hanged Mukeza high, and it's not because the Belgians so thoroughly revile Adolf Hitler. It's more a desperate hush from the subjects of a Nazi-occupied state, uncertain who is on which side, and on which side it's safe to be. To the distinctly limited extent that they have any idea what's up in Zunguland, Elizabeti and Stefania are most likely rooting for the Germans. I would be too. For one, they have no good reason to favor the Allies. What have the Allies ever done for them? For another, a proximate colonial is more distasteful than a departed colonial. The Belgians are proximate; however fond they say they are of the Batutsi, the Batutsi are not fond of them. The Germans are colons several decades removed. However beastly they were with the Herero, and in Tanganyika, they weren't all that beastly in Ruanda-Urundi. This deep in Africa, there just weren't enough of them to do much damage, and the few who were here were closer in temperament to Emin Pasha than Karl Peters—and then there were the exploits of Tembasi's Tutsi lads during the Great War in East Africa, exploits that so appealed to the Tutsi love of war.

But this line of thought doesn't bear much scrutiny, if for no other reason than that there's not much to scrutinize. For Africans in Africa, World War II isn't simply far off. It also puts Europe a long way off. In the event,

Elizabeti and Stefania never have to utter the word *Hitler* anyway. Hitimana is a common Rwandese name. Hitler becomes Hitimana. Now, go jail the two wives of Chief Rubasha for gossiping, sister to sister, about the witch medicine of this man Hitimana.

Of this we can be sure: Their gossip is utterly, sublimely, blessedly uninformed. With no idea what Fascist ideas have done to the world, nor what they've done to Ruanda-Urundi, they wonder what all the fuss is about. They hear nothing of mass murder. Certainly they never hear of General Patton's remark upon first seeing the inmates of a concentration camp, that the camps are just where such socially contagious losers belong. Movies like *The Great Dictator* won't even reach us until well after the war, when they're worn and scratchy and taking up too much shelf space somewhere else in the world. Nor will the latest books, or the latest versions of old books, or the latest comic books, or the latest versions of old comics. Here in Belgian Africa, Tintin will keep on teaching us about our motherland, even as Éditions Casterman rubs its corporate chin and gives Hergé the go-ahead to clean up the copy.

Every bit as much as Alabama, we're a backwater. But these shifts in fashion won't get to us until the Fascists are finished, and Mama (by then grown, married, and with three children) and Elizabeti and Stefania are standing and squinting skyward at clouds drifting in on fronts of balmy postwar weather, sprinkling Kigali-ville with showers of Star-Spangled America: LifeSavers, Lucky Strikes, Alka-Seltzer, Bromo Seltzer, Pepsodent, Pepto-Bismol, Zippos, and oh my aching back, Vicks VapoRub; goodies that will be quickly collected and stacked ceiling-high in dusty Hendi dukas on Muhima hill in the center of town, where spotted hyenas yet prowl by night.

The ladies will even spy, now and then, a rare thunderhead purple with weight and moment, a fridge or hippo-heavy jukebox, bound for some pigeonhole juke joint. Now, a quarter century late, comes swing. All the way out here beyond the Rift, the ladies hear those moody trombones, led by a solitary, soulful clarinet, half-asleep . . . and isn't there something Tutsi about that languor? And not just easy swing but jumping jitterbug, bubble gum, and the "Sales Tax Boogie." The sales tax who? Call it "value-added," call it "*à l'achat*," we still won't get the idea. Come the late forties, we'll still be getting used to cash, and just barely getting used to the flip in Zungu fashion now that Tintin's naïve colonial preening before a class of pickaninnies has gone out of vogue.

As Africa now rallies for independence, Batutsi lead the movement in Rwanda, and this dismays the colonials no end. How could it be that their infatuation with the Tutsi "race" has gone so thoroughly unrequited?

Meantime, Hitler's disgrace has made an embarrassment of their old racial stereotypes. Quickly they drop them for new racial stereotypes. Quickly, but far from adroitly. It's a clumsy about-face, and it takes time to catch on. First, fashion-forward Belgian missionaries and proconsuls in Rwanda begin to use *Tutsi* as a word meaning either "stingy," or "cruel," or "shifty," or you name it. Then, alas, the roar of turbojets is heard over Africa, and Belgian money sniffs profit in the tour business. So even as Belgium abuses Batutsi in Rwanda, Belgian business churns out ads that glamorize us even more than in the old days.

But these are grace notes. The policy chiefs bad-mouthing the Batutsi are calling the real tune. For the past half century, Belgian planters have exploited Hutu peasants. As Zungu authority now spells matters out to a still unschooled majority of Hutu peasants, holding souls in serfdom is an evil peculiarly inherent in "the Tutsi race." It proceeds to sack legions of educated Tutsi civil servants, hire legions of hastily educated Hutu replacements, and draw up plans to grant independence to an authoritarian Hutu regime. The new fashion rules. Among the few arenas in which it doesn't are racial pass cards. They will remain law to the bloody end of Belgium's official watch in 1961—the graceless year of my birth—and they will remain law after the new Hutu elite takes over.

A WOMAN WHO KNOWS HER PLACE

Elizabeti is above all a *grand rassembleur,* a grand assembler of people, and especially of children. It's nothing official. It's the way things are. It's as if, without laws or proclamations or budgets or codes (Zungu medicine, all), buildings were to be built, and when they were built, children would begin showing up, along with teachers, and the children would learn, and people would call it a school. That's how it is with Elizabeti. They don't even have to build a schoolhouse, or bother to call it a school. Children just show up, and sweet Jesus help the laggard.

She also assembles smaller groups. For instance, households . . . and all the clannish Batemura instantly and insistently question her wisdom in finding for Mama the widower Bitsindinkumi. This aging, tongue-tied yeoman who goes by the name of "he-who-seduces-young-women"; does Elizabeti actually feel so sorry for him that she gives him their beauty? Well, no; it's clear she sees quiet strength in the man. But she never feels obliged to put it that way, and certainly her wisdom is more homely than Solomonic . . . though there are signs that she sings in key with the oracles.

Shortly after marrying Papa, Mama follows Elizabeti to Butare, where they visit the queen, recently married and almost exactly Mama's age. The queen is a young woman whose grace has stood, and will long stand, in contrast to the irascible royalty of Rwanda's recent years. There are few people about. The queen hugs Elizabeti, she hugs Mama, they gossip, Elizabeti moves on with Mama, and soon a lady-friend approaches them. The lady says, "He saw you. When you were with the queen, he saw you."

"Saw who?" Elizabeti.

The lady looks at Mama. "Saw you. Bibiane."

"Who saw Bibiane?"

"The *mupfumu.*" A *mupfumu* is a witch doctor.

"So . . ."

"So he saw the two of them, the queen and Bibiane, and he said, 'Those two girls, the queen and the other one, both of them have just been married. One of them is going to have a big family. The other will be barren.'"

"Did he say which?"

"He doesn't know which."

("But we know, don't we," Stefania will wink in later years, as we the proliferate siblings Bitsindinkumi squeal in delight at her tale, and in our squeals forget the sorrow of a barren queen.)

SO ELIZABETI'S WISDOM IS SAID TO STAND UP TO TIME, HER WISDOM NOT JUST IN husband-picking but in so many other matters, and what do you know—when Chief Rubasha dies, the court is in a quandary over whom to appoint, and its quandary results in the capstone of Elizabeti's career as a *grand rassembleur.* No, she doesn't find the king a new chief. She would never presume to do that. The king's ministers say the king needs some time to decide, which means *they* need time to decide, and so she just folds her heavy arms and sits and waits in silence, just like everybody else, just like obedient children in a classroom, except that it's different when your teacher folds her arms and waits. When a teacher folds her arms and waits, something is expected. The king needs a few months, the ministers say. Maybe a year.

Oh yes?

Yes, they affirm, not firmly at all.

"Mmmh," says Elizabeti.

"Mmmh," they assert, altogether uncertainly. "But . . ."

"Yes?"

But in the meantime, perhaps they can announce an interim chief.

"Perhaps?"

Not perhaps. *Will* announce. *Are* announcing. "The court is pleased to announce the appointment of Interim Chief Gatukwa Elizabeti."

Grins all around.

. . .

NOW, TRULY, COMES ELIZABETI'S DAY AS A *GRAND RASSEMBLEUR,* WHICH ALAS, DESPITE her strong feminine identity, means a *grand rassembleur* of men, and moreover, a *rassembleur* of men as a Tutsi woman would assemble them.

As in all things Tutsi, there are excruciating balances to be achieved by the woman who gathers men about her—the most telling instance of which may be food.

How is a Tutsi woman to cook for men who aren't supposed to enjoy food? I don't think I ever really understood how abstemious our men can be (or are supposed to be) until one afternoon at the library in Ruhengeri, an afternoon in the stacks. It was there in the imagination of Anton Chekhov, or more exactly in "On Human Frailty: An Object Lesson for the Butter Festival," that I made the acquaintance of one Semyon Petrovich Poditkin. Dear Semyon Petrovich—gourmet, gourmand, councilor at law. He was everything a Tutsi male should never be . . . and there in this complete antithesis of Tutsi manhood I discovered how antithesis may define thesis. Semyon Petrovich sits with a napkin tucked neatly under his chin. His plump fingers drum his belly in anticipation of a feast to come.

> Ranked in the middle of the table were lines of tall, slender bottles—three kinds of vodka, a Kiev cordial, Rhine wine, and even a potbellied bottle filled with the concoction of the Benedictine Brotherhood. Arranged around the drinks in artistic disorder were heaps of herring in mustard sauce, pickled smelts, sour cream, black caviar (3 rubles, 40 kopeks per pound), smoked salmon. . . . Finally the kitchen maid appeared with the blini. . . . Risking a severe burn, Semyon Petrovich grabbed at the two topmost (and hottest) blini, and deposited them, plop, on his plate. The blini were deep golden, airy, and plump—just like the shoulder of a merchant's daughter. . . . Poditkin glowed with delight and hiccupped with joy as he poured hot butter all over them.

They say that hidden deep within some white men of America's South is a horror of African blood lurking somewhere in their veins. Thus do Tutsi men fear some Semyon Petrovich lurking in them. A Tutsi man will no more present himself as Semyon Petrovich than Queen Victoria would expose herself indelicately to the affections of a household horseman. Chekhov's creation represents perfectly the taboo side of Tutsi manhood. Not that underground feasting is the scandal of Rwanda. But a Tutsi *mugabo* catching a waft of roasting pork (a dirty animal, dirty) has much in common with a Victorian schoolboy catching a glimpse of a French postcard.

A fact not lost on Padiri Kagame, son of Elizabeti's brother Bitahurwina, and ever a guest at Elizabeti's family sit-downs. During the rugo suppers of

1928, he turns up as a young seminarian; during the rugo suppers of 1962, he shows up as a bishop; and at some point during these years he pens a popular children's tale in verse in which the aroma of roasting pork drives Rwanda's austere Tutsi chiefs to such delirium that they abandon their storied decorum and get into a food fight over who gets the biggest portion.

The hard cores of these suppers are the brothers and sisters who grew up with Mukeza as either father or stepfather—Bitahurwina, Kabenga, Elizabeti, and Stefania—but they always include, as well, grown children like Bitahurwina's son Kagame and husbands like Chief Rubasha and cousins like Alexis Karekezi.

At the hard core of the hard core are Elizabeti and Stefania. As children tear this way and that, the men, on the men's side of the passageway, will now and then hail a little one for recitation. Oh, to be that child, all alone amid the smoke of their pipes, their stern glares, the alcohol on their breath! Some quail, some are brazen, but facing the men is nothing next to finding yourself alone before either Elizabeti or Stefania, on the women's side of the passage. No child is brazen before Elizabeti and Stefania.

Only by repute will I know Elizabeti, but Stefania's glare endures deep inside me, the source of my picture of the Elizabeti rugos that I never knew firsthand. We children rip and tear, but within fearsome bounds. Any transgression is met by that glare; and in the case of Stefania, by her ultimate judgment, rendered in terms of cold minuses or a rare plus. You rush in from play. "Good day, Auntie." You rush out. Or rather, you try to rush out.

"What? No kiss?"

Silence.

"Not so much as a 'By your leave, Auntie'?"

Silence.

"Minus five."

The sexes do not listen to each other during these grand suppers; that is, the men do not listen to the women. The women most certainly listen to the men.

Somehow the ladies manage to listen to the gents gossip, and carry on with their own gossip at the same time. Should they hear something questionable across the passage, a mortar round may well go sailing out of the women's quarter in a perfectly aimed trajectory that arches the passage and explodes squarely amid the men.

"Says who? Says you?"

Should one of the men say something truly balmy, what he might hear is, "Might we offer some guidance? You're balmy." "Daft."

What the men might hear should one of their number say something downright outrageous is a solitary but devastating, *"Minus ten."*

"Ewww," say the kids in a hush.

The men tend to look much alike, tall and stern, even those in Western dress like Karekezi who wears kneesocks and starched khaki shorts with a khaki shooting vest, starched and pressed. But they're so different. Uncle Bitahurwina is the big warrior with the gentle tongue, this man recruited by the court and the Germans to join the 1912 raid deep into Uganda, to Jinja on the far side of Victoria, there to dispatch the pretender to the throne. As he sits with his son, Kagame, he is all placid composure amid the jokes and provocations, puffing on his long pipe. After all these years, his wife has borne him only two children, but he loves her dearly, spending hour upon hour composing love songs with which to croon her grace. As she sits with us on the women's side, with chatter and children all around, she is the picture of pinched disdain. Thus is she known to everyone but her son, Kagame, and her devoted husband, Bitahurwina.

Kabenga is the born host, though you'd think that as host he'd be more politic, certainly less provocative than he is, especially as the positions he takes (hapless royalist that he is) are so open to challenge by Young Turks. Likewise, you'd think that as a modern man ready to jettison tradition, Karekezi would be the provocateur. He's not. He's forever on the defense.

It's hard to feel sorry for Karekezi. As early as 1928, he's doing well and does ever better as these years go by, traveling to Belgium, winning promotion after promotion from the Belgians, and even, in his own way, defying the Belgians. In 1959, Belgium's military governor—the colonel Guy Logiest—engineers what he fancies a revolution, a move that incites the pogroms that kill thousands of Batutsi and chase Papa off his farm in Ruli. But the Belgians still need skilled mandarins like Karekezi, and Karekezi chooses just this moment to buy the one grand indulgence of his abstemious life, a big black 1959 Chevrolet Impala with Hydromatic Drive and fins that outsoar all fins, a nuncio of Western industry shipped straight to Kigali prefecture from Antwerp (well, almost straight from Antwerp; Antwerp by way of Mombasa, Nairobi, Kampala). In short, he chooses this moment of Tutsi vulnerability to flaunt, for the first time in his life, his Tutsi station, or I should say, his seeming Tutsi station, for in reality, Logiest has by this time stripped Batutsi of all station; the status Karekezi now enjoys he enjoys in spite of his Tutsi blood. And as if this tail-finned flaunting of station were insufficient to annoy the Belgians, he begins arguing the cause and the case of the Congo's elected hero, Patrice Lumumba, a bane of the Belgians if ever there was one.

I wasn't even born during the heyday of these evenings, but well into the sixties, Karekezi will be bumping up and over the ruts of Kabuye hamlet in his big black Impala. In class, we schoolchildren hear the purr of that vehicle. We hear its springs, engineered for Route 66, strain and groan at the challenge of Africa. We let our torsos drift in unison toward the window. Our eyeballs snap as one. Ah, the delight to know that this is the carriage that took my mother to the hospital and drove us home! "Attention!" barks the nun. Attention, indeed. Attention for Alexis Karekezi, the builder of our school, so felicitously dubbed Saint Alexis Primary by the White Fathers.

Yet he seems so off balance during these family sit-downs. Here he is, beneficiary of the powers that be, rejecting those powers even as their victims, victims like Kabenga, defend the old ways, and he, Karekezi, is the one off balance. You'd expect Kabenga and Bitahurwina to be off balance, confused. But they're not. Only Bitahurwina's son, Kagame, can provoke them.

During these evenings, it seems hardly to matter (though most certainly it does) that after the pogroms of 1959, the family is especially vulnerable, especially dependent on Karekezi. Down in Nyanza, still the royal court, we still have cousins and they have their own storied paterfamilias, Uncle Ruboya; it's during these years that one of the worst pogroms hits Rwanda. The royal court, including Uncle Ruboya, barely escapes. Muslim merchants hide them amid goods on lorries headed for Tanganyika, from which Uncle will never return. Then a wave of pogroms chases Mama and Papa from their farm in Ruli. Then the same wave of massacres chases Uncle Rwankumbili and his family from their farm into Kigali's Swahili quarter where Uncle scrapes by selling this and that. His eldest son, Karani, our cousin Karani, flees the country altogether. He moves upcountry beyond the Uganda Virungas to the banks of the Simliki River in the Simba Hills beneath the Mountains of the Moon, where he marries, competes with Simliki lions for turf on which to scratch a new living, scratches out a successful one, and becomes known as "the tall one." But his success is the exception, as is our escape to a new, albeit smaller, farm near Kigali, thanks to Karekezi, who bankrolls Papa.

SOMETHING RUMBLES; APOCALYPSE WHISPERS; YEARS GET LOST

From where I sit at century's end, it's too easy to form a pearl of perfect forgetfulness around the pain of those days. In 1959, I was still two years from birth. In my mind those years are still that series of silent snapshots, brother Nepo, high on a hill, his eyes keen for trouble on hills in the distant west, spying wisps of smoke, whistling the alert down to Papa. They dash from the house and onto the bed of that borrowed flatbed lorry; the dresser just sitting there, holding the cash savings they forget and leave behind; infant Wellars's mouth wide in the scream that remains forever silent in my head, unable or unwilling as I am to hear these screams that attend the birth of our generation.

My story of bloodlines, without which we have no story, is over. Now Mama has married the seducer, and you know the rest, more or less through the events of 1990.

The events of 1990 signal the coming of the Thing Itself in 1994. They signal the season, the weeks, days, hours that begin on April 6, 1994, and blaze so white that in their brilliance they burn out most of their own features and the features of the years before and after, creating a white-hot hole in my universe. Entire years get lost in it. Well into the twenty-first century, I'll gaze at the bright shining haze of those years and be able to make out only the palest pictures, leached of all color, bleached of all shadow.

All the same, there are a few brief pictures I can and know I must pick out, and the first is a September midnight in 1990. On that night, Tutsi units desert Uganda's army, and make ready an assault on Akazu Rwanda.

· PART IV ·

INTERLUDES WITH THE THING ITSELF

Glimpses
1990–1994

· 27 ·

THE DOOR CRACKS

September–December 1990

Comes at last that September midnight in 1990. Tutsi troops in Yoweri Museveni's National Resistance Army begin deserting their units, and with that a crack opens in the door to Providence, giving us a glimpse of the future the past has given us, the century and a half since Mutemura, Burton, Speke, the fat man, the white man, King Rwabugiri, the Dowager Kanjogera.

WHAT THE INKOTANYI PLANNED WAS A BLITZKRIEG, AND BY THE END OF THE FIRST DAY, everything has gone to plan. They've taken a border post; the avant-garde is marching smartly on. By the end of the second day, disaster is marching smartly on.

Inkotanyi planners have simply not seen how rumor would race through villages and refugee camps holding half a million souls dreaming of Rwanda. In a rush to join the invaders, refugees and their cows and their great clouds of red dust choke the roads south. The Inkotanyi main force, marshaled behind the avant-garde, ready for action, can hardly move. Desperate for Zion, refugees with their life's possessions on their backs choke every track into Rwanda. Blitzkrieg has bogged down to sitzkrieg. And at just this moment Rwigema Fred, the Inkotanyi's chief, out front with his avant-garde, leading from the front, is shot dead.

By now—late 1990—the United States has long been on good terms with the once-dreaded red revolutionary, Uganda's Museveni. Museveni has hardly changed his revolutionary mind, and the United States knows it. But the Cold War is over, he's keeping the peace as no Ugandan ruler has, and he's fighting AIDS as no African ruler has. The red revolutionary is now a darling of a State Department that once recoiled at his very name. Officers of Uganda's National Resistance Army now attend U.S. Army training schools at posts like Fort Leavenworth in Kansas. Which is where one Paul Kagame is just now because he's a major in that army. But that's not all he is. He's also a Mututsi, and a member of the Inkotanyi brain trust. Kagame rushes back to take charge; he finds the Inkotanyi reeling.

THROUGH A RAVEL IN THE WEAVE OF RWANDA

People stop coming to Chez Lando. The place turns deathly quiet. Still, for Lando and Hélène, there are weekends with the kids, times for high discussion. Sunday morning, October 7, 1990, is a weekend morning full of plans, and let's forget the world out there. Lando is up as usual at six thirty. Fresh from the shower, he's about in an old red robe, a present once grand, now threadbare. He's trudging and reading, limping and reading, his eyeglasses low on his nose. The kids, Malaika, now fourteen, Patrick, thirteen, are up too, but they have long since gotten the aide-mémoire: No noise before ten. At ten, Hélène, rested at last from yet another late night at work, is up and the kids are in from the garden. Now it's time for mangoes, papaya, and that high discussion. Coffee is brewing. There's a knock. Lando answers. Troops. The family falls silent. Mumbles at the door. "Bien sur. Just let me get dressed." Then to Hélène: "I should be back in . . . no, wait; I should get a book to read." He gets a book, probably some much-thumbed paperback. He heads for the door. Hélène and the kids just stare. He mumbles, his words half-lost in the slam of the door, "Back in a couple hours."

He isn't. Hélène calls me.

"They took him. They say they just want to talk to him. I'm sure it's okay. I'm sure they won't keep him overnight." Later the same day she calls again.

"They just took Joseph and Anne-Marie. I'm sure they're okay."

They're not. Nobody is.

AS LANDO WALKS OUT THE FRONT DOOR, HE VANISHES THROUGH A RAVEL IN THE WEAVE of Rwanda. He's simply gone. Not a word is forthcoming. Then Joseph and Anne-Marie vanish through the same ravel. Muzungu goes out to Kabuye to check on Mama, who still holds down the homestead there, and he discovers that Dr. Zitoni is gone. One day Dr. Zitoni was at his little surgery, and the next day, no Dr. Zitoni. Then the ravel claims Muzungu. Anne-Marie's kids (Safari is twelve now, Shara eleven, Nana nine, and Kazuba aka Little Sunshine is four) won't leave the house.

Anne-Marie had come to know her pediatrician personally. A born wit, he's Belgian; his name is Philippe Lepage. His wife's name is Colette. They live nearby. Colette keeps an eye on the kids; either Hélène or Gaetan will come by once a day. As it turns out, Colette can't just come by. She makes a pot of tea and sits with them all day, chain-smoking, anxious.

When it can no longer be kept quiet, someone dispatches a messenger up Kabuye Hill to let Mama know. Mama sends back a message from another world: "My children, be strong. I will sleep tonight. Be careful with messengers."

After a week or so, a Zungu friend, a diplomat, manages to get some bars of soap and a couple of books to Lando. Thus do we learn that he's still alive. Hélène rings up Georgette van Hyfte, who lives near Bruges; the next thing Malaika and Patrick know, they're flying to Bruges. When they land, they hear they've already been registered for school. Malaika looks at Georgette and smiles the stiff smile of the anxiety-ridden. "Papa," she says, "where he's at, *there*. He's going to be there a long time, isn't he."

DEEP UNDER WASHINGTON

I wanted to be ready; I'm not.

It's strange, hoping people you love are in prison, but that's what I hope. Prison is at least this side of the place where the Church resides triumphant. I write, I wire, I call. Nothing. We can't see them, talk to them, write to them. We try, but we might as well be posting notes to the moons of Jupiter. Waking with a start in the hours before dawn, I sense a chill that tells me I'm just fooling myself, that they aren't in prison, that they've been consigned to the nowhere that's forever.

Every time I turn around, I find myself telling myself, There's something I've got to take care of. One after the other, I read numbing newsmagazines. I read items that begin, "From Maine to California, from Alaska to Florida . . ." I read every item, from the back all the way to the front.

I'm on a Metro car deep under Washington. The neighborhood is called Shaw; kids get on with boom boxes. Now Chinatown. A roly-poly Buddha in a fedora gets on. He sits down next to me. Gallery Place; the National Gallery, Gilbert Stuart. Tourists get on. Tangerine tank tops. Chartreuse shorts. Fanny packs. I read the paper: sales on shoes, sales on exercise gimmicks, sales on something called a "stair climber" (which I imagine is for fat people whose houses don't already have stairs), sales on Barcaloungers, and buried beneath all this, a brief item on how America has more of its population behind bars than Russia. As I'm reading, I run across a name, an outfit the item says is based in London, Amnesty International. "Right," I say to myself. It's a name I run across now and then. I remember once running across it at school in Ruhengeri. There too I was reading a newspaper, an item about Ngugi wa Thiong'o, about how the authorities in Kenya had locked him up, and how this very outfit was trying to help.

Do they have an office here in Washington? I'll find out at the next stop. I'll get out and look them up in the book. Next to me my venerable Buddha in a fedora has his nose deep in the bond tables at the back of *Barron's*.

I get off to look them up. They're here. I ring. A lovely lady gives me an appointment. I go to see her. On the way, I rehearse what I will say. First I will say this. No, first I will say that. No, first I will . . . and now I'm confused. I have to write it down; I pull out an envelope, scratch something down, scratch it out, scratch something else down. I try putting it to memory. I find the building. In the elevator, Muzak tries to soothe me.

I'm in the waiting room. Now I'm in her office. Now there she is. She interviews me, asks me questions. I have so much to tell her. I open my mouth. No words come out. Just like that, I'm a uniformed schoolgirl at the Kansi mission on the Burundi frontier, in the headmistress's office, on a chair facing her desk, my legs dangling in the air, struck dumb. I have to leave.

"You have to leave?"

"I'll have to come back."

· 28 ·

WHERE THE WARDER IS DESPAIR

October 1990–July 1992

All that we know who lie in gaol
Is that the wall is strong. . . .
OSCAR WILDE, *The Ballad of Reading Gaol*

Still no Lando. No Joseph. No Anne-Marie. No Muzungu. I picture those walls in the dead weight of their red-brown brick, with their red-brown arch set with that tile, 1930.

Another week drags by. I've got to do something. I should fly to Paris and stand in the rain in the cobbled courtyard of the Élysée until they let my brothers go. Another fortnight drags by, a fortnight or so in which I'm present but unaccounted for, simply a presence, half-listening to whoever sits in front of me, and whatever gets clicked on TV. *Patton,* for the umpteenth time. The incident where he slaps some poor kid who's down with shell shock. I need a slap.

This is when I first hear, from someone there, that story about how the general, upon first seeing inmates of a concentration camp, said the camps were just where such socially contagious losers belong. Is that what my brothers, my sister, are becoming? Is that what we already are?

At last Anne-Marie gets out, then Muzungu, then more weeks.

At last, Lando. Relief but little joy. Instead, from him, inscrutable jail-house funk.

A month later, Anne-Marie's Joseph gets out. They have not simply beaten Joseph. Warders whose minds are off have assigned him to warders whose minds are gone. They don't hate Joseph because he's Tutsi. They hate him because he's Hutu; to the Akazu, a Hutu married to a Mututsi is worse than a Mututsi.

A CALL FROM STANISLAS

Less than two months ago, in the hot late summer of 1990, François Mitterrand invited French-speaking Africa to holiday with him at posh La Baule on the cool summer coast of Brittany. No sooner were they settled with their Orangina and Pernod than he told them the days of the police state were over. No sooner did the Habyarimanas get home than Juvenal announced that come June of 1991, political parties would be legal. Mitterrand was serious, but he started more of a revolution than he could have imagined. The air immediately filled with expectation. Political parties are starting without waiting for June.

Now it's starting to look like the October attack will let the Habyarimanas welsh. Mitterrand sympathizes with Habyarimana. He's been embarrassed. A crew from English-speaking Uganda has assaulted the French-speaking community of Africa—*la francophonie*. But it's too late for Habyarimana and Mitterrand to reverse course. Too many have been too stifled and abused, too many too stirred by Mitterrand's words at La Baule. Their eyes have seen the glory of Liberty Leading the People. They won't shut up, and it's all the harder to shut them up because Habyarimana and his Akazu crew may well have a wink from Mitterrand to reverse course, but they can't cancel outright the go-ahead for political parties in June. That would be too embarrassing for Mitterrand. But the big No has begun, and it won't stop.

INSTEAD, CHEZ LANDO STOPS. BUSINESS PICKS UP SOME FROM THE IMMEDIATE AFTER-shock of the attack—some but not much. Everyone's scared. Jailhouse funk still grips Lando.

At last he begins to stir—a wrangle here, a joke there—and just as he does, he gets a call from Mbonampeka Stanislas.

Mbonampeka practices law; he's a temperate man amid building hysteria. He invites Lando for a drink. When Lando gets there, he finds Mbonampeka with a known opportunist-about-town, Mugenzi Justin. Mbonampeka wants to know if Lando has any interest in starting a new political party.

Why not? What sort of platform does Mbonampeka have in mind? Mbonampeka asks what Lando has in mind, and Lando answers, "Democracy."

"And?"

"Minority rights."

At this moment, parties are being put together all over Rwanda. The

Habyarimanas are still welshing, still trying to squelch any legal opposition. But the organizing goes on.

Until June, it's still illegal. Until then, Mbonampeka and Lando are simply what I find myself calling Rwandese refuseniks. I've been reading the construction so often these days, it's insinuated itself—and I must say, it fits Lando just right. To the day they walked him into prison, our happy Lando wouldn't fool with politics. For Lando, politics were about as amiable as nagging in-laws; he was our Rwandese Falstaff. Now our saloon keeper is turning serious, organizing the moderate Liberal Party in a desperate effort to heal the nation before it's too late. The big powers assure the moderates of support.

OF ALPHABET SOUP AND DOSTOYEVSKY

Please don't call Lando's party "the PL." For Lando and for Stanislas, it's honest work, and so it is for others, but for many, this party craze now upon us is an exercise in deceit, and neatly packaging deceit in brave new acronyms and abbreviations—PL, CDR, MDR, MRND—is one of the ways in which we the educated of Rwanda will try to give the spectacle a nice civic gloss. In fact, this eruption of progressive-looking abbreviations marks us like measles on the face of a miserable child.

Initial-letter labels are giving power players a certain modern dash, at once enlightened and spurious. It's the same spuriously progressive decorum that denatures torment with names like the Office of Information or (as in Idi Amin's Uganda) the Bureau of State Research. On top of this, some alphabet outfits now cropping up in Kigali are simply shell corporations concocted by the Akazu to multiply its influence.

Zungu social scientists, familiar only with democracy and its legislatures and courts and its conflicting interests neatly balanced and ordered by name, with each name neatly abbreviated, are showing up in their scores at Chez Lando. They seem schooled from birth to parse all humanity in terms of such abbreviations. They take ours at face value, they take the talk at face value, and they parse away. Soon I will be running across our alphabet outfits discussed at face value in scholarly print; the articles will read like Dostoyevsky denatured as a topic for a current events club.

What matters, of course, is not the abbreviations. They reflect scarcely more than distracting riffs on two core constituencies at play. What matters are the two constituencies:

First, there's the ruling clique itself, the Akazu in all its factional totality; plus that portion of the population, by now a large portion, that Akazu propaganda has animated; plus those whose livings depend on Akazu patronage.

Then there's the south, Nduga country, and its out-of-power constituency of southern Bahutu, all indelibly Hutu and Nduga, split among several acronyms and abbreviations, just two of which are substantial, a socialist party and the mainstream Nduga party to which the intrepid Agathe Uwilingiyimana, the other Agathe, belongs. To this group also belong the nation's disenfranchised Batutsi. In all, it's even less uniform in character than the Akazu-dominated group, but as a matter of practical fact in the roads, no matter what their internal diversity, these are the two core constituencies at play.

Looking at Rwanda from a similar but somewhat different angle, you could say that on one hand there's the ruling elite and its minions, and on the other hand, a nationwide constituency of workers and peasants, both Bahutu and Batutsi.

Lando is neither worker nor peasant, but his hand is the other hand. Not that he fancies himself the clenched fist of the people. So far he hasn't been a political man at all, and on top of that, he's a Mututsi, a son, no less, of the *abiru,* the court ritualists. His father was a yeoman. Stanislas is a moderate— a Whig. They call themselves the Liberals. Their natural constituency, the only constituency to which they have some access, is the non-Akazu portion of the 15 to 20 percent of Rwanda that can read, the portion that crowded in to see *Topaze* and made a success of La Fringale and Chez Lando. Yet for all that, the Rwanda Lando has always known, the Rwanda in which we grew up, the Rwanda he remembered in Montreal and to which he was driven to return, is more a people than a place, and Rwanda's people are above all its peasants, the wellspring of its fundamentally Bantu character. They never did well; these days, drought and bad prices for crops are hammering them. They are multiplying. When in a couple of years he puts himself forward for a post, it will be the Ministry of Labor and Social Welfare.

He insists he has no illusions. He has barely more than word of mouth to reach people. As it turns out, he reaches more than just the literate few, but just now, they're the only ones he's certain he can reach. And he knows that many will say the literate few are simply the Batutsi and the rich.

In fact, the rich are almost all Akazu and few. The literate, by contrast, are a significant, seldom rich, minority. These are the schoolteachers, engineers, clerks, nurses, professional men and women, small-businesspeople, students, doctors—the sort of people who still collect about him at Chez Lando. This is where he sees promise. This is his horizon. Where once he'd perched on the kerbstone of Chez Lando's beer garden to talk football and music with friends, now he sits and talks politics.

ANNE-MARIE NEVER JOINS LANDO'S PARTY OR ANY FACTION, BUT THERE IS ONE REfusenik, one *rifiutatrice,* who impresses Anne-Marie no end. It's the other

Agathe, Agathe Uwilingiyimana. The other Agathe is now helping marshal what looks to be, come next June, the most popular resistance party, made up mostly of Bahutu from the Nduga south. From where I sit, on the wrong side of an ocean, it seems like Anne-Marie is looking to Agathe for both personal friendship and ideas.

How do you measure a soul's valor? By any measure, this new figure on the Rwandese stage is a woman with an attitude, an insistent advocate of her Nduga Bahutu, who at this moment are of no mind to let up on the Akazu. They won't be stopped.

The Habyarimanas won't be stopped either. Agathe U's refuseniks are marching, but the Akazu have a tight apparatus in place, a legacy of Rwanda's anciently totalitarian past. The Habyarimanas have no trouble cutting orders and passing them down from presidency to prefecture to commune to sector to cellule, and the orders are clear. Local officials are to get to work, and that's just the word the apparatchiks use, "work," *gukora.* The people grasp the word in its fullest sense. Beginning with the "Hutu Revolution," *gukora,* "work" has come to mean the work of burning Tutsi homesteads, of killing Batutsi, of killing as community labor. Karangwa says that people just keep disappearing. He says bodies are starting to show up by the roads. In Rwanda, "work" now means what "ethnic cleansing" will soon mean in Serbia, Croatia, and Bosnia-Herzegovina—local massacres as a run-up to worse. Oh, the care with which the party (still the one party of a one-party state) frames its intentions. Thanks to Akazu foresight, murder is now rendered with a talkable, nay, positive, word, "work." How much more simply and elegantly euphemistic than "ethnic cleansing."

Nor are propriety and appearances all they seem to have in mind with their wordplay. It seems, looking back, that they are creating conditions for bigger things. Maybe I'm wrong; maybe their greater ambitions do not begin this soon. But if all that the bosses want now is some people killed, they have all the thugs they need for the job. They have no need yet to induce the public to do their dirty work, and hence no need for euphemisms to disguise public dirty work. Only if they someday want truly large numbers of people killed (a virtually industrial task) do they need to enlist the public. To kill the public, it will take the public.

QADAFFI AND FIREWORKS

Come December of 1990, the intellectual lights of the Akazu publish something they call "The Ten Commandments of the Bahutu," among which are injunctions to see all Batutsi as enemies, to see all Bahutu who marry Batutsi as traitors, to avoid "contamination" with Batutsi, and to show Batutsi no pity. It defines as traitors all Bahutu who consort with or do business with Batutsi. The ink with which they penned this screed must have been concocted of honey wine and crocodile bile. Here in official print are the racial musings of Burton, Speke, Stanley, Nietzsche, rendered in modern words immediately comprehensible to a deliberately deluded public.

Come the end of the following month, the end of January 1991, Paul Kagame's Inkotanyi show they're still alive, if just barely. They attack the prison in Ruhengeri, that battlement in the heart of Akazu country, where the population is less than 1 percent Tutsi, the Akazu keep for political prisoners. A few years ago, our uncle Ntukanyagwe shocked everyone by coming out alive—and even fit. He came out after such a long time, looking so well, that people nicknamed him "Mandela." He walked upright and straight, like a soldier in good spirits, but the work the place did on his spirits became clear soon enough. When in a few years he dies in the genocide, he's already a bitter man, estranged from all. Now the Inkotanyi greet 1991 by attacking Uncle Mandela's old home, Ruhengeri prison.

UNKNOWN TO ANY OF US AT THE TIME, FRENCH INTELLIGENCE NOW SENDS A CONFIDENtial aide-mémoire to the Élysée. It names Habyarimana's wife, Agathe, *his* Agathe, and her family as prime movers in a network intent on stopping democracy by promoting race hate. The Élysée, chastened, sends one of its own on a mission to the Habyarimanas. By February 1991, the results show. The Habyarimanas at last deliver on the commitment they made just after La Baule. They sanction opposition parties.

By August, Bahutu in their tens of thousands have joined opposition parties. Lando is there with them, building the Liberal Party.

Come November, Lando and his refusenik mates begin putting together plans for a mass rally. Before the month is out, they schedule it. At dawn of the scheduled day, in scattered groups, people are already filing down from the hills. Steadily, up this road and down that, people walk, coming together at last in a mass movement that chokes the roads into Kigali. The *rifiutatori* had planned, but not for anything on this scale. Much of this demonstration, this mass *manif,* is spontaneous. People of every stripe are calling for Habyarimana to get off the dime. They demand reform.

Two months on, the guns at last go silent on the war front, and with monitors on station, this cease-fire holds. On the phone, Lando says, "It's all over but the bargaining."

Would that it were.

AGATHE UWILINGIYIMANA

The momentum of the new political parties is unstoppable through the spring of 1992. They rally. They bargain with Habyarimana's party over who will get which posts in any new government that might be put together. Comical cartoons of Habyarimana, something previously unheard of, start showing up in new opposition newspapers. In April, Habyarimana, caught between the Inkotanyi and La Baule, finds himself obliged to accept a new government under his presidency. I still jump when the phone rings, but at least I can pick it up.

Wellars: "Looks like three slots are going to the Liberals. Commerce. That will be Justin the Notorious. Justice to Stanislas. Labor to Lando."

How about that? Then comes news even more delightful.

"Eugénie had her baby. It's a girl. Kayitesi."

And from Anne-Marie: "Education is going to Agathe U."

Is this really happening? Agathe U, the woman with an attitude who has so impressed not just Lando but Anne-Marie. Anne-Marie still won't join the Liberal Party. She is a strong woman, but she still has that queasy stomach. Politics seem to back her up, and not just with caution. Politics gets to her viscerally, the way the sight of running sores might get to you when suddenly you encounter them on some poor soul suffering a vile disease.

Both Anne-Marie and Lando have watched Agathe grow within her faction, which her Nduga Bahutu have made the most popular opposition party. Neither Lando nor Anne-Marie has to tell me that Agathe's post now as education minister is more important than it sounds. For Rwandese, education is the direct and tangible key to success, and access to education is controlled by the Akazu. It is a critical element of their patronage. Less than a tenth of Rwandese children make the cut for secondary school, and it's the Akazu that decides the cut. There are entrance exams, but the testing regime is rank with corruption.

From the moment she takes up her job in April, Agathe is determined to reform it, and she does. Quiet wails issue from privileged families—and then they're not so quiet.

The very next month, May of '92, Anne-Marie gets a call at home from a long-time friend, a nurse named Marie, a staunch Hutu advocate, but who nonetheless gets on famously with sister. Marie tells Anne-Marie that Akazu rounders are about, boasting that just the night before they did a job on Agathe U in the bungalow she rents off the airfield road, not far from Chez Lando. Marie says she can't get through to Agathe on the phone.

"We should go," says Marie.

Anne-Marie asks, "Can you get bandages? Anesthetic? Antiseptic?"

"Yes. Can you drive?"

"I can drive."

They park well away, picking their way through bush well back from the road. On the road, business goes on as ever, buses claxon, lorries grind their gears, air brakes hiss, bicycles career, hawkers peddle gum, cigarettes, warm sodas; on a hillside, an enterprising entrepreneur stands watch over ranks of sneakers laid out in neat rows. Marie and Anne-Marie pick their way up to Agathe's bungalow through back gardens where laundry hangs on lines. They try to be discreet, but both of these women are tall. The house is quiet. They knock, wait. Nothing. At last, Agathe opens the door. Just Agathe. By herself in that house. Her head is swollen, her features distorted, but they can see the relief on her face. "Ah, it's you," she says. "Saw you coming but didn't know who. Just shadows through the back. Big shadows."

She laughs—or tries. "Big." They sit her down in a chair. They pull out their gear, draw water, boil it, daub.

She's been gang-raped. There were twenty of them. Her legs are striped with angry welts. Since last night when it happened, no one has come to help.

Anne-Marie looks at her and says to herself, "Is this a government minister in front of me? Can this happen to a government minister?"

Within the month, I hear from Anne-Marie again. She can't go out. She's getting reports that rounders are on the roads in force, beating on cars, beating on people. "Anybody in their way." World Bank President Lewis Preston, a tall, calm man, asks Habyarimana to stop "military spending." A request like that from the man who provides most of your cash should be taken seriously—if you will, as a "proffer of guidance," but it is not, and the World Bank does not crack down. Cash keeps flowing to the Akazu, and my sister is afraid to go out.

JUSTIN MUGENZI

Later the same month, May of '92, Justin Mugenzi—the Liberal Party's opportunist-about-town—finds the cash to fly to Brussels, and so does another Liberal Party player, Agnès Ntamabyariro. Which, of course, we won't know for some time, nor for some time will we know what transpired in Brussels, and even then, it will take some putting together. At just this moment, May of '92, Agnès is in Washington on the U.S. tab. I'm Lando's sister. She visits me. I escort her about town. One day, she comes up to our flat, tells me she'd like to call Mugenzi in Brussels, I give her the phone, then she checks herself. "No, I think I'll wait."

An hour later I offer again. Again no. She'd already made it clear that she needed to talk to him. It's starting to look like she doesn't want to talk to him in front of me. That much I can tell. What I don't yet know is what, in fact, she's up to: conspiring with Mugenzi to break up the Liberal Party and deliver a slice to Habyarimana.

NOW THE STOVE IS GETTING HOT. NOW I CAN'T GET OFF THE PHONE WITH ANNE-MARIE. Sometime in June, she says, *"Zut alors.* Your Lando is finally waking up to his party's *grande responsabilité."* Ordinarily Lando is "our Lando." Except when he makes a mistake. Then he's mine. Immediately, I know the mistake he's made. It's Justin Mugenzi, the charmer and fawning toady who went to prison for killing his wife, conned Habyarimana into pardoning him, and then conned his way into Stanislas Mbonampeka's plans for the Liberal Party, which included conning Stanislas into conning Lando into accepting Justin as party cochief—although I sometimes wonder how hard it was to persuade Lando. Those days, our Lando, once so apolitical, was fresh out of prison and hell-bent on politics. Not even getting Justin as a bedfellow was going to stop him. Regardless, no leader, no *responsable*, was ever less *responsable* than Justin. I don't have to ask her who. But I do.

"Justin?"

"Le luminaire lui-même."

"What's he up to now?"

"No idea. But he's up to something. The Habyarimanas are handing out stacks of cash all over town, trying to break up the parties. Already they've split Agathe's party. You think they won't try to bribe Justin? You think he won't . . ."

"Sell out?"

"Loulou, Justin will grin and grab."

Soon enough we will learn that Mugenzi has done just that, defected with a chunk of the Liberal Party and pledged it to the Akazu. Soon, a slew of sellouts fracture the other refusenik parties.

· 29 ·

THE GENOCIDE GROUP, SA

December 1991–April 1994

In a mimeographed document entitled, "Note relative à la propagande d'expansion et de recrutement," found in Butare prefecture [amid the detritus of a killing field], one propagandist tells others how to sway the public most effectively. Obviously someone who has studied at university level, the author of the note presents a detailed analysis of a book called *Psychologie de la publicité et de la propagande*, by Roger Mucchielli, published in Paris in 1970.

ALISON DES FORGES, *Leave None to Tell the Story: Genocide in Rwanda*

The footprint of astute planning in the epigraph betrays a source of the seeming hysteria shortly to grip us, a source of the seemingly spontaneous but in fact well-planned hysteria about evil Batutsi, about Batutsi whose shoes hide feet that if you will but look are not feet at all, but hooves, and cloven. In such cool planning will be found the businesslike elements of bureaucratically organized hysteria.

Like so many engineers of grand corporate scams, the engineers of this one will one day induce wonder. How could anyone, in this day, in this world, expect to get away with a stunt so outrageous, so evident, so vulnerable to the common decency of the big powers? Forget any armed action against them, not even cutting off the killers' gas or electricity or turning off the radio it will use to incite, explicitly, the mass murder of a civil population. (Freedom of expression, after all.) Who are the victims of genocide to expect an effort that someone might someday describe as heroic? For that matter, who are they to take seriously that heroic business "Never again!" Simple cancellation of the Akazu machine's credit and credentials will send a message that can be ignored only by a truly reckless outfit—and that this outfit is not.

They are not bent on their own destruction. For all the authentic race hate your Akazu duc nurses, it's most likely less rabid than the hate the Nazi bore the Jew. Akazu duchesses and their ducs want racial purity for Rwanda, but not as much as they want business success for their families, and even, if you can digest the notion, business success with a certain respectability. These are men and women who with all due solemnity keep the holy days of obligation; and with more solemnity do they keep the ledgers. However much hate they indulge, they are nonetheless intent on keeping alive and solvent the franchise that is their Rwanda. Throughout the crime that lies ahead, the *génocidaires* will fix a steady eye on the big powers, watching closely who backs them as they kill (France) and who pretends not to know what they're up to (the United States, Belgium, and Britain).

As now in the early nineties the first few of the Akazu ducs sit about cooking up genocidal schemes, they have to know that after the comprehensive murder of planned genocide begins, the big powers who bankroll them will at some point finally have to say, "Enough, no more cash." Given this reasonable expectation, their enterprise is a wonder, regardless how base their morals. Simply as a practical matter, committing genocide with the West's money, under the noses of the West, is so outrageous on the face of it that one must ask how intelligent, educated people can waste their time on so stupid an errand.

This last in particular is the business question—and the bottomless mystery. Who has the answer? Why am I so compelled to find one? Of course I must first ask myself if their genocide is in fact so stupid an errand. They will, after all, get away with it. Right enough, their ultimate fate is to waste in exile or in prison, but not until their task, the essential task of genocide, which is exterminating a people, is three-quarters done, and even then, who will, in fact, put an end to it? The intent face of the West? The steady hand of the West?

For now, let's just say this: These men who now fantasy genocide are intelligent and educated and know that, given any will whatever on the part of the big powers, they cannot act with impunity.

It may even be this: At this early moment in the early nineties, they may not imagine that they will convince their own Akazu comrades to go along with their homicidal daydreams. In fact, this may be the reason, during these early days, that they can let their imaginations plunge ahead with such impunity, why they can let their creative juices flow.

As flow they must. The franchise is still theirs, but it needs help, creative help, and desperately. It's in jeopardy, and shrinking. Many Akazu men no longer have the jobs they had just a year or so ago. One of Mme. Habyarimana's own brothers, Rwagafilita Pierre-Celestin, has somehow been downsized out, as has another big dog, another colonel, Pierre-Celestin's comrade and would-be dauphin, Laurent Serubuga, fingered by Radio Trottoir as the man who put out the contract on the president's good friend Stanislas Mayuya. As loose lips have it, Habyarimana's chum Mayuya stood in the way of Serubuga's own ambitions to one day succeed Habyarimana. Now Mayuya is gone, and Habyarimana is all the more isolated within the Akazu, without even a dauphin, for he will not abide the rumored contractor, Serubuga. Habyarimana won't even restore Serubuga's old job, and we don't need Radio Trottoir to tell us that. That's a matter of fact. Both Pierre-Celestin and Serubuga still have little to do but sit and stew—often enough, we may reasonably assume, with Pierre-Celestin's sister, the madame of *le clan de madame,* Queen Kanziga herself, our latter-day Kanjogera and increasingly known by just that name.

Akazu men everywhere see less coming in. Mitterrand's warning words at La Baule meant that directly (if only for show) the network had to cut some of the worst excesses of its patronage machine, and now the parleys with my *rifiutatori* and the Inkotanyi mean that soon they must share power, and sharing power hurts more than just the ego. It means sharing patronage, and the little grass shack has no patronage left to spare. Something must be done.

Directly in December of 1990, well before the Arusha deal is at last signed, they publish their "Ten Commandments of the Bahutu" in which they tell the pure of race how they must prevent defilement by the impure and evil Batutsi. But that's just a tone-setter. An action plan is called for, something well beyond pogrom, and now here they sit, a select few of the old grass shack elite, the senior ducs, the *abategetsi,* authors of a gathering action plan.

What's it like as they sit about, planning? I see them only from afar; I can barely hear them, and what I hear, I hear secondhand. We will someday learn what they're now dreaming up—thanks mostly to the paper trails their planners famously leave behind, memos, ledgers, requisitions, orders. If just barely, my mind can picture them talking, but I can't make out a word they're saying, and you must remember that during these days when they actually sit about, brainstorming, planning, nobody but them knows that any of this is going on.

As now I write I find my mind circling them, looking them over one by one, up and down, much as Tipoo Tib and his Arab slavers circled us so long ago, casing our "infidel sultanates" for an opening they never did find, for all the impunity of their predatory eyes. My roster of Akazu ducs is simply mine, what I know from what I hear. Others may protest that I neglect this one or overrate that one. They may well be right. Lando could likely come up with a better list, and some of his bartenders might be able to come up with lists yet better. Be all that as it may, this is my list, and thus, like Tipoo Tib, does my predatory mind now circle these Akazu predators, never finding that opening that will let me catch and devour them word for word, but nonetheless gazing at each of them, one by one, up and down.

PROFILES IN IMPUNITY

I want to go back to my little grass shack
In Kealakekua, Hawaii
—BILL COGSWELL, TOMMY HARRISON, AND
JOHNNY NOBLE, "My Little Grass Shack"

The Beulah Land of which these lordlings dream as they relish their grass shack moniker is a tropical paradise along ukulele lines (most of these ducs covet money, comfort, even glamour more than power), but much more is it a paradise without Batutsi.

Here in Kigali, here beyond the Akazu northwest, Beulah Land is often the poured concrete fantasy of the Habyarimanas' hotel, pleasant minivillas near the top of an artfully carved and planted hillside, graced by palms, kissed by breezes, pretending it's somewhere else. They call it the Rebero, but its formal name is the Rebero l'Horizon, so named for its commanding view of the Kigali horizon. Kigali is still just a town, but it's feeling the surge of the world out there, showing polyps of growth at every hand, on every hill. It's a town still ordered but set to go metastatic with the growth and fever patches of poverty that by now blight most big towns in Africa. Overlooking all this from the terrace bar of the Rebero, seated about metal tables set with fresh flowers and overstuffed ashtrays and littered with litrons of Primus and Mützig and half-empty glasses of gin straight up, our Akazu men take up the creative challenge.

They laugh. I can't claim they laugh in sadistic anticipation of events to come; these are not leering Svengalis. Their laughs are more the laughs of old comrades. Forgive me, though, if I describe their camaraderie as less than easy, their guffaws as forced. Forgive me if I describe them as a joyless lot, however much they may dream of a paradise full of Dorothy Lamours. Seldom, if ever, do they repair to billiards or the gaming table. These are men properly and even severely brought up, brought up by nuns and pious mothers, and faithful, let me not forget, to the holy days of obligation. They are men grimly pious in their dissolution. They just drink, and use their leftover beefsteaks as ashtrays.

A SLUG AT THE CENTER OF FAMILY LIFE. M. Zed is assertive, an aristo who tries gamely, in the midst of this indignity, to cut a glad figure. "Good families are generally worse than any others," says Anthony Hope in *The Prisoner of Zenda,* and M. Zed, né Protais Zigiranyirazo, is a man of good family indeed. He's another of Queen Agathe's brothers, and for years, until just a couple years ago, he was the prefect of Ruhengeri, home to our old republic of letters up on the Uganda frontier. If you want to offend him, you could catch him as he slips out of line for a breather, buy him a drink, and suggest, purely by way of small talk, that when he was up in Ruhengeri, he was really just one more outside chief, like Auntie Pascazie's husband, Kabano, Ruhengeri's old Tutsi chief who met us in the cold dawn of a track in Goma the morning we escaped Rwanda.

Zed will get the insult. M. Zed is a Hutu native of the heavily Hutu northwest in which Ruhengeri prefecture sits. Zed's family, Queen Agathe's family, enjoys in these hills a past that is at once Hutu and princely. Old Chief Kabano, by contrast, was neither a native of the northwest nor Hutu. Kabano's past was Tutsi, and it was a past far south, in royal meadows. But the very fact of Zed's patrician past, while thoroughly Hutu, and thoroughly of the northwest, nonetheless endows him with a manner that many Rwandese, Hutu and Tutsi alike, regard as "Tutsi," which is to say insufferably stiff in contrast to the glad Bahutu, who often enough live up to their glad image. Meanwhile, with tanking coffee prices beggaring Akazu patronage, the outfit was already scrapping over diminishing spoils when M. Zed was prefect. The privileged northwest was already fracturing between Ruhengeri ducs on the Uganda frontier and Gisenyi ducs on Lake Kivu—and by birth, M. Zed is a Kivu duc. Which made him, as prefect of Ruhengeri, an outside chief, indeed, a patrician outsider—just like old Kabano.

Thus, I imagine, does rule by racket play itself out, and for that matter, any lucrative business whose success pivots on clubby connections; thus does connected business end up in disconnect. Early in the game comes the man, or in this case, perhaps, the woman, the queen bee, M. Zed's sister, Habyarimana's wife, Queen Agathe. Then comes family. Then business grows beyond family, becomes a network of connections, an outfit, and the outfit is the great multiplier of power and influence. It provides not just the boss's eyes, ears, and strong right arm; in the trendy parlance of these ducs who would be businessmen, it grows the franchise. Pretty soon it's the only game in town, as the Akazu indeed became, with lordlings running about with such impunity that impunity gets into their blood. Meantime, with maturity comes slower growth. Profits lag. There's less to go around. Bosses get nervous, nasty. They retreat to secure redoubts. They start muscling each other the way they muscle the public, and just like that—bad blood on the inside. The big boss, now precarious, starts "retiring" underbosses too powerful. Thus has Habyarimana's precarious clique, with one foot in the Akazu and one foot out, retired several of Madame's brothers along with Théoneste Bagosora and Laurent

Serubuga—the colonel widely believed to have put the contracts out on Hab-yarimana's crony Stanislas, then on the sergeant jailed for actually shooting Stanislas, and then on the public prosecutor pursuing the case. And thus do such men now sit festering in retirement. Now all over again it's a matter of family, the one repository of trust. Nepotism rules. I picture enforcers plagued with congenital disease becoming the slugs at the center of family life.

I've got to get a grip. I'm letting my anger boil over. I find myself think-ing figuratively, in hyperbolic excess, and that's so unlike Batutsi. "Con-genitally diseased." I have no evidence whatsoever that any of these men and women are congenitally diseased. Indeed, by painting them with con-genital disease I defame the congenitally diseased. I defame slugs.

Be all this as it may, that sergeant did in fact kill Stanislas, and regi-mented Rwanda is hardly an exception to the rule that sergeants generally act on orders. Likewise, M. Zed did in fact find himself an Akazu insider en-forcing Akazu will in a corner of the Akazu hills that has been fracturing off in nervous self-interest—and looking at him as an outsider.

Alas, these are also the hills in which Africa's mountain gorilla is making her last stand. According to Radio Trottoir (not to speak of Zungu re-searchers), M. Zed ran, and may yet run, the bush meat racket, which is to say, the market in gorilla meat and gorilla parts. (Given adequate taxidermy, hands make handsome ashtrays.) According to the same so far elusive sources, M. Zed may be the enforcer who contracted the murder of Dian Fossey, that chain-smoking harridan of the volcanoes now some years dead.

He doesn't come off a killer. His manner is engaging, even corporate. He's successful. He looks and smells like success. If you run into him in the first-class lounge of a continental airport and ask him what he does, he might tell you he's "engaged in the field of wildlife management." In a more candid moment, he might call it "the pest control industry." M. Zed, perhaps even more than his brothers, his sister, and his comrades, is in it for the coins. Wherever he is, he's likely to have a black Mercedes that needs its shine kept glowy and a mistress whose cheeks must keep their bloom.

In early 1990, months before the Inkotanyi attack, he suddenly moved to Montreal. "To advance my education," he said at the time. Radio Trottoir said he was running. Some said that in the wake of Mme. Fossey's murder, the poaching trade was getting too hot. Others said he was on assignment to keep Akazu dollars in secure coffers, setting up nominee accounts, Inter-net accounts, numbered accounts, haggling over Krugerrands and Mikimoto pearls. Still others said the upside potential in Ruhengeri no longer war-ranted the downside risk. Who knows? Two things are certain. He has no academic ambitions, and he is still a controlling partner, if not *the* control-ling partner, in the franchise.

TWO FINE FIXERS. In no particular order: Séraphin Rwabukumba (he of "errors and omissions," which translate to under-table commissions) and Elie Sagatwa, the president's right hand.

Séraphin is another of Agathe's brothers, an even more patrician brother. As our Gaetan is somehow endowed by his name with a certain Gaetan look—suave, charming—so does this angelic Séraphin shine with the visage of the seraphim. This most *doux* of Queen Agathe's brothers is called Prince Charming for the womanizing glint in his eye. He'd be the least embarrassed to kick out a leg in my conga line. Once a junior executive under Lando's chum Augustin at the Central Bank, he now moves money about like a born central banker. He knows how to quarter-fold a crisp new fifty-dollar bill with deft discretion, slip it between his second and third fingers, and grease your palm—or as it's put, *"graisser la patte."*

Likewise elegant and almost as handsome is their cousin Elie Sagatwa. He too is a charmer, but of a different stripe. What Sagatwa courts is power, and his genius for it is crocodilian. He doesn't just have looks that can kill, he has looks that do kill, and he wants you to know it. With patrician discretion, he has created a myth around himself. He's the maximum man's immediate right hand, and just between you and him, he wants you to know that he directs, as he puts it, "counterintelligence." But beyond that there is much that he does not want you to know. Perhaps more than any other man in Rwanda, Elie Sagatwa can see with cool dispassion where the interests of the Akazu lie; perhaps more than Habyarimana, perhaps more than his cousin M. Zed or even his cousin Queen Agathe, he runs Rwanda. For now.

THE FAMILY MAN. Théoneste Bagosora likes to run with the big dogs. Some say he's the cur given to getting things wrong, to misreading signals. Periodically, this gets him yapped briefly from the pack, to which he returns, tail between his legs, doing some dirty deed to get back in the pack's good graces. Such matters can be pictured in more than one way. His own malign musings in print indict beefy Bagosora Théoneste, but let's picture him as a family man. Perhaps we can even picture him as a man of some character, the strength of which has been tested, a man who stood by his woman when the Akazu wanted him to drop her. Now the pair has a fine family, and he has more of which to be proud. Educated as a soldier in France—indeed, the first Rwandese ever to study at the select École Militaire Française—Bagosora springs from the once-princely realms of Queen Kanziga and her highborn brothers. His own brother Pasteur is the director general, or as they like to say, "the DG," of the Banque Continentale.

Among Bazungu, Bagosora circulates a résumé that sparkles with achievement, not the least of which, it tells its readers, is his "management" of the

1963 operation that in fact was the slaughter of Tutsi civilians in Gikongoro. Do those events ever give pause to this proper family man? I have no idea, and as far I know, he never describes himself as "engaged in the field of population control." But my brain keeps rerunning a stray remark overheard from the mouth of another Akazu man. "Someone has got to provide these services."

THE IMPRESARIO OF OLD CLOTHES. Chief financial officer of what is becoming the Genocide Group is Félicien Kabuga. Mild-mannered Félicien is hardly a Young Turk, nor a captain of great industry, yet in his conservatively turned-out way, he sets more of an example for the younger generation than do the mighty in their fine array. Nor is his "industry" lightly to be dismissed. It may not appear impressive, but when it comes to business, Kabuga doesn't care about appearances. He cares about profit, and he knows where to find it. He has made a fine success importing used clothes (most particularly T-shirts), recruiting adolescents to hawk them in the roads, reinvesting the profits in coffee, selling the coffee to Rwandex (the state-run exporter), and using the foreign exchange credits to buy construction materials, foodstuffs, and of course, more used clothes.

Thus do you see, here in deepest Africa, grown men running about not just in T-shirts but in T-shirts that read MY COUSIN WENT TO SIX FLAGS OVER TEXAS AND ALL HE GOT ME WAS THIS LOUSY T-SHIRT. (And no, Mr. Ambassador, that fellow with the panga is not likely to have a cousin who went to Six Flags Over Texas.)

Catch one of Félicien's grown sons in conversation and he may well tell you, "Dad is engaged in the field of dry goods distribution. Dry goods and consumer staples. I'm middle management."

By now, Félicien also benefits from all manner of graft, especially when it comes to taxes and avoiding foreign exchange controls. Kabuga is an authentic businessman; he'd be doing handsomely without the connections. But with success, connections have come, and in spades. Not long ago, the Habyarimanas' son married Kabuga's daughter.

OUR YOUTH AND THEIR NAMELESS NUMBERS. Now come the younger bosses, the Mod Squad, and here's what sets them apart:

Superficially, our Akazu men, old school and new alike, are garden-variety gangsters of the African stripe. They cosset power. They spend money. However scant the financial acumen of the common African gangster, it doesn't matter. Power gets him all the cash he can spend, and power is a game at which he's skilled. The Genocide Group doesn't conform all that neatly to the picture. Even the old school has more business savvy than that, and the Mod Squad, in its nameless numbers, is yet more business minded.

That hoary fixture of Zungu Africa, the old hand, doesn't find this entirely credible. It doesn't fit his picture of "the African," and here we have a cartoon figure—"the African"—invoked by another cartoon figure—"the old Africa hand." My old hand is drawn from life, but he's nonetheless, I must allow, a cartoon, a ruddy regimental given to grumbling in his gin. Forever grumpy, he rustles his week-old *Telegraph,* slumps in a club chair in a threadbare club in some lost outpost of empire, and gripes about how "the African," in sudden power, sees business simply as an entitlement.

"Here he is," he says, "the African, in sudden ownership of an enterprise that some poor wretch had to dump at fire sale prices. And what does he do? Runs it to ground. Never reckons that here's something he could put some capital into, some work into, and keep it ticking. No more than fruit for the plucking. That's how he reckons it."

I wonder, is there a farmer anywhere—and the Bantu is above all a farmer—who reckons that the fruit of his work is simply there for the plucking?

Right enough, there are Africans who have snapped up businesses during the fire sales of decolonization, and "run them to ground." Mobutu ran all the wide Congo to ground. More to the point, Lando isn't unique. Not every African with a business got it through his cousin in government. If anything, Lando is a disenfranchised African, and in this he's kin to most of Africa, this continent that wears its struggling small businesses like gaily colored bangles, right down to the mammy-wagons that everywhere grace the gridlock of West Africa. Just look at Kigali-ville. Here in deepest Africa, in the moving shadows of buzzards circling above, and countless furlongs from the Peoria Chamber of Commerce, there's more than enough earnest commerce to win admiring clucks in Peoria, or Dubuque, or Dayton.

Kigali has plenty of Rwandans trying to put a little something together by working, saving, and risking their savings. One is Michael Shyirakera, a middleman in general trade. Another is Alphonse Gatarama, a thriving distributor of beer and soft drinks. The Iris Flower Shop on the market road near Kigali's roundabout does an exuberant business with rich Rwandese and Zungu expats; Sieva, a stationer near the central post, does well; the Boulangerie Athenée sells its baked goods like, well, hotcakes, and if you tell me it's run by Greeks, I'll tell you it's run by Greeks settled for so many generations, and so fluent in their Kinyarwanda, that they are as Rwandese as I am. The locally owned Hotel Bienvenue, where we all go for grilled chicken, holds its own against competition from flush Europeans and connected Akazu men.

Commerce is everywhere, and exuberantly promoted. Much of it is run by Bahutu like Shyirakera and Gatarama, good businessmen with no genocidal pastimes. Development banks are actively and successfully promoting a business mentality, lest their loans be wasted. Meantime, the Mod Squad is neither dumb nor besotted with greed. Indeed, in their way, these younger under-*abategetsi* are more dangerous than the ducs, and the fact that they talk more like junior executives than gangsters makes the threat all the greater. It's these inoffensive-looking junior enforcers who supply the Akazu's muscle in the offices, meeting halls, and scattered backcountry missions where the company meets the customer.

The rub is not that they see businesses as fruit for the plucking. It's that in hate they see business opportunity. This is hardly the case with all Bahutu in business. The beer and soda man, Alphonse Gatarama, like many Hutu businesspeople, will never be implicated in genocide. But others will, and they will determine much of the character of the genocide. They aren't the thugs in the road. They aren't out to milk good businesses dry. They are good businesspeople. They will put together a businesslike apocalypse.

As the genocide's original thinkers (mostly but not entirely senior bosses) see matters, killing will have to be so quick and so widespread that no central apparatus will be able, physically, to do it. They will have to dupe the public into doing it. They will have to marshal the marketing and advertising skills to convince the public to do it. On top of this, they are sophisticated enough to handle the two tasks, marketing on the one hand and advertising on the other, as discreet tasks, calling for discreet skills. They may not be that good at such tasks themselves, but the kids are.

Lando's old chum from Montreal, Jacques Roy, knows especially what the kids are like. Jacques is now in Rwanda working on a World Bank project. Forever at Chez Lando's bar, he's given to talking, in quieter moments, about Mod Squad kids he works with at the Ministry of Public Works. Jacques describes them as sharp, well spoken, well educated, and arrogant, living lives for which their government salaries could not possibly pay. He says they understand marketing. They know a product must be given popular appeal. They use phrases like "youth-oriented product position." Likewise they know advertising, and as matters progress, advertising will get even closer to the point where company meets customer. Here, most particularly, the younger generation, the underbosses, come into play.

OUR NIETZSCHE. Tonton Kagame had Ferdinand Nahimana as a student in Butare. By the time I enrolled at school in Ruhengeri, he'd become a professor there, a distinguished professor of history. He'd make me feel so good as he'd pass me on campus and nod, such a genteel generosity for Tonton's niece. "*Enchanté*, young lady. Completely *enchanté*." He was building a reputation, a justifiable reputation, as a bright scholar, some would say brilliant. He was on his way to becoming Rwanda's Nietzsche. But not as puny as Nietzsche. He is instead tall, slim, handsome; he smiles a lot.

Now in the early nineties, Nahimana provides the intellectual credentials that permit his chums to speak of Batutsi as creatures meant for extermination. You could say he's become Rwanda's distinguished professor of
genocide. He is the apothecary general of their latter-day witch medicine.
Once the picture of cool in his writing, he is now simply the picture of cool
in person; nowadays, his written words, his newspaper articles, his scholarly papers, are forever sailing off into screed.

Most recently, he's stopped lecturing and taken on a more rewarding
job. He's moved down from Ruhengeri to Kigali, where the Habyarimanas
have decided they need him to run Radio Rwanda. But staid Radio Rwanda
is no canvas for this artist. Before long, Félicien Kabuga, the impresario of
old clothes, puts together the cash to start that independent station, the
one that the Habyarimanas can plausibly deny is theirs, one worthy of Nahimana's talents, namely RTLM, Radio/Télévision Libre des Mille Collines,
the free voice of the thousand hills.

To coin a proverb, he's the right man in the right place at the right time.
His station fakes news, invents fake bulletins. He is now *libre* to intoxicate
the masses, who now have cheap transistor radios aplenty and stand ready,
ears to the speakers, to hear him out; before long he has a runaway hit,
broadcasting pop and hate in one bubbly confection. He is now effectively
the director of advertising and communications for the Genocide Group.

PAULINE SWEET AND SOUR. *Abategetsi* cover a multitude of sins and sin-
ners. For example, Jean Kambanda, director of the Banque Populaire, is nothing like Pauline Nyiramasuhuko, the minister of social affairs. Banker
Kambanda, along with a number of other bosses, is much a nonentity, a man
distinguished above all by how seamlessly he fits the Akazu mold. Pauline,
by contrast, is an authentic figure, part of the vital cadre of bosses. As minister of social affairs, she has a big Peugeot and a driver, and travels about the
country, especially her native south, Nduga country, standing before one
quietly respectful audience after another, gazing at them from behind wire-
rimmed bifocals, sweetly, earnestly lecturing on sanitation and the dangers
of AIDS.

In news stories yet to be reported, she will figure prominently, perhaps
more prominently than any other Rwandese woman. As the century turns,
she will be the highest-ranking woman in the world ever indicted on
charges of genocide, and two years later, *The New York Times Magazine* will
run a profile. But now, in the early nineties, she is not (nor for that matter
will she ever be) the most prominent female during this period, nor the second most, nor even the most prominent from Nduga country. The most
prominent is our *rifiutatrice*, our prime minister, Uwilingiyimana Agathe,

"that woman with an attitude," the brave Agathe, the decent one, who's also from Nduga. And Pauline is hardly more significant than her patroness, the queen bee herself, our latter-day Kanjogera, the dark Agathe, the madame in what French intelligence calls *le clan de madame*, Juvenal Habyarimana's invisible wife, Kanziga Agathe.

Pauline is nonetheless notable. For one, she has that modern background so characteristic of the new generation of Hutu leaders. No, she hasn't studied in Europe, and she comes from a backward household, but she has a good education, including a stint in Israel. (She's named her son Shalom.) For another, she's the proximate hand of our approximate Kanjogera, indeed her protégée. As Queen Agathe sits aloof atop her palace hill, Pauline is a visible, public hand.

Her value to Queen Agathe is not that she's brilliant. She isn't. Her value is that she's ambitious to the point of craven loyalty to her betters. This in itself is not unique. This is, after all, Rwanda, lockstep Rwanda. But these days that see Pauline's sweet face frozen in a craven smile are days in which it's crucial for the Akazu to have in its pocket a favorite daughter of Nduga country, where the Akazu does so need support. Southern Bahutu do not favor Pauline nearly as much as they do Agathe Uwilingiyimana, but she's nonetheless theirs. Her success, engineered by Queen Agathe (they both went to the same lycée), has made her popular at home, and thus a valuable shoehorn for the Akazu into the south, where Bahutu and Batutsi are heavily mixed (it's hard, in fact, to be certain of Pauline's origin), and where Hutu opposition to the Akazu has its base. The Akazu needs to denature Nduga country however it can. Among some northern Bahutu it is said, "there are no Bahutu in the south."

Pauline's lectures, of late, have been taking on a sharp tone. Sanitation means not just cleaning up the filth that breeds dysentery and hepatitis. It means cleaning up the filth that breeds cockroaches (*inyenzi*), Batutsi, AIDS. Fastidiously, before each talk, she takes out a pocket mirror and powders her nose. With each visit, her tone becomes more strident, to the point where she commandeers audiences by setting up roadblocks, and the hills begin calling her drives among them "ghost days."

She pulls a local official from the crowd, chews him out, he returns to the crowd, and a fellow official asks, "She isn't mad at me, is she?"

As time goes on, as the war wears on, Pauline is taking on more of Queen Agathe's aloof qualities, clearly offended by these depths where coughs and hepatitis and AIDS, chiggers and jiggers and worms, all breed. Some say that even as she spreads her message to the common folk, she's putting distance between herself and her own mother and siblings, still leading the common life in the hills.

All of which marks her as a woman transfixed and enveloped by that greater She, the whirring silence at the heart of the hive, worrying Her rosary in Her own private chapel.

EICHMANN. Tharcisse Renzaho is a clerkly man in a soldierly outfit. Like so many officers in so many of today's armies, he wears the field utilities that once were uniform of the day mostly for dogface grunts, fatigues cut for men fatigued by physical work, which Renzaho and his officer lot are not. His fatigues are freshly pressed, starched, distinguished by creases razor sharp. His brass gleams. His boots sport a high shine. He shines neither his boots nor his brass.

Four days after the Inkotanyi attacked from Uganda in 1990, the Akazu handpicked Renzaho to take over as prefect of Kigali. He is a colonel, but he was not picked for any ability to lead men in combat. He was picked for his training as a military administrator. He is the consummate military bureaucrat, or as they say in Uganda, "your right staff wallah."

But let's not patronize. Whether your military is beastly or brilliant, administration is critical. Great armies have been run by midlevel leaders less accomplished than Tharcisse Renzaho. Adolf Eichmann wasn't cut out for combat either. Hitler was a corporal. He was brave in war (in the Great War, that is), but his genius was not for war. His genius was for cajoling and flattering a Wehrmacht already of a lockstep, goose-step mind into a grotesque cartoon of itself. Indeed, Hitler's genius was for cajoling and flattering an already lockstep nation into a grotesque cartoon of itself. And who gets the ultimate credit for that? Hitler and his Fascists? Or a nation discovering its awful potential? Or humankind discovering its awful potential? On parade, Rwanda's army goose-steps just like Hitler's; indeed, the goose-step comes easy to us lockstep Rwandese.

To which you may well reply: Goose-steps do not a Wehrmacht make. True enough, but don't snicker at Renzaho's bookkeeping. Administration *is* a crucial war-making skill. (Logistics, logistics, logistics.) The rub comes with the sort of books he keeps. They don't enable combat. They bring production-line order to the business of making sausage of ordinary folk.

In his preference for doing battle on ledger pages, he's not alone. If you're of a generous mind, you could say that the officer corps of Rwanda's army is simply too enlightened to be much good at physical war-making. The skills these officers prize above all are business skills—and I don't intend this as code for greed, nor do I intend to be snide. They genuinely prize administrative talent, and in the arena of administration, Tharcisse Renzaho is a first among equals. As they say, he runs a tight ship.

His offices are in a gleaming new city hall, great halls of jasper, built with donor funds. While the idea men cook up their schemes at redoubts like the Rebero, Renzaho's offices are where bureaucrats, in rank behind desks, translate ideas into practical plans.

He's Akazu, but he isn't from Akazu country. He's from the east, where the hills roll more easily. In Renzaho country, patches of dry East African savannah show up amid the hills, and the Uganda kob whistles warning. (Yes, a gazelle that whistles.) Renzaho knows how to organize muscle to break up refusenik parades without leaving Akazu fingerprints. He knows how to turn dreams of democracy into nightmares. As a captain commanding a battalion under enemy assault, he might well be worthless, but from his offices, he can marshal entire regiments of the ragged, and that is no negligible skill. He counts them. He makes sure that now and then someone slips them some pocket money. He makes sure they get free beer. He makes sure they show up where they are supposed to show up when they are supposed to show up. He is the link between the Akazu's dreamers and schemers and the legions of young men with empty stomachs newly idle in the roads; he's the clerk who lets the dogs out.

THE AKAZU'S FACE FOR THE WORLD. And that face, I regret to say, belongs to one of ours; our old and dear friend, Barayagwiza Jean-Bosco, he of the crew that included Augustin, now chief of the Central Bank, Lando, Gaetan, and the one we call Sacré—Jean-Baptiste, a Mututsi who migrated to the States, became an engineer, and out of sheer love of Rwanda has come back, teaching now at the university in Butare.

When Gaetan wanted to come home from Kinshasa in 1985, it was Jean-Bosco to whom Lando went for help. Jean-Bosco was then a deputy secretary in the foreign ministry. He was also an old *copain* of both Lando and Gaetan at the Collège Saint André. He came through for Gaetan.

At this point, Augustin is firmly, if not strategically, entrenched at the Central Bank. Jean-Bosco is just the opposite. Regardless, he's the one, not Augustin, to whom Lando goes for help getting Gaetan out of the Congo. Why? It's hard to say, but he's where the action is. If you want, you could say that I'm including Jean-Bosco because we know him so well, not because his power, just now, justifies it. Be that as it may, I include Jean-Bosco in the genocide group.

Short, another smiler, a womanizer, he's now the ministry's secretary-general. He likes Tutsi women but wants to send their men "back to Egypt." One wonders why he helped get Gaetan back from Kinshasa. Radio Trottoir says that he beats his wife, and many people seem to believe it. All I know for sure is that Barayagwiza Jean-Bosco's wife, Asumpta, is an engaging woman from an engaging Hutu family. At school in Ruhengeri her niece Monique befriended me; now and then I'd encounter Asumpta when I'd stop by for Monique at Jean-Bosco's house in Kigali. As Karangwa puts it, she and Jean-Bosco are among Kigali's Muscovy ducks, lured to the Soviet Union during the Cold War; it was at the university there that she had the misfortune to meet him.

Just now, Jean-Bosco is one of two leading figures in a new Akazu enterprise that is an intensely racial offshoot of the president's already racial party. Karangwa has proved right; the difference between the two parties is more apparent than real. If anything, Jean-Bosco, like so many insiders, is more Akazu than the president himself. In June of this year, June of '92, Habyarimana got rid of some entrenched establishment types, among them his wife's brother Rwagafilita and Laurent Serubuga, nemesis of Habyarimana's late confidant, Stanislas. At the same time, he brought in a non-Akazu professional, James Gasana, as defense minister. These were smart moves. In virtually one stroke, he got rid of some antagonists within the Akazu, tossed a sop to the banks pressing for reform, and picked up someone he can use—is now using—as a stalking horse when he senses Akazu pressure. The idea is that instead of gunning for him, they can gun for his new defense minister, Gasana, and in short order that is just what they will be doing. By August of '93, Gasana will be out, and Jean-Bosco, a diplomat with no military background, will be muscling the professional military.

Now, in 1992, Jean-Bosco is getting together with Nahimana to put Radio RTLM together, meantime setting new horizons for his new operation. He not only operates as a separate political party (even though he's at least as Akazu as the Akazu party), but in addition, he's putting together a second Akazu militia, the Impuzamugambi, to back up the Interahamwe. His new party may exist mostly on paper, but his Impuzamugambi boys exist on a lot more than paper. They exist in the roads.

The foreign press pictures Jean-Bosco's new party as more extreme than the old-guard party, and this is true as far as it goes. But the toxin it spreads is not that new. What's new is that since Mitterrand's summit at La Baule, the Habyarimanas' Akazu party has to watch what it says. Which is where Jean-Bosco comes in. They use him and his party as a mouthpiece they can disavow. They can use Jean-Bosco to keep toxin pumping through the body politic. What's also new, and what now gives the toxin special wallop, is the club-swinging Impuzamugambi boys. They show up in the roads with their faces chalked white. The formal name of Jean-Bosco's outfit is the Coalition for the Defense of the Republic. For me it's simply the Akazu in chalk-face.

Jean-Bosco's mistress is Tutsi.

CASTOR. Lingering here near the end of all these *abategetsi* is Nsabimana Déogratias, and I must allow it's an odd place for the man, here at the end. Nsabimana is no colorless apparatchik. Ugly things are said of him. It's said that well before the genocide, he raped Tutsi girls. Is the accusation fair? Perhaps not, though I hear it too insistently to rule it out, and in any case, we will learn that he at least sits in on sessions during which genocide is planned. At least pro forma, he outranks men like Kigali prefect chief Renzaho, who is his military inferior; Nsabimana is the commander of the armed forces. And beyond the merely pro forma, he's still a cut above men like Renzaho, even if men like Renzaho are more tightly plugged into the Akazu. Nsabimana is a born battlefield commander. He is by all accounts a brave man, and accomplished in combat. "War is the father of us all," says Heraclites. War is manifestly the father of Déogratias Nsabimana.

Even as the Akazu is sick at heart, even as doom stalks it as certainly as doom stalked Sparta, it is betimes heroic in its individuals.

It would seem. How little I know. Like Mama, Rwanda is a grand mistress of secrecy.

Castor's role in those meetings at which genocide is planned is uncertain, as is much about the man. To his enemies in combat, the Inkotanyi, he is known more as a warrior than either a rapist or a killer of innocents. From the moment of the 1990 attack from Uganda, he does not leave the country, and he seems forever at the front, getting shot at, leading from the trenches. As a fighting force, Habyarimana's army gets shabby notices, but Nsabimana is neither a fool nor a coward nor a slouch. He rallies many Hutu stalwarts, chastens his Tutsi enemies, and much of his bad press may begin with old-shop Akazu, those pious dissolutes who find horrid scandal in his off-hours carousing. This Castor, this Spartan son of Zeus and Leda the swan, is known for rolling down from the hills after battle and repairing, battered and exhausted, to a quarter known for its brothels. This is clearly too much for the royal, Kanziga Agathe, daily saying her rosary at her very own chapel, just a few hills off. From within her shining nimbus, the queen of the Akazu looks down on all this with a twinge.

Would that Queen Agathe were a blunt woman. Would that she were the sort to dress a sanctimonious husband down with a curt "Let's not forget, *mon chéri*. We're scoundrels. Let's conduct ourselves like scoundrels." Alas, it's the other way around. She's the pious one, our lady of sanctimony, our *sainte nitouche*, our Saint Don't-Touch. She admonishes her husband to send an armed squad to drag Castor from his brothel. He stalls. She hectors, and at last Habyarimana, much hectored, sends an armed squad to drag Nsabimana from his brothel.

And that they do. But the next time Nsabimana rolls down from the hills, he rolls down in a *char*—a tank. He parks the monster out front, along with a corporal in the turret manning a fifty-caliber machine gun. Walking wearily to the front door, Castor says, "Now let's see her drag me out."

Castor freely distributes condoms to his troops, which hardly pleases the pious Queen Kanziga, for whom birth control is a scandal, just as it is for her protégée, Minister of Social Affairs Pauline, lecturing earnestly about the dangers of AIDS. Haranguing crowds from over her wire-rimmed glasses, she declares that abstinence is the answer.

FOR WHOM THE ANGELS WEEP. Let us not neglect Nzirorera Joseph, veteran minister of public works, the man to whom Jacques Roy's young friends in the Mod Squad report. Radio Trottoir has Joseph a garden-variety embezzler of state funds. He shows up regularly at Chez Lando just after last call and picks a fight if he doesn't get served. One night he shows up as everyone is leaving and encounters a Tutsi lass of the sort that men find it pleasant to encounter. She, however, does not find him so pleasant, and so what if he's a big *légume.* So what if she's whatever. However much the vamp, she's of no mind to vamp this blotto *soulard,* this plastered drunk, who smells like Satan. It's bedtime, she insists. He insists on confiscating her pass card. At last he leaves, getting home, no doubt, in something of a state. Within a few days, word gets back to Chez Lando that in a fury the morning after, his wife went through his clothes where he dropped them, item by item en route to bed, found a certain pass card, saw the word *Tutsi,* and oh the angels then did weep.

For high discussion with his comrades, a bruised Nzirorera hangs out at the Habyarimanas' Rebero.

DO I DO THESE CREATURES A DISSERVICE? RADIO TROTTOIR, AFTER ALL, IS BUT A TISSUE OF rumors. Nor does identifying rumor as rumor excuse repeating it. If anything, it may betray a certain intemperance I feel in the matter of M. Zed, Jean-Bosco, and their ilk. So be it. Rwanda is a nation that lives on rumor; the old way was to keep silent, to reveal nothing, and things haven't changed all that much. Rwanda believes that truth can be found through a careful parsing of rumor. I invented none of these stories, but I make no claim to impartiality. I despise these men.

As a group they are in the act of committing a crime of some measure. They are conjuring genocide. This is beyond dispute. Someday they will sit in cells blaming ghosts of antique Batutsi for making them hate. In other words, the devil made them do it, the same royal devil that forced suicide on two of our own grandsires and tormented countless others. Is it only because we're Tutsi that we won't blame these same devils for our own failings, that we don't judge antiques by modern measures? The ghosts who truly pollute aren't antiques. They're the ghosts of corpses still fresh in the fields of modern history, the ghosts of Bazungu in love with the idea of race, from Rider Haggard's naïve love affair to Burton's deadly serious one.

They're the ghosts of the bigots who educated the bigots who educated the priest who lent Bagosora *Mein Kampf* for inspiration. They're the ghosts of the bigots who educated elite squads of *Übermenschen*—in random sample, the second Baron Redesdale, der Volksführer Adolf Hitler, our Father Claes, Sir Oswald Mosley, America's Father Coughlin, America's Avery Brundage; for that matter those two well-educated American superboys, Leopold and Loeb. Tin toy iterations of these are among Zunguland's biggest gifts to Africa, and especially to Rwanda.

Nor is it simply hate that now drives the *responsables* of the Genocide Group. It's love-hate, in any number of perverse displays. Look at how these Hutu lordlings mimic the impunity of the old Tutsi court. Look at how they exalt Zungu notions of race. They're not led astray by ghosts. They're conspiring with them—or at least trying to. These men who would never disco in public now switch off the lights, grab a ghost—or a pasteboard image of a ghost—and fandango, one minute with an unresponding Speke, the next with a priest, then with a pasteboard Mutemura, grandsire, baron, brigand, and a model for these baronial *responsables* whose daylight reserve masks mania. Lie twirls after lie, and on they rip. Here's a pasteboard Muganza, fat as life. In Kinyarwanda his name means "the one who wins"; in fact, he's the one upon whom fate forced suicide. Here's Muganza, who stood fast and imparted so much, and there an unresponding Emin Pasha, who stood alone and imparted so much. There—Ismail Pasha Ayoub, who forced Egyptian will up the Nile. There's his lieutenant, General Gordon, who wanted to exchange his command at Khartoum for Mombasa, the better to reach what he reckoned the Nile's true prize, its source in our green hills—and in his own scripture-ridden, whiskey-ridden fantasies carried the banner of Zungu will into our slice of Africa, inspiring generations of the Bazungu who descended on us with their ideas of men and supermen. There in habit is Rwanda's Father Claes himself, who wrote of men and supermen; there, Mukezarugamba, grandsire, image of strength and resistance, the first man hung by the Belgians. There's the Dowager Kanjogera, the image of conspiracy; there her husband, Rwabugiri, the greatest of conspirators. There's Grandfather Kabenga, who hunted with the king and choked to death on buttermilk force-fed him by goons in a Belgian lockup; there, his brother, Bitahurwina, who chased a pretender to the throne on foot all the way across Uganda to Jinja on Lake Victoria, and there killed the man; and just there, Bitahurwina's son, Tonton Kagame, with his lessons of Bantu redemption. There's Guy Logiest, Belgian colonel, who conjured a false state. There President Kayibanda, who drove a Volkswagen because he feared making ghosts jealous. Over there is a clutch of Egyptian ghosts—the purest phantoms, for they don't even know who we are, and have only come because Bazungu and Akazu ducs (who hate them) have made them part of the show.

A STAR IS BORN

It's the summer of 1993, and the star is Radio RTLM, the free voice of the thousand hills, a product of the business genius of Félicien Kabuga, emperor of old clothes, multiplied by the propaganda genius of Ferdinand Nahimana, late of Tonton Kagame's classes in Butare. It's soon to be known as Radio Hate, at times as Radio Panga. "Turn it up!" their talk-jocks shout whenever they get truly mad with hate, telling their listeners how the evil Batutsi have turned even our ever-forgiving Lord Himself against them, turned sweet Jesus against them, sweet Jesus in his all-encompassing grace. "Turn it up!" they shout to a nation with straining transistor radios to their ears. "Turn it up!"

THE LAW MUST GO ITS WAY

December 1993–February 1994

It's been six years, six years, and here I am in Kigali, my first holiday home in six years. Can anyone call this Rwanda a holiday? I can. There on the other side of passport control is nearly all the family, Mama, Lando, Anne-Marie, Karangwa, Hélène, kids and more kids. Mama. She looks at me as if she never expected to see me again.

LANDO AND I ARE COLLABORATING ON SUPPER. THE PHONE RINGS. IT'S SEEMS AS IF SOME official or other on the other end needs a routine party document. I listen. I realize who it is. It's Judge Kavaruganda. "Oh, Lando . . ." I say.

We don't really know Kavaruganda. I don't even know what he looks like. But Rwanda is a small town. I feel like I know him. I feel kinship. He's no *rifiutatore*. He's a judge, which means he's Hutu. In fact, he's worked for years for the two great stalwarts of Hutu power (lowercase power), old President Kayibanda and then Juvenal Habyarimana. He's stern. He also seems upright, and if it's true, that's both brave and perilous.

"Kavaruganda," I say to Lando, which confounds him because he's trying to deal with me and talk to Kavaruganda at the same time. I don't let that bother me. I say, "Wasn't he the one on the radio—"

Lando shakes his head in irritated confirmation. I say, "The one talking about people afraid of what was it?"

"The rule of law," says Lando, then, "No, Your Honor, I wasn't talking to you. I was talking to little sister."

"Ask him if he wasn't afraid," I say. I'm a shameless intruder. "I mean taking a stand like that. Out front."

"She wants to know weren't you afraid? Taking a stand like that?"

There's a pause. Lando's lids droop slightly, as they might listening to someone hem and haw. I'm such an intruder. Asking somebody I don't know such a personal question. What can he do but hem and haw? At last Lando says "Mmmh," wraps up his business with the judge, and we make plans for supper. At supper I ask him what Kavaruganda said.

"He said, 'Oh well, you know. . . .' "

"That's all?"

"He said, 'Oh well, you know . . . the law must go its way.' "

"That's all?"

"That's all he meant to say. But then he said, 'Put yourself where I am. You're a Muhutu. Your fight has been the Hutu fight. Your life is winding down. You're thinking about gravestones. Two gravestones, actually. One says, *Here lies a man who loved justice*. The other says, *Here lies a man who hated Batutsi*. The law must go its way.' "

"THEY'RE NOT AFTER FAMILIES; AT WORST, POLITICIANS."

I'm alone with Lando at his place. I'm in his kitchen, getting a drink. A bang at the door; it's the watchman. He says, *"Interahamwe, Monsieur le Ministre . . .* headed this way." Now I hear them.

> *That's the house.*
> *The cockroach house.*
> *That's the house.*
> *The cockroach house.*

Lando clumps out front, clumps back, phones a UN post.

> *That's the house.*
> *The cockroach house.*
> *That's the house.*
> *The cockroach house.*

Lando hangs up; he says they said that if they threaten us directly, then he should call back.

The chants fade. They're gone. I tell him he's got to get Mama, the entire family, to move.

"Loulou, they're not after families. At worst, politicians."

At once I know he didn't mean to say that. As if he's not now a politician.

. . .

NEW YEAR'S EVE. HÉLÈNE AND I HAVE BEEN ON EDGE ALL DAY, AND FOR NO PROPER REA-son. After all, family is on the way, kids and their friends, the start of a year full of dread, to be sure, but dread that is the foam on bubbling promise. Habyarimana has already signed a solid peace agreement, and he's under enormous pressure, inside the country and out, to quit dragging his feet. Straightaway, Hélène and I fetch Mama from Kabuye and have her nap so she can stay up with us past midnight. Then I pull myself up on a high stool and use the kitchen counter to iron a lace tablecloth and linen napkins from Hélène's Special Collection. Mama, too excited to nap, comes in to chat. To get her back to bed, I switch on RTLM; just like that she's back to her nap. Whatever RTLM's faults, indeed its sins, one of them is not boring its listeners to sleep. Except Mama. It's less a matter of the anti-Tutsi hate they sing than that old Tutsi impatience with foolishness.

Ironing done, I fold it all neatly, slide it carefully into a plastic shopping bag, and head for the kids' bathroom for a shower. On the way, I peek in on Lando in the study, where he's deep in the composition of some deep letter. I don't even want to know what it is. I just peek in the door. I get my robe and turn on the shower. Good; there's water. I just finished a session with a hot iron, and America has addicted me to endless, humming showers.

With Mama yet asleep, Hélène and I walk from chez Lando to Chez Lando to put our heads together with the cooks and plan the meal. We'll be eating at Chez Lando's restaurant, which they call La Fringale, after the old saloon in town. It's just a family affair, Mama's family, but it will be some feast. A maître d' will seat everyone along a prize possession dragged from the old place in town, a grand table that seats eighteen. Then French starters, Belgian starters, great platters of Rwandese entrées, magnums of cham-pagne, great calabashes of banana beer with honey, flowers of every sort, and sweets and juices of every sort for the kids. I think briefly that it would have been nice to have little Brother Marko at the Polish Mission on Gikondo Hill print up the menu at his press. He's such a lovely man. He does first-rate work. But that would be too extravagant for a family affair. Too pricey. It will look just fine printed up by hand. Through all the getting ready, I hold fast to the plastic bag that secures our freshly pressed linen.

When we get back to the house, it's late afternoon and Lando is still deep in his library. In the front room, I hear the VCR. Patrick and a school-mate are gazing wide-eyed at Colonel Jack Nicholson as he barks at them, "The *truth*! You can't handle the truth!"

"Auntie, you've got to catch this," says Patrick, and at last I settle down. I'm from Rwanda. For me, handling Colonel Nicholson is a break.

About five, the study phone tingles. At last, the buffalo lumbers out. "Habyarimana's man, Enoch," he mumbles. "Says his boss wants to talk. He's sending a car." I look at him in brow-speak. My brow wants to know if anything is wrong, and how wrong. He answers matter-of-factly, "Back by seven."

The slow crunch of tires on gravel wakes Mama; the car, come for Lando. She asks, "Are the guests here already?" Once again, we speak in failed unison, and this time it's four of us, me, Hélène, Patrick, Malaika: "No, Mama/Grandma. It's Lando/Daddy. He's leaving/leaving. He'll be right back/back. Seven/seven/about seven."

Seven comes, and no Lando. Seven goes, and no Lando. We say nothing. We just look at each other. Mama goes to her room. Gaetan is in his office at Chez Lando; we send word.

Just after eight, we muster at the door for the walk to Chez Lando. We're a glum crew. Gaetan is waiting for us. This evening Gaetan has none of his usual smolder about him. This evening Gaetan has a great broad grin. He sees Mama. He takes her by the shoulders, hugs her, and now the ever-lambent Gaetan shines through as he holds her back at arm's length, looks at her face-on. "Mama, come on. You know how it is. Politics takes time. He'll be here in no time."

I look at the table. It looks so grand, so long, bright with Hélène's linen freshly pressed and punctuated by bouquets of purple and white orchids that reach out extravagantly but won't force anyone to crane a neck to chat, or argue, or rail (this is, after all, a family table). Serving carts stand by, stacked with plates, a size for each course, and likewise standing by is Mama's favorite staffer, Ruhumuliza, *Jean-Baptiste* Ruhumuliza, a longtime Chez Lando maître d'hotel, and our maître d'extravagance for this family evening. He wears black tie, a grin, and a fresh white serviette over a half-folded arm.

It's a picture pluperfect, too perfect for life. Everything that's needed is here—and nothing that isn't. And most especially, Jean-Baptiste is here. Trained *à point* by Belgians, this man is impeccable in his drill, in his French, in his expertise in all matters culinary, indeed in all matters hospitable, from the oenological all the way to tipsy conclusion in the oeno-illogical.

A state, by the way, with which Jean-Baptiste is familiar; he's been sacked more often than anyone cares to remember for vanishing on week-long romances with the bottle. But this is an evening for Mama, the only soul this side of kingdom come who can get him his job back after one of those benders. This evening, Jean-Baptiste bears the world a big grin.

"*Bonne année, Jean-Baptiste,*" says Hélène. "Between cups?"

"Between cups, madame," says Jean-Baptiste. "And a *bonne année* to you."

Where will Lando sit? What place should I keep for him? Why does it matter? It's time to enjoy. Hélène has set out tiny handwritten nameplates. I settle down by my nameplate and gaze at a menu I already know by heart, intending to make none of the choices indicated but instead demand a little of everything, or maybe a lot of everything, most particularly the champagne:

Menu du Réveillon, 1993–1994

Toast aux champignons
ou
Crevettes à l'avocat

Sombe
ou
Steak au poivre vert
ou
Brochettes de tilapia

Riz à la vapeur
ou
Pommes de terre sautées
ou
Bugali

Mousse au chocolat
ou
Sorbet aux fruits de la passion

De la passion, indeed. No *ou*'s for me, and never mind the trouble on Mama's face. I'm sure it's Lando she's fretting about, not the flute that is forever and frequently finding its way to my lips. (*"Jean-Baptiste, s'il vous plaît. Encore du champagne."*) I catch Mama's eye and laugh. She laughs back, and stage-whispers to Gaetan, "Tell her not to drink like she's worried about something." Gaetan, of course, does nothing of the sort, doubtless thinking to himself, as I'm thinking to myself, Oh those confounded Tutsi ways, never let them see what's bothering you. That's not me, not tonight. *"Jean-Baptiste, encore du vin."*

Normally I eat so slowly I drive people mad. Now I bolt down a feast, and who knows how much champagne, in no time flat. So much and so fast that the new year *boings* in with hugs and kisses and half an hour later I'm dead in bed.

I wake up. Gentle shakes; someone is shaking me. The clock says two. It's dark. It's Lando, whispering. *"Bonne année, Loulou."*

As I fall back to sleep, I hear the soft tinkle of plates and forks, Mama's murmur in the kitchen, her bustle, Mama whispering questions, fixing a little something for Lando, who would much rather be asleep.

HAPPY NEW YEAR

Blackouts. Each blackout is a cover for assassination. We press Lando to tell us what went on in Habyarimana's office. All we know is that the president's office is still tinselly with Christmas. Spread out on sofa tables, side tables, and bookcases are American Christmas cards, families in Agfacolor and Kodacolor grinning out from cards full of cheer. We won't let him go. We press him for more. He slips every question. There must have been veiled threats, and how can he deny that? But just how veiled? Just how serious? He slips the subject. He sticks to vague descriptions of what Habyarimana wants. Juvenal wants him to bring what remains of the Liberal Party into the government fold. But what, in fact, did he say?

"He bellyached."

Besides that.

"He talked pieces."

Pieces?

"Piece of this. Piece of that. Percentages."

Percentages?

"Percent of this. Percent of that. Before special items. After special items. Off the top. Off the books. I couldn't do the math."

What did you tell him?

"I told him I couldn't do the math."

It's clear there's an "or else" bite to Habyarimana's cozening, but Lando dismisses it as if it were of no consequence. He shifts, he distracts.

"We'd get up and just walk around. First around the office; not as big as a basketball court. Then we wander through the halls, in and out of empty offices, empty halls. Lots of echoes. He says to me, 'Tell me, Lando, do you believe I really hate Batutsi?' and I say, 'Yes, I do, I just don't know how much,' and he says, 'But just between men, Lando, *inter nos*, do you believe that as a man I hate Batutsi?' I tell him we're dying; he says, 'But what about you?' I say, 'You put me in prison. You beat me.' He says, '*Aliko ye*, Lando, come on, your party split and it was your fault. You had a chance to create a loyal party, and you blew it—and now, do you know that you still have a last chance?' "

THIS IS THE MORNING, THE MORNING OF THE DAY I LEAVE. ON THE WAY TO THE SHOWER, I check in on Mama. She's up. She's fixing her hair. She holds a mirror in front of her, but mostly she's staring out at the dew in the yard. It is such a familiar ritual. I smile at the memory; ointments and unguents, lotions and creams, small remedies and analgesics, perfumed spirits, alcohol, damp cloths, soft towels, the shifts and tricks beauty deploys to keep a corner of heaven in precincts without running water. All that so long ago; Mama fixing her hair, fixing mine, working magic with a long thin stick, her wand, to coax stray strands into place. So cool; such a pretence of cool. I sit down next to her. She pulls me next to her. "Now go and shower. Your tears are messing my hair."

I switch off the BBC, switch on RTLM. It's having its day. It's less than a year since its star was born, and now you can start at the top of the road, squeeze your way through the crowd to the bottom, and hear it blaring from one duka to the next. You can hear the DJ start one of his nonstop sentences at the top, hear him carry on from blaring duka door to blaring duka door, and at the bottom you can hear him put full stop, period, to the sentence. Won't miss a word. RTLM, Radio Hate, Radio Panga, blasts from every duka, every bakery, every butcher, every cooper, cobbler, dairy, every kiosk. It blasts in digital stereo and it squawks from the speakers of cheap transistors held to every other ear in the pressing crowd. "Turn it up," the DJ shouts, and they do. "Turn it up! God himself has abandoned them! Do you hear that, brothers and sisters? God himself! Tell the world! Turn it up!"

RTLM's Rwanda is awash in RTLM's paranoia. RTLM has taken a Rwanda already soaked in bigotry and taught it to fear and loathe the peace worked out in Arusha. RTLM may be the deadliest weapon in the brick arsenal of the ducs against the peace, and they use it brilliantly. All the same, there's at least one problem: bad press abroad. It's getting creditors testy. Likewise East African neighbors.

AND THUS IT IS THAT TODAY, APRIL 6, 1994, HABYARIMANA IS FLYING TO DAR ES SALAAM to commit himself once and for all to the deal he's already signed, and doing so because he must, because Rwanda is broke and the message from his Zungu patrons is that they can't keep underwriting him if his Akazu keeps embarrassing them with its excesses, its pogroms, its impunity.

By now Dar is bathed in the orange light of late afternoon. Habyarimana has assured the bosses that this time he means it, that within a few days he will put formally to work the power-sharing agreement he first signed months ago. He will remain president, but with half the army's officer corps and 40 percent of its enlisted men supplied by the Inkotanyi, thus guaranteeing the end of pogroms, the end of abuse, the end of impunity.

Back in Kigali-ville, the retired colonel who likes to run with the big dogs, Théoneste Bagosora, *chef du bureau* at the defense ministry, has ordered troops to cordon off the reservation that includes the airfield and the presidential palace. Habyarimana's jet takes off from Dar for home; by seven forty-five or so, his pilots initiate early radio contact with the tower. Fifteen minutes later, Anne-Marie and her family sit down to supper. Habyarimana's plane is beginning its descent. From just outside the airfield—but by most evidence inside the cordoned reservation—two missiles hiss up through the dark. At least one hits. Habyarimana's plane goes down. Anne-Marie's family hears it. "Artillery practice," says her Joseph, but just in case, he turns on the radio. Martial music signaling official announcement, then the announcement itself—the president is dead. On the roads the word is the Inkotanyi did it. Or the Belgians did it. Or they both did it.

Bagosora's troops roar into Masaka Hill, the hill near the airfield that's almost entirely Hutu—turf from which missiles might theoretically have been fired. The troops begin killing. The killing is under way and the first victims are the Bahutu of Masaka Hill. Bagosora will soon report that his troops are searching out (read killing) "people implicated in the crime." What does he mean, "implicated"? Does he mean that these people may have been witnesses?

· 31 ·

THE DAY ITSELF
April 6, 1994

> The many men, so beautiful!
> And they all dead did lie:
> And a thousand thousand slimy things
> Lived on; and so did I.
> —SAMUEL TAYLOR COLERIDGE, "The Rime of the Ancient Mariner"

In Washington, it's three thirty in the afternoon of the same day, an afternoon struggling out of winter. I'm at my desk at the African Development Bank. I get a call. I learn. At first I think: This obstacle to peace, Habyarimana—gone at last. Gone; this wretched man is gone. Then I think again; suddenly I'm jelly with fright. I don't know why.

About the same time in Kigali, General Dallaire is rushing up the outdoor staircase to his office. His phone is ringing. It's our Agathe, the first minister. She tells him she won't surrender, that she must address the nation. If she can get on the radio by first light, she has a chance. First light is when all Rwanda listens. If she can get on the air then, she has a chance to stop the killing, stop the putsch. Dallaire says UN troops will get her to the station.

IN DC, I SLOWLY SENSE, WITH A CHILL, THE SOURCE OF MY FRIGHT. I CAN'T SAY THAT AT this instant I know that genocide is starting to roll over us but I do sense, bearing down on us, the malice of that century-plus just passed that is now so much a part of me. I don't know what's coming, but I know the engine behind it; I feel its force. And I fear for myself, here in DC where I couldn't be safer. I fear my head reaching some critical coefficient beyond which there is nothing but brain-lock.

At Force HQ, four men huddle: Dallaire; the Ghanaian general Henry Anydiho (his second in command); Major Brent Beardsley, the skipper's Canadian aide-de-camp; and Luc Marchal, the major seconded to the UN by Belgium. Marchal dispatches a squad of Belgian paracommandos to Radio Rwanda to secure the station for Mme. Agathe. A squad has already been dispatched to protect her, but if she's to speak in the morning, they must also secure the radio station.

Just before dawn, the squad deploying to guard her calls Force HQ on their failing UN radios on failing UN batteries. They're taking rounds.

Over on Lando's Kimihurura Hill, watch is nearly up for one of the guards in the contingent from the Rwandese gendarmerie. The officer of the guard relieves him. He quits his duty station and heads for his barracks. On the way he sees a comrade. The comrade says he's just seen the Presidential Guard, "and they're going after Lando. They're headed for his place."

The gendarme ducks back by a shortcut.

At about the same time, events are taking shape at a Jesuit community called the Christus Center just a few blocks away. It's now about six thirty: Christus Center priests are preparing mass at its chapel. As they are wont to do during emergencies, Tutsi families have fled here for safety. The priests begin saying mass. Three Presidential Guards stride in. They interrupt the mass. They have lists. They order a sister to get the register. They check the center's lists against their lists. They separate out the Europeans. One by one, they begin scrutinizing pass cards. They separate out most Bahutu. They order everyone else to room 28. Those left behind drift nervously away; some drift to the library. Now and then they peek out. They catch sight of an officer showing up. They hear him order the troops to lock room 28. A few minutes pass, and they hear two explosions, the sort made by hand grenades, then brief silence, then automatic weapons fire. The troops leave with their officer. The group in the library edge out. Inside room 28 are seventeen dead—seminarians, visitors, a sixty-seven-year-old Jesuit priest.

PROCEEDINGS OF THE UNITED NATIONS COMMISSION
INQUIRING INTO THE PERFORMANCE OF
UN MISSIONS TO RWANDA
PRIOR TO AND DURING THE 1994 GENOCIDE

Date of proceedings: 12/08/99
Location: Rayburn House Office Building, Hearing Room 2255.

Extract:

MR. [Michael] HOURIGAN: What was the security circumstances of your family...

MS. MUSHIKIWABO:...My brother's house...was guarded by United Nations troops. He was also escorted to work and to social events by both Rwanda police gendarmes and United Nations troops....

MR. HOURIGAN: Did Landoal [*sic*] express confidence in the safety of his family because of the presence of UN troops?

MS. MUSHIKIWABO: Oh yes, He—Landoal knew that he was top of the list of the most wanted in Rwanda at that time. He knew that he would be one of the first people to be targeted by the Death Escadron. [But] Hotel Chez Lando...was just a couple of steps from the UNAMIR headquarters....

MR. HOURIGAN: Louise...the United Nations...received [from intelligence agents] a document about a death threat against your brother. Louise, did Landoal ever discuss the existence of this document...?

MS. MUSHIKIWABO: No....we talked about how dangerous things were in Rwanda and the need to probably leave the country, and—but he didn't know of any serious, reliable information about his assassination in the hands of the United Nations. He did receive a number of anonymous letters asking for money so that he could be given information on all these assassination plots against him, but as far as I know, and I have spoken with my brother many times...he never mentioned any document or any type of information related to his assassination.

MR. HOURIGAN:...What is the significance of this document?

MS. MUSHIKIWABO: It is hard for me to describe this document. When I became aware of this document in the fall or winter of 1998, I was stunned. I had been invited to a kind of briefing...and I was just sitting in the room to listen to Michael Hourigan, whom I didn't know at that time, and...he mentioned a memorandum dated February 17, 1994, and as he started reading the memorandum, I realized one of the men he was talking about was my brother, and I was speechless. I was speechless.

I went back home that evening, and I faxed a copy of this memo to [my family] in Kigali, without any comment.

My feeling toward the United Nations that day was very confused. I knew of the difficulty of the United Nations to protect civilians, to basically try to stop the genocide, and I knew that things were not easy...but I could not believe that an institution like the United Nations would have had this precise information, including the names of the killers [assigned to kill] my brother, and that [we were never told these specific orders were out there and in UN hands].

On Lando's Kimihurura Hill, the gendarme just relieved is back. His shortcut has worked. He's here before the Guard troops. It's about six thirty. He blurts the news to his mates. They charge the bungalow, bang on windows, the front door. "Lando! Patrick! Up! Out! They're coming."

"Hide. You've got to hide."

PROCEEDINGS OF COMMISSION ... ON UN PERFORMANCE
IN RWANDA/1994, CON'T

Date of proceedings: 12/08/99

Location: **Rayburn House Office Building,** Hearing Room 2255.

Extract:

Commission Investigator MR. [Michael] HOURIGAN: ... we'd like the Commission to understand the importance that Landoal [*sic*] played in the critical resolution of the Arusha process....

MS. MUSHIKIWABO: I guess as Minister of [Labor and] Social Affairs ... [he] played a critical role ... specifically the social protocol [for] refugee repatriation. He was also a leader of one of the most powerful opposition parties in the pro-democracy movement. In 1994, in the transitional government, Landoal was the single Tutsi in the cabinet, so that placed him in a position of danger.

MR. HOURIGAN: Louise, actually that's the exposure to danger that we were speaking about earlier ... perhaps you could speak about that....

MS. MUSHIKIWABO: ... There was no secret for anyone ... that there was a lot of political tension in Rwanda. There were many incidents of violence ... there was a newly created radio, RTMN [*sic*] that was basically the voice of the extremist Hutu movement in Rwanda, which was also supported by many of the members of the government at that time. I heard my brother's name mentioned many times over the radio.... He was called a traitor, a man who deserved to die....

I left Kigali on January 13, 1994, and my brother told me he was happy I was leaving.

At about seven, Anne-Marie on Kicikuro Hill rings Lando on Kimihurura Hill. He tells her troops are outside his place too. The gendarmes have warned him and run—the UN troops have gone over the back fence. He's there with Mama, Hélène, and the kids—Malaika, Patrick, and the kids' half cousin Rudasingwa.

Lando says to Anne-Marie, "We've rung up Dallaire. We can't get through. Can you try?"

"We'll try."

"Anne-Marie, what hurts is that . . ."

"We'll try."

"I always had a feeling I'd die. What hurts is that we're all going to die. I always thought I'd die alone."

PROCEEDINGS OF COMMISSION ... ON UN PERFORMANCE
IN RWANDA/1994, CON'T

Date of proceedings: 12/08/99

Location: **Rayburn House Office Building,** Hearing Room 2255.

Extract:

MR. HOURIGAN: What do you think this information would have done to his decision, whether to leave his family in Rwanda or remove them? You, as a Rwandese, knowing of the reputation of this group, how important would this have been to Landoal's decision making on whether to keep his family there or remove them?

MS. MUSHIKIWABO: There is no doubt in my mind, there is no doubt that had my brother been given this piece of paper with this information, with the people planning to kill him—he knew them very well—with the names of the members of the Death Escadron, the soldiers that were going to kill him, he would at least, at the very least, have sent his children, his wife, and other family members away. I have no doubt about that.

For him, personally, I cannot really tell. He might have decided to stay, regardless. I'm not sure. But what I know is that he would have put his family in safety.

MR. HOURIGAN: Do you think that, had he been told this information, would he have shared that with you?

MS. MUSHIKIWABO: Absolutely. Absolutely. We talked many times from his hotel in Arusha and then from Rwanda about going or not going. It was something we discussed in the family, not just myself and my brother, but inside the family, we discussed going away.

Back in 1990, when his—when he was arrested and detained in Rwanda, his two children [left Rwanda] for protection. So they went back when their father was released from prison, and things were looking good at that time, '91. The creation of all these parties, and then the United Nations mission, things were looking bright. The peace negotiations in Arusha were going well, so he decided to bring back his children.

So it is something—it's a topic we had discussed many times before about who should go, who should stay, is it really dangerous, is this the time to go? It is something that came up in our conversation constantly.

At Lando's place on Kimihurura Hill, Hélène is now on the phone. It's about seven thirty. At last she's gotten through to Dallaire at Force HQ. She tells him that she and Lando and the kids and Mama are inside and Akazu troops are outside. He tells her to sit tight, why it's important to sit tight. Suddenly she interrupts him. She tells him she hears the troops. Dallaire hears her become "indescribably calm." He will write that she talks as if there's "no choice now but to be resigned to her fate." She says good-bye.

TRANSCRIPT OF AN INTERVIEW WITH LUC MARCHAL
BY THE PUBLIC BROADCASTING SERVICE PROGRAM *FRONTLINE*

Date: 1/26/99

Extract:

What happened to Monsieur Lando?

In the morning of the 7th I received a phone call from Mrs. Lando requesting me to send security because she was afraid for the safety of the Lando's family . . . she told me the presidential [guards] were preparing an attack....I tried to get some more information and I promised to try to send some detachment to secure the location. But at the same time we were confronted with a lot of incidents in the Kigali area. Two or three minutes later, Mr. Lando himself phoned me and he asked me again to very quickly send some people to secure his residence, and he described the situation outside his residence. I heard him [say] that more or less 15 presidential guards were preparing an attack against his residence, and he gave me some details, real details, about the preparation of the presidential guards. And then at a certain moment I heard an explosion of hand grenades, firing and so on, and Mr. Lando told me, "It's too late," and it was his last words.

From the memoirs of Roméo Dallaire: "Luc . . . heard them being murdered over the phone." Not just Lando. All of them. Hélène, Malaika, Patrick, Mama, Rudasingwa.

MEMORY-LOCK

By midmorning, nearly every decent leader in Kigali is dead. A reporter will put it this way: "Everyone, whether Hutu or Tutsi, who wanted power-sharing, or who had spoken out against Habyarimana and Hutu Power . . . every journalist, every lawyer, every professor, every teacher, every civil servant, every priest, every doctor, every clerk, every student, every civil rights activist [has been] hunted down in a house-to-house operation." Among the few exceptions are some notables who escaped to the Mille Collines, plus the first minister, the other Agathe.

In Burundi, Muzungu's Canadians get a call from Kigali. "Return without delay."

At the first minister's residence in Kigali, the Belgians not yet captured hustle her, her husband, and their five children out a back door.

By midmorning, she too is under fire. About half the ten Belgians sent to protect her are looking down Akazu rifle barrels.

The phone rings at the residence of the deputy chief of the U.S. mission. Her next-door neighbor, Prime Minister Agathe, wonders if she could stop by.

Agathe; dear, gracious Agathe. She's pregnant. She tries to jump the fence into the yard of the U.S. diplomat; she can't. A shot rings out. The diplomat on the other side gets scared. She thinks they've been spotted. She tells Agathe to quit trying. They run to the garden's opposite wall, on the other side of which is a UN aid compound. This wall is lower; this time they make it. The prime minister hides her children, then she and her husband find their own hiding places. By now, Akazu troops have taken prisoner the entire ten-man Belgian squad. Within minutes they have them under guard at Camp Kigali—Akazu army HQ. Back across the road at Agathe's place, Akazu troops are fuming. They can't find her.

Just before noon, hoots rise from the road, then howls of victory. They've found her. They've found their commander in chief. They've found her husband. They haven't found the kids. In a short while, friends will spirit the kids away.

It's high noon when they finish her. Accounts vary. Dallaire says Agathe and her husband try to escape, then surrender quietly to save the kids. By all accounts she's mutilated. By all accounts, her legs are spread and a trooper advances with a broken bottle. My mind seizes up.

When I hear accounts of Lando's end, I have a chance to get my head ready for it. I'm never really ready, but at least I can tell myself not to let it lock me up. Hearing about Agathe takes me by surprise. I'm not ready for it. My mind locks up. It's hot. These Akazu killers are working hard. They must be sweating. I can smell their sweat. Where I write, the day is even hotter, but where my mind resides it's thirty below, and all I get when I turn the key is a feeble effort. Something has dropped my head in a deep freeze.

What about the rest of the day? Matters hardly stop with Lando, Mama, Agathe. Our notes on the rest, so preciously collected over so many years, sit paper-clipped at my left, the season's, the month's, the week's, the day's events, precious clues we've obsessively collected and picked apart and poked, scrutinized as closely as a witch doctor scrutinizes entrails or a Harvard scholar picks apart precious coprolites. And it's not just the remains of this day I've got to get on with. There's the next. Again, cold click. What's wrong? Has critical temperature intersected with critical pressure? Have I reached the critical coefficient that spells lock-up? Key. Click.

A SINGLE DEATH, A TRAGEDY; A MILLION, A STATISTIC

April 7–July 20, 1994

At seven thirty of the mongrel day at hand I'm just getting up in Silver Spring, listening to the news and trying not to, afraid what I might hear, afraid to miss it.

The next morning is the same.

And the next. Seven thirty and I'm getting ready for mass. I listen to the news. My heart's in my mouth. Nothing. Back after mass, and again I turn on the news. I learn that a rock star got high and killed himself. Nothing else. I have to get through. I try and try again. At last I get a line: One of Lando's old chums, Monseigneur Bertello, at Kigali's Vatican Embassy. People are shouting in the background, yelling, crying. I can barely hear him. Just barely, beneath chaos, I hear him say, "My daughter, we have got to pray. We have got to pray. I have got to go." The line goes dead.

The following night, I get a call. It's *jolie* Judith from Kigali, now working in Montreal. "Oh Louise, I just saw Muzungu on TV." It was a Canadian TV report; Muzungu has just been evacuated to Ottawa from Kigali by his Canadian employers, and "Oh Louise! he looks awful." Then: "Louise, they said Muzungu's whole family was killed. Louise, please, get up here. Louise, sweet Jesus, even Mama." It isn't her own mama she's talking about. It's mine. Judith knows nothing of what's happening to hers. We're all dangling by the same thread. We all have the same mama.

I fly up to see Muzungu. His mind has reached the critical coefficient. He keeps repeating: "They're all right. I know it. I'm sure. The Canadians got me out. They'll get them out. I'm sure. Soon. I'm waiting here." A friend puts him up in Ottawa's French quarter.

. . .

I CAN'T RECALL WHERE OR WHEN. I CAN ONLY RECALL THE DATELINE, REUTERS, MONDAY, April 25. That's the day I read in the papers that UN agents at the refugee camp just over the frontier on the road to Emin Pasha's Bukavu say they're witnessing the greatest mass movement in the UN's history.

A few days later, a family friend living in Virginia rings up. Gaetan is dead. Karangwa is dead. Wellars, Anne-Marie, Joseph, Shara, Nana are safe at a refugee camp in Inkotanyi-held Byumba; Safari is dead.

By day's end, April 7, Wellars, his wife, their baby, had escaped to Amahoro stadium. It's just around the corner from Chez Lando. It's under UN control, and hard by the airfield. A stray story about Wellars leaks through: In the dark before first light of that day, he heard planes over head. The French. Flying pachyderms circled, dropped, touched down. Bays swung open. The Foreign Legion charged out. They deployed to UN positions controlling the field; one by one, they ordered UN troops to quit their posts. They took control of the UN positions.

Late June, I hear that Anne-Marie, Joseph, Shara, and Nana might be turning up soon in Kampala. Come the fourth of July, the Akazu troops begin filing out of Kigali, a broken force, headed west. The same day I catch a flight for Kampala.

"MY MISSION HAS FAILED"

Reunion after such absence. I see them. They see me. There's nothing I can say. I try to speak up. I'm mute. At last a word comes out, "Safari." I can form no other.

Anne-Marie and family have been staying at the house of a friend. At this moment, nothing is further from Rwanda than posh Ntinda. Their friend is a businessman from Kigali, Assinapol Rwigara, and it's at his dream-song house that I hear bits of this, bits of that . . . and later I'll hear more bits, and collect them like precious coprolites. But randomly—and in any event, they'll end up frozen in a mind locked by that critical coefficient.

Anne-Marie is the sort who takes first things first. She begins by telling me about that unholy day, April 7. It's early evening. Chez Lando is burning. Her kids are huddling under UN guard at Dom Bosco School in the south end of Kigali. Some four thousand souls huddle there under UN guard. Safari, Shara, and Nana are but three specks among them. A Belgian squad drove them there early that morning. The Belgian lads tried to bring Anne-Marie and Joseph, but there wasn't room. Anne-Marie and Joseph hustled the kids into the Belgian jeep. Akazu troops then took the two of them. Just where, they had no idea—and most especially, the kids, on their way to Dom Bosco, had no idea. The kids were utterly confounded.

Chaos somehow arranges for Joseph and Anne-Marie to get back to their place—where they know they aren't safe. They go over the back fence to a house under construction. It's owned by one of Joseph's friends, a Muhutu who has himself fled with his family to the safety of his hometown. Here they hide, and will for weeks to come, crouched much of the time in a two-foot-high crawl space under the roof of that house under construction, wondering desperately about the kids. Their one connection with the world outside is a man in whom they must have total faith, their friend's young cook and house-guard, Eliya.

Right through the end of April, one thing unites an otherwise fractured Kigali: Almost uniformly, the town expects the Inkotanyi to show up at any minute. The same Inkotanyi who had made deadly mistakes in their 1990 attack, mistakes that tore them up.

At month's end, the Akazu still has robust French help. It sits comfortably in the UN and in embassies in every big power you can name. There's no question that it outguns and outmans the Inkotanyi. The Inkotanyi are led mostly by Batutsi, some 10 percent of the population. They're guerrillas—and not even the guerrillas Mao saw swimming among a sympathetic population. And meanwhile, on quite different killing fields, mobs marshaled by Akazu grind on with their "work."

Still, the power of myth and fear being what it is, Kigali expects the Inkotanyi any minute. It's an event you either dread or just as desperately want, but everyone expects, and at any time.

Great expectations—and doomed. It's more than two months before the Inkotanyi make their move on Kigali, two months during which random cannonades nightly rattle the town out of fitful sleep. The one escape is fatigue-induced slumber often as not, what rips you out of it isn't Inkotanyi at all. It's an Akazu unit firing at dodging phantoms. The Akazu troops seldom know what's out there. Inkotanyi dodgers are at work, and no one is more keenly aware of this than Roméo Dallaire. He's certain they can take the town any minute. But the general is a man under many guns. He's often reduced to a state in which he can do nothing but get mad as hell—and the Inkotanyi are hardly exempt. Where *are* they?

He's even harder on himself. Every day he wakes up breathing despair. "The mangled bodies of my Belgian soldiers. Helen, Lando, and their beautiful children crying for help and then resigning themselves to their fate. The congealed blood and screams in the Kigali hospital compound. Bagosora's deceptive smile. The Presidential Guards and Interahamwe militiamen at the roadblocks, their faces filled with blood lust. The enigma of Ndindiliyimana [the gendarmerie chief]. The voice of Prime Minister Agathe as she realized she could not get to the radio station to speak to her nation. Her children cowering in a dark corner of the bedroom, expecting the next footsteps to be those of their executioners. . . .

"My mission ha[s] failed."

"YOU DON'T HAVE TO WORRY ANYMORE. I'M HERE"

Thanks in good part to the lad Eliya and another Muhutu both brave and resourceful, Shara and Nana make it to their parents' hiding place. Shara and Nana; not Safari. Along the way, Safari had run and vanished into the oven of that first day.

This I've already learned over the phone; now in Kampala I feel Safari's absence, and now I learn how fraught matters were after Eliya found Shara and Nana and took them to the house under construction. By late April, all five of them are running low on water. You'd think that as a Muhutu, Eliya could get out and get some water, but he can't, not even a drink for himself. Chanting mobs of painted hypnoids have made the roads lethal for everyone . . . and even if the roads were safe, there's scant water to be had. Nothing runs from the taps. Meantime, as Kigali expects the Inkotanyi any day, they expect a knock from Akazu agents any day. As far as they can tell, Akazu troops are digging in all around them.

They're right. The Akazu's best troops are digging in for a determined stand to defend the airfield and the Guard's Camp Kanombe, and the family hideout is just inside the perimeter. Every day they hear the scrape of spades; soon they seem to hear (or is it just nerves?) one spade in particular. Every day it gets more distinct, closer. By the first few days of May, it's right next door—at least to their ears. They're wired. They're out of food and water.

At last, the scraping stops. Silence. Then bangs at the door. Anne-Marie is at the end of her rope. Is it Jean-Bosco's crew? Or the Interahamwe? Will they be any better off if the goons have to break in? She answers the door.

The first thing she sees is the rifle. The next thing she sees is the face of the lad holding it. A face that looks nearly as young as Shara's. Then she sees the body, so skinny, so straight. Then she sees the left hand grab the rifle's barrel and drop the piece crisply to the ground on his left. She sees the drab East German kit; the lad's right hand snaps to a salute in smart British style, palm forward. (I could just as well call it, as now I write, "snappy French style," but I'm not in the mood.) His heels click. He says, "You don't have to worry anymore. I'm here."

THE INKOTANYI HUSTLE THEM TO A REFUGEE CAMP IN BYUMBA. MATTERS ARE CHANGING.

Known but to a few, the Inkotanyi have somehow managed to swing around Kigali from the north to the south. By mid-June, they have the town in a vise. France lets the UN know that "for humanitarian purposes" it's dispatching an expeditionary force immediately.

Radio Hate is ecstatic. The French are coming. "Let's rejoice!" they forever boom over the airwaves. "Let's rejoice!" That and *"Vive la France!"* Banners span the roads, *"Vive la France!"* Militia goons dance in the roads.

But no military force, not even the French Foreign Legion, can swing into action just like that. Base camps must be set up. Strategy focused. Tactics developed. Orders cut. Orders issued. Before the full force of the French operation can be brought to bear, Akazu forces just might have to beat some strategic retreats.

SHARA

It's July 5 by the time I get to Kampala. Anne-Marie taps her credit in this world outside Rwanda and they move out of Assinapol's posh digs and into a small hotel on Kampala Road—two adjacent rooms on the second floor for two weeks. "Jammed up" is how I describe Kampala Road to a stateside friend. If I weren't so low, Kampala Road wouldn't be jammed up. It would be "bustling with life." Anne-Marie's Shara squeezes my hand. I look at him. He grins.

"Loulou, think how happy we are to see you. We never thought we'd see you again. Don't cry."

I squeeze his hand and promise not to cry. He says, "From now on, everything's going to be clean sheets and feather beds."

The hotel is run by a fat lady. Fat and friendly. She grins as I pass. "Welcome to Uganda, sister." She doesn't pry, we don't cry.

Much of what remains of the family is still at the camp in Byumba. Rwanda is still at war. The genocide is still on. The plan is to head for the Byumba "house" where the family stayed after the Inkotanyi smuggled them out of Kigali. "The house" is in fact a classroom at the École Sociale de Byumba. Gaetan's wife, Eugénie, is still there with their two kids. So is Wellars, his wife, their child. So are others I long to see. A cousin arranges for the three of us—me, Anne-Marie, and Joseph—to ride along with three young men headed for Byumba in a banged-up Toyota Land Cruiser.

We set off; we'll be crossing the frontier at Gatuna. Three hours later we're halfway to Gatuna and stop for supper. It's past nine. It's dark. We stop at a vest-pocket restaurant-bar in the middle of the thickest banana plantation I've ever seen. The food takes forever, but the beer comes straightaway. Back in the truck, we bump and thump over rutted roads. I'm so far gone we seem to breeze through the winding black desolation. I fight sleep.

Gatuna Post is the picture of normalcy, at least under the circumstances.

Uganda Customs is here, wanting to see our IDs, asking when we expect to cross back. Just like that we're through, and just like that (because I've been asleep) we're in Inkotanyi-held Byumba.

RWASUBUTARE

Just after first light, there he is, Wellars. First an apparition, then a jolt—the first of two. My ever-immaculate brother is filthy. His face is scrubbed shiny. The rest of him reeks. For a shadow of a second he disgusts me—and with that comes jolt number two.

Jolt number two isn't him; it's me. How could I let the signs of his suffering disgust me?

This worship of strength above all else! Could it lurk in me? Stoic creed is seeded deep in every Mututsi, but souls who have endured what Wellars has endured are nothing if not stoic. How could I read signs of suffering as stigma? As shame?

Muzungu's wife, Tabu, is here. Karangwa's son Richard is here, his sisters, Chantal and Sandrine, are with an Inkotanyi unit near Kigali. Richard tells me that a good week into the killing, an Inkotanyi soldier found them dodging along the Byumba road, Interahamwe just behind them. I hear that their brother Nyarugabo is still alive—and not just alive, but Inkotanyi. An old friend from Karuruma Hill was making her fugitive way along a road between Kigali and Byumba and saw him red-eyed and mud-splattered behind the wheel of a commandeered Toyota short bed flying a shredded Inkotanyi flag. I try to picture it: Karangwa's twelve-year-old Nyarugabo with a gun and a lorry. "He gave us a big wave," someone says. "A big wave and a grin. As if he weren't frightened to death, and the flies weren't biting."

Out of the corner of my eye, I see two old professors from Ruhengeri. Anastase Gasana. Joseph Nsengimana. It's dreamlike. I see them, someone somewhere says something, my head is turned, they're gone.

The sight of them prompts questions. I ask about. I find out. Rwasubutare didn't make it. He was on a list. Rwasubutare, who lived in such fright of those he so unwittingly frightened. He was so right to fear them. They were so right to fear him. In the most inexplicit but fundamental way, he challenged their impunity, and so they put him on a list and now he's dead. He's run his race.

"PRINCES WERE PRIVILEGED TO KILL"

Back in Kampala, I take hot baths in the morning, hot baths in the afternoon, a hot bath before bed, and with each I sink blessedly into fond appreciation of the kids still with us, of Anne-Marie's Shara and her Nana, of

Karangwa's Richard, his sisters Chantal and Sandrine and their brother Nyarugabo—NYAHRoo-gahbo, the family's rascal, our adolescent Inkotanyi, soon to demob. Where will we send him to school? Would that all our problems fell into such a category!

By the end of July, I'm back in the States and still it's hot baths twice a day; thoughts of the kids. From all accounts, Shara is still the Shara who squeezed my hand when the story of Safari's end had me choking, still the lad who told me I shouldn't cry, still forever plunging into the limpid blue of a hotel pool, as if each dive through those clear waters washes away more and more bad luck, clearing the way to the future. Just watching him was infectious. One step, two step, spring, jackknife, and then straight down into the pool. I watched and knew that from then on I didn't have to jump at the jangle of every phone. His dives were almost magical, ritually repeated, one step, two step, spring, jackknife, then straight down. Over and over. It was mesmerizing. It was as if the higher he sprang, the more crisply he folded, the more steeply he dove, the more evil he washed from the family's fortune. The more, the better; the better, the more. "Everything's going to be clean sheets and feather beds."

LORD KNOWS PAPA TRIED, BUT HOW COULD HE POSSIBLY HAVE PREPARED US FOR WHAT was to come? He knew something was coming. *"Ibihe n'ibindi,"* he was forever saying. "Things are changing." But he was making a mistake. In the midst of all that insecurity, he was giving us too much security, too much love. We lived too happily behind the protective walls he laid by hand, tile by heavy tile, leveling each chalk-lined course like a man who would be a master mason. When our father died he left Mama the rugo, and all of us a millennium of heritage recorded in the heads of his clan's *abiru* . . . plus an imaginary bank vault full of real stratagems and real shifts and real ambition left to Rwanda by King Rwabugiri, that nineteenth-century autarch who had us hell-bent before the white man ever got to Rwanda. And then the white man left us with yet more for Papa to pass on, an imaginary pharmacopoeia stocked to the eaves with real witch medicine.

All this on the shoulders of a bent farmer in somebody's cast-off overcoat and shoes with no socks. He left us more than we could possibly grasp.

FITFULLY, INCOMPLETELY, I TRY TO GET THE REMAINS OF THE STORY DOWN ON PAPER. I try to write; I'm assaulted by numbers. In Gikongoro, forty to fifty thousand died in less than a week. My head can't grasp it. Forty to fifty thousand? Numbers that big in a town so small in a time so short, it just doesn't register. It's just statistics.

. . .

IN THE BISESERO HILLS, TWENTY THOUSAND NEARLY DEFENSELESS SOULS (THEY HAD bows, they had pangas, rocks) gathered to defend themselves. Kalashnikov-armed killers reduced them to a few hundred. At my first boarding school— the one Tonton drove me to in Kansi—agents of the state killed the headmistress and most of her pupils, almost all of them Hutu. At Notre Dame d'Afrique, high in Akazu Gisenyi, at our boarding school there, agents of the state killed the headmistress and most of her pupils, almost all Hutu. In the cathedral at Kibuye on Lake Kivu, where the helpless retreated for safety, goons broke stained glass with rocks, lobbed in grenades; birds flew out in a rush, followed by the helpless stampeding, and then a hail of automatic weapons fire that cut them down. It's not a unique event. Priests do kill. On the high plains of Rusomo, a young duka wallah named Paul Kamanzi sheltered dozens of fleeing Batutsi in his boutique. Kamanzi Paul was a Muhutu; he sheltered them, fought the goons as they attacked, died with his wards.

And on without end, amen. They killed children on sight in the roads. They raped, gutted alive, rent from crotch to neck, took sex slaves, beat them daily, abandoned them to die as derelicts, some of them as derelicts with genocide-contracted AIDS, many with bastard infants, some with AIDS, loved as mothers love all their children, held close as only a mother with AIDS can hold close her child dying of AIDS.

There comes a point where my brain freezes up, and all I hear is numbers—numbers so great they stand massively between me and the people they stand for. With each new statistic the thermostat on the deep freeze that locks my brain drops another degree, and the statistics won't stop, still haven't stopped. Every day more war widows with genocide-contracted AIDS die; numbers mount; heads stop absorbing. At some point, nearly everyone finds their mind freezing, and after that there's little to do but count.

In this matter, Stalin has the last word: "A single death is a tragedy. A million is a statistic." Psychotic Stalin and one Edward Young, writing about two hundred years earlier: "One to destroy is murder by the law, / . . . To murder thousands . . . / . . . glorious art." Stalin and Young and one Beilby Porteus, nearly as old: "One murder made a villain, / Millions a hero. Princes were privileged / To kill, and numbers sanctified the crime."

I'M IN THE TRANSIT HALL AT ZAVENTEM AIRPORT IN BRUSSELS. IT'S JULY '94; A STOPOVER. An old friend from Kigali, Georgette van Hyfte has come all the way from Bruges to greet me. Hugs, kisses, tears; she hands me an impossibly old letter addressed to me from Lando. She explains that shortly after Lando got out of prison in '90, her husband was flying back to Belgium and so Lando gave him the letter to post from there; it would be much quicker than posting from Rwanda. I begin slowly tearing it open, not even looking at it, listening to Georgette. She says they'd posted it and it had come back, "ADDRESS UNKNOWN." All these years they'd kept it.

The letter isn't quite registering and neither is Georgette. My brain is still falling back into Stalin and statistics. I think, "I hope at least to have kept myself from counting skulls," and all the while I just keep counting.

Slowly I unfold the letter, struggling to stop the counting. I'm thinking, "Give us just one skull, just one slim anecdote, just one faded snapshot of someone now gone—and if there are more, please don't deliver them by the gross. Give them to us one by one, beat the drum in measured triplet, and hold to the cadence as we catch brief sight of them. Brave Judge Kavaruganda, who never has to worry about what his tombstone might read; frightened Professor Rwasubutare, who worries so; duka wallah Paul Kamanzi; Agathe Uwilingiyimana (forever our first minister); her husband, Ignace; the headmistress of our mission school at Gisenyi; the headmistress of our mission school at Kansi."

Almost idly, I look at the letter. The date reads "*le 17 décembre, 1990.*" The prison year, 1990. I wonder: Will I learn what I don't want to learn? I don't. He's gentle:

> . . . *it would be unwise to describe the times we are going through in a letter or by word of mouth. We will have to wait until things calm down. You must be patient. The ways of the Lord being unfathomable, we shall probably have the chance to meet soon and talk face to face.*

And one by one, his face, those faces, forever gone, on and on. I can't help working it out statistically. I can't help counting:

We'd need nearly twenty Vietnam Memorials for all their names.

Family, the kids: Lando's Malaika and Patrick; their cousin Rudasingwa (riddled in the same rented bungalow at the same sickening moment); Safari; Shara; and Kazuba (Little Sunshine). Lando; Hélène; Gaetan; our half brother Nyagatare; Karangwa; Karangwa's beautiful Donatilla; Mama.

To prison Lando's letter only alludes, and just once.

> . . . *It's not the physical humiliation but the moral breakdown. . . . I kept telling myself this can't be happening. I've never betrayed my country and I never will. . . . how selfish of me, not telling you that Hélène, the kids, the whole family were sharing every instant of my distress . . . But hope reappears . . . hope is on the horizon.*

Ah, yes, the horizon. That imaginary line you can never catch. Who knew that however futile your efforts to catch it, it could catch you.

"From a single crime, know the nation. I shudder to say it." Thus spake Virgil, and so speak I, and shudder to say it: From a single crime, know our nation. Without ever knowing who we were, Rider Haggard made so much of us. Without ever knowing who Haggard was, we made so much of ourselves. Must we now be defined mostly by victimhood and a squalid crime?

Our Rwanda? Our tiny world, which in our language still means the universe?

How is it that the old meaning hangs on?

Maybe it's this: Rwanda, once so alone, then so aloofly above the swamps and the dry savannah below, was ultimately hit so hard by the larger world . . . and Rwandese don't like picturing themselves as victims. Steadfast to the last, our father refused to be a victim. Whatever we did, we were steadfast, and who is to say who was the more so? Those who struggled in Diaspora? Or those like Papa, who refused to let the pogroms of '59 chase him out of Rwanda? This refusal to accept victimhood was the very air we breathed in our Bujumbura exile, and I somehow managed to pack it like a mini-respirator, right there next to my toothbrush, when fate took me back to Rwanda and school with the nuns at the Kansi mission. Items like invisible mini-respirators fit easily in the tightest suitcase.

This refusal to accept victimhood, to hang on, is what kept Lando in Rwanda after he got out of prison, and one friend after another was warning him, "Lando, get out." He asked them how he could abandon all the people who by then were counting on him, all those who had no way to get out. It's what sat silent and steadfast in Anne-Marie's mind in that little hotel in Kampala as I pleaded with her to start filling out Canadian immigration papers, U.S. immigration papers, for her and what was left of the family. There was no way she was going to do that; within weeks, she, and they, were back in Kigali. It was the air I gasped to breathe when at last I got back to Rwanda, that kept me coming back—twice a year, every year, in all the years since then.

Perhaps in remembering that Rwanda is the universe, we, all of us, Hutu and Tutsi, see ourselves not as victims of the world, but simply as part of it, that what the universe has done to Rwanda, it is doing to itself. Rwanda is the universe. The universe is Rwanda.

To no one in particular, in the vast emptiness of an international airport filled with people, I say, "Your honor, I protest." I glance again at Lando's letter. I'd missed the ending: "*Ne cèdes jamais au découragement.*"

"Never give up."

· ACKNOWLEDGMENTS ·

Writing this book began with a posthumous letter, read in a moment of profound desolation in the vast emptiness of a busy airport in July 1994; it ends with the serenity that hope brings. We are grateful to Lando, the author of the said letter, for the inspiration. Anne-Marie Kantengwa and Milagros Ardin-Kramer were of immense help in obtaining material for the book and critiquing it; we are deeply grateful to them. Norman Gleason's unwavering support for this story and his technical skills were invaluable. We want to express our gratitude to Alphonse Ruboya, who gave us access to his writings and knowledge of the Batemura clan, and provided valuable examples of how ordinary Rwandans of all ethnicities lived together as one people for centuries until the 1950s. François Kayiranga told us stories of the Batsobe clan and genealogy: we thank him. Many individuals in Rwanda gave us stories that are not easy to tell, and we thank them all. We want to thank the following people for making various contributions: Smithsonian archivist Amy J. Staples, Barbara Halpern, Joan Diamond, Miriam Kerson, Lou Lapidus, Craig and Linda Laughlin, Carol Ludwig, Carey Winfrey, Gwenda de Moor, Nepo Ntaganda, Nausicaa Habimana, Vincent Gleason, Sabine Levy, Steve Bradshaw, Philippe Lepage, Roy Furchgott, Zeke Kramer, Judith Kabanyana, Jean-Pierre Mutangana, Judith Musabyimbabazi, Pelagie Kamanya, Egide Muzungu, Wellars Kayiranga, and Etienne Sayinzoga. Special thanks go to Mike Hamilburg for making sure this story gets published, and to Daniela Rapp for her editorial expertise.

Note: Foreign terms used just once, and defined in the text, are not included; no abbreviations or acronyms are included because we use only commonly understood abbreviations like US and UN, preferring to define all groups by why they matter; abbreviations with which other books are commonly peppered appear here as part of the common name by which the people know and speak of them. (For example "Inkotanyi" The insurgents fighting the Akazu state; officially the RPF, the Rwandese Patriotic Front or the FPR (French), the *Front Patriotique Rwandais*."

Abadage   Kinyarwanda for Germans.

abategetsi   leaders; singular: **umutegetsi**, leader.

abaterambabazi   Affected high-society ladies; singular: **umuterambazi**.

abiru   Court ritualists, generally of the Tsobe clan, responsible for the transition from king to king and other court matters.

Akazu   In English, the little grass shack. In the old days the king's small circle of advisers. The well-educated power brokers of Rwanda's northwest mountains. Name given in coy understatement of their weight; an unofficial organization, and therefore usually lower case; we upper-case because it is more powerful, and more tightly organized, than any publicly chartered organization in the nation. Its top bosses and highly educated junior cadre organized the genocide. Until insurgents defeated its French-supported military three months after the genocide began, it was the nation's Hutu power elite.

aristo   French slang, an aristocrat.

askari   Kiswahili for a uniformed guard or trooper, widely heard among whites throughout East Africa, but seldom used in Rwanda, where the Kinyarwanda term is **umusilikare**.

Bakiga   Mountain people, hillbillies, said of both Bahutu and Batutsi, and also used in Uganda.

Banyarwanda   In Kinyarwanda, the people of Rwandan culture; they speak that Bantu language; the prefix **banya** indicates "people."

Batemura Singa subclan, founded by Louise's maternal grandsire, Mutemura.

Bega One of the many Rwandese clans; the clan of the powerful dowager queen, Kanjogera.

bella figura In Italian, a man on unsteady ground who nonetheless cuts a fine figure and a sweet deal.

bwana "Good Sir," a strictly Swahili honorific title that Banyarwanda seldom use in conversation among themselves. As Kiswahili is East Africa's *lingua franca,* and as it is closely related to its Bantu cousin, Kinyarwanda, Banyarwanda often use it to address officials in formal written or oral communications, and to address Bazungu, who prefer Swahili.

demob British army slang for "demobilize." It is thus Ugandan army slang for the same. A soldier who is "demobbed" is released from service to civilian life.

duka Urdu for a shop, and the common word for a shop throughout East Africa, where shops are often run by "Hendis," "Indians." In Rwanda, even shops not run by Hendis are called "dukas," though among the more literate they may be called, in the French manner, "boutiques." A related expression is **duka wallah,** Urdu for a shopkeeper.

facho French slang, a Fascist.

gacaca Originally just a grassy patch, often beneath a shade tree, then a place where elders dispensed justice. Now a means for expediting judgment of the tens of thousands in prison on charges of genocide.

godown Local (from China to East Africa) term for a warehouse; somewhat less in use now, in wide use during period in which we use the term.

ibihe n'ibindi "Things are different now, times are changing."

ibyitso Kinyarwanda for "accomplices," with the added implication of treason.

Imana God.

imbunda Rifle, from Arabic *bundegeya* and Swahili *bunduki.*

Inkotanyi The insurgents fighting the Akazu state: officially the RPF, the Rwandese Patriotic Front or the FPR (French), the *Front Patriotique Rwandais.*

Interahamwe Literally, "those who attack together"; officially, the youth movement of what was long the state's one legal party; actually, the Akazu's equivalent of the Nazi blackshirts; thugs trained to kill on the road.

Intore Originally, the king's elite warriors. Under Belgian rule, which forbade the king a military, they became dance troupes. Today, dancers of that characteristic Rwandais warrior dance.

inyenzi Literally cockroach. During the period when Belgium handed power to a new Hutu elite, it was an epithet for Tutsi renegades. Commonly used to mean Tutsi people.

Inzu A word with two related meanings, either "house" (and as such the closest Kinyarwanda equivalent to the English, *rondavel*) or "bloodline."

kalinga The royal court's sacred drum, tassled with the testicles of its enemies, which Akazu propagandists later contorted to mean the court's enemies, the Hutu. In fact, almost all the court's enemies were rival Tutsi kingdoms or principalities.

kwitonda Reserve; the Tutsi stiff upper lip, from one point of view, poise, from another; flat affect, lack of evident emotion.

litron French slang for a *litre,* commonly used for a liter of beer.

mmmh A very important word in Kinyarwanda, used to convey a variety of emotions such as surprise, skepticism, approval, denial, or shock.

mushanana Rwandan traditional garment made of a wrap-around skirt and a top piece tied on the shoulder in a knot; once worn in different form by both men and women, now worn only by women.

mwami King. Variations of the word have similar meanings in most Bantu nations.

Nduga South. In Rwanda, the South, the region where Bahutu and Batutsi are so mixed that Bahutu in the north say, "There are no Bahutu in Nduga country."

ngw'iki "What's that? What are you saying? What do you mean? Are you serious?"

Nyiginya Rwanda's kingly clan.

politicard French slang, a politico.

right staff wallah British army, and thus Ugandan army, slang for a staff officer with scant field experience making field decisions for troops in the field. The term can be applied to any out-of-touch functionary or bureaucrat.

rondavel An English term commonly used through eastern and southern Africa for round African huts, though many are too big to be called "huts."

rubanda nyamwinshi A favored term meaning the Hutu masses; more literally translated as the common people, the majority.

Singa One of the uxorial clans; that is, one of the few clans from which the king could choose a wife.

soulard French slang, a drunk.

Tsobe The clan that provided most of the king's *abiru*: highly influential in matters of protocol, doctrine, and succession.

ubuhake Occasional labor owed the court, in the manner of the feudal corvée.

uburetwa A more severe form of *ubuhake,* introduced by the powerful King Rwabugiri, Kanjogera's husband; later exploited by the German and then the Belgian colonial authorities.

umugabo A man.

umusozi The hill, the fundamental unit of Rwandese social organization; made up of family rugos.

umupanga Kinyarwanda for "machete"; throughout East Africa, it's called **panga**.

umuyaga Wind.

urugo A family compound, consisting of several structures surrounded by a palisade. Also, the center of life.

waramutse Good morning.